Eight Days
at Yalta

Eight Days at Yalta

How Churchill, Roosevelt, and Stalin Shaped the Post-war World

DIANA PRESTON

Atlantic Monthly Press
New York

Originally published in the UK in 2019 by Picador
an imprint of Pan Macmillan

Published simultaneously in Canada
Printed in Canada

First Grove Atlantic hardcover editon: February 2020

ISBN 978-0-8021-4765-3
eISBN 978-0-8021-4766-0

Library of Congress Cataloging-in-Publication data is available for this title.

Atlantic Monthly Press
an imprint of Grove Atlantic
154 West 14th Street
New York, NY 10011

Distributed by Publishers Group West

groveatlantic.com

20 21 22 23   10 9 8 7 6 5 4 3 2 1

In memory of Leslie and Mary Preston

CONTENTS

LIST OF ILLUSTRATIONS ix

MAPS xi

DRAMATIS PERSONAE xiii

PROLOGUE 1

PART ONE
PERSONALITIES, POLITICS AND PRESSURES

CHAPTER ONE 'The Big Three' 7

CHAPTER TWO 'We Ended Friends' 26

PART TWO
PREPARATIONS, MALTA
AND ELSEWHERE, EARLY 1945

CHAPTER THREE Argonaut 45

CHAPTER FOUR 'One Tiny Bright Flame in the Darkness' 71

PART THREE
'JAW TO JAW', YALTA, 3–11 FEBRUARY 1945

CHAPTER FIVE 'All the Comforts of Home' 93

CHAPTER SIX 'Uncle Joe and Stone Arse' 112

CHAPTER SEVEN 'To Each According to his Deserts' 128

CHAPTER EIGHT 'The Monstrous Bastard of the
Peace of Versailles' 148

CHAPTER NINE 'The Riviera of Hades' 172

CHAPTER TEN 'The Broad Sunlit Plains of
Peace and Happiness' 188

CHAPTER ELEVEN 'Quite a Decent Arrangement
About Poland' 208

CHAPTER TWELVE 'Judge Roosevelt Approves' 225

CHAPTER THIRTEEN 'A Landmark in Human History' 243

PART FOUR
AN ALLIANCE UNDER PRESSURE,
FEBRUARY TO AUGUST 1945

CHAPTER FOURTEEN Elephants in the Room 259

CHAPTER FIFTEEN 'A Fraudulent Prospectus' 271

CHAPTER SIXTEEN 'I Liked the Little Son of a Bitch' 291

PART FIVE
AFTERMATH

CHAPTER SEVENTEEN The Iron Curtain Descends 313

EPILOGUE 323

ACKNOWLEDGEMENTS 328

NOTES AND SOURCES 331

BIBLIOGRAPHY 370

INDEX 381

LIST OF ILLUSTRATIONS

1. Roosevelt, Stalin and Churchill and the US, Soviet and British delegations at the 1943 Teheran Conference. (Heritage Image Partnership Ltd / Alamy Stock Photo)
2. The destruction caused in Chiswick by the first Nazi V2 rocket to hit Britain, 8 September 1944. (Trinity Mirror / Mirrorpix / Alamy Stock Photo)
3. The *Ferdinand Magellan* railcar that carried Roosevelt on the first phase of his journey to Yalta. (By courtesy of the author)
4. Roosevelt and Churchill aboard the USS *Quincy*, Valetta Harbour, Malta on 2 February 1945, eve of the Yalta Conference. (Franklin D. Roosevelt Library)
5. Roosevelt and Churchill on arrival at Saki airfield in the Crimea on 3 February 1945. (Franklin D. Roosevelt Library)
6. Roosevelt aboard the USS *Quincy* in Malta with Leahy, King, Marshall and Kuter. (Franklin D. Roosevelt Library)
7. The Italianate Livadia Palace built by the last Tsar where Roosevelt stayed and the plenary sessions of the Yalta Conference convened. (By courtesy of the author)
8. Soviet women working to prepare the Livadia Palace. (Franklin D. Roosevelt Library)
9. The Vorontsov Palace where Churchill stayed during the
& 10. Conference. (By courtesy of the author)
11. One of the lions of the Vorontsov Palace, admired by Churchill. (By courtesy of the author)
12. The Yusupov Palace, admired by Church at Koreiz, once owned by Rasputin's assassin Prince Felix Yusupov, where Stalin stayed during the Conference. (Юлия Соловъева [CC BY-SA 3.0 https://creativecommons.org/licenses/by-sa/3.0])

13. Photo call for Churchill, Roosevelt and Stalin during the Yalta Conference with their respective foreign ministers, Eden, Stettinius and Molotov. (Franklin D. Roosevelt Library)

14. Menu of the dinner hosted by Churchill at the Vorontsov Palace on the night of 10 February 1945. (Franklin D. Roosevelt Library)

15. Stalin in Moscow, August 1945, with Malenkov, Beria, Molotov and his eventual successor Khruschev. (Pictoral Press Ltd / Alamy Stock Photo)

16. Stanisław Mikołajczyk, Prime Minister of the Polish Government in exile in London during most of the war and briefly post-war deputy Prime Minister. (Popperfoto / Contributor)

17. Cadogan and Eden during the Teheran Conference, 1943. (Pictoral Press Ltd / Alamy Stock Photo)

18. Churchill's daughter Sarah, Roosevelt's daughter Anna and Harriman's daughter Kathleen at Yalta. (Franklin D. Roosevelt Library)

19. General Charles de Gaulle, leader of the Free French, who was not invited to Yalta. (Serge DE SAZO / Contributor)

20. Roosevelt and Churchill with Chinese Nationalist leader Chiang Kai-shek at their pre-Teheran meeting in Cairo. (Bettmann / Contributor)

21. Roosevelt's meeting with King Ibn Saud of Saudi Arabia on 14 February 1945 aboard the USS *Quincy*. (Interim Archives / Contributor)

22. German refugees forcibly expelled in the latter stages of the war from Eastern Europe. (Library of Congress / Contributor)

23. The results of the RAF/USAAF bombing raids on Dresden in mid-February 1945. (Photo 12 / Alamy Stock Photo)

24. A staged photograph of the capture of Berlin by the Soviet Red Army. (Shawshots / Alamy Stock Photo)

25. Delegates at the first meeting of the United Nations, San Francisco, 25 April 1945. (Everett Collection Historical / Alamy Stock Photo)

26. Churchill, Truman and Stalin at the Potsdam Conference held in Allied-occupied Germany between 17 July and 2 August 1945. (Everett Collection Historical / Alamy Stock Photo)

27. The atomic bomb 'Little Boy' exploding over Hiroshima, 6 August 1945. (Image from the collection of the Australian War Memorial. AWM 043863.)

PRE-SECOND WORLD WAR NATIONAL BOUNDARIES

Inset map (top right):
Odessa
ROUMANIA
CRIMEA
U.S.S.R.
Sebastopol
Yalta
Black Sea
Istanbul
TURKEY

Main map:

ICELAND

Norwegian Sea

Faroes

Shetlands

Orkneys

NORWAY

SWEDEN

FINLAND

Helsinki
Leningrad

Oslo

Stockholm

Tallinn
ESTONIA

North Sea

Riga
LATVIA

IRELAND
Dublin

DENMARK
Copenhagen

Baltic Sea

LITHUANIA
Kaunas
Vilna
Vitebsk
Smolensk
Minsk

UNITED KINGDOM

London

The Hague
Antwerp
HOLLAND

Hamburg
Bremen

Königsberg
Danzig
GERMANY

Berlin

BELGIUM
Brussels
LUX

Warsaw

U.S.S.R.

Ardennes

GERMANY
Leipzig
Dresden
Breslau

POLAND
Lublin
Kiev

Paris

Prague

Kraków
Lvov

Strasbourg

CZECHOSLOVAKIA

FRANCE

Munich

Vienna
Bratislava

Berne
SWITZER

AUSTRIA
HUNGARY
Budapest

ROMANIA
Odessa

Lyons

Milan

CRIMEA →
(See inset map
above at the
same scale

SPAIN
Barcelona

Marseille

Bologna

ITALY

YUGOSLAVIA

Belgrade

Bucharest

Black Sea

Balearic Islands

Corsica
Rome

BULGARIA

Sardinia

Naples

Tirana
ALBANIA

Istanbul

TURKEY

Mediterranean Sea

Sicily

GREECE
Athens

300 miles

400 kilometres

TUNISIA

MALTA
Valetta

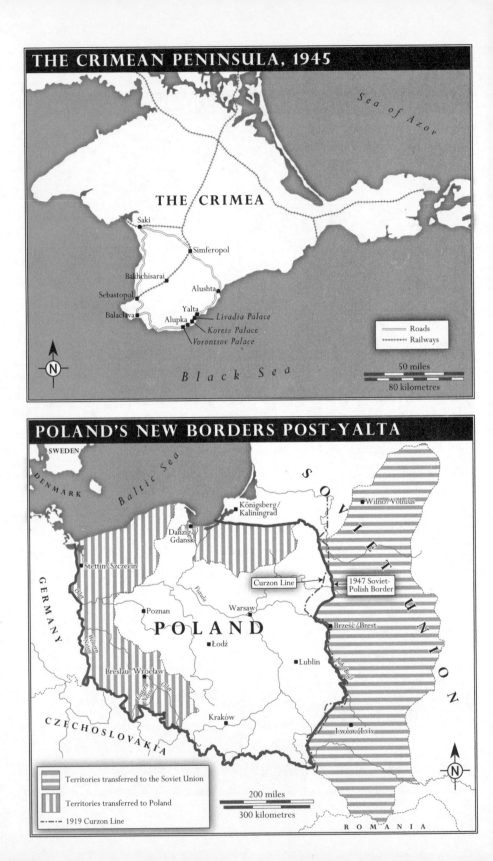

THE CRIMEAN PENINSULA, 1945

Sea of Azov

THE CRIMEA

Saki

Simferopol

Bakhchisarai

Sebastopol

Alushta

Balaclava

Yalta

Alupka

Livadia Palace

Koreiz Palace

Vorontsov Palace

Roads
Railways

Black Sea

N

50 miles
80 kilometres

POLAND'S NEW BORDERS POST-YALTA

SWEDEN

DENMARK

Baltic Sea

Königsberg/
Kaliningrad

Danzig/
Gdansk

SOVIET

Wilno/Vilnius

Stettin/Szczecin

Oder

GERMANY

Curzon Line

1947 Soviet-
Polish Border

UNION

Vistula

Warsaw

Poznan

POLAND

Brześć/Brest

Łódź

Western Neisse

Breslau/Wrocław

Oder

Bug (Buh)

Eastern Neisse

Lublin

CZECHOSLOVAKIA

Kraków

Lwów/Lviv

N

Territories transferred to the Soviet Union

Territories transferred to Poland

200 miles
300 kilometres

1919 Curzon Line

ROMANIA

DRAMATIS PERSONAE

In alphabetical order

AT YALTA

The American Delegation

Anna Boettiger, Roosevelt's only daughter.

Charles Bohlen, assistant to the Secretary of State, adviser to Roosevelt and his interpreter at Yalta.

Wilson Brown, Vice-Admiral, Roosevelt's senior naval aide.

Howard Bruenn, Lieutenant-Commander, cardiologist in attendance on Roosevelt.

James Byrnes, Director, Office of War Mobilization.

Averell Harriman, diplomat and from 1943 to 1946 ambassador to the Soviet Union.

Kathleen Harriman, Averell Harriman's daughter.

Alger Hiss, Deputy Director, Office of Special Political Affairs, State Department, and Soviet agent.

Harry Hopkins, Roosevelt's close adviser.

Robert Hopkins, Harry Hopkins's son and US army photographer.

Ernest King, Fleet Admiral, Chief of Naval Operations and Commander-in-Chief US Fleet.

Laurence Kuter, Major-General, US Army Air Force.

William Leahy, Fleet Admiral and US Navy Chief of Staff.

George Marshall, General of the Army and US Army Chief of Staff.

Ross McIntire, Vice-Admiral, Surgeon General US Navy, and
   Roosevelt's personal physician.
Robert Meiklejohn, personal aide to Averell Harriman, US Embassy,
   Moscow.
Mike Reilly, head of White House Security.
William Rigdon, Lieutenant and White House naval aide.
Franklin D. Roosevelt, President and Commander-in-Chief.
Edward Stettinius, Secretary of State.
Edwin 'Pa' Watson, Major-General and Roosevelt's military aide and
   appointments secretary.

The British Delegation

Gladys Adams, shorthand writer.
Harold Alexander, Field Marshal and Supreme Allied Commander,
   Mediterranean.
Arthur Birse, Major, British Military Mission, Moscow, and
   Churchill's interpreter at Yalta.
Joan Bright, assistant to General 'Pug' Ismay.
Alan Brooke, Field Marshal, Chief of the Imperial General Staff.
Alexander Cadogan, Permanent Under-Secretary Foreign Office.
Winston Churchill, Prime Minister and Minister of Defence.
Andrew Cunningham, Admiral of the Fleet and First Sea Lord and
   Chief of Naval Staff.
Anthony Eden, Foreign Secretary.
Joan Evans, one of Churchill's cypher clerks.
Marian Holmes, one of Churchill's secretaries.
Hastings 'Pug' Ismay, General and Chief of Staff to Churchill as
   Minister of Defence.
Archibald Clark Kerr, ambassador to the Soviet Union.
Elizabeth Layton, one of Churchill's secretaries.
Hugh Lunghi, Captain, British Military Mission, Moscow, and
   interpreter for British Chiefs of Staff.
John Martin, Churchill's principal private secretary.
Lord Moran (Charles Wilson), Churchill's doctor.
Sarah Oliver, Churchill's second daughter.

Richard Pim, Captain, naval officer in charge of Churchill's Map Room.

Charles (Peter) Portal, Marshal of the RAF and Chief of the Air Staff.

Joyce Rogers, stenographer.

Frank Sawyers, Churchill's valet.

James Sommerville, Admiral and Head of Admiralty Delegation, British Joint Staff Mission, Washington.

Maureen Stuart-Clark, Wren officer and aide to Admiral James Somerville.

Jo Sturdee, one of Churchill's secretaries.

Henry Wilson, Field Marshal and Head, British Joint Staff Mission, Washington.

The Soviet Delegation

Alexei Innokentievich Antonov, Army General and First Deputy Chief General of Staff, Red Army.

Lavrentii Pavlovich Beria, head of the Soviet secret police, the NKVD.

Sergo Lavrentievich Beria, Lavrentii Beria's son and NKVD surveillance operative.

Andrei Andreyevich Gromyko, ambassador to the US.

Fedor Tarasovich Gusev, ambassador to the UK.

Valentina 'Valechka' Vasilevna Istomina, Stalin's mistress and housekeeper.

Nikolai Gerasimovich Kuznetsov, Admiral and People's Commissar for the Navy.

Ivan Mikhailovich Maisky, Deputy People's Commissar for Foreign Affairs.

Vyacheslav Mikhailovich Molotov, Soviet Foreign Minister.

Vladimir Nikolaevich Pavlov, Stalin's principal interpreter.

Joseph Vissarionovich Stalin, Marshal and Chairman of the Council of People's Commissars of the Soviet Union and, of course, Soviet dictator.

Andrei Yanuarievich Vyshinsky, Deputy People's Commissar for Foreign Affairs.

ELSEWHERE

Americans

Dwight D. Eisenhower, Supreme Commander Allied Forces in
   Europe.

Douglas MacArthur, General and Supreme Allied Commander,
   South-West Asia.

Henry Morgenthau, Treasury Secretary.

Frances Perkins, Secretary of Labor, first female US cabinet member.

Eleanor Roosevelt, the President's wife.

Elliott Roosevelt, the President's third son.

James Roosevelt, the President's eldest son.

Lucy Mercer Rutherfurd, Roosevelt's sometime mistress.

Joseph 'Vinegar Joe' Stilwell, General, commander of US forces in
   China and Burma until 1944.

Henry Stimson, Secretary of War.

Margaret 'Daisy' Suckley, Roosevelt's distant cousin.

Harry Truman, Roosevelt's Vice-President and successor as
   President.

Britons

Clement Attlee, Deputy Prime Minister in the wartime coalition
   government, leader of the Labour Party and Prime Minister
   following the July 1945 elections.

Clementine Churchill, Churchill's wife.

Mary Churchill, Churchill's youngest daughter.

Pamela Churchill, wife of Randolph Churchill and sometime
   mistress and later wife of Averell Harriman.

Randolph Churchill, Churchill's son.

John (Jock) Colville, one of Churchill's private secretaries.

George VI, the King.

Bernard Montgomery, Field Marshal and Commander-in-Chief of
   Twenty-first Army Group, Western Europe.

Louis Mountbatten, Admiral and Supreme Allied Commander South-
   East Asia Command.

Arthur Tedder, Air Chief Marshal and Deputy Supreme Allied
Commander Europe.

Soviets

Georgii Konstantinovich Zhukov, Marshal and Stalin's most senior
military commander.

Chinese

Chiang Kai-shek, Chairman of the Nationalist Government.
Meiling Kai-shek, Chiang's wife.
Mao Zedong, Communist leader.

French

Charles de Gaulle, head of the Provisional Government of the
French Republic.

Germans

Joseph Goebbels, Minister of Propaganda.
Heinrich Himmler, Interior Minister and Chief of the SS and
Gestapo.
Adolf Hitler, Chancellor of the German Reich.
Joachim von Ribbentrop, Foreign Minister.

Poles

Władysław Anders, General and Commander Free Polish forces.
Tomasz Arciszewski, Prime Minister of the Polish government in
London.
Stanisław Grabski, member of the Soviet-controlled 'Lublin Group'.
Stanisław Mikołajczyk, former Prime Minister of the Polish
government in London and briefly post-war deputy Prime
Minister of Poland.

PROLOGUE

'Statesmen are not called upon only to settle easy
questions. These often settle themselves. It is
where the balance quivers, and the proportions
are veiled in mist, that the opportunity for
world-saving decisions presents itself.'

Winston Churchill

'We cannot get away from the results of the war.'

Joseph Stalin

Under leaden skies shortly after noon on Saturday 3 February
1945, greatcoated Soviet soldiers lining the runway at Saki aerodrome on the west coast of the Crimean Peninsula snapped to
attention as a Douglas C-54 Skymaster transport swooped in over
the Black Sea. Moments later the aircraft touched down on the
short runway in which Russian labourers had only recently filled
large holes and from which well-muffled women had struggled
right up to the last minute to brush away the fallen snow with
birch-twig brooms. Despite their efforts the surface still retained
an icy film, making the landing a tricky one.

Twenty minutes later another Skymaster landed. As soon as it
had taxied to a halt and its pilot had shut down its four engines
and the propellers had ceased to rotate, a short bulky figure
wearing a military cap and greatcoat and with a cigar clamped
between his teeth – Winston Churchill – disembarked. He hurried
over to the other aircraft and waited while its purpose-installed

lift lowered to the frozen ground a man sitting in a wheelchair
and protected against the cold by a velvet-collared thick woollen
US naval officer's boat cloak. The Prime Minister stepped forward
and greeted his wartime ally Franklin Delano Roosevelt. Then
the President's head of security, Mike Reilly, pushed Roosevelt's
wheelchair from his Skymaster – nicknamed the '*Sacred Cow*' by
Roosevelt's advisers because of the amount of protection it
received – over to an open jeep. He gently lifted the President
onto the back seat, which was covered by a red and blue Kazakh
oriental rug, and tucked thick blankets around him.

Preceded by photographers walking backwards as they took
their shots, the jeep headed slowly across the airfield towards a
Soviet guard of honour. Wearing brass-buttoned tunics, trousers
tucked into highly polished, knee-high black boots and white
gloves, the troops stood rigidly to attention holding aloft standards resembling those of Roman legions. A military brass band
waited beside them.

Churchill walked close alongside the President's jeep, holding
on to the door frame near where Roosevelt's elbow was resting,
just 'as in her old age an Indian attendant accompanied Queen
Victoria's phaeton', Lord Moran, Churchill's physician, thought.
Scrutinizing Roosevelt closely, Moran gave him only a few months
to live. Sergo Beria, the twenty-year-old son of the Soviet security chief Lavrentii Beria, claimed that through his carefully
positioned long-range directional microphones he could overhear
the way Roosevelt refused to talk to Churchill and 'cut him short,
saying that everything had been discussed and decided'. Churchill
remained at Roosevelt's side while the band struck up first 'The
Star-Spangled Banner', then 'God Save the King' and finally the
'Third Internationale' and the two leaders reviewed the guard of
honour.

Shortly afterwards, under the watchful gaze of the fur-hatted
Soviet Foreign Minister Vyacheslav Molotov, known as 'Stone
Arse' for his ability to sit for hours in negotiations saying 'no',
sent by Soviet leader Joseph Stalin to welcome his wartime allies,
Roosevelt, Churchill and their teams transferred to a fleet of
limousines, many of them black Packards supplied by the US

under Lend-Lease. The vehicles would carry them to the seaside resort of Yalta, with Roosevelt and his daughter Anna Boettiger travelling in the lead motorcade. Yalta was only ninety miles away but the journey over potholed, slushy, war debris-lined roads which Vice-Admiral Ross McIntire, Roosevelt's physician, thought 'a Sherman tank would have found tough going' took nearly as long as their seven-hour flight from Malta.

Once they had arrived and settled into their accommodation in two hastily rehabilitated, war-damaged palaces and Stalin, their host, had joined them at the end of his thousand-mile journey by armoured train from Moscow, the three would embark on the conference, code-named Argonaut, that had brought them all to Yalta to decide the post-war order. Their decisions would define the world for decades to come, long after all three were dead.

Controversy continues as to whether the price the Western leaders paid for the 'golden fleece' that was peace was too great, whether the stability of Western Europe was bought at the cost of the loss of freedom in the East and whether the terms Stalin won for his agreement to enter the war against Japan were too generous, providing Soviet Communism with a foothold in East Asia, and on the Korean Peninsula in particular. Many have thought so and have dated the beginning of the Cold War from Yalta. In 2005, President George W. Bush, speaking in Latvia, compared the Yalta agreements to the 1938 Munich Agreement and the Nazi Germany–Soviet pact of a year later and suggested Yalta had left Europe 'divided and unstable'. Thereby it 'had been one of the greatest wrongs of history . . . Once again, when powerful governments negotiated, the freedom of small nations was somehow expendable.'

Such views have long found favour in Continental Europe and particularly in France, whose wartime leader General Charles de Gaulle never forgave his exclusion from the conference by the instant, unanimous agreement of the other three leaders. Yalta's position as a pivotal event in European eyes is well illustrated by a remark by the then supermodel Carla Bruni in 1996. Attempting to compare the relative triviality of her role as a fashion model to truly important events, she said, 'I mean, the worst thing that can happen to me is I break a heel and fall down. This is not Yalta, right?' Years later, she would marry the French President Nicolas Sarkozy who also damned the conference decisions. He ascribed the reason for his aristocratic Hungarian father leaving his homeland to 'the tragedy of Yalta' and in 2008 prior to a visit to Moscow insisted, 'The revival of spheres of influence is unacceptable. Yalta is behind us.' Similar views were earlier expressed by, among others, Germany's Chancellor Helmut Kohl and France's President François Mitterrand. Even immediately following the Yalta Conference, some British parliamentarians lamented its failure to do more for Poland, for whom Britain had gone to war in the first place, and for the Poles who had fought bravely at Britain's side for five years.

Others, however, have questioned what more the Western leaders could have done when Soviet troops were already in occupation of so much of Eastern Europe and concluded that even if this imperfect 'jaw-to-jaw', as Churchill might have put it, led to a Cold War, it helped end a hot war which cost some 60 million lives and avoided another in its immediate aftermath.

In all negotiations, as in poker games, not only the nature of the hand each participant holds but also their character and the way that leads them to play their own cards, and to anticipate, interpret and manipulate their opponents' moves, are important. The story of Yalta, its context and consequences, reveals the thinking, tactics, available options and reactions of each of the main players: the wily, enigmatic but seriously ill Roosevelt; the war-weary, eloquent if loquacious Churchill, conscious of Britain's already diminishing place in the world; and Stalin, an autocrat determined to make no concessions and of all three leaders the most certain of what he wanted to achieve and at what price.

PART ONE

Personalities, Politics
and Pressures

'No more let us falter! From Malta to
Yalta! Let nobody alter.'

Winston Churchill to Franklin Roosevelt,
January 1945

CHAPTER ONE

'The Big Three'

The three leaders who would at Yalta decide the end of the war and the shape of the future peace shared completely only a single common goal – the speedy defeat of Nazi Germany. Just as their backgrounds and their route to power varied markedly, so too did their aspirations and ambitions, both for themselves and their countries.

Churchill, seventy in the previous November, was the oldest; Stalin, born in December 1878, was sixty-six; and Roosevelt, the youngest, would be sixty-three on 30 January 1945 as he journeyed to the conference. The stresses and strains of office and of the war had taken their toll on all three. None was in particularly good health, with that of Roosevelt being conspicuously the poorest. A bout of polio in August 1921 had paralysed him from the waist down – a paralysis which he refused to believe was permanent and tried numerous therapies to alleviate. Even in January 1945 he had a new masseur and healer, ex-prize fighter Harry Setaro, who told him 'Mr President, you're going to walk.'

With the acquiescence of a media more compliant than now, Roosevelt concealed from the public the extent of his paralysis, often using a system of heavy steel leg braces to allow him to stand at important events and even to walk short distances with the help of a stick or the arm of an aide, swinging his legs from the hip. In this he was helped by the determined way he built up his upper body strength, even becoming a better swimmer than any of his White House staff. An aide recalled, 'You did not really notice he could not walk. He was a sort of Mount Rushmore being wheeled around, and all you noticed after a while was the Mount Rushmore part.' However, approaching his sixty-third birthday Roosevelt was also suffering excessively high blood pressure, had an enlarged heart with a weak left ventricle leading to reduced blood supply throughout his body, chronic sinus and bronchial problems, frequent headaches, chronic insomnia, and bleeding haemorrhoids – several of which conditions were exacerbated by his enforced sedentary lifestyle.

Stalin suffered from chronic psoriasis, tonsillitis, rheumatism and foot problems, among which was that two toes on his left foot were fused together. His face was marked by boyhood smallpox. Following an infection his left arm hung stiff, sufficiently so for him to be declared unfit for military service in the First World War. In spring 1944 his aides had found him unconscious at his desk from an unknown cause. Although almost certainly the fittest of the three, he had developed a hypochondriac's sensitivity to any small health problem, probably heightened by fears of poison and increasing paranoia in general.

Churchill was so overweight that in 1942 he had to have a new desk installed in his Cabinet war rooms beneath London's Whitehall because he could not fit behind the previous one. Throughout his life he had been subject to depression which he likened to having 'a black dog on one's back'. He routinely took barbiturate sleeping pills. He had suffered a heart attack when visiting President Roosevelt over Christmas and New Year 1941 / 2 and had had several bouts of pneumonia. During the worst of them, which occurred in mid-December 1943 in Morocco as he returned from the first meeting of the 'Big Three' – as newspapers habitually labelled the three leaders – in Teheran, his doctor Lord Moran told one of Churchill's ministers that he expected him to die. He had had several previous brushes with death, not only in action during his early career as an army officer and war correspondent, but also due to accidents, as when in 1931 a car knocked down and nearly killed him in Manhattan. The aftermath of this incident provides a major clue to one of his habits. It was Prohibition time in the United States and Churchill demanded that the doctor treating him write a note stating, 'This is to certify that the post-accident convalescence of the Hon. Winston S. Churchill necessitates the use of alcoholic spirits especially at meal times. The quantity is naturally indefinite but the minimum requirements would be 250 cubic centimetres.'

Churchill habitually used alcohol. He enjoyed whisky – a favourite was Johnny Walker Black Label – which he always drank without ice but with sufficient soda or water for one of his private secretaries to describe it as 'really a mouthwash'. He loved champagne, particularly vintage Pol Roger, fine wine and brandy.*

Whether Churchill was an alcoholic has been much debated. He himself said, 'I have taken more out of alcohol than it has taken out of me.' But many suspected he was addicted. Sumner Welles, one of Roosevelt's first envoys to Britain, dismissed him as 'a drunken sot'. When he heard Churchill had become prime minister, Roosevelt told his cabinet 'he supposed Churchill was the best man that England had, even if he was drunk half of the time'.

Roosevelt too enjoyed alcohol, though he did not drink so much as Churchill. He particularly liked to mix cocktails 'with the precision of a chemist', as a friend observed, a social ritual he could still perform despite his disability. Churchill detested these cocktails and would sometimes slip to the lavatory with his glass to pour his away and replace it with water. Invited to taste one of Roosevelt's cocktails, Stalin described it as 'Alright, cold on the stomach.'

Stalin drank spirits, particularly vodka, but preferred the white wine of his native Georgia – said to be the first place wine was ever produced – and could sometimes become drunk. However, his Foreign Minister Molotov suggested that more often he used alcohol to test people, insisting they keep on drinking to see what true opinions they might express in their cups or simply for the

* Even today the only champagne served at Cambridge University's Churchill College receptions is Pol Roger, donated by the company.

amusement of seeing them fall down dead drunk. According to Beria's son Sergo, 'Stalin loved that. He delighted in the spectacle of human weakness.' Averell Harriman, Roosevelt's envoy, detected a similar trait in the President, 'He unquestionably had a sadistic streak . . . [and] always enjoyed other people's discomfort . . . it never bothered him very much when other people were unhappy.'

All three men smoked heavily. So did many of their aides. Any room including those at Yalta where they met would have reeked of their various tobaccos and been truly smoke-filled with a blue-grey haze. Roosevelt was a virtual chain-smoker, inhaling through a holder usually Camels but sometimes Lucky Strikes, both of which were untipped – as were nearly all cigarettes of the time. Stalin also chain-smoked. He enjoyed American cigarettes but was more often pictured using one of his pipes, some of which were imported from Dunhill in London, frequently gesturing with them to underline a point in debate. Churchill only smoked large, long cigars, also purchased from Dunhill, often eight or nine a day.

In physical appearance Churchill and Stalin were stout and short, even if according to one of his interpreters Stalin wore 'special supports under his heels built into the soles of his boots to make him look taller than he was'. Milovan Djilas, a Yugoslav Communist visitor to Moscow in 1944, described Stalin as:

> of very small stature and ungainly build. His torso was short and narrow, while his legs and arms were too long. His left arm and shoulder seemed rather still. He had quite a large paunch and his hair was sparse though his scalp was not completely bald. His face was white, with ruddy cheeks . . . His teeth were black and irregular, turned inward . . . Still the head was not a bad one . . . with those amber eyes and a mixture of sternness and mischief.

Churchill's daughter Sarah Oliver recalled Stalin as 'a frightening figure with his slit, bear eyes' although sometimes 'specks of light danced in [them] like cold sunshine on dark waters'.

A guest at a White House dinner party described the five foot six inch Churchill as:

> a rotund, dumpy figure with short, slight arms and legs, narrow in the shoulders, mostly stomach, chest and head, no neck. Yet, as he advanced into the room, a semi-scowl on his big, chubby, pink-and-white face with its light blue eyes, the knowledge of his performance since Dunquerque and something about his person gave him a massive stature. He moves as though he were without joints, all of a piece: solidly, unhurriedly, impervious to obstacles, like a tank or a bulldozer.

Roosevelt's distant (sixth) cousin and frequent companion Margaret 'Daisy' Suckley thought Churchill 'a strange looking little man. Fat & round, his clothes bunched up on him. Practically no hair on his head . . . He talks as though he had terrible adenoids . . . His humorous twinkle is infectious.'

Roosevelt was more than six inches taller than either of the others, being six foot two when standing in his leg braces. The same dinner guest who described Churchill depicted Roosevelt's 'ruddy' face, 'broad-shouldered torso and large head' with 'close-set square eyes [which] flashed with an infectious zest . . . His hands gesturing for emphasis, lighting one cigarette after another, and flicking the ashes off his wrinkled seersucker coat, shook rather badly. The rings under his eyes were very dark and deep.' One of his interpreters described how Roosevelt 'thought he had a sense of humour' but in fact it was 'exceptionally corny'. He 'loved to tell jokes . . . and roar with laughter, very visibly savouring and enjoying his own humour'.

Theatricality is a facet of many politicians. Roosevelt's security chief Mike Reilly thought there was 'a good deal of the actor' about both Churchill and Roosevelt. Roosevelt had a habit of throwing back his head in a motion which he himself attributed to 'the Garbo in me'. He once told Orson Welles that the two of them were the finest actors in the United States. An American diplomat recalled of Churchill and his British bulldog image, 'Everything felt the touch of his art, his appearance, his gestures . . . the indomitable V sign for victory, the cigar for imperturbability.' Milovan Djilas found it difficult to assess how much of Stalin's behaviour was 'play-acting' and how much was real, since 'with him pretence was so spontaneous that it seemed he himself became convinced of the truth and sincerity of what he was saying'. He also detected in Stalin 'a sense of humour – a rough humour, self-assured, but not without subtlety and depth'. However, behind his teasing, particularly of subordinates, there was often 'as much malice as jest'. Sergo Beria recollected how Stalin mocked Malenkov, one of his senior ministers, for being overweight, telling him it was ideologically unsound for a senior party official to be so fat and ordering him to exercise and take up horse riding 'to recover the look of a human being'.

The working hours, habits and approach to government of the three varied considerably. Roosevelt worked 'office hours', often with his black Scottish terrier Fala at his side, usually halting and taking a swim before dinner. Churchill, according to his daughter, 'never wanted to switch off'. He sometimes worked into the night. When he had no meetings in the morning he would remain in bed working on his papers lying scattered over the bedclothes, and sometimes wearing his 'siren suit' – a 'onesie' or all-in-one piece of clothing. A British diplomat described it as 'a dreadful garment that [Churchill] claimed to have designed himself to wear during air raids . . . like a mechanic's overalls or more still like a child's rompers or crawlers'. Churchill often took a siesta after lunch. Sometimes he would dictate to one of his secretaries while soaking in the bath.

Stalin, who had Lenin's death mask beside his desk in his small spartan office in the Kremlin, was even more nocturnal, routinely working late into the night and sleeping until eleven or so in the morning. According to Sergo Beria, 'He always locked himself in when he slept, but it would be wrong to put that down to cowardice. My father said that Stalin did not fear death. He simply did not want anyone to see him asleep and defenceless. When he was ill he concealed his weakness.' Andrei Gromyko, who was present at Yalta and other conferences as Soviet ambassador to Washington, 'never saw a doctor with him throughout all the

Allied conferences'. If so, Stalin was the only one of the three leaders who did not have a personal doctor in close attendance at Yalta.

As befitted a man who had uniquely already served three presidential terms and embarked on a fourth, Roosevelt always kept a close eye on domestic politics. He never went further than he thought a majority of public opinion would allow and made sure through his 'fireside' radio chats that the electorate understood and empathized with his message and motives. Roosevelt's desire to have public opinion with him led a presidential rival to call him 'a chameleon on plaid' as he fitted his policies to the public mood. Churchill told his son Randolph, 'The President for all his warm heart and good intentions, is thought by many of his admirers to move with public opinion rather than to lead and form it.'

Churchill – the only British prime minister ever to wear military uniform regularly in office, and his own Defence Minister – focused his attention on the conduct of the war and the relationship between Britain and its allies. He had not only little time but also little inclination to attend to domestic policy. Thus he left the members of his coalition Cabinet significant freedom of action in that area. Labour members took major roles in planning for post-war reconstruction and indeed laid the foundations of the National Health Service without interference from him. One of Churchill's private secretaries, John 'Jock' Colville, noted that Churchill's focus was on 'defence, foreign affairs and party politics', much less on 'domestic problems or the home front except when he was aroused for sentimental reasons'.

Churchill rarely held a grudge. The morning after they had had 'a sharp and almost bitter argument', a colleague found him 'benign and smiling and affectionate'. Roosevelt's wife Eleanor described the Prime Minister as 'lovable and emotional and very human' even if she disagreed with many of his political views. Churchill's daughter Mary considered that her father 'was not complicated in his approach to people. He was trusting and very genuine. He could be wily if he had to, but it did not come naturally.' Again according to Colville, 'Patience [was] a virtue with which he was totally unfamiliar.' Churchill recognized how his impatience, allied to his impulsiveness, led him to go off at tangents into oral flights of fantasy by telling his civil servants only to accept written instructions. He always liked an audience and tended to monopolize conversation.

Churchill's deputy Clement Attlee believed, 'Energy, rather than wisdom, practical judgment or vision, was his supreme qualification' but 'it was poetry coupled with [that] energy that did the trick.' However in mid-January 1945, just before Yalta, Attlee typed himself – with two fingers 'so that none of his staff should see it' – 'a very blunt letter to the P.M.' It included a complaint about 'the P.M.'s lengthy disquisitions in Cabinet on papers which he has not read and on subjects which he has not taken the trouble to master'. Colville wrote in his diary, 'Greatly as I love and admire the PM, I am afraid there is much in what Attlee says.' Churchill's wife, to whom he showed Attlee's letter, thought it 'both true and wholesome'.

Roosevelt was much less emotional and much more restrained, calculating and enigmatic than the easily moved to tears, voluble and rarely dissimulating Churchill. He chose his words carefully, kept himself at the centre of the web of his administration and compartmentalized both his personal and political lives. His wife Eleanor warned Churchill, 'when Franklin says yes, yes, yes it doesn't mean he agrees . . . It means he's listening.' She also believed he had 'a great sense of responsibility . . . And the great feeling that possibly he was the only one who was equipped and trained and cognizant . . . of every phase of the situation'. General Dwight D. Eisenhower, the Supreme Commander of the Allied forces in Europe, considered him 'almost an egomaniac in his belief in his own wisdom'. Roosevelt's vice-president for his third term, Henry Wallace, was not alone in thinking that he was 'strictly opportunistic'. He worked 'by intuition and indirection' and could 'very successfully go in two directions at almost the same time'.

Roosevelt's last vice-president and successor, Harry Truman, described him as 'the coldest man I ever met. He didn't give a damn personally for me or you or anyone else in the world, as

far as I could see.' He 'liked to play one outfit against the other'.
An aide went further:

> He would send messages out through one department and have
> the replies come back through another department because he
> didn't want anyone else to have a complete file on his commu-
> nications with Prime Minister Winston Churchill, for
> example . . . he didn't want anybody else to know the whole
> story on anything . . . Because Roosevelt didn't ever take people
> fully into his confidence, it left his subordinates always uncer-
> tain of where they stood. They had to be loyal to him, but they
> didn't really know how loyal he was to them.

Roosevelt acknowledged the truth of some of these criticisms:
'You know, I am a juggler and I never let my left hand know what
my right hand does . . . I may be entirely inconsistent, and furthermore I am perfectly willing to mislead and tell untruths if it will
help win the war.' The respected Washington correspondent of the
New York Times, Arthur Krock, summed up this ambiguity in him:

> I think you'd have to go back to Jefferson to find another
> President like him. He was quite as inconsistent as Jefferson
> and at times as dishonest as Jefferson – but really a great man.
> There were a good many resemblances between him and
> Jefferson, and he always thought there were too.

Both Roosevelt and Churchill were – and had to be – good
orators although in very different ways. Roosevelt was innovative
in his use of friendly radio fireside chats. Churchill successfully
adapted Roosevelt's use of the radio to boost public morale in
wartime but was a much more flamboyant and emotional speaker,
a conjuror of quotable sound bites. Eisenhower recalled of
Churchill he was 'a master in argument and debate . . . intensely
oratorial', even one to one: 'He used humor and pathos with
equal facility and drew on everything from the Greek classics to
Donald Duck for quotation, cliché and forceful slang to support
his proposition.' Even the curmudgeonly Free French leader

General Charles de Gaulle acknowledged Churchill's ability 'to stir the dull English dough'.

Whatever the men's colleagues, friends and families made of their abilities, Roosevelt's wife Eleanor – niece of his fifth cousin former President Theodore Roosevelt – wrote, 'A man in high office is neither husband nor father nor friend in the commonly accepted sense of the words.' She acknowledged the bond her husband and Churchill formed, which helped them win the war – 'a fortunate relationship', she called it. The two men shared an extraordinary self-confidence, resilience and determination which allowed them, in Churchill's words, 'to keep buggering on' to overcome any setbacks, whether political, military or, particularly in Roosevelt's case, physical.

Not surprisingly, since Stalin had instant power of life or death over his colleagues, they wrote much less about his personality and methods of working. At home he was undisputed leader in both political and military matters, trusting few and taking the big decisions himself. His daughter Svetlana said, 'Human feelings in him were replaced by political considerations. He knew and sensed the political game, its shades, its nuances. He was completely absorbed by it . . . Cold calculation, dissimulation, a sober, cynical realism became stronger in him with the years.'

Sergo Beria wrote:

Stalin was supremely intelligent. He had a cold heart, calculated every action and remained invariably master of himself. He took all his decisions after having carefully weighed them. He never improvised. When he was obliged to depart from his original plan he never risked doing it until he had worked out a replacement strategy. It was not that he was slow in his reactions but he undertook nothing lightly. Every one of his actions formed part of a long-term scheme which was to enable him to attain a particular aim at a particular moment . . . Methodical in the extreme, Stalin's vast memory constituted a veritable collection of archives and he drew from it at will the data . . . he needed . . . to achieve an aim. He prepared carefully for every meeting, studying the questions he meant to raise.

Sergo also said to enforce his will Stalin encouraged government organizations to report on each other and state security to
report back on them all. He used hidden microphones to bug his
colleagues' conversations and 'set those around him one against
another. He was a master of this art.'

On a more personal level Andrei Gromyko recalled,

> I was always aware, watching Stalin speaking, of how expressive
> his face was, especially his eyes. When rebuking or arguing with
> someone, Stalin had a way of staring him mercilessly in the
> eyes and not taking his gaze off him. The object of this relent-
> less stare, one has to admit, felt profoundly uncomfortable.

Foreign diplomats, however, were surprised by the dictator's
seeming charm, the softness of his voice and how, unlike others,
including Churchill, he often seemed prepared to listen to what
they had to say, rather than to speak himself. Even if some of
their praise of him was pragmatic, based on the wartime necessity of appearing to be on good terms with an ally, by and large
they, like Churchill and Roosevelt and later Truman, formed much
more favourable impressions of him than his known deeds should
have warranted.

Churchill and Roosevelt were much closer in background to each
other than to Stalin. They even shared common ancestors from
the late Princess Diana's family, the Spencers. Churchill was a
nephew of the Duke of Marlborough and was born at the family
seat, Blenheim Palace. His father was the Duke's brother – the
mercurial, talented, shooting star of a politician, Lord Randolph
Churchill. His mother was an American beauty and heiress, Jennie
Jerome and as a consequence Churchill claimed he 'could trace
unbroken male descent on my mother's side through five generations from a lieutenant who served in George Washington's
army', giving him 'a bloodright to speak to the representatives
of the great Republic in our common cause'.

Recent research suggests that Churchill's childhood may not

have been quite as lonely and isolated as his own writings suggest. Nevertheless he often pleaded for more attention from his parents, writing to his mother from school, 'I am so wretched. Even now I weep. Please my darling mummy be kind to your loving son . . . Let me at least think that you love me.' Lord Randolph Churchill certainly questioned his son's abilities, telling his own mother that Winston 'has little [claim] to cleverness, to knowledge or any capacity for settled work. He has great talent for show-off exaggerations and make believe.' When Churchill wrote to his father, exulting in getting into the military academy at Sandhurst on his third attempt, Lord Randolph's reply was crushing, condemning him for not doing well enough to get into an infantry regiment, continuing, 'If you cannot prevent yourself from leading the idle, useless, unprofitable life you have had during your school days and later months, you'll become a mere social wastrel . . . and you will degenerate into a shabby, unhappy and futile existence.'

Lord Randolph died when Winston was twenty. After Sandhurst, Churchill went both as an army officer and a successful reporter wherever the military action was – Cuba, the North-West Frontier in India, the last great cavalry charge of the British army at Omdurman in the Sudan, and South Africa, where he was captured in a Boer attack on an armoured train. His spectacular escape, and his thrilling first-person account of it for the *Morning Post*, made him a national hero. For the first time his mother took notice and promoted his career using the influence she had built up through her many affairs, including with Edward VII when he was Prince of Wales. In September 1900 Churchill was elected a Member of Parliament, which he was to remain, with one short break, until just before his death sixty-five years later. 'Restless, egotistical, bumptious, shallow-minded and reactionary but with a certain personal magnetism, great pluck and some originality' was how the socialist Beatrice Webb described him during his early years in Parliament. Originally a Conservative, he crossed the floor to join the Liberals, serving as Trade Secretary before being appointed Home Secretary and then in 1911 First Lord of the Admiralty, the political head of the Royal Navy.

Early in the First World War, Churchill – already a Cabinet minister for six years – was the major proponent of landings at Gallipoli in the Dardanelles, designed to knock Turkey swiftly out of the enemy alliance. The disastrous failure of the landings led in late May 1915 to his dismissal from the Admiralty. His wife later remembered, 'The Dardanelles haunted him for the rest of his life. He always believed in it. When he left the Admiralty he thought he was finished . . . I thought he would die of grief.'

For some months in late 1915 and early 1916, Churchill became a front-line infantry battalion commander in the trenches of the Western Front – the only one of the Big Three leaders ever to see front-line action. Returning to Britain, he became Minister for Munitions and in 1919 Secretary of State for War. Before that in 1918, Churchill had attended a talk by Roosevelt at one of London's Inns of Court. According to Joseph Kennedy, at the outbreak of the Second World War US ambassador to Britain and no friend to Churchill, Roosevelt told him Churchill had been rude and 'a stinker . . . lording it all over us'. When they first met during the Second World War Churchill could not recall meeting Roosevelt before – somewhat to the chagrin of the President.

Churchill, as a British Cabinet minister, was among the most vociferous in urging armed intervention against the Russian Revolution. He condemned Bolshevism as a 'foul baboonery' and 'a pestilence more destructive of life than the Black Death or the Spotted Typhus' and approved the dispatch of support to White Russian forces around Archangel and Murmansk and the use of British naval forces to help ensure the independence of the Baltic states as agreed at the Versailles Peace Conference in 1919.[*]

By the early 1930s, Churchill was in the wilderness. Having rejoined the Conservative Party and served five years as an undistinguished Chancellor of the Exchequer, he had become distanced from the leadership of his party following the Conservative defeat

---

[*] A bronze plaque in the Holy Spirit Church in Estonia's capital Tallinn celebrates the British intervention and the award of the Cross of Liberty to Churchill and others.

in 1929, originally owing to his opposition to the smallest concessions to Indian Home Rule and later to efforts by the British
government to appease Hitler.

Churchill condemned the Indian independence leader Mohandas
Gandhi as a 'half-naked fakir'. When told by Lord Halifax, a
former Viceroy of India, that he held views of India 'similar to
those of a subaltern [second lieutenant], a generation ago' and
that he might wish to update them by meeting some Indian
political activists, Churchill replied, 'I am quite satisfied with my
views of India, I don't want them disturbed by any bloody Indian.'

Churchill's campaign against appeasement reached a peak after
Neville Chamberlain's notorious abandonment of Czechoslovakia
under the 1938 Munich Agreement with Hitler. Churchill told
the House of Commons,

> Parliament should know there has been gross neglect . . . in
> our defences . . . we have sustained a defeat without a war the
> consequence of which will travel far with us along our road . . .
> the whole equilibrium of Europe has been deranged . . . this
> is only the beginning of the reckoning . . . the first foretaste
> of a bitter cup which will be offered to us year by year – unless
> – by a supreme recovery of our moral health and martial vigour,
> we arise and take our stand for freedom.

Franklin Roosevelt came from a long-established Anglo-Dutch
family and enjoyed a happy childhood on his family's Springwood
estate at Hyde Park overlooking the Hudson River near
Poughkeepsie. An only child with a devoted if somewhat domin-
eering mother, he was the only one of the three leaders to attend
university – in his case Harvard. However, he did not excel
academically there or subsequently at Columbia Law School,
perhaps justifying Supreme Court Justice Oliver Wendell Holmes's
later comment, 'A second-class intellect. But a first-class
temperament.'

In 1910, as a Democrat in contrast to his Republican fifth
cousin Theodore, Roosevelt secured his first elected position –

that of a New York State senator. He later suggested that he needed this apprenticeship before moving on to the federal level, writing, 'I was an awfully mean cuss when I first went into politics.' Three years afterwards, he was offered his first federal office – that of Assistant Secretary of the Navy, a position which fostered his love of the sea, just as Churchill's Admiralty posting had for him. In his very first message to Churchill, Roosevelt noted their common naval experience. Throughout the Second World War Churchill's messages to Roosevelt were often signed 'Former Naval Person'.

Roosevelt was in France on an inspection tour during President Wilson's negotiations at the Versailles Peace Conference which led to the creation of the League of Nations. The League was Wilson's brainchild and he received the 1919 Nobel Peace Prize for his part in its foundation. Roosevelt returned to Washington from Versailles on the same ship as Wilson. During the voyage Wilson said of the League, 'The United States must go in or it will break the heart of the world for she is the only nation that all feel is disinterested and all trust.' Roosevelt agreed and stored the quote for future use – the sentiments would underlie his future advocacy of the United Nations at Yalta and elsewhere.

However, that same year the US Senate vetoed Wilson's proposal that the US should join the League as impinging upon US sovereignty. Nevertheless the League was still a live issue when, at the age of thirty-eight, Roosevelt ran as the Democratic vice-presidential candidate to James Cox in the 1920 US presidential election. Roosevelt strongly supported the League during the campaign. After the landslide victory of Republican Warren Harding, the US remained outside the League, leaving that organization even more toothless than it might have been.

In August 1921, sailing in his yacht off New Brunswick, Roosevelt fell overboard as a sudden weakness deprived him of his balance. He had contracted the polio which paralysed his legs. In 1927 he founded an institute for the treatment and rehabilitation of polio patients at Warm Springs in Georgia. In line with the policy of the southern states, it was segregated – black people were not admitted. Like Churchill in his thinking about the races of the British Empire at this time, Roosevelt would go beyond casual racism, arguing in the newspapers against Japanese immigration because 'Japanese immigrants are not capable of assimilation into the American population . . . the mingling of Asiatic blood with European and or American blood produces in nine cases out of ten the most unfortunate results.'

In 1928 Roosevelt ran for the governorship of New York State, winning by 25,000 votes out of 4.2 million when the Republican Herbert Hoover was winning the presidency by a landslide. Re-elected governor by a larger majority in 1930, Roosevelt then won the Democratic presidential nomination in 1932 when, following the economic crash of 1929, Hoover's reputation had degenerated to the extent that the joke was, 'If Hoover won, Mahatma Gandhi would make the best-dressed list.' Roosevelt defeated Hoover in a landslide and immediately embarked on his New Deal revolution, telling the American people, 'the only thing we have to fear is fear itself,' launching public works programmes, regulating the banks and stock market and thereby restoring confidence in the economy, and giving direct assistance to the unemployed, who then numbered more than a quarter of the industrial workforce. In all he did he showed great ability as 'a reconciler' of seemingly diametrically opposed factions. Using what Henry Wallace called his 'feminine intuition about people', Roosevelt improvised solutions to solve immediate problems 'at least for the present'. In 1936 he was re-elected with an even greater majority, won an unprecedented third term in 1940, and had started his fourth just before Yalta.*

By the time the Versailles Peace Conference assembled in 1919 to decide the shape of Europe after the First World War, Stalin had achieved considerable power. According to a contemporary, 'Stalin did not like to speak about his childhood'. He was born Joseph Vissarionovich Djugashvili in December 1878 to a drunkard father who beat him and his mother. Both Stalin's parents had

---

* In December 1933, Roosevelt had found time to repeal Prohibition, something which would have undoubtedly appealed to Churchill.

been born serfs. They lived in Gori, a small town on the Kura River in Georgia.

Stalin was the only one of four siblings to survive a harsh childhood. After his mother threw out his father she took in washing from the local merchants and priests. Perhaps with the latter's help, in 1894 Stalin won a scholarship to the Orthodox seminary in the Georgian capital Tiflis (Tbilisi), where he was paid five roubles a month as a choirboy. Stalin later said his father once appeared at the seminary asking him for money, pleading, 'Don't be as mean as your mother!' Stalin told him to leave or 'I'll call the watchman'.

Stalin was expelled from the seminary in 1899. Shortly afterwards he became a full-time revolutionary and in 1902 was first exiled to Siberia. In 1907 he robbed a bank in Tbilisi of 250,000 roubles to fund the revolutionary cause. Afterwards he visited several European countries including Britain – he first met Trotsky in London – to attend revolutionary meetings. A visit to Prague and Kraków at the end of 1912 was his last outside Russia until the first 'Big Three' conference at Teheran in 1943. Some time before then he had begun writing in Russian rather than Georgian. His spoken Russian retained a strong Georgian accent throughout his life. In 1912 at Lenin's urging he was elected a member of the Communist Party's Central Committee and began using the name Stalin, meaning 'steel'. At around this time he is believed to have acted as a double agent, betraying his opponents among the revolutionaries to the Tsarist secret police, the Okhrana. This may explain why the further period of exile to which he was sentenced shortly afterwards was less than might have been expected.

Following the abdication of the Tsar in March 1917, Stalin fled his exile and travelled to St Petersburg where he took over the editorship of *Pravda* (*Truth*), the Bolshevik newspaper, from his future Foreign Minister Molotov. After the Bolshevik Revolution of October 1917 he rose in the party hierarchy. In spring 1918, Lenin dispatched him on an armoured train with 400 Red Guards to bring order to the chaos and treachery in the strategic city of Tsaritsyn on the Volga, a gateway to the Caucasus's oil and grain supplies threatened by advancing White Russians. There, from his blue-silk decorated railway lounge car, Stalin completed 'a ruthless purge of the rear administered by an iron hand'. Tsaritsyn was renamed Stalingrad after him in April 1925.

Other important tasks followed until in 1922 Stalin was appointed General Secretary of the Central Committee of the Communist Party. Following Stalin's merciless behaviour in suppressing dissent in his native Georgia and elsewhere, Lenin became disillusioned with his protégé, warning towards the end of 1922, after he had suffered his first stroke, that Stalin 'has concentrated immense power in his hands, and I am not certain he will always know how to make use of this power with sufficient caution'; a little later he warned, 'Stalin is too rough and this defect becomes . . . intolerable for one who holds the office of General Secretary [of the Communist Party].' Nevertheless, in the years following Lenin's death in January 1924 Stalin achieved complete power at the expense of Trotsky, not least by arguing that the Communist Party should concentrate on 'Socialism in one Country', the USSR, rather than on the rolling international revolution favoured by Trotsky.

Stalin oversaw a disastrous forced collectivization of peasant farmers, leading to a mass famine in 1932/3. Thirty-two million of the Soviet Union's 70 million cattle died or were killed in the upheaval, together with nearly two-thirds of the goats and half of the horses. Tragically some 6–8 million people died, among them 4–5 million from the fertile Ukraine. Going through a Ukrainian village, a journalist found messages scrawled beside bodies, 'God bless those who enter here, may they never suffer as we have.'

Dissatisfied with the lack of party discipline and firmness in the response of some colleagues to the turmoil of the collectivization and fearing attempts to usurp him both from the Trotskyite left and the Bukharinite right of the Communist Party, Stalin embarked on a series of great purges during the middle and late 1930s. On trumped-up charges – or even without charge – he had 93 of the 139-strong Central Committee and 89 of the 103 Soviet generals and admirals executed. Up to a third of the 3 million or so members of the Communist Party were also killed. Estimates vary, but many millions of ordinary civilians suspected of disloyalty or of being kulaks – former landowning peasants too rich for their own good – or simply innocents denounced by a personal enemy were deported or sent to the gulags, where they died in great numbers.

Although reports of the suffering and of the trials reached the West, many, particularly socialists and liberal thinkers sympathetic to communist ideals, refused to credit them, believing them exaggerated or that there was truth in the confessions at the trials – denying or not realizing they had been tortured out of the accused. In 1944, an American adviser who accompanied Vice-President Wallace on a visit to the Kolyma Gulag where 3 million died between 1937 and 1953 wrote a magazine article comparing the gulag to the Tennessee Valley Authority, a centrepiece project of Roosevelt's New Deal. Roosevelt himself underestimated Stalin's crimes when he found him guilty of 'the indiscriminate killings of thousands of innocent victims'.

Reluctance on the part of the Western Allies to recognize the truth about the extent and gravity of the Soviet regime's excesses, or at the very least a conviction that they were committed by dark forces outside the control of Stalin and the leadership, persisted throughout the war years.

CHAPTER TWO

'We Ended Friends'

Churchill and Roosevelt's first meeting during the Second World War took place at Placentia Bay in Newfoundland in August 1941. It followed France's capitulation, Churchill's appointment as prime minister and his formation of a national government (he would not face an election as prime minister until 1945) and Roosevelt's re-election for a third term in November 1940. The President and Prime Minister were already well into their wartime exchange of nearly 2,000 messages, of which Churchill sent three to Roosevelt's every two, and the two men would spend four out of the next thirty months in each other's company and even more time travelling to their meetings. In March 1941, Roosevelt had instituted the Lend-Lease programme whereby America provided its allies with equipment and services to be repaid in kind after the war. Churchill described it as 'the most unsordid act in the history of any nation'. From the earliest days Churchill had cultivated the relationship, calling the President 'sir' during their first telephone conversations and always playing the humble suitor, later recalling, 'No lover ever studied every whim of his mistress as I did those of President Roosevelt.'

Aboard the new battleship HMS *Prince of Wales*, with Roosevelt's two advisers Harry Hopkins and Averell Harriman, who had travelled with him to Placentia Bay, Churchill nervously awaited the arrival of the President on the USS *Augusta*, all the time wondering 'if he will like me'. Several times during the ensuing discussions he quizzed Harriman about the impression he was making. He need not have worried. As Harriman wrote to his daughter Kathleen, 'Historic meeting of the great men . . . has taken place . . . The P.M. has been in his best form. The President is intrigued and likes him enormously.'

The main product of their Newfoundland meeting would be this burgeoning friendship, but to the outside world it was the agreement of the Atlantic Charter. This aspirational document – Churchill would later call it 'not a law but a star' – committed the two men to democracy and to basic freedoms such as those of speech and religion, and freedom from want, as well as the establishment after the war of an international system to ensure them. The aims of freedom of trade and self-determination posed some difficulties to the British with their imperial possessions but they were soon glossed over. The two leaders sent the charter to Stalin for comment since he was now Britain's formal ally following the German invasion of the Soviet Union in Operation Barbarossa on 22 June 1941 – before which Stalin had ignored warnings from both the UK and the US of the imminence of the attack. Churchill and Roosevelt had immediately recognized the need to embrace Russia in their anti-Nazi coalition. As Churchill said, 'If Hitler invaded hell, I would make at least a favourable reference to the devil in the House of Commons.'

By the time Churchill, the first of the two Western leaders to meet Stalin, visited Moscow in August 1942, the President and Prime Minister had met twice more in Washington, deepening their all-important personal relationship. Much had changed in the war. Japan had attacked Pearl Harbor – an attack about which the American high command had ignored warnings just as Stalin had about Barbarossa. Hitler had released Roosevelt from a dilemma by declaring war on the United States. The war had gone badly for all three Allies with the loss of the Philippines, the fall of Singapore and Hong Kong, with Leningrad besieged and vast swathes of Russian territory, including the Crimea, occupied by the Nazis.

Perhaps the most important decision taken by Roosevelt and Churchill at their Washington meetings was one with which Stalin wholeheartedly agreed: priority should be given to the European theatre and the defeat of Germany, rather than that of Japan, with whom the Soviet Union was not at war. The US had also extended Lend-Lease to the Soviet Union. However, Stalin had been less pleased that a full-scale cross-Channel invasion by the Allies was not foreseen until 1943, and at his second Washington meeting with Roosevelt Churchill had begun to query even that date, proposing Allied landings in Tunisia in North Africa instead.

Churchill flew to Moscow in a converted B-24 Liberator bomber for his first meeting with Stalin. According to Harriman, who was present, Stalin spoke with 'bluntness almost to the point of insult' about the delays in the cross-Channel invasion, urging Churchill, 'No risks taken; no victories gained. Just don't be afraid of the Germans,' only to be partly mollified by news of the planned Tunisian landings. At one of their dinners Stalin raised Churchill's prominent support for British intervention on behalf of the White Russians in 1918/19. Churchill agreed, 'I was very active in the intervention, and I do not wish you to think otherwise.' Stalin smiled and Churchill asked, 'Have you forgiven me?' 'All that is in the past, and the past belongs to God,' the ex-seminarian and formally atheist dictator replied.

Not to be outdone, Churchill asked Stalin about Trotsky, the problems of collectivization of farming and the deaths of the kulaks, which Stalin brushed off as 'very bad and difficult – but necessary'. On several occasions Churchill felt the meetings were going so badly he ought to return home. However, a final dinner and hard drinking session lasting six hours produced a thaw in relations. Churchill returned to Britain believing he had achieved such a relationship with 'this hard-boiled egg of a man' that 'I was taken into the family . . . We ended friends.' Stalin, though, privately remained distrustful, fearing as he would throughout the war that the British and Americans might intend to make a separate peace with Germany when the latter was sufficiently weakened at the cost of Soviet blood.*

---

* During the course of the dinner Churchill watched with some awe as Stalin 'offered me the head of a pig and when I refused, he himself tackled it with relish. With a knife he cleaned out the head, putting it into his mouth with his knife. He then cut pieces of flesh from the cheeks of the pig and ate them with his fingers . . .'

The two men had stressed the desirability of a meeting of the 'Big Three', but this did not occur until November 1943 in Teheran. Before then Churchill and Roosevelt had met four more times, including a pre-Teheran meeting with the Chinese Nationalist leader Chiang Kai-shek in Cairo. By then the war had swung towards the Allies, with victories at Stalingrad, Kursk, Midway and El Alamein, followed by the successive Anglo-American invasions of North Africa, Sicily and southern Italy and the Italian surrender. At Casablanca in January 1943, Roosevelt and Churchill announced that they would only accept unconditional surrender of their enemies – a stance which somewhat eased Soviet fears that they might make a separate peace, but ran the risk of hardening German resistance.

During the next two conferences in Washington and Quebec and amid not a little acrimony between the American and British General Staffs, the date for the cross-Channel invasion – Operation Overlord – was pushed back at British urging to May 1944. Over the course of the year Churchill became increasingly conscious of his country's diminishing role as US forces built up and began to outnumber Britain's and as an American – General Dwight D. Eisenhower – not a Briton, was appointed to command Overlord. Not without a hint of irony Churchill continued to describe himself to Roosevelt as his lieutenant. He was more than disappointed to discover that Roosevelt was secretly attempting to set up a private meeting between himself and Stalin. When Churchill found out, Roosevelt falsely claimed that the idea had been Stalin's and in any case that Stalin might 'be more frank' without Churchill present. He wanted 'to explore his thinking as fully as possible concerning Russia's post-war hopes and ambitions'. That meeting never took place.

At the Teheran Conference Churchill wryly illustrated his diminished status, describing himself as 'a poor little English donkey' in between 'the great Russian bear' on one side and 'the great American buffalo' on the other, but he was still self-confident enough to suggest he was 'the only one of the three who knew the right way home'. An aide described Roosevelt as 'always thinking he could "handle" people, no matter who . . . He had

that self-confidence that he would be in control no matter who
or where . . . that he would pull through as the top dog.' Roosevelt
deliberately set out to woo Stalin, whom he saw as the leader of
an emerging superpower. One means by which he hoped to win
Stalin's trust was by distancing himself from Churchill, the leader
of an empire in decline, much to the latter's dismay. Pleased with
the opportunity it gave him to engineer separate meetings with
Stalin, Roosevelt acquiesced in Stalin's proposal that he should
stay in the Soviet Legation in Teheran so he would be safer from
Nazi agents. At their private meetings he emphasized disagreements with Churchill on issues such as India, the role of France
and the date of the cross-Channel invasion.

At the subsequent full conference sessions when Stalin attacked
Churchill for his tardiness about the cross-Channel invasion
Roosevelt did not come to Churchill's assistance. The President's
interpreter, diplomat Charles Bohlen, recalled, 'I did not like the
attitude of the President, who not only backed Stalin but seemed
to enjoy the Churchill–Stalin exchanges.' On another occasion,
in Roosevelt's own words,

> As soon as I sat down at the conference table, I began to tease
> Churchill about his Britishness, about John Bull, about his cigars,
> about his habits. It began to register with Stalin. Winston got
> red and scowled, and the more he did so the more Stalin
> smiled . . . I kept it up until Stalin was laughing with me and
> it was then that I called him 'Uncle Joe'. He would have thought
> me fresh the day before but that day he laughed and came over
> and shook my hand. From that time on our relations were
> personal . . . The ice was broken and we talked like men and
> brothers.

Churchill's daughter Mary recalled, 'My father was the odd
man out. He felt that very keenly. [He] was very hurt, I think.'
Nonetheless, partly through his intelligence information and the
result of bugging during the conference and partly due to his
inherent suspicion, Stalin was never fully convinced of Roosevelt's
sincerity in distancing himself from his loyal ally Churchill.

The substance of the Teheran Conference centred first around Churchill and Roosevelt reassuring Stalin of their commitment to launching the cross-Channel invasion Overlord in May 1944, backed up by operations in the Mediterranean. They then turned to preliminary discussions of some of the topics that would take prominence at Yalta: the organization that would become known as the 'United Nations', the role of France and the irksome de Gaulle, the fate of Poland and its future borders, Soviet entry into the Pacific conflict, war reparations and the punishment of war criminals. Speaking about the latter at one of the heavy-drinking dinners, Stalin – jocularly, according to most of those present – said, 'The German General Staff must be liquidated. Fifty thousand officers and technicians should be rounded up and shot . . . at the end of the war Germany military strength would be extirpated.'

Churchill, perhaps already irritated by his treatment by Roosevelt and Stalin, took him seriously and snapped back, 'The British Parliament and public will never tolerate mass executions . . . The Soviets must be under no delusion on this point.' 'Fifty thousand must be shot,' Stalin insisted. A deeply angered Churchill said, 'I would rather be taken out into the garden here and now and be shot myself than sully my own and my country's honour by such infamy.' Roosevelt's son Elliott, who was present, then according to Churchill 'made a speech saying how cordially he agreed with Marshal Stalin's plan and how sure he was that the United States army would support it'. Churchill got up and left the room to be followed by Molotov and Stalin, 'both grinning broadly', who reassured him that it was a joke. Mollified, he returned.

At the end of the conference the communiqué issued by the three leaders looked forward to 'the day when all peoples of the world may live free lives, untouched by tyranny and according to their varying desires and their own consciences' – a pious hope far from fulfilment with the Soviets already deporting hundreds of thousands of their own citizens and even further away when the Yalta Conference opened thirteen months later with millions of displaced persons and prisoners on the move.

During these intervening months the fighting had gone well for all three Allies, with the D-Day invasion removing one bone of contention between them. But few other outstanding issues had been resolved. As the British envoy for North Africa and future British Prime Minister Harold Macmillan observed at this time, 'It is clear that Washington and London are not as close as they were. The honeymoon stage between the President and the Prime Minister is over, and the normal difficulties and divergences, inseparable from staid married life, are beginning to develop.'

Churchill and Roosevelt met again in Washington and Quebec in September 1944 and Churchill visited Stalin in Moscow the following month. Churchill's discussions with Roosevelt were notable for the signing of a secret agreement between the US and UK to continue to collaborate post-war on atomic research, but also for an extraordinary debate about the future of Germany, once defeated. Henry Morgenthau, the US Secretary of the Treasury and a long-time friend of the President, joined Roosevelt and Churchill at their discussion in Quebec. There he argued vociferously for the plan on which he had been working for some time for the 'pasturalization' of Germany under which all its factories would be dismantled and their machinery distributed among the Allied nations as reparations, and for the German state to be broken up.

Churchill, backed by his Foreign Secretary Anthony Eden, at first disagreed. 'You cannot indict a whole nation.' The proposals were 'unnatural, un-Christian and unnecessary'. However Roosevelt, who believed that 'The German people as a whole must have it driven home to them that the whole nation has been involved in a lawless conspiracy against the decencies of modern civilization,' supported Morgenthau. Since, as the Prime Minister recorded in his memoirs, he had 'so much to ask' from his American counterpart, in particular a renewal of Lend-Lease, Churchill made a U-turn and agreed to the proposals – to Eden's openly expressed disgust. However, when the plan was leaked to the US press, probably by the US Treasury Department itself, there was an outcry in the country against its severity in which the British War Cabinet joined. In Germany, Goebbels told the German people in a radio broadcast, 'The plan proposed by the

Jew Morgenthau would rob 80 million Germans of their industry and turn Germany into a simple potato field.' A headline above a newspaper article encouraging Germans to fight on read, 'Roosevelt and Churchill Agree to a Jewish Murder Plan'. Sensitive as ever to American public opinion, Roosevelt soon dropped the proposal, professing privately that it was 'nonsense' and that he had 'not the faintest recollection of having approved it'. He and Churchill would thus arrive at Yalta with no firm plan for the treatment of a conquered Germany.

Churchill's visit to Moscow in October 1944 was even more controversial. Despite knowing Roosevelt's opposition to discussion of what were euphemistically known as 'spheres of influence', Churchill did something which in his own words was 'naughty'. Motivated in part by his desire to preserve the British position in the Mediterranean and in part by practicalities, he proposed a division of influence in Eastern Europe, scribbling it on a piece of paper in percentage terms, suggesting 90 per cent British influence in Greece, 90 per cent Soviet influence in Romania, 75 per cent Soviet in Bulgaria and 50/50 for both countries in Yugoslavia and Hungary. Churchill made no mention of Poland nor the Baltic states. Making clear it was a personal, not even a British government, let alone an American, initiative, he passed the note to Stalin. Saying that 'the US claims too many rights for itself' and did not leave enough initiative to the Soviets and Britain, Stalin ticked the paper with a blue pencil and handed it back.

Perhaps already a little worried at his impetuosity in disposing so cavalierly of the fate of whole populations without any pretence of consulting them, Churchill said, 'Might it not be thought rather cynical if it seemed we had disposed of these issues so fateful to millions of people in such an offhand matter? . . . Let us burn the paper.' Stalin told him to keep it, which he did. Following pressure from Averell Harriman, US ambassador to Moscow since October 1943, whom Churchill told about it, he never sent a promised follow-up letter to Stalin, and the discussion and some follow-ups between Eden and Molotov were not referred to again either at Yalta or elsewhere. However, the divisions so lightly agreed would influence both of the leaders' future thinking, including at Yalta. Most fortunately, unlike the Morgenthau Plan, the division was never leaked to the press.

During the visit to Moscow, Churchill had emphasized the importance of the planned second Big Three meeting for which all three had expressed enthusiasm, originally proposed for late summer 1944, but for which no timing or location had yet been established, telling colleagues, 'We can settle everything, we three, if we come together.'

On 19 October, Stalin paid Churchill the rare compliment of going to the airport to see him off in person. The same day in a telegram to Roosevelt headed 'Secret and Personal' Stalin wrote that Andrei Gromyko, the Soviet ambassador to Washington, had told him Harry Hopkins had suggested the idea that 'you could arrive in the Black Sea at the end of November and meet with me on the Soviet Black Sea coast'. Stalin welcomed the proposal and so, he believed, did Churchill.

The idea of the Black Sea indeed originated with the President's adviser, Harry Hopkins. Knowing Stalin's dislike of travelling and keen to get plans for a conference moving, he had suggested the recently liberated Crimea to Roosevelt, whose only caveat had been that no conference take place until after the presidential elections in early November. Thus encouraged, Hopkins had discussed suitable Black Sea locations with Gromyko.

On 22 October, Churchill assured the President he would 'come anywhere you two desire'. Roosevelt then hesitated. He planned to travel by ship and thought sailing through the heavily mined waters of the Dardanelles might be too risky. That same day he therefore asked Churchill, 'Do you think it is possible to get U. J. to come to Athens or Cyprus?' Churchill thought it unlikely, 'there would be the same difficulties in Russian warships coming out of the Black Sea as of American and British warships coming in'. In the same telegram, Churchill raised his own misgivings about the Black Sea region, which he had seen when his plane landed there during his recent journey from Moscow: 'From what I saw of the Crimea it seems much shattered and I expect

all other Black Sea ports are in a similar state. We should therefore in all probability have to live on board our ships.' He agreed
that Athens would be more suitable or indeed Cyprus, 'where
absolute secrecy, silence and security can be guaranteed together
with plain comfortable accommodation for all.' He added, 'Will
you telegraph to U. J. on the subject or shall I? Or, better still,
shall we send a joint message?'

Roosevelt chose to write on his own to Stalin, saying, 'I would
appreciate suggestions from you. I have been thinking about the
practicability of Malta, Athens, or Cyprus if my getting into the
Black Sea on a ship should be impracticable or too difficult. I
prefer travelling and living on a ship.' Stalin, however, would not
be moved, responding:

> If the idea that was expressed earlier about the possibility of
> our meeting on the Soviet Black Sea coast appears to be accept-
> able for you I would consider it extremely desirable . . . The
> conditions for a meeting there are absolutely favourable . . .
> Since the doctors do not recommend me to undertake any big
> trips at the present time, I have to give consideration to that.

On 2 November – five days before the presidential election
– Roosevelt complained to Churchill that 'U. J.' was not being
'very helpful in the selection of a place for our next meeting . . .
His doctors to whose opinion he must give consideration do not
wish him to make any "big trips".' Roosevelt's own doctor, Vice-
Admiral Ross McIntire, had warned him 'that health conditions
in Black Sea ports such as Odessa are very bad, and we must
think of the health of our staffs and our ships' crews as well as
ourselves'. Roosevelt asked Churchill for 'any information you
may have in regard to a suitable place for the meeting, danger
from enemy action, living conditions etc.' However, his message
ended with a weary fatalism: 'I fear that Uncle Joe will insist on
the Black Sea. I do think it important that we three should meet
in the near future.'

Churchill, whose doctor Lord Moran warned diseases 'from
dysentery to bubonic plague' were rampant in the Black Sea area,

suggested Jerusalem – 'Here there are first-class hotels . . . and
every means can be taken to ensure security.' The British and
American warships could dock in Haifa. As for 'Uncle Joe', he
could travel by special train from Moscow 'with every form of
protection'. Churchill urged Roosevelt to put the ball back in
Stalin's court 'and throw on him the onus of refusing'.

Roosevelt, however, gave little further attention to the conference until after his re-election for a unique fourth term when he
irritated Churchill by telling him that he wanted to postpone any
tripartite meeting from late November until after his inauguration.
On 18 November, Roosevelt wrote to Stalin formally proposing
that the conference be delayed until 'about the twenty-eighth or
thirtieth of January'. He also said, 'My Navy people recommend
strongly against the Black Sea' and suggested that instead Stalin
should travel to a port on the Adriatic and there board an American
warship for Jerusalem, Alexandria, Rome or perhaps Taormina
in Sicily.

This latest note annoyed both Churchill and Stalin. Churchill
complained to the President,

> Your message to U. J. will, of course, make it certain that he
> will not come anywhere before the end of January . . . Even
> if a meeting can be arranged by the end of January, the two
> and a half intervening months will be a serious hiatus . . . The
> treatment of Germany and the future world organization, rela-
> tions with France, the position in the Balkans, as well as the
> Polish question . . . ought not to be left to moulder.

Significantly, the ten-week delay together with the speed of the
Soviet advance rendered some questions – in particular that of
Poland – much more difficult since Russian troops in the interim
occupied much of the territory that would be discussed. Stalin's
equally prickly reply deplored the US's negative view of Soviet
Black Sea ports and reminded Roosevelt that the idea of meeting
there had originated on the American side.

Accepting it was unlikely that Stalin could be induced to change
his mind, Roosevelt asked Averell Harriman to advise on possible

Black Sea locations. The ambassador consulted two US naval officers who had visited Yalta and Sevastopol and told him Yalta was 'by Russian standards . . . extremely neat and clean . . . The winter climate is reasonable. Average temperature in January and February 39 degrees Fahrenheit.' To avoid food poisoning Harriman suggested that the President bring his own mess crew to cook for him.

This was the first mention of Yalta specifically. Encouraged by Harriman's report, Roosevelt told Churchill it might be suitable. Even so, the battle of wills between Roosevelt and Stalin was not quite over. Harriman on Roosevelt's behalf made a last attempt to persuade Stalin to travel further afield. Stalin tried to coax Roosevelt to come to Odessa, claiming he had already begun to make arrangements there – no doubt a device to make it appear that when he agreed to Yalta if that was what the President preferred, he too could be seen to make a concession. Two days before Christmas Roosevelt instructed Harriman to agree to Yalta which, to keep the location secret, would be code-named 'Magneto'. Churchill suggested that the conference itself should be code-named 'Argonaut' after the classical myth of the voyage of Jason and the Argonauts into the Black Sea in search of the golden fleece.

Churchill also suggested that he and Roosevelt should fly to Yalta from the Allied airbase at Caserta in southern Italy. However, the President's medical advisers worried about him having to fly at altitude over high mountain ranges and instead recommended that he sail to Malta and fly on from there. 'I liked this', Churchill recalled. On New Year's Day 1945, he cabled 'I shall be waiting on the quay . . . No more let us falter! From Malta to Yalta! Let nobody alter!' Inordinately proud of his doggerel, he repeated it to anyone who would listen over the next few weeks.

Churchill also attempted to convince Roosevelt that the stop-over in Malta – code-named 'Cricket' – was a good opportunity to discuss joint strategy for the coming talks, and he asked Roosevelt to spend two or three nights there: 'You have but to say the word and we can arrange everything.' When Roosevelt replied that shortage of time would make this impossible,

Churchill pressed him at least to send his military staffs and his newly appointed Secretary of State, Edward Stettinius, ahead for discussions with their British counterparts: 'I do not see any other way of realising our hopes about world organisation in five or six days. Even the Almighty took seven,' he urged.

Churchill's 'pertinacity', as he called it, paid off. Roosevelt refused to alter his own plan of staying in Malta only one night but agreed that the heads of the military and Stettinius would arrive in time to hold joint talks. However, concerned what Stalin might infer about collusion against him if he knew the Americans and the British were getting together at Malta, he insisted no publicity be given to their meeting.

At no stage did any of the leaders contemplate inviting to Yalta either Chiang Kai-shek, the Nationalist Chinese leader who had attended the Cairo pre-Teheran Conference summit with Churchill and Roosevelt, or the French leader Charles de Gaulle who, hearing of the conference, had sought an invitation.

Although China had been at war longer even than Britain and would lose at the most conservative estimate 14 million of its inhabitants and at other estimates double that number between 1937 when the Japanese invaded and 1945 when the Second World War ended, China's absence from Yalta in part reflected the fact that the Soviet Union was not at war with China's sole adversary Japan. However, it also demonstrated the United States administration's growing disillusionment with the Nationalist regime of Chiang Kai-shek, whose armies were still conceding territory to the Japanese and whom the US had backed to the virtual exclusion of Chiang's rival, Mao Zedong and his Communist-inspired army.

As it entered the war, the US administration had placed considerable hopes in Chiang Kai-shek and his forces tying down and defeating the large bodies of Japanese troops opposing them and in consequence provided them with great amounts of funds and equipment. Their confidence in Chiang Kai-shek, who did not speak English, was enhanced by his attractive, politically influential wife, American-educated Meiling Soong. 'Vinegar Joe' Stilwell, then head of American forces in the region, described the woman he called 'Madam Empress' as 'quick, intelligent. Wants to get things done. Wishes she was a man. Doesn't think deeply but catches on in a hurry. Impulsive . . . Direct, forceful, energetic, loves power, eats up publicity and flattery . . . The Chinese were always right; the foreigners were always wrong.'

In 1943, in discussions about the embryonic United Nations China, on US urging, was named as one of the powers that would have a permanent seat on the future organization's Security Council and help 'police' the world. The President's adviser Harry Hopkins described Roosevelt's view that 'China, in any serious conflict of policy with Russia, would undoubtedly line up on our side.' Churchill complained, 'I cannot regard the Chungking government [Chiang's] as representing a great World Power. Certainly they would be a faggot vote on the side of the United States in any attempt to liquidate the British overseas Empire.'

However, as 1944 drew towards its close, Roosevelt and his advisers had become increasingly disillusioned with Chiang Kai-shek, given his regime's massive corruption, which siphoned off a great deal of the money and materiel the Americans supplied, and Chiang's insistence on keeping a large force to guard against his compatriot Mao's Communist armies, despite considerable American pressure to cooperate with Mao against the Japanese. Even more disillusioning was the poor performance of those armies which Chiang did commit to battle. Japan's Operation Ichigo offensive in the summer of 1944 conquered further large swathes of south-east China including all the air bases from which the US air force had hoped to bomb Japan in the lead-up to any invasion. In these circumstances, in Roosevelt's mind there was no question of Chiang being invited to Yalta or to any pre-summit.

Churchill, who once dismissed the Chinese as 'four hundred million pigtails', had no reason to encourage their leader's attendance at Yalta, where he would describe the Roosevelt administration's desire to increase the status of China as 'the Great

American Illusion'. The Prime Minister's main concern in the Far East was to retain Britain's influence and trading position, together with, when liberated, the colonies in the area, Singapore, Malaya and Hong Kong. Roosevelt knew this, telling his Treasury Secretary in autumn 1944, when Churchill was pressing for the British Pacific Fleet to join the American naval advance on Japan, 'all they want is Singapore back'. Many senior American officers claimed to believe that the acronym SEAC, which stood for the British-dominated South-East Asia Command, actually stood for Save England's Asian Colonies.

Roosevelt, Churchill and Stalin all agreed that France and de Gaulle should not be represented at Yalta. This was despite Churchill's worry throughout the latter stages of the war, 'What are we going to have between the white snows of Russia and the white cliffs of Dover?' He was therefore keen to restore France's status as a major power to relieve Britain of some of the burden and cost of maintaining the peace in Western Europe. However, his relationship with de Gaulle was fraught with difficulties as the Frenchman – described by Lord Moran as 'an improbable creature, like a human giraffe sniffing down his nostrils at mortals beneath his gaze' – took for granted concessions which Churchill had previously worked hard to obtain for him and simply demanded more as if his by right.

De Gaulle's obduracy and refusal to compromise were what had seen him emerge as the foremost Free French leader after he fled France in 1940 and allowed him to see off other contenders better favoured by the Allies. Churchill would tell one American official who enquired about the general, 'Oh, don't let's speak of him. We call him Jeanne d'Arc and we're looking for some bishops to burn him.' One of de Gaulle's advisers explained the general's attitude: '[He] believes that Frenchmen always try to please the man to whom they are talking. The General thinks they overdo it and he adopts a different attitude. He makes no effort to please.'

In the hours before D-Day a fierce row erupted between de Gaulle and Eisenhower about whether de Gaulle should be named in the propaganda leaflets being dropped on France in advance of the invasion. When as a consequence of Eisenhower's refusal to include him de Gaulle in turn refused to broadcast to the French people in support of the landings, Churchill called his behaviour 'treachery in battle' and demanded he be flown 'to Algiers in chains if necessary'. De Gaulle backed down and made his broadcast just before the invasion began.

Roosevelt found the Frenchman even more difficult than did Churchill, calling him 'a well nigh intolerable figure', 'a narrow-minded French zealot with too much ambition for his own good' and a potential future dictator who behaved as if France were still a world power rather than defeated and dependent on the sufferance and sacrifice of the US and the UK. The President told Churchill de Gaulle disliked both the British and the Americans 'and would doublecross both of us at the first opportunity'. De Gaulle reciprocated Roosevelt's dislike, writing, 'Roosevelt regarded me without benevolence. He meant the peace to be an American peace, convinced that he must be the one to dictate its structure . . . and that France in particular should recognise him as its saviour and arbitrator.'

Stalin no more than either of the other leaders took a liking to de Gaulle when they met. Like Roosevelt he deplored France's caving in to Germany in 1940. He queried how, with insignificant numbers of troops in the field, de Gaulle could claim to be an equal with the other Allies. In this same spirit, Churchill wrote to Eden, after de Gaulle's request to go to Yalta, that he was strongly opposed. If he attended, de Gaulle would be:

forever intriguing and playing off two against the other . . . France contributes a very small fighting stake to the pool at present. It is not French blood that is being shed to any extent in any quarter of the globe . . . I cannot think of anything more unpleasant and impossible than having this menacing and hostile man in our midst, always trying to make himself a reputation in France by claiming a position far above what France occupies, and making faces at the Allies who are doing the work.

Roosevelt and Stalin agreed wholeheartedly. As a sop de Gaulle was offered the prospect of a meeting soon afterwards with Roosevelt. To the satisfaction of all participants, the Yalta Conference would be an exclusive club of three.

PART TWO

Preparations, Malta and Elsewhere, Early 1945

'The misery of the whole world appals me.'

Winston Churchill to Clementine Churchill,
February 1945

CHAPTER THREE

Argonaut

On 20 January 1945, Roosevelt's thirty-seven-year-old eldest son James, a colonel in the marines, and a secret service man, helped the dark-suited President in his painful steel leg braces to the lectern set up on the White House's South Portico. Since George Washington's time the Capitol had hosted presidential inaugurations, but with America at war the President had decided on a more modest and subdued ceremony with no Inauguration Day parade, partly on secret service advice that a small event would be easier to protect. A crowd of only 5,000, compared to 100,000 at his first inauguration, stood watching from the White House grounds, still covered by the previous day's light fall of snow, while Roosevelt's thirteen grandchildren were grouped on the steps leading up to the portico. Chief Justice Harlan Stone held the seventeenth-century Roosevelt family bible open at the same verse from the thirteenth chapter of First Corinthians as at Roosevelt's previous three inaugurations – 'And now abideth faith, hope, charity: these three; but the greatest of these is charity.' Putting his hand on the bible, Roosevelt swore the oath of office for the fourth time.

His inaugural address was the briefest in US history – less than 600 words – and his message simple: the people of America were 'passing through a period of supreme test' during which they had learned 'to live as men and not as ostriches' and to be 'citizens of the world'. He promised that, 'In the days and the years that are to come, we shall work for a just and honorable peace, a durable peace, as today we work and fight for total victory in war.'

As he spoke, Roosevelt felt sharp chest pains, probably angina. Once back inside the White House in the privacy of the Green Room he immediately asked his son for a stiff whisky and downed it in one. Despite his determination to conceal his frailties – only his physician, Vice-Admiral Ross McIntire, was allowed to disclose information about his health – he could not deceive those close to him about his deteriorating condition. Former Vice-President Henry Wallace, who had just sworn in Harry Truman as his own successor, noticed Roosevelt's whole body 'and especially his right arm' shaking as he grasped the lectern.

President Woodrow Wilson's widow was also watching. When the ceremony was over, in a White House corridor she grabbed Frances Perkins, Secretary of Labor and the first female US cabinet member, and said, 'I feel terrible . . . He [the President] looks exactly as my husband looked when he went into his decline.' Frances Perkins recalled, 'She looked really stricken . . . That sort of frightened me, and I said to her, "Don't say that to another human soul." And I put my finger on my lips.' At the inauguration lunch Frances Perkins told the President she would pray for him. 'I need it,' he replied.

Mike Reilly, head of White House security, was not at the inauguration. A week before, he and a team had flown from Washington to check security for the President's journey to Yalta. In Naples harbour Reilly inspected USS *Catoctin*, shortly to sail to the Crimea to serve as a supply and communication ship during the conference and be available in case the President wanted to live aboard. Reilly had wooden ramps installed for Roosevelt's wheelchair, checked the range of the ship's radio communications and ordered sufficient supplies to feed a large group for up to ten days to be taken aboard.

Next Reilly flew to Malta to review facilities at Luqa aerodrome from where the conference delegates would leave for the Crimea. Then, with a small team, he boarded one of two aircraft setting out overnight to test the route the President would take to the

Crimean airfield of Saki – one of the most heavily bombed of the war and the base from which Russian fighters claimed to have shot down nearly 1,000 Luftwaffe planes.

Over the Black Sea turbulence became so violent that, though Reilly's C-54 Skymaster battled on, the other plane turned back. To escape the buffeting, Major Ed Coates, piloting Reilly's plane, climbed to 15,000 feet, only for the wings to ice up. Even after he descended to 2,000 feet ice continued to form. 'We ain't gonna make it, boys. I think we'll have to ditch this thing. Anyhow put on your parachutes,' Reilly recalled him saying 'as the plane lurched crazily'.

Somehow, Coates kept the Skymaster airborne until in the pale dawn light Saki airfield appeared ahead. Coates swooped low in a pre-arranged signal to the aerodrome's Soviet controllers that they were friend not foe. However, as he approached the runway, hundreds of Russian women were still shovelling snow away. Coates had to circle to give them time to finish before landing.

Everything Reilly had experienced convinced him that the President should not fly to Saki. As soon as he stepped onto the frozen runway, he told Artikov, the high-ranking member of the People's Commissariat for Internal Affairs (Narodnyi Komissariat Vnutrennikh Del – NKVD, the Soviet secret police) waiting to greet him, exactly what he thought. They had met before, and if Reilly was blunt – so was the Russian. When Reilly argued that the President should arrive by ship, Artikov pointed out that the Black Sea was heavily mined. When Reilly queried how many mines there were, he snapped, 'Who knows. The Germans put them there. They didn't leave a map.'

Relations improved as Reilly, Artikov and their teams set off in convoy for Yalta. After three hours, Artikov halted at an inn. Reilly, who had experienced Russian hospitality before, warned his less-seasoned colleagues to expect 'gallons and gallons of that rubbing alcohol they call vodka'. For diplomatic reasons they would have to endure it: 'They call it a party but it's a contest.' And so it proved. The Russians proposed toast after toast – to Stalin, Churchill, Roosevelt, even to the American film star Paulette Goddard. Reilly recalled that 'early Russian casualties were heavy' – one NKVD man tumbled down some stairs. He himself was soon wondering how he kept upright: 'It must have been sheer patriotism.'

Reilly and his men arrived in Yalta with aching heads to be greeted by a sight that 'did nothing to ease the pain'. Before the war, over 20,000 people had lived in the town but barely more than 200 remained with only nineteen undamaged houses to shelter them. The rest of the buildings lay in ruins. However, the Allied delegations were to be accommodated a little way outside Yalta in two palaces – the Americans in the fifty-room Livadia and the British in the Vorontsov. The retreating German troops had left both standing but stripped the Livadia of even basic fittings such as the plumbing and smashed the windows. The Vorontsov had suffered less because Hitler had given it to one of his generals who, planning to occupy it after the war, had ordered none of the original furnishings to be removed. These included a huge banqueting table and what appeared to be 'a lead-lined mahogany bathtub', in fact for chilling champagne. Artikov promised that everything needed to make both palaces fully habitable was on its way to Yalta.

Stalin had ordered Moscow's leading hotels such as the National and the Metropol to be denuded of anything and everything that might be useful. Furniture, bed linen, curtains, cut-glass wine goblets, china, cutlery, even light switches and door knobs had been loaded onto trains already trundling south through the snows to the Crimea. Stalin had also commandeered the hotels' staff to wait upon his guests, including some from the Metropol who had served the food and topped up the glasses at the gala dinner given by Stalin in Moscow in 1939 for his German guests to celebrate the Molotov–Ribbentrop Pact.

Craftsmen assisted by soldiers and even members of the NKVD were working from 5 a.m. until midnight, painting walls and installing kitchens, bathrooms and electricity to renovate the palaces. Despite the winter weather, half-starving Romanian prisoners of war clad only in rags had been put to work to restore the rutted, long-neglected gardens.

As well as the President's comfort, Reilly worried about the listening devices he knew his Soviet counterparts would install.

He decided it would be pointless to sweep the Livadia Palace for bugs until after the President had arrived, when it would be much more difficult for the NKVD to replace any removed.

Sergo Beria, 'entrusted with eavesdropping on Roosevelt and his entourage' – the same function he had fulfilled at the Teheran Conference – had high expectations of the more sophisticated equipment he had been given, including the directional micro-phones which could pick up sounds 200 metres away. He anticipated these would be especially useful when the paralysed President asked to be wheeled outside to take the air as the Russians were certain he would. He later claimed that the improved microphones which he placed in every room 'contained no metal' and were therefore 'undetectable'. Many of the NKVD agents posted to Yalta to help him were young women.

A different kind of bug – the lice and bed bugs for which Yalta was notorious – appeared easier to deal with. Reilly arranged for a team from USS *Catoctin* to delouse the Livadia before Roosevelt arrived.

Despite the presence at Yalta of British women as stenographers, cypher clerks and administrative aides, and Russian women in similar positions as well as domestic staff, the most prominent female roles would be played by daughters. On the evening of the President's inauguration, his wife Eleanor, to whom 'it was clearer every day that Franklin was far from well', suggested she accom-pany him to Yalta. By this time the union between Roosevelt and his strong-minded and intelligent wife, who had turned sixty in October 1944, had become more of a political than a conventional marital one. The cause dated back over two decades when on his return from a First World War visit to Europe Eleanor had found love letters from her social secretary Lucy Mercer in Roosevelt's baggage. He had confessed to the affair and, under pressure from his mother that a divorce would destroy his political career, prom-ised not to see Lucy again – a promise he had reneged on, entertaining Lucy after her marriage to wealthy Winthrop Rutherfurd and later widowhood without Eleanor's knowledge.

In the interim, according to his son Elliott, Roosevelt had also had an affair with his then secretary 'Missy' LeHand who died in 1944. He clearly enjoyed relaxing in the company of women and in particular that of Laura Polly Delano, his first cousin, and Margaret 'Daisy' Suckley, his more distant cousin. Both women were unmarried and devoted to him, providing the easy but entertaining companionship he wanted away from his political duties. Many writers have speculated about an affair between Roosevelt and Daisy. who wrote in her diary, 'The President is a MAN – mentally, physically and spiritually. What more can I say.' However, there is no conclusive evidence.

Although even prior to her discovering the relationship with Lucy Mercer Eleanor had considered sex with Roosevelt 'an ordeal to be borne', she had given him six children – five boys, one of whom died in infancy, and a daughter, Anna, born in 1906. Subsequent to the affair Eleanor lived an independent life, re-putedly indulging in both heterosexual and lesbian relationships. Nevertheless, although they spent many days and nights apart, she continued to be an active political First Lady, pressing her various liberal causes upon Roosevelt and offering more advice than he sometimes welcomed.

Replying uncomfortably to his wife's request to come to Yalta, Roosevelt told her, 'If you go they will all feel they have to make a great fuss.' If he took their daughter Anna it would 'be simpler', adding that Churchill was bringing his daughter Sarah, while Averell Harriman would be accompanied by his daughter Kathleen.

Eleanor acquiesced in his wishes but the incident did nothing to help her already strained relationship with her twice-married thirty-eight-year-old daughter Anna Boettiger who had become a major interface between her ailing father and the world. One commentator even suggested, 'Daddy's girl has her work cut out for her, running Daddy.' Nor was Eleanor's disappointment less-ened by her husband's half-humorous suggestion that once his term expired four years later they might visit the Arabian desert and show the Arabs how to make it bloom or take a slow cargo boat around the world.

During her husband's absence Eleanor Roosevelt would busy

herself representing him at various inaugural functions and pursuing her own liberal causes. Among them were civil rights, of which she was a strong supporter in contrast to her husband who passed no civil rights legislation during his twelve years in office. In 1939 she had resigned from the Daughters of the American Revolution because they refused the use of a hall to a prominent black American singer. Anna Boettiger would meanwhile be listed in State Department documents on Yalta as a 'lady private secretary'. Her code name in internal communications was 'Topaz'.

Churchill's marriage to his wife Clementine, ten years his junior, was undoubtedly a happy one. She put him at the centre of her life and subordinated her own interests and indeed sometimes those of their four surviving children to his. She both accompanied him on wartime visits and, like Eleanor Roosevelt, also undertook independent tours. Although Clementine confessed to a brief shipboard romance, none of his biographers has alleged that Churchill had any extra-marital relationships, often maintaining that he was not highly sexed.*

Neither the Churchills' nor in particular the Roosevelts' children found it easy to establish happy marriages – the Roosevelts' five children who survived into adulthood would be divorced a total of fourteen times between them. At the time of Yalta the marriages of two of the Churchills' children were in difficulties. Sarah, an actress and dancer who performed with Fred Astaire but now a wartime Women's Royal Air Force officer, was separating from her show business husband Victor (Vic) Oliver, of whom the Churchills had never approved, and was developing a relationship with the new US ambassador to Britain, John Winant.

The marriage of the Churchills' only son, the hard-drinking,

---

* Roy Jenkins, the former British Chancellor of the Exchequer, wrote in his biography of Churchill that he was 'probably the least dangerously sexed major politician on either side of the Atlantic, let alone across the Channel since the Younger Pitt'. However, in 2018 a TV documentary suggested Churchill had a brief affair in the 1930s with the socialite Lady Doris Castlerosse but the relatively insubstantial evidence has been widely questioned.

difficult Randolph, had also broken down. His striking, aristocratic, flame-haired wife Pamela, whom he had married within weeks of meeting, had begun an affair with Averell Harriman when he was Roosevelt's envoy in London. After separating from her husband she had lived for a considerable time with Harriman's daughter Kathleen, who remained a good friend. After Harriman left London Pamela had several other romantic relationships, including with US Army Air Force General Frank Anderson, who would attend the Yalta Conference, as would another of her close male friends British Chief of the Air Staff Charles (Peter) Portal, who would write to her from Yalta. One of several bones of contention between Randolph Churchill and his parents was that they had known of and condoned Pamela's affairs – in the case of his father at least because of the access to American thinking they provided since both he and Clementine remained on close terms with Pamela.

At the time of Yalta, Pamela was conducting an affair with Edward R. Murrow, the celebrated CBS broadcaster who spent the war in London and lauded Churchill as a leader and orator, praising him for 'mobilising the English language and sending it into battle'. In a further complication, Kathleen Harriman was said to have had a passionate affair with Roosevelt's son Franklin Delano Roosevelt Junior.

Stalin had no wife to bring to Yalta. His first wife had died of tuberculosis in 1907. His second, the highly strung Nadya Alliluyeva, committed suicide in 1932 following a dinner party at which Stalin had paid too much attention to the wife of a colleague. Stalin was devastated. 'She broke my life. She's crippled me,' he said. Their daughter Svetlana wrote, 'My mother's death was a dreadful, crushing blow, and it destroyed his faith in his friends and people in general . . . He viewed her death as a betrayal and a stab in the back.' Several biographers have agreed, suggesting her suicide scarred his personality, increasing his indifference to the suffering and death of others.

Stalin had three children. Yakov, the son of his first marriage, a pilot captured by German forces, was in a prisoner of war camp, and neither of his two children by Nadya – Svetlana, then aged eighteen and heavily pregnant, and Vasily, a heavy-drinking fighter pilot – accompanied him to Yalta. According to Sergo Beria, Stalin retained a weakness for opera singers 'and not only for their talent. My father did not fail to tell smutty stories about their relationships. They were all very big, well-endowed blondes with blue eyes who were at least a head taller than Stalin; Valkyrie types'. However, it was not a voluptuous opera singer but Stalin's faithful mistress for the last quarter of his life, his housekeeper the buxom Valentina Istomina, 'Valechka', who came to Yalta with him. As ever and in accordance with Stalin's wishes she would keep quietly in the background.

Averell Harriman and his twenty-seven-year-old daughter Kathleen travelled by train from Moscow to Yalta in advance of the conference to check on the arrangements. The tall, darkly handsome, twice-married fifty-three-year-old ambassador to the Soviet Union was the son of a Union Pacific Railroad baron. His second wife remained in the United States, while Kathleen acted as his hostess at the embassy. His previous business contacts with the Soviet Union and his time in the Moscow embassy had left him with no illusions about those the President would have to deal with on the Soviet side during the Yalta Conference. He had already explicitly warned the President that Stalin, Molotov and Stalin's other close associates were men 'bloated with power' who expected to 'force acceptance of their decisions without question upon us and all countries' and that their approach towards Poland in particular was one of 'aggressiveness, determination and readiness to take independent action'.

The Harrimans' journey was, Kathleen recalled, long – 'three days and three nights – most of the time spent standing in bombed-out stations'. As their train ambled through snow-covered countryside they passed many freight trains loaded with American Lend-Lease trucks. A female attendant made the beds on the train 'and every hour or so walked down the passage cleaning up the dirt – a wonderful procedure – She'd spray water through her teeth on the carpet to dampen it, and then sweep'. Though the beds were comfortable, bugs bit Kathleen so badly on the first night that one of her eyes closed up. 'It itched like mad. After that I bombed everything thoroughly with DDT.'

Throughout the journey NKVD guards kept a close eye on the party, which included Harriman's personal aide Robert Meiklejohn. The travellers had come prepared. Meiklejohn wrote in his diary, 'We have brought with us bottled water and all the food needed . . . as there are no dining cars on the train – and if there were any we wouldn't dare eat in them.' Hawkers on station platforms offered bread and other eatables but 'all we bought were some eggs with which [we] compounded eggnogs that were almost pure bourbon.' Otherwise they lived on bouillon which they made by crumbling stock cubes into cups of hot water from a samovar at the end of the carriage, ham and turkey sandwiches and hard-boiled eggs. When they noticed that the female attendant eagerly 'seized upon some crusts of bread that were left on the plate' they took care to leave food after each meal.

At Simferopol, the railhead for Yalta, the Harrimans' Soviet escort urged them to spend the night in the town, claiming it was too dangerous to drive on through the mountains in the dark. The ambassador, however, insisted and despite having to battle through a snowstorm they reached Yalta safely. Two days later Harriman left again to rendezvous in Malta with Churchill and Roosevelt, leaving his daughter to oversee the frantic activity still under way to prepare the Livadia Palace for the President's arrival – 'hanging draperies, upholstering chairs, installing glass in windows, painting everywhere . . .'

On 1 February – forty-eight hours before Roosevelt was due to arrive – Kathleen wrote, 'I never quite realized that so many things could go wrong in so many ways . . . The rugs for the President's suite have been changed four times. Each time all the furniture had to be moved out – and it's big and heavy and Victorian. The Soviets just couldn't make up their minds which oriental colors looked best.' Even though Moscow hotels had been stripped, there were still not enough 'shaving mirrors, coat hangers and wash bowls' so that the surrounding area was 'being scoured for such things'. One china ashtray bore a manufacturer's mark proudly advertising that the company had served five tsars.

She also realized that, large though the Livadia was, living quarters would be cramped – only 'full generals and admirals and chiefs of state' would get their own room.

Kathleen invited Joan Bright, assistant to British General Hastings 'Pug' Ismay, who had arrived in Yalta to oversee the arrangements for the British delegation in the Vorontsov Palace, to dinner. Before the war, Joan had refused an offer to teach English to Rudolf Hess's family in Germany. One of her wartime boyfriends was Ian Fleming who, some believe, later drew on her ironic sense of humour and effortless efficiency for the character of Miss Moneypenny in his James Bond books. While still in London, telegrams from the British military mission in Moscow such as one suggesting 'plenty of flea powder and toilet paper be issued to all ranks' had alerted her to the challenges. So had a message from the Soviet People's Commissariat of Foreign Affairs saying it was 'much perturbed at the extent of overcrowding there would be'.

Entering the Vorontsov Palace for the first time, Joan thought it 'a dream. Inside the large hall there blazed two wood fires in two baronial fireplaces.' Maids in black dresses and white aprons hurried about and immaculately dressed waiters served her food, which after the 'poverty and misery' she had seen on the drive to Yalta, seemed 'out of a fairy-tale'. Among the staff she recognized a woman from one of the Moscow hotels, 'tall, dear Nina Alexandrovna'. Only the more senior British delegates would live in the Vorontsov itself. The rest would stay in two sanatoria some distance away in the palace grounds. Inspecting them, Joan was dismayed, 'Though they were clean, with new paint, their amenities were meagre, and I could not see my military and diplomatic charges exactly greeting with joy dormitories for six without bath.' She telegraphed General Ismay: 'accommodation will stretch people's tempers to limit'.

As Kathleen showed her around the Livadia Joan realized 'my mathematical problem of six brigadiers into one room was elementary compared with theirs; they were sleeping eight generals to one room, sixteen full colonels to one and forty middle ranks to one.'

*

The British and the American 'Argonauts' set out in late January, their destination a closely guarded secret though it was common knowledge the three leaders were about to meet. Despite attempts to keep it out of the news, the arrival in Europe in late January of Harry Hopkins, sent by Roosevelt for talks with the Pope, de Gaulle – to try to placate him about not being invited to the conference – and Churchill, was widely reported on both sides of the Atlantic. Hopkins's conversations with newsmen left them in little doubt that the long-awaited second gathering was imminent. In the US reporters noted Roosevelt's and Anna Boettiger's sudden absence from Washington and that White House officials refused to discuss their whereabouts, while in the UK the absence of both Churchill and Eden from the House of Commons fuelled the speculation.

Churchill's journey of about 3,000 miles would be shorter than Roosevelt's but still somewhat of a challenge to a seventy-year-old who had already suffered one heart attack. Nevertheless, Churchill who was out of Britain for over a year of his five-year wartime prime ministership, travelling more than 100,000 miles by land, sea and air and on his more risky journeys telling his bodyguards to shoot him rather than allow him to be captured, resented the destination far more than the risks of travel. Five days before departing he complained to Harry Hopkins, 'if we had spent ten years on research, we could not have found a worse place in the world'. Two days later, on 26 January, Churchill sent Roosevelt a telegram warning that a team of American and British officers had twice attempted to reach Yalta, only to be forced back by mountain blizzards – a 'most terrifying experience', a British officer had reported.

At 9.30 on the evening of 29 January, Churchill's Skymaster took off for Malta from RAF Northolt outside London earlier than originally planned to avoid anticipated bad weather, with Churchill travelling under the code name Colonel Kent. His thirty-year-old daughter Sarah Oliver and his physician Lord Moran were among others on board. At first the plane was freezing, so cold that, as Sarah wrote to her mother:

Papa sat huddled in his great coat – then it began to get hot and in a minute we were all pink as tomatoes screaming for air. More re-adjustments but Papa looked like a poor hot pink baby about to cry! He took his temperature – it was up . . . It was about one o'clock before we settled in for the night but nobody slept much.

Churchill blamed his temperature on some sulphonamide pills Moran had given him but his doctor denied they were the cause.

At 4.30 a.m. in the darkness of a winter morning, the plane touched down in Malta. With Churchill's temperature still high, Moran contemplated having him admitted to hospital rather than transferring, as planned, to the light cruiser HMS *Orion*, moored in Valetta's battered Grand Harbour. 'It was touch and go between the ship and the hospital for a few hours,' Sarah Oliver recalled. 'The hospital was laid on – the ship was cancelled – the hospital was cancelled, and the ship laid on.' With Churchill starting to feel a little better he boarded the *Orion* only to find the vessel too cold for his liking and 'the bed round the wrong way'. Churchill 'sat in a dejected lump' while the furniture was shifted, before retiring to bed to be comforted with hot-water bottles.

Eden, who had left England twelve hours earlier than Churchill, flying separately from the Prime Minister for security reasons, also had a bad flight. He recalled, 'we flew high and were not given oxygen with the result that I arrived with a headache, not feeling too good'. The British military Chief of Staff, the forthright Field Marshal Sir Alan Brooke, who left at the same time as Eden, wrote:

A poisonous cold morning, driving through a snow covered Hyde Park in half darkness. I loathed the idea of launching myself out into cold space and longed to be able to remain at home! However we had a wonderful trip mostly at 12,000 ft height over the clouds in brilliant sunshine.

A week earlier he had railed:

I don't feel that I can stand another day working with Winston, it is quite hopeless, he is finished and gone, incapable of grasping any military situation and unable to give a decision. We met him this morning to try [unsuccessfully] and get from him some decisions prior to our meeting with the American Chiefs of Staff.

On his arrival in Malta, Brooke plunged into these strategic discussions with his American counterparts. By this time Allied victory in Europe seemed virtually assured. With some notable exceptions, such as northern and western Holland, where hundreds of thousands in cities like Amsterdam were being reduced to eating tulip bulbs and sugar beets in what became known as the 'Hunger Winter', nearly all the lands seized by the German armies since war began in 1939 had been liberated. However, although the main uncertainty seemed not if but when the Nazis would be defeated, much serious fighting clearly still lay ahead and the strategy for the future was the main item for discussion among the chiefs.

In the west the invasion of France, much disputed and debated not only at Teheran in 1943 but also between the two Western Allies themselves, had succeeded. Paris had been liberated in August 1944 and nearly all of France was now free. Further north the German army's December Ardennes offensive, in which a quarter of a million troops had been intended to drive through the wooded countryside to recapture the strategic port of Antwerp, had been blunted in the Battle of the Bulge following breaks in the winter weather allowing Allied air superiority to be used to the full.

Nevertheless, German resistance to American forces, some of whom their general, George Patton, considered very green, was proving skilful and stubborn. The initial Ardennes advance had caused some panic in Antwerp and elsewhere behind the lines and led General Eisenhower to give the British Field Marshal Bernard Montgomery overall command of the defence. Although he had contributed significantly to the organization of the predominantly American defenders, not unusually for him Montgomery behaved tactlessly and at a press conference claimed more than his due share of credit for the successful defence, exacerbating existing tensions between British and American generals.

In early January 1945, the German army launched a diversionary attack code-named 'North Wind' against Strasbourg. Eager to conserve his forces for the Ardennes defence, Eisenhower urged the city's abandonment. French leader General de Gaulle objected, threatening to withdraw his troops from the joint Allied command, and ordered his French forces to defend the city. They did so successfully, repulsing the attackers at the last bridge before Strasbourg – an incident that did nothing to improve relations between the Allies and their prickly French colleague.

In Italy, whose government had surrendered in 1943, the Allied armies' hard slog up the mountainous spine of the country against the determined resistance of Italy's former German allies – a campaign in which Free Polish forces were playing a considerable role – was almost at a standstill. This was due in part to poor winter weather, in part to the terrain and stubbornness of the defence, but also to the diversion of some British troops to newly liberated Greece to combat what the British saw as a Communist insurrection. Behind the German lines Italian partisans, many also Communist inspired, harassed and harried the German defenders.

In Eastern Europe, Stalin had responded as a good ally to a visit to Moscow by British Air Chief Marshal Arthur Tedder, Eisenhower's deputy as supreme commander, urgently requesting the Soviets to relieve some of the German pressure in the west with the Ardennes and Strasbourg offensives not yet defeated. In what Churchill hailed as 'a fine deed of the Russians and their chief to hasten their vast offensive, no doubt at a heavy cost in life', Stalin brought forward the planned Soviet westward campaign from 20 to 12 January 1945, telling Tedder,

We are comrades. It is proper, and also sound, selfish policy, that we should help each other in times of difficulty. It would be foolish for me to stand aside and let the Germans annihilate you; they would only turn back on me when you were disposed of. Similarly, it is to your interest to do everything possible to keep the Germans from annihilating me'.

The Soviet advance was swift and over a broad front, covering 300 miles in just eighteen days. On 17 January, Marshal Georgii Zhukov's forces took Warsaw – a city where Stalin's failure to support the previous late summer's rising had caused great tension between himself and his allies. That same day Russian troops advancing into the already besieged twin Hungarian cities of Buda and Pest arrested on suspicion of spying Raoul Wallenberg, a Swedish envoy to Hungary who had over the previous months saved many Jewish people by issuing them with passports and other papers. Wallenberg was never seen again. The following day, 18 January, German troops withdrew from Pest across the Danube River to Buda, blowing up the celebrated and beautiful Chain and Elizabeth Bridges.

On 21 January the German army abandoned Tannenberg, the scene of their great August 1914 victory over the Russians, taking with them the bodies of Field Marshal Paul von Hindenburg – the battle's victor and subsequently First World War Chief of the German General Staff and President of Germany during Hitler's rise to power – and of his wife, which had been buried there. On 27 January Russian troops seized Hitler's 'Wolf's Lair' headquarters near Rastenburg in Eastern Prussia where in the 'Valkyrie Plot' of July 1944 Claus von Stauffenberg's bomb had failed to kill Hitler. In Germany itself trials and executions of plotters and suspected plotters continued, including on 23 January the killing of Erwin Planck, the son of the Nobel Prize-winning physicist Max Planck. By the time of Yalta, Marshal Zhukov's advance units were within fifty miles of Berlin, Hitler's capital, with their spearhead across the frozen Oder River.

Germany's forces still had some important novel weapons in their armoury. One innovation feared by the Allied Chiefs of Staff and targeted by their airpower was the production of a new generation of U-boats. These partially prefabricated submarines had improved batteries and torpedo tubes which could fire more than one torpedo at a time. Most importantly they deployed 'schnorkels' – a ventilation tube allowing the submarine to remain submerged at virtually all times, rendering the vessels highly difficult to detect and destroy as they attacked Allied convoys.

The largest version of the new submarine – the 1,600-ton Type XXI – according to intelligence reports could cruise as far as the Pacific without refuelling and reach a submerged sprinting speed of more than sixteen knots.

The new weapon produced in greatest numbers was the world's first ballistic missile, the V2 ('Vengeance Weapon Two'). It had a range of 200 miles, travelled at 3,600 miles an hour and rose to a height of some seventy miles before crashing to earth with its warhead of three-quarters of a ton of high explosive. The first V2 to hit Britain struck Staveley Road in Chiswick in West London on Friday 8 September 1944, killing three people in what the British government told the public at the time was not a rocket attack but a gas explosion. The blast caused a crater thirty-two feet across and ten feet deep outside six-year-old John Clark's house. He was in the upstairs bathroom at the back of the house: 'You're deafened, that's what it comes down to,' he recalled. 'Seeing an airing cupboard crumpling in front of you without a sound is an eerie experience.' John's sister, three-year-old Rosanna, in her cot in the front bedroom, was killed. 'There wasn't a mark on Rosanna,' John remembered, 'the blast had collapsed her lungs.'

Not until 10 November, after more V2s had fallen, did the British authorities admit the rocket attacks. Their greatest fear was that rockets could be used to spread poison gas. German scientists had produced an adaptation of the warhead for this purpose, but it was never used. By January 1945, V2s were falling on London, according to Jock Colville 'like autumn leaves'. The speed of the rocket meant the public had no warning before it struck. A Londoner described it as 'a terror weapon – you didn't hear it arriving'. Its distinctive double thunderclap as it broke the sound barrier and exploded less than a second later could be heard up to sixty miles away. Hence, although casualties were much lower than in the bombing blitz, the V2s unsettled the British public, who had believed aerial attack was over. 'These latest attacks were the last straw,' another Londoner recalled. 'It is difficult to describe the tension under which we lived – twenty-four hours a day we were vulnerable. Only the belief the war was likely to end within months kept us going.'

As well as London, Paris and Antwerp were favoured targets. On 16 December 1944, the same day as the German Ardennes offensive began, a V2 fired from the occupied Netherlands hit Antwerp, causing the greatest number of deaths from a V2 attack – 567 people including 296 Allied service personnel who had been in a cinema watching the popular film *Buffalo Bill*. V2 rocket attacks would continue throughout the Yalta Conference despite intensive Allied bombing of launch sites.

German scientists and engineers produced two other new weapons but in insufficient numbers and too unreliable to be effective militarily: the world's first jet fighter, the Messerschmitt Me 262, first operational in small numbers in summer 1944, and the Arado 234B jet bomber which first flew operationally when, on Christmas Eve 1944, sixteen Arados attacked factories and marshalling yards near Liège in Belgium in support of the Ardennes offensive.

The Western Allies' most secret programme, the Manhattan Atomic Bomb Project, was still in the development stage although confidence in the viability of a nuclear weapon was growing with the first weapons-grade uranium produced on Christmas Day and the first plutonium ready for shipment from the Hanford facility in Washington State at the end of January 1945. In that same month aircraft from the squadron of Boeing B-29 Superfortresses commanded by Paul Tibbets and specially modified to carry the atomic bomb flew down to the Batista field, twelve miles from Havana in Cuba, to practise bombing runs and cross-water navigation in the fine weather of the Caribbean.

As yet uncertain about the potential of the Manhattan Project and in most cases ignorant of it, American generals at the beginning of 1945 feared that it might take well into 1947 to defeat the Japanese Empire. General Douglas MacArthur, Supreme Allied Commander in South-West Asia, estimated that 5 million men might be required to invade and conquer the Japanese home islands, of whom a fifth could prove casualties. One of the main objectives of Roosevelt and his military advisers at Yalta would be to bring the Soviet Union into the war against Japan to alleviate their burden. The American military concerns were stimulated by the stubbornness of Japanese resistance despite the tide of war flowing in the Allies' favour everywhere other than in eastern China.

At the battle of Leyte Gulf in October 1944, despite suffering the first concerted attacks by kamikaze planes, the US navy destroyed the Japanese surface fleet as a significant fighting force in what was the largest naval engagement in the Second World War and, on most criteria, in history. The battle was fought to defend the landing on the Philippine island of Leyte by General MacArthur's troops. After defeating the Japanese on Leyte and on Mindoro, MacArthur's forces on 9 January invaded Luzon, the largest of the Philippine islands on which the capital, Manila, stands. Meanwhile, in Burma British and Indian troops were fighting hard as they advanced south in their campaign to recapture the country from the Japanese.

In Malta the American and British generals argued over how to deliver the final knockout blow to Germany. In talks which American Chief of the General Staff, General George Marshall, described as 'the stormiest of the entire war', the sticking point was General Eisenhower's strategy of two separate, simultaneous broad thrusts deep into Germany after the essential crossing of the River Rhine. One would be a northern advance skirting the Ruhr and across the German portion of the north European plain towards the Baltic, and the other a push from Karlsruhe towards Kassel. The British, who thought Eisenhower too cautious, were keen to move quickly towards Berlin in a single, narrower thrust and, in any case, doubted whether the Allies were strong enough to mount two such operations. Marshall at times 'brutally frank . . . stood four square behind Eisenhower' in opposing what the latter called 'a pencil-like thrust' to Berlin. In what Brooke thought 'the most washy conclusion', the British eventually and somewhat ungraciously accepted Eisenhower's strategy and American assurances that resources for the British advance beyond the Ruhr, to be commanded by Montgomery, would not be prejudiced by American offensives elsewhere.

The two air staffs – headed by Major-General Laurence Kuter of the USAAF and Peter Portal of the RAF – in general had a more cordial relationship, small differences overshadowed by their consensus on the greater war-winning ability of air services. At Malta, they worked on plans to realign Anglo-American bombing priorities to support the Soviet advance into Germany. They agreed not only to attack German tank factories but also to launch 'heavy attacks in the four cities, Berlin, Dresden, Leipzig and Chemnitz' which would be 'most likely to hamper enemy efforts to transfer forces between the Western and Eastern fronts'. They also agreed arrangements for a force of RAF bombers to be deployed to the Pacific to aid in bombing Japan. Probably wisely, they decided to abandon Project Weary Willie – a proposal to launch battle-weary (worn-out) heavy bombers into Germany as pilotless missiles each packed with twenty tons of high explosive.

As Churchill recovered and waited for the President to arrive, he was briefed on the military discussions. His temperature soon returned to normal, he became 'cheerful and eating and drinking everything within reach' and, to Lord Moran's annoyance, sat up late at night playing one of his favourite card games, bezique, with Averell Harriman. 'Surely this bout of fever should put sense into his head. But Winston is a gambler, and gamblers do not count the coins in their pockets. He will not give a thought to nursing his waning powers . . . Damn the fellow, will he never give himself a chance?'

Yet though Churchill outwardly appeared his usual ebullient self, his mood as he contemplated the challenges ahead was sombre. On 1 February he wrote to his wife:

> my heart is saddened by the tales of the masses of German women and children flying along the roads everywhere in 40-mile long columns to the West before the advancing Armies . . . The misery of the whole world appals me and I fear increasingly that new struggles may arise out of those we are successfully ending.

His closing words reflected his melancholy:

> Tender Love my darling.
> I miss you much.
> I am lonely amid this throng.
> Your ever loving husband.

The rapid Soviet advance was indeed pushing before it a bow wave of misery in the form of struggling, straggling humanity. More than 2 million people were on the move in the harsh winter conditions. They included German civilian refugees from East and West Prussia and inmates of concentration and prisoner of war camps forced onto death marches. In its wake the advance left hundreds of thousands of others, some apprehensive civilians rightly fearful of being displaced from their homes and lands, others disoriented refugees and despairing, starving ex-prisoners overtaken by the speed of the advance.

On 20 January a British prisoner of war on one forced march which had become mingled with refugees recalled 'marching all night to cross the Oder before bridges blown . . . Intense cold. Six refugee children died en route – many falling out of ranks exhausted – frostbite gets a grip.' Another British prisoner of war, Stan Wells, and his companions concealed, fed and cared for a young Jewish woman who had escaped a death march from the Stutthof concentration camp. Wells wrote in his diary,

> God punish Germany. I have seen today the filthiest foulest and most cruel sight of my life. At nine a.m. this morning a column straggled down the road towards Danzig. I was struck dumb with a miserable rage a blind coldness which nearly resulted in my being shot. Never in my life have I been so devoid of fear of opening my mouth. They came straggling through the bitter cold, about 300 of them, limping, dragging footsteps, slipping and falling, to rise and stagger under the blows of the guards – SS swine. Crying loudly for bread, screaming for food, 300 matted haired, filthy objects that had once been – Jewesses!

On 27 January, advancing Russian units reached the Auschwitz-Birkenau concentration camp near the pre-war Polish–German border. In the previous few days guards had forced 60,000 ill-clad, starving inmates capable of walking to march thirty miles over seventy-two hours in the snow and ice to be loaded on railway trucks and taken to other camps. A quarter of those who set out – 15,000 people – died on the march as guards shot out of hand any who collapsed. About 7,000 of the weakest, sickest inmates had been left behind in the abandoned camp. Among them was Italian chemist and later celebrated author Primo Levi who was suffering from scarlet fever. He recalled, 'We lay in a world of death and phantoms. The last trace of civilisation had vanished around and inside us. The work of bestial degradation, begun by the victorious Germans, had been carried to its conclusion by the Germans in defeat.'

Mounted on their shaggy-haired ponies, twenty-one-year-old Lieutenant Ivan Martynushkin and his comrades of the Soviet 322nd Rifle Division entered cautiously, on the alert for any ambush. Then he spotted:

> some people behind barbed wire . . . I remember their faces, especially their eyes which betrayed their ordeal. At first there were worries on both our part and theirs but then they apparently figured out who we were and began to welcome us . . . to signal that they knew who we were and shouldn't be afraid of them – that there were no guards or Germans behind the barbed wire, only prisoners. We could tell from their eyes they were glad to be saved from the hell. Happy to be freed.

Between 1941 and that January, the Nazis had killed at least 1.1 million people at Auschwitz, about 90 per cent of them Jewish, nearly a sixth of those who died in the Jewish genocide. Martynushkin and his men found some 600 decaying corpses, piles of teeth from which gold fillings had been removed, 370,000 men's suits, 837,000 items of women's clothing and 7.7 tons of human hair as well as indications of hurried unsuccessful Nazi attempts to destroy camp equipment such as the gas chambers.

Primo Levi recalled that he was carrying out the 'very light' body of another inmate on a stretcher with a friend when, as they 'overturned the stretcher on the grey snow', they saw the Russians arrive.

Ten-year-old twins Eva and Miriam Mozes Kor had been held in the Birkenau part of the camp as subjects for the infamous Dr Josef Mengele's experiments on 'hereditary biology' on twins. A few days before their liberation, they had been marched to the sound of Soviet gunfire to the main camp. Very ill from one of Mengele's injections, Eva kept telling herself she must survive. 'If I had died my twin sister Miriam would have been killed with an injection to the heart and then Mengele would have done comparative autopsies.' The two emaciated girls did reach the main camp and a day or two later heard a woman in the barracks they had been confined in shout 'We're free! We're free!' Eva ran to the door but could see only snow. Then she made out Red Army soldiers dressed in white camouflage uniforms. 'We ran up to them and they gave us hugs, cookies and chocolates,' she remembered. 'Being so alone a hug meant more than anybody could imagine because that replaced the human warmth we were starving for. We were not only starved for food but . . . human kindness.'

During January, German Grand Admiral Karl Dönitz, head of the German navy, assembled a fleet of 800 vessels of all sizes from liners to fishing boats for an operation code-named 'Hannibal' to evacuate German troops and civilians from the Baltic coast of East and West Prussia which were now effectively cut off. Among the largest vessels was the 20,000-ton *Wilhelm Gustloff*. She left Danzig just after midday on 30 January 1945 with some 10,000 people aboard, mostly civilians and refugees but also wounded troops, over 300 female naval auxiliaries and 1,000 U-boat crewmembers.

In the winter darkness that evening – the twelve-year anniversary of the Nazi Party's rise to power – the Soviet submarine *S-13* commanded by Captain Alexander Marinesko sighted the *Gustloff* and fired three torpedoes. They struck the liner on the port side just as Hitler's familiar harsh yet hypnotic voice was being transmitted over the ship's loudspeaker system as for the final time he addressed his people over German radio: 'I expect every German to fulfil his duty to the utmost, to make every sacrifice that will be and must be demanded of him . . . every healthy man to risk life and limb in this battle . . . every woman and girl to fight with the utmost fanaticism!' One torpedo hit the engine room, disabling it and cutting off all power and communication. Another slammed into the emptied swimming pool where many of the 300 female naval auxiliaries were sheltering, killing most instantly.

Only nine lifeboats could be launched from the listing ship. Many people plunged into the freezing Baltic waters which were strewn with small ice floes. There most quickly died of hypothermia. Within an hour or so the liner had sunk bow first. An accompanying torpedo boat rescued nearly 1,000 people. The rest − around 9,000 − perished, the largest loss of life in a single sinking in history. A female survivor in a lifeboat recalled:

> I cannot forget the loud clear sound of the siren as the *Gustloff* . . . made the final plunge. I could clearly see the people still on board clinging to the rails. Even as she went under they were still hanging on and screaming. All around us were people swimming, or just floating in the sea. I can still see their hands grasping at the sides of our boat. It was too full to take on any more.

While some were liberators, many advancing Soviet troops brutalized the civilian populations of countries they occupied, raping and looting and shooting any who resisted their depredations. A group dragged fifteen-year-old Agnes Karlik and her fourteen-year-old sister into a tent. 'They were screaming . . . I felt absolutely so frightened that I was just rigid . . . they raped us. We were just young. Very young. And we didn't know what they were doing because at that time children were brought up differently.'

A report from the Swiss embassy in Budapest stated:

The worst suffering of the Hungarian population is due to the rape of women. Rapes – affecting all age groups from ten to seventy – are so common that very few women in Hungary have been spared . . . The misery is made worse by the sad fact that many Russian soldiers are diseased and there are absolutely no medicines in Hungary.

The Hungarian Communist Party made a contemporaneous report to the Soviets confirming the situation. Stalin responded to one complaint, 'Can't [one] understand if a soldier who has crossed thousands of kilometres through blood and fire and death has fun with a woman or takes some trifle?'

In the German Reich, effectively devoid of European allies with the defection of Bulgaria, Romania and Hungary, the mood among the people varied. Some remained fiercely loyal to Hitler and the Nazi cause. On New Year's Day 1945, a Junkers 87 Stuka pilot, Hans-Ulrich Rudel, credited with destroying 500 Russian tanks, went to the Fuhrer's western headquarters at Bad Neuheim to receive from him 'the highest decoration for bravery, the Gold Oak-leaves with Swords and Diamonds to the Knight's Cross of the Iron Cross' and promotion to group captain. Hitler offered to remove him from operational duties but Rudel told him he could not accept the decoration and promotion 'if I am not allowed to go on flying with my wing'. 'Looking me in the eyes', Hitler smiled and agreed. A senior officer told Rudel, 'the sheet lightning in the Fuhrer's face does not always resolve into a smile'.

In a Berlin suffering increasingly from hunger and ever more intensive Allied bombing, however, a woman newspaper journalist Ursula von Kardorff wrote in her diary that she and her colleagues were in 'a madhouse . . . robots, performing a senseless role. For example, every day we have to fill long pamphlets with atrocity stories about the Russians or with idiotic exhortations. "Hold firm" because Goebbels insists that we are on the brink of victory. "We shall win because we must win!" is typical.' People had, however, to exercise great caution in speaking against the Fuhrer. In mid-January Gertrude Seele, a nurse, was executed as a 'recognized enemy of the state' because at a private party she had spoken of her loathing for Hitler.

On 23 January, returned from Bad Neuheim to Berlin where he now spent much of his time in his bunker fifty feet below ground, Hitler seemed to lose faith in his generals when he appointed Heinrich Himmler, who was entirely without military experience, to command the German army's Vistula Group.

At the end of January the most costly film ever made by the Nazis, Kolberg, had its premiere. According to its director Veit Harlan, 187,000 German soldiers were released from operations to act as extras in this colour film. Designed to raise public and military morale, it depicted the heroic German defence of Kolberg on the Baltic in 1807 against Napoleon's French forces. Copies were distributed to German troops everywhere. Shortly afterward, Kolberg itself fell to the Soviets, a fact concealed for some time from the German public.

In the port city of Hiroshima, as elsewhere in the Japanese home islands, cinemas were also showing uplifting material. A newsreel, The Divine Wind Special Attack Forces Take Off, glorified the first kamikaze pilots as, before their one-way missions, the young suicide bombers vowed fealty to their Emperor and smiling climbed into their cockpits. Neighbourhood associations began to organize air-raid drills and to give guidance on rallying areas in case of attack. They distributed little brown and white pottery cups with bracing inscriptions such as 'neighbourhoods unite and resist'. Those whom neighbourhood leaders observed or overheard engaging in defeatist talk were reported to the secret police, the Kempei Tei. Schoolchildren of thirteen years and older had already been conscripted to work for up to eight hours a day in weapons factories. Now, in their spare time, they were ordered to dig trench shelters in hillsides.

Such was the state of the war and the world as Churchill waited in Malta for Roosevelt to arrive.

CHAPTER FOUR

'One Tiny Bright Flame in the Darkness'

In Washington on the evening of 22 January after some early birthday celebrations – Roosevelt would be sixty-three on 30 January – the President and his daughter Anna descended to the basement of the Bureau of Engraving and Printing, close to the White House. Here, on a subterranean spur line built to transport fresh-printed dollar bills in secret, Roosevelt's private Pullman railroad car, the *Ferdinand Magellan*, awaited. Only one other president – Abraham Lincoln in the early 1860s – had had a railcar built for his specific use. During his lifetime Lincoln refused to use it because it was 'too fancy and ornate' but it had carried his body to its final resting place in Illinois. In early 1942, after America entered the war, Roosevelt approved Mike Reilly's suggestion that for security reasons he should have his own railcar. The choice fell on the *Ferdinand Magellan*, originally built in 1928 as one of six Pullman railcars all named after famous explorers. The Pullman Company's workshops near Chicago were tasked with rebuilding it. Roosevelt's only request was that it be made 'a little more comfortable'.

The accommodation in which the President and his daughter settled down comprised four bedrooms, a dining room with an eight-seater mahogany table and a green-carpeted, cream-painted observation lounge. The car weighed 140 tons and its sides, floor, roof and ends were sheathed in nickel-steel armour plating, the windows were three-inch-thick bulletproof glass and the doors were waterproof when closed. In an emergency the President had the option of two escape hatches – one in the ceiling of the observation lounge, the other in a side wall of the bathroom. Every room had a telephone which, when the railcar was in a station, could be linked to a trackside telephone outlet. When the carriage was moving, the diesel-powered radio in the communications car, operated by Army Signal Corps personnel, kept the President in touch with the outside world. Leaning from the train to wave goodbye to her husband John, a former newspaperman now wartime army officer, Anna Boettiger 'got deluged with soot' from the train's steam engine.

The rest of the train comprised four additional sleeping cars, a dining car and lounge car. Travelling with Roosevelt were his two doctors – his personal physician Vice-Admiral Ross McIntire and Lieutenant-Commander Howard Bruenn, chief of cardiology at Bethesda Naval Hospital. Since diagnosing Roosevelt's hypertension and enlarged heart the previous March, Bruenn, who privately described the President's condition bluntly as 'God-awful', had been in constant attendance on him. Also aboard were Filipino stewards from the presidential yacht *Potomac* who would cook many of his meals at Yalta. Equally important to Roosevelt's well-being was the familiar presence of Alabama-born Major-General Edwin 'Pa' Watson, his military aide since 1933 and later also his appointments secretary. The two had long been friends. The President enjoyed playing poker with 'Pa' and ribbing him about his obvious liking for pungent aftershave. Watson had accompanied Roosevelt on nearly every important presidential journey, including to the Teheran Conference.

A more challenging companion was James Byrnes, a sixty-two-year-old lawyer. Of Catholic Irish stock, he was born in Charleston, South Carolina. He had served in the House of Representatives from 1911 until in 1924 he ran for the Senate but lost when opponents attacked his refusal to join the Ku Klux Klan because of its anti-Catholic stance. Ironically, in many areas Byrnes's views coincided with the Klan's. Finally elected to the Senate in 1930, he was an outspoken segregationist adamantly opposing racial integration and in the mid-1930s helped block anti-lynching legislation, claiming lynching was the most effective way of preventing the rape of white women by black men. Roosevelt himself felt unable to support the bill for fear of antagonizing southern voters. (At the time of Yalta segregation remained entrenched in American society. Not until 1948, for example, did President Truman announce the desegregation of the US military.)

In 1941, partly as a reward for Byrnes's help in shepherding the Lend-Lease programme through Congress, Roosevelt appointed him to the Supreme Court. In 1942, Byrnes resigned from the court to head up first the new wartime Office of Economic Stabilization and then the Office of War Mobilization, responsible for a vast range of wartime domestic matters from public procurement to wage control and rationing. Subsequently, however, the President had twice disappointed Byrnes, first by failing to support him as his running mate in the 1944 presidential elections – Byrnes believed that Roosevelt had broken his word to him and raged about his hypocrisy – and second by appointing Stettinius, not him, as his Secretary of State. By inviting Byrnes to Yalta to advise him on economic issues, Roosevelt was offering him a small consolation though Byrnes took some persuading before he accepted.

A notable absentee from the presidential party was the man on whom Roosevelt would rely most at Yalta, his special adviser Harry Hopkins, who had departed the previous day for his meetings with Churchill, de Gaulle and the Pope, and who would join Roosevelt in Malta. The President affectionately called him 'Harry the Hop'. Others described him as the President's eyes and ears. A celebrated American political journalist thought he had a natural instinct for working with Roosevelt:

Many New Dealers have bored Roosevelt with their solemn earnestness. Hopkins never does. He knows instinctively when to ask, when to keep still, when to press, when to hold back; when to approach Roosevelt direct, when to go at him round-about . . . Quick, alert, shrewd, bold, and carrying it off with a bright Hell's bells air, Hopkins is in all respects the inevitable Roosevelt favorite.

Another commentator observed Hopkins's 'almost "feminine" sensitivity to Roosevelt's moods'. Hopkins shared Roosevelt's suspicion of State Department officials as 'cookie pushers, pansies – and usually isolationists to boot' and together the two men often bypassed the department – a circumstance that may well explain economist John Maynard Keynes's comment that communicating through the State Department was 'like making love through a blanket'.

Eight years younger than Roosevelt and the son of an Iowa harness-maker, Hopkins had worked on social and public health projects. In 1933, Roosevelt appointed him head of the Federal Emergency Relief Administration whose purpose was to fund job creation – an integral part of the New Deal. Hopkins's work brought him into close contact with the Roosevelts. In May 1940, the President invited him to dinner at the White House and, when the hour grew late, to spend the night. Hopkins remained living in the White House, occupying the Lincoln Room where he could be on constant call to Roosevelt, for three and a half years until December 1943, when his new, and third, wife Louise Gill Macy insisted on a home of their own.

In early 1941, Roosevelt chose Hopkins as his emissary to Churchill in London where by proxy he laid the foundations for the close relationship between President and Prime Minister. Hopkins saw himself as 'a catalytic agent between two prima donnas'. Roosevelt believed him 'the perfect Ambassador for my purposes. He doesn't even know the meaning of the word "protocol".' Churchill called him 'Lord Root of the Matter' and early identified him as a friend to Britain, 'worth more to us than any battleship'. The emotional Churchill was greatly moved when at his farewell dinner before he returned to America after his 1941 visit, Hopkins quoted from the Book of Ruth: 'Whither thou goest I will go and where thou lodgest I will lodge, thy people shall be my people, and thy God my God.'

Tall and gangling, Hopkins cared little for appearances. A profile in the New Yorker called him 'an animated piece of Shredded Wheat'. British General 'Pug' Ismay thought him 'deplorably untidy', writing with military starchiness, 'his clothes looked as though he was in the habit of sleeping in them, and his hat as though he made a point of sitting on it'. The physical frailty of Hopkins, who seemed to exist on a diet of coffee and cigarettes, was obvious. The stomach cancer that would eventually kill him first appeared in the late 1930s, precipitating many gastro-intestinal problems, and was probably why he never ran for political office. Churchill's daughter-in-law Pamela described him as:

> small, shrunken, sick . . . and always kind of a dead cigarette out of the side of his mouth, looking sort of like a very sad dog . . . If you just came into a room and saw him sitting there, you would feel sorry for him. But if you heard him talk, you would listen with great respect.

With soldiers guarding the track, particularly at junctions, the *Ferdinand Magellan* travelled south at the steady forty miles an hour Roosevelt preferred to avoid painful jolting, to arrive just before dawn at Newport News in Virginia. The crew of the heavy cruiser USS *Quincy* were waiting to pipe the President aboard to begin his nearly 5,000-mile voyage across the Atlantic and into the Mediterranean to Malta. The 13,600-ton *Quincy* had a main armament of nine eight-inch guns and carried four catapult-launched Kingfisher observation planes. She had seen action on D-Day, firing on German shore batteries on Utah Beach. In preparation for the voyage to Malta, she had, like the *Catoctin*, been fitted with special ramps to enable Roosevelt to embark, disembark and move around in his wheelchair.

Protected by a screen of destroyers and cruisers and with air cover from aircraft carriers and US bases in North Africa, the *Quincy* remained blacked out during the voyage, zigzagging as a defence against enemy submarines. The precaution seemed all the more necessary when, on the *Quincy*'s first full day at sea, US intelligence radioed that the German government might well have discovered the conference location. Twice escort ships thought they detected enemy submarines but they proved false alarms. Among the more extreme security arrangements was the inclusion in the secret service team aboard of a particularly strong swimmer. His orders, in the event of a sudden need to abandon ship, were to get the President over the side and keep him floating until rescue came. Before leaving Washington Roosevelt had taken the precaution of telling his eldest son James that his will and the instructions for his funeral were to be found in the White House safe. He also told him, 'I want you to have the family ring I wear. I hope you will wear it.'

During the voyage, Roosevelt surprised James Byrnes by how 'little preparation for the Yalta Conference' he made. He did not read the detailed studies aboard on the issues to be covered prepared by the State Department. Only four or five times, usually after dinner, did he raise questions to do with Yalta, and then principally about his proposals for a United Nations. Otherwise in the evening he preferred to watch films, which he much enjoyed, as did Churchill and Stalin, the latter being a fan of Tarzan and cowboy films. In the daytime, Roosevelt seemed more interested in looking at stamps – philately was his favourite hobby – and watching a 'field meet' staged on deck in which sailors ran three-legged races and competed in tugs of war.

On 30 January, the President's actual birthday, the *Quincy*'s crew gave him a brass ash tray made from the casing of a five-inch shell the *Quincy* had fired on D-Day, and in private he opened a package containing 'a lot of little gadgets' from Lucy Mercer Rutherfurd and his cousin Daisy Suckley, including pocket combs and a cigarette lighter that would function out on the windy deck. At his birthday dinner that evening Anna arranged for him to be presented with five birthday cakes – one from the *Quincy*'s officers, one from the non-commissioned officers and one from the rest of the crew, together with one from his own Filipino cooks and one from his travelling companions. The first four cakes symbolized his four terms in office while the fifth – an afterthought – was decorated with a large question mark made of icing. Roosevelt chuckled at the allusion to a possible fifth presidential term. Later he played a few hands of poker, winning 'all the money' and enjoying 'the game more than anyone else'.

At around 9.30 a.m. on 2 February, with Spitfires overhead,

bands on the British and American warships playing 'The Star-Spangled Banner' and marines lining the decks, the Quincy edged past anti-submarine nets into Valletta's Grand Harbour at the end of her ten-day voyage. To Churchill's daughter Sarah Oliver the American vessel dwarfed the 'more modest' Orion. As the Quincy passed the British cruiser, Roosevelt, wearing a brown coat and a tweed cap, and Churchill, in naval uniform and according to Anna Boettiger 'standing stiffly and trimly at attention', exchanged waves. Beneath cloudless skies people crammed every roof and vantage point around the harbour, craning for a view of the President. Eden, also watching, reflected that in Roosevelt's 'hands lay much of the world's fate . . . a sudden quietness fell. It was one of those moments when all seems to stand still and one is conscious of a mark in history.'

Two hours later, Churchill and Eden visited the President. Churchill claimed to believe him 'in best of health and spirits'. Others disagreed. Marian Holmes, one of Churchill's secretaries who, like him, had last seen Roosevelt at Quebec four months previously, was shocked by how much weight he had lost, by the dark circles beneath his eyes and his general fragility, 'as if he is hardly in this world at all.' Eden thought his powers visibly failing.

Eden had held the only serious political discussions so far at Malta about the forthcoming conference. They were with his newly appointed counterpart, US Secretary of State Edward Stettinius, something of an unknown quantity. Roosevelt's choice in late November 1944 of the genial forty-four-year-old busi-nessman, inexperienced in foreign affairs, had surprised many, not least because the outgoing Secretary of State Cordell Hull, a powerful political figure from Tennessee, had favoured Byrnes to succeed him. State Department official Charles Bohlen thought his mild-mannered, prematurely white-haired new boss 'a decent man of considerable innocence' sometimes 'unaware of political nuances' and 'no intriguer, no infighter, no politician'. He concluded shrewdly that since Roosevelt relied on Harry Hopkins 'as his chief instrument in foreign affairs' these characteristics might be a positive asset. Unlike the forceful Byrnes, Stettinius 'would not be disposed to disagree with anything Roosevelt or

Hopkins wanted to do' but would direct his 'Boy Scout enthusiasm' to reorganizing the State Department. Roosevelt's friend,
Treasury Secretary Henry Morgenthau, agreed that Roosevelt was
looking for a 'good clerk'. Others were more damning. Roosevelt's
long-serving Secretary of the Interior Harold Ickes thought the
appointment was 'a douche of cold water to most of the intelligent people in the Administration'. One of Stettinius's juniors
thought he was 'about as much Secretary of State as I was King
of Spain'. In June 1945 Truman would replace him with Byrnes.

In Malta Stettinius's discussions with Eden ranged widely from
zones of occupation in a conquered Germany to control of Iran's
oil fields to the future of Poland. Eden worried that the Americans
were so preoccupied with Roosevelt's brainchild, the United
Nations, that they were neglecting Poland. Indeed, together with
bringing the Soviet Union into the war against Japan, the United
Nations would be the main priority for Roosevelt at Yalta.
Roosevelt's vision was of the nascent UN as a post-war international structure ensuring peace, with the leading role of enforcers
being entrusted to five 'policemen' – the US, UK, USSR, Chiang
Kai-shek's China and in due course France. He also foresaw a role
for the UN in undertaking trusteeships for new nations emerging
from colonial rule. The organization would have a charter based
upon the principles underlying the Atlantic Charter and President
Wilson's cherished League of Nations charter.

The name 'United Nations' had emerged from discussions
between Roosevelt and Churchill over Christmas and New Year
1941/2. Late one evening in the White House they had been
discussing several suggestions before agreeing to sleep on it. By the
next morning Roosevelt had firmed up on the name. He wheeled
himself to Churchill's room and entered, only to find Churchill
'stark naked and gleaming pink from the bath'. Roosevelt prepared
to retreat but Churchill made his often-quoted remark, 'The Prime
Minister of Great Britain has nothing to hide from the President
of the United States.' Thereupon Roosevelt said, 'The United
Nations,' and Churchill replied simply, 'Good!' The title was first
used officially in the United Nations Declaration issued in Washington
on New Year's Day 1942, and signed that day by Churchill, Roosevelt

and representatives of the Soviet Union and Chiang Kai-shek's China and the next day by those of twenty-two other nations. It committed signatories to maximum war effort and not to make a separate peace. The aim of their struggle was, 'to ensure life, liberty, independence and religious freedom, and to preserve the rights of man and justice'.

Churchill in general supported Roosevelt over the next three years as he worked up his plans for the new organization, particularly once he had received assurances that there was no question that any British colony would become a trusteeship, although he continued to be uneasy on this latter point. Stalin too was prepared to go along with Roosevelt's proposals.

After an international meeting lasting over seven weeks at Dumbarton Oaks, a mansion in Georgetown, Washington DC, in late summer and early autumn 1944, the broad structure of a United Nations organization was becoming clearer. A General Assembly in which all eligible nations would have a seat would give the smaller nations a voice but be very much a talking shop. A Security Council comprising representatives of eleven members – of which only the 'five policemen' would be permanent members, the other seats would rotate – would take and implement decisions including the use of force 'to maintain peace and security'. Much, however, remained to be clarified, including voting procedures in the Security Council, any veto arrangements and whether any Soviet republics would become members of the General Assembly in addition to the Soviet Union's membership of both the Assembly and the Security Council.

On Poland, Eden urged Stettinius that Roosevelt insist to Stalin that the country be treated 'with some decency', arguing that it was America's turn 'to take up the burden on this issue. We would back them to the full but a change of bowling was needed.' They agreed that the best solution for Poland would be the formation of an interim government followed by free elections.

Now that Roosevelt and Churchill were together Eden hoped for more co-ordinated preparations but he was disappointed, writing of the ensuing lunch aboard the *Quincy*: 'Pleasant, but no business whatsoever done.' In fact, during the voyage from

Newport News, according to Anna Boettiger, there had been ' a lot of amused talking about the fact that Churchill insisted on meeting us when we docked at Malta . . . the joke was that a cable came through from Stalin saying, "I said Yalta, not Malta."' Intending to take the lead and talk 'man to man' with Stalin as he had at Teheran, Roosevelt remained determined not to allow Churchill to push him into prior commitments that might suggest to Stalin that Britain and the United States were ganging up against him. Churchill sensed Roosevelt's reluctance to engage. His daughter recalled, 'My father and all the British party felt a with-drawing of the former easy understanding [with Roosevelt].'

Although not to be drawn on matters of substance, Roosevelt paid Churchill a thoughtful small attention at lunch which, as it was designed to, touched the sentimental Prime Minister: 'He must have noticed the candle by my bed when we were at the White House, because there was a small lighted candle on the luncheon table by my place to light my cigar.' The President had also recently sent Churchill three bow ties which Churchill had sworn to wear in Yalta.

After lunch, Malta's Governor-General and his wife took Roosevelt, Anna Boettiger and Sarah Oliver on a sightseeing drive. Sarah, who had not met Anna before, 'thought at once how amazingly like her mother she was although of course so *much* better looking . . . She is very easy and I like her, but I think she is quite nervous about being on the trip.' As they toured the island, Anna Boettiger recalled, 'The immense amount of destruc-tion hit me between the eyes because it was my first glimpse of mass destruction in this war.' Though small – just seventeen miles long and nine miles wide – Malta's strategic position as a British possession and supply base had made it a prime enemy target. During 154 days and nights of constant air raids, German and Italian air crews, many taking off from Sicily less than one hundred miles away, had dropped 6,700 tons of bombs on the rocky island, twice the amount dropped on London during the Blitz. In April 1942 at the height of the raids, King George VI had conferred the George Cross, Britain's highest civilian medal for gallantry, on the entire population.

The island had also endured a lengthy naval blockade that brought its people close to starvation and was not lifted until August 1942. In 1943 Malta was one of the launch pads for the Allied invasion of Sicily. In December that year, while in Malta on his return from Teheran, Roosevelt had presented the island with a letter in the name of the people of the United States praising how 'Under repeated fire from the skies, Malta stood alone, but unafraid in the center of the sea, one tiny bright flame in the darkness.' Now the Governor-General showed Roosevelt where those words had been engraved on a plaque mounted on the facade of the Grand Master's Palace in Valletta.

More junior members of the delegations were also taking the opportunity to enjoy Malta. A British stenographer, Joyce Rogers, had first been struck by the presence 'all around us in the water of gondolas manned by one or two men with long oars which they used . . . standing up' and by 'terrible bomb damage'. Later she luxuriated in not having 'to bother about the black-out' and the availability – unlike in rationed wartime Britain – of 'grapefruit for breakfast'.

On the evening of 2 February, after a meeting of the Combined Chiefs of Staff with Churchill, Roosevelt entertained Churchill and Eden to dinner. In the latter's view it 'was no more successful than the luncheon' in terms of business done. The British and the Americans 'were going into a decisive conference and had so far neither agreed what we would discuss nor how to handle matters with a Bear [Stalin] who would certainly know his own mind'.

Eden's views were somewhat exaggerated. Even if, as Hopkins once remarked, Roosevelt 'loves Winston as a man for the war, but is horrified at his reactionary attitude for after the war', the US and UK positions were reasonably closely aligned on nearly all issues. Yet, however much discussion there had been, there could never have been a full meeting of minds on Churchill's pre-eminent objective – to preserve and protect the position not only of Britain but of the British Empire, which ruled over some quarter of the world's population.

Churchill was an unreconstructed imperialist. His obsession with the empire was an anachronistic Achilles heel which led him to devote to the topic much time and energy which might have been better spent elsewhere in achieving concessions more crucial for Britain's future than those for which he pleaded on the empire's behalf. In the 1930s Churchill had confessed to being 'a child of the Victorian era . . . when the structure of our country seemed firmly set, when its position in trade and on the seas was unrivalled, and when the realisation of the greatness of our Empire and of our duty to preserve it was ever growing stronger'. His outlook combined an often colourfully expressed racism directed at most other nations with an undoubtedly sincere belief in the superiority of the Anglo-Saxon, and in particular the 'British race'. For example, when speaking of South Africa to one of Roosevelt's advisers he said, 'We will not let the Hottentots by popular vote throw the white people into the sea.' In 1940, as Prime Minister Churchill railed, 'I hate Indians . . . They are a beastly people with a beastly religion.'

Churchill's fellow anti-appeaser but reluctant wartime Secretary of State for India, Leo Amery, could never convince Churchill to conciliate the Indian Congress Party leader Jawaharlal Nehru with offers of post-war concessions. Nehru had since the mid-1930s often condemned Hitler and vigorously criticized Chamberlain's policy of appeasement and if treated differently might well have been prepared to give some support to British war aims. Amery complained that Churchill had a 'Hitler-like attitude towards India' and was 'shouting' about India and claiming its then 500 million inhabitants were 'breeding like rabbits'. On one occasion Amery questioned whether 'on this subject of India he [Churchill] is really quite sane – there is no relation between his manner, physical and intellectual, on this theme and the equability and dominant good sense he displays on issues directly affecting the conduct of the war.'

Perhaps partly because of his generally hostile attitude, Churchill had been slow to realize the seriousness of the 1940s Bengal famine in which more than 1 million people died. The press in America as well as in Britain and India castigated the feeble relief attempts by the British government and also by local Indian authorities. Nevertheless, it took considerable pressure,

including a threat to resign by the British viceroy in India Lord
Wavell, as well as from Leo Amery and Parliament to overturn
the government's 'scandalous' inaction. Finally convinced, in April
1944 Churchill wrote to Roosevelt asking to borrow American
merchant ships to import wheat to India from Australia. A million
tons would be required 'to hold the situation, and so meet the
needs of the United States and British and Indian troops and of
the civil population'. Roosevelt would not assist for fear of
damaging the transport of supplies to American forces in the
Pacific. However, the increased efforts of the authorities began
to ameliorate the worst effects of the famine and by the time of
Yalta the topic had dropped from public attention. Despite both
the independence struggle and the Bengal famine, the British
authorities in India had by 1945 raised from the subcontinent the
largest all-volunteer army in history, increasing its size from
189,000 in 1939 to some 2.5 million.

Churchill's almost hysterical opposition to any suggestion of
Indian independence was well known to both Roosevelt and
Stalin. Roosevelt himself at Teheran discussed Churchill's stance
privately with Stalin, who agreed that the empire was a sore
spot for Churchill. In Washington over the New Year of 1941/2,
Roosevelt suggested that Churchill promise India independence
and propose a timescale for achieving it as the US had for the
Philippines. Churchill responded that he would resign before he
would 'yield an inch of the territory that was under the British
flag'. On the fringes of the Casablanca Conference, after jocularly
offering to hand Gandhi over to the United States – 'He's awfully
cheap to keep, now that's he's on hunger strike' – Churchill
continued:

> There are always earnest spinsters in Pennsylvania, Utah,
> Edinburgh or Dublin persistently writing letters and signing
> petitions and ardently giving their advice . . . urging that India
> be given back to the Indians and South Africa back to the Zulus
> or Boers, but as long as I am called by His Majesty the King
> to be his First Minister, I shall not assist at the dismemberment
> of the British Empire.

From Malta Churchill wrote to his wife:

> I have had for some time a feeling of despair about the British
> connection with India, and still more about what will happen
> if it is suddenly broken . . . However out of my shadows has
> come a renewed resolve to go fighting on as long as possible
> and to make sure the Flag is not let down while I am at the
> wheel.

In any case the time for prior discussion had run out and what
Churchill called 'the exodus' began that same evening of 2 February
– for security reasons the decision had been taken to depart after
dark. Twenty Douglas Skymasters and five RAF Avro York transport
planes waited by the control tower at Luqa aerodrome to carry
some 700 people 1,400 miles to the Crimea. They included the
'Sacred Cow', the modified Skymaster about to make its first flight
with Roosevelt aboard who, in turn, would be the first US president to visit the Soviet Union. When he saw the plane's cage-elevator,
specially fitted to raise his wheelchair to the cabin, he grumbled,
'I never authorised that. It's quite unnecessary.'

Just before midnight the first aircraft took off into the darkness,
followed at regular ten-minute intervals by the twenty-four
others. To allow the President time to settle down for the night,
lying on a wide couch, the 'Sacred Cow' did not depart until 3.30
a.m., five minutes before the plane carrying Churchill lifted into
what its navigator John Mitchell recalled as 'a cold, starlight night'.
Cardiologist Howard Bruenn sat up all night on a chair positioned
against Roosevelt's couch, to make sure the President did not fall
from it in the event of turbulence or if he became ill.

Every possible precaution was taken. Edward Stettinius recalled,
'the planes were to fly without lights and their radios were to be
silent. In case any plane was attacked there was an agreed-upon
radio frequency to be used to warn the other planes. If an attack
did occur all the planes had directions to fly to bases in Africa.'
Relays of American Lockheed P-38 fighters – German troops
nicknamed them 'fork-tailed devils' because of their twin tails –
would escort the President's and the Prime Minister's planes. Since

the Nazis still occupied Crete, the Allied pilots would sheer away north-west as they approached the island. After passing over Athens around dawn, they would turn again for the Dardanelles and head onwards, like Jason and the Argonauts of mythical times, over the empty expanse of the Black Sea. Allied air-sea rescue ships were stationed along the route in case of incident.

To avoid any risk of being mistaken for the enemy, as they approached the Soviet radio transmitter near Saki aerodrome, the planes would, in agreement with the Russians, make a right-angled turn. As another precaution against trigger-happy anti-aircraft batteries – so recently engaged in desperate fighting against German forces – mistakenly firing on incoming Allied aircraft, Mike Reilly had told Artikov, his NKVD counterpart, that unless a non-commissioned US air force officer was permitted to be stationed with each battery, the President would not come. A startled Artikov had consulted Stalin, who had instantly agreed.

Yet, however careful the planning, things could still go wrong. A York bringing members of the British delegation to Malta, including Brooke's ADC, had crashed after the pilot had mistaken the island of Lampedusa for Malta in the darkness. Unable to establish communications with the ground, he had circled until, with fuel running out, he had attempted to land on water. By bad luck the place he chose was over a submerged wreck which ripped the belly out of the plane, killing most on board. Elizabeth Layton, one of Churchill's secretaries, recalled how she and the fourteen other young female staff she was travelling with 'all felt uncertain after the bad news of the day' as, lying in rows on the floor of their York aircraft, they waited to take off to Yalta.

However, every plane that left Malta that night reached its destination safely. Roosevelt had been the first president to fly in office – his cousin Teddy had been the first to fly. Now Roosevelt's doctors insisted that the 'Sacred Cow', flying at its cruising speed of 200 miles per hour and unpressurized like all the planes, keep low throughout the flight – no more than 6,000 feet – because of the President's breathing problems and high blood pressure. Nevertheless, Bruenn recorded that the President 'slept rather poorly because of the noise and vibration'.

Captain Hugh Lunghi, a young translator from the British military mission in Moscow, watched the President's plane land at Saki and was shocked to see Roosevelt 'being decanted . . . it's the only word I can use' from the *Sacred Cow*. Lunghi had never seen the President before and was taken aback by:

> this gaunt, very thin figure with his black cape over his shoulder, and tied at his neck with a knot, and his trilby hat turned up at the front. His face was . . . a sort of yellow, waxen and very drawn, very thin, and a lot of the time he was sort of sitting, sitting there with his mouth open . . . staring ahead.

In fact, the slack jaw was a consequence of medication Roosevelt was taking for hypertension. Churchill's doctor Lord Moran agreed with Lunghi: 'The President appears a very sick man. He has all the symptoms of hardening of the arteries of the brain in an advanced stage.'

The 'care taken of their disabled President by his bodyguards' impressed Sergo Beria, also watching the new arrival closely. 'It was obvious that they loved him. One had only to observe the way they put him in his car, doing everything to conceal his infirmity.'

The welcoming ceremonies included the offer of caviar, sturgeon, smoked salmon, eggs, champagne, vodka and tumblers of what the new arrivals took to be apple juice but was in fact Crimean brandy. Then the delegations set out south to Yalta, ninety miles away, 'under lowering clouds that spat rain and a little wet snow' along roads from which all other traffic had been banned. The unpaved surfaces were so rough that Admiral William Leahy was soon complaining that the journey 'was breaking every bone in his body' and that he was 'being asphyxiated by the engine exhaust'. As the most senior in the car Leahy was at least in the front seat. Roosevelt's naval aide Vice-Admiral Wilson Brown, bouncing about in the back, remembered 'The driver's tenacity in holding his place in the line despite hell and high water was a fine example of discipline through fear. We were soon convinced that he would keep his place or die with the rest of us in the attempt.'

Seeing her father's weariness, Anna Boettiger had arranged that only she would travel with him 'so that he could sleep as much as he wanted and would not have to "make" conversation'. They drove through flat, featureless terrain strewn with ruined buildings, burned-out tanks and gutted German freight trains destroyed during the Nazis' recent retreat. Hitler had boasted of making the Crimea 'our Riviera' and Nazi troops had occupied it for two and a half years. Roosevelt told Anna the devastation made him even more determined 'to get even with the Germans'.

In preparation for the conference, on Lavrentii Beria's orders the NKVD had carried out security checks of the area resulting in the arrest of more than 800 supposed security risks. With scarcely a civilian to be seen except for 'a few grim-faced peasants' Sarah Oliver, sitting by her father's side, thought the view 'as bleak as the soul in despair!' Greatcoated soldiers, some wearing astrakhan caps and all armed with elderly American Lend-Lease Springfield rifles, stood sentry every 200 yards of the route, saluting each car that passed. Many were female and, Sarah thought, magnificent-looking. As they bumped along the slushy road at only twenty miles an hour, it was not long before Churchill asked his daughter how long they had been going. When she told him only an hour, he replied, 'Christ, five more of this.'

The convoy passed through the drab town of Simferopol where Averell Harriman and his daughter had arrived a few days before and where Stalin had also recently ended his own 1,000-mile rail journey from Moscow. Stalin disliked flying. His only experience of it had been a knuckle-whitening turbulent journey in an American Douglas Dakota Lend-Lease transport plane from Baku across the Caspian Sea to the Teheran Conference. It had brought on not only a severe nosebleed but an earache lasting two weeks. On 30 January, wearing his customary peasant garb of baggy trousers, plain khaki tunic and boots and chain-smoking his favourite American cigarettes – like Roosevelt he particularly liked Camels, Chesterfields and Lucky Strikes – he had left Moscow in a green armoured train carrying no special markings but with copious protection including troops with anti-aircraft guns mounted on flat cars, and in Stalin's carriage bulletproof glass just as the *Ferdinand Magellan* had.

The dictator's journey of three days and nights had carried him through the bleak battle-ravaged regions of Tula, Orel and Kursk. The latter had been the scene less than eighteen months previously of the Second World War's largest tank battle involving 8,000 tanks and a pivotal engagement in which the Red Army had blunted the last great German strategic offensive on the Eastern Front. Major Arthur Birse of the British military mission in Moscow, who would act as Churchill's chief interpreter as he had at Teheran and had made the same journey a few days before, was struck by the spectacle of whole forests felled by machine-gun fire and homeless, helpless refugees milling around the makeshift wooden shacks erected in place of stations destroyed in the fighting. From Simferopol, Stalin had continued by car down to Yalta along the same potholed roads his guests were now enduring.

As their motorcade ascended into the mountains between Simferopol and Yalta, many American and British delegates noticed with relief the air growing warmer and the climate milder. Cypress trees softened the landscape and soon any trace of snow disappeared. The Black Sea, as it came into view near the seaside town of Alushta, glinted blue. By now Women's Royal Naval Service Officer (Wren) Maureen Stuart-Clark, travelling with Admiral James Somerville whose aide she was, and Field Marshal Henry Wilson urgently needed a lavatory stop:

> Finally I could exist no longer so I turned round to Field Marshal Wilson and said, 'Do you mind if we stop soon, Sir' to which he replied rather ponderously, 'No, No, but *you'd* better choose the place'. I did – one of the derelict Russian tanks to which I plodded through the snow.

Sarah Oliver was also focused on 'the call of nature . . . pretty desperate by now!' She too would have liked to find a convenient derelict tank or a bush, but with 'cars in front – press photographers behind!!' felt too inhibited – 'obviously no future in that!

At last when hope had nearly died', the convoy stopped at a rest house. It was more than a comfort stop. Inside, they found a room laid out with every luxury including caviar again and presided over by a smiling Molotov. Roosevelt and his daughter had halted earlier for coffee and sandwiches. Concerned her father should reach Yalta as quickly as possible and without consulting him, Anna got quickly out of the car, found Molotov's interpreter and 'pave[d] the way . . . for a refusal from Father'. Rejoining Roosevelt, she told him no one would mind if they pressed on to Yalta which, to the Russians' evident disappointment, the President agreed to do. However, 'that tough old bird' Churchill settled down to an enjoyable lunch during which the popping of champagne corks 'went on all the time like machine-gun fire'.

From Alushta, the final part of the journey followed the 'Route Romanov'. Completed in 1913 for the last Tsar Nicholas II, it was far from 'imperial'. The sharp hairpin bends which, despite the precipice below, had no retaining walls alarmed one of Roosevelt's naval aides – 'passengers were thrown about in the constant change of direction; one escape from the edge was quickly followed by another hairbreadth escape'. Churchill distracted himself by reciting 'practically all' of Byron's lengthy poem 'Don Juan' to his daughter.

Darkness had fallen as the tired visitors finally approached Yalta, their vehicles' headlights picking out the soldiers still standing sentinel. Two miles south-west of the town, Roosevelt's convoy turned up a drive. A few moments later the Livadia Palace, camouflage-painted pink and brown for security, loomed out of the trees. Kathleen Harriman was standing in the entrance to welcome the President after a journey that had brought him a third of the way around the world.

Twelve and a half miles away at the Vorontsov Villa, Joan Bright waited apprehensively, feeling like 'a hotel housekeeper'. This was her 'D-Day – Damned Day – the day the main delegation would arrive'. She doubted 'whether anyone would be pleased with our arrangements' but she had done her best including getting hold of the large double bed she knew Churchill would insist on to work as well as sleep in, which had been sent specially from Moscow.

When Churchill eventually arrived, he seemed in 'an ill humour'. 'What a hole I've brought you to!' he apologized to his secretary Marian Holmes.

PART THREE

'Jaw to Jaw', Yalta, 3–11 February 1945

'If we cannot get a meeting of minds when our armies are converging on the common enemy, how can we get an understanding on even more vital things in the future?'

Roosevelt to Stalin, February 1945, Yalta.

CHAPTER FIVE

'All the Comforts of Home'

Though Churchill was dismissive of Yalta, others had once considered it a place of charm and grace. In 1860 Alexander II, the liberator of the serfs, purchased the Livadia estate where he built two palaces as summer homes for his family. The Russian aristocracy followed their Tsar, constructing their own airy villas overlooking the Black Sea. Mark Twain, who arrived by ship in 1867, admired 'the great parks and gardens of noblemen' and 'the bright colors of their palaces' against the dramatic backdrop of 'tall, gray mountains . . . their sides bristling with pines'.

A British guidebook of 1875 likened Yalta's 'charming situation' to that of 'Naples on a small scale . . . The number of Russian families that go there for the purpose of bathing is increasing from year to year and bids fair to make Yalta the Russian Brighton.' A later guidebook called Yalta:

> the gayest, the most exclusive, and the most expensive Russian resort. As always with modish Russians, everything is done on a large scale. The hotels are enormous and very grand. The casino and café life is typically extravagant . . . The Yalta planet revolves from midnight to midnight. It is the social capital of the Crimea.

Despite the freneticism of the summer season, Tolstoy and Gorky found peace and inspiration in Yalta. The balmy climate suited Anton Chekhov, who lived out his last tuberculosis-ridden years in his white-painted hillside dacha shaded by the cherry, mulberry and almond trees he planted and where he wrote *Three Sisters* and *The Cherry Orchard*. Yalta's fashionable visitors amused Chekhov, and he noted 'two peculiarities of a well-dressed Yalta crowd . . . the elderly ladies were dressed like young ones, and there were great numbers of generals'.

In 1909, Alexandra, wife of Nicholas II, persuaded him to build a new palace at Livadia because she believed unwholesome conditions in the old buildings had caused their young son Alexei to catch typhoid. By 1911, their new three-storey, fifty-room Italianate Renaissance-style mansion of white limestone with white Carrara marble detailing was finished. Nicholas and Alexandra had clearly been demanding patrons. A report on the palace prepared for the American delegation to the Yalta Conference described how the architect had slyly incorporated caricatures of the Tsar in the lion's head armrests of two marble benches flanking the main door: 'when a cap is placed atop the lion's head' the likeness to the Tsar was 'striking'. Nicholas and his family only spent four summers at the Livadia, boating, picnicking and walking in the grounds. The Tsar reputedly slept in a different bedroom every night, even swapping rooms in the middle of the night, for fear of assassination. During the Yalta Conference Stalin would joke that the only place Nicholas II could certainly be found in the morning was the bathroom.

After the Tsar's abdication in March 1917, Alexander Kerensky and the new Menshevik government rejected his request for the imperial family to live quietly in the Livadia. Instead the palace became first a home for 'victims of Tsarism' and, after Lenin and the Bolsheviks seized power from Kerensky in the October 1917 revolution, a sanatorium for workers suffering from tuberculosis. During the Nazi occupation, Wehrmacht units quartered themselves there. A witness described them as 'like animals, getting drunk and sometimes throwing their wineglasses and plates off a balcony overlooking the Black Sea'. Hitler subsequently presented the Livadia to Field Marshal Karl von Runstedt as a reward for capturing the Crimea, but Runstedt left the Eastern

Front at the end of 1941 and by the time the Russians retook Yalta in April 1944 retreating German troops had thoroughly looted the palace.

The Nazis' occupation and their later expulsion also devastated the town. Arthur Birse wrote that 'though the town looked attractive as we approached it, a closer look revealed its tragedy. Each house was a roofless shell, the destruction had been systematic, and before evacuation the Germans had left no house untouched.' He realized, 'there was also another reason for the desolation: the Crimean Tatars – the largest separate nationality in the Crimea – had been deported'.

The previous year, at Lavrentii Beria's urging, Stalin had ordered the forcible deportation of more than 230,000 of the Crimea's inhabitants, including 180,000 Tatars – a Turkic ethnic group settled for over a millennium in the peninsula they called Qirim, perhaps the origin of the modern name Crimea, Krym in Russian. His justification was that after the Nazi occupation of the area in September 1941, 20,000 Tatars had served in so-called German 'self-defence' battalions. They included prisoners of war who preferred to fight for the Nazis rather than starve in their camps and others angered by the pillaging of their villages by Russian partisans who viewed Tatars with contempt. The price for their decisions was the collective punishment of the entire Crimean Tatar population.

A twenty-eight-year-old teacher, Crimean-born Russian Olga Korniyasenko, lived in a village where all but seven of the 120 families were Tatars, but 'We did not make a distinction such as "I am a Tatar or you are a Russian".' She watched helplessly as soldiers forced her friends and neighbours from their homes. With the Tatars' departure, 'our village turned into a ghost town'.

The deportations were swift, savage and without warning. 'All was calm the day before the exile,' sixteen-year-old Arire Idrisli recalled. Then, in the early hours of 18 May 1944 Russian soldiers arrived. They pushed Idrisli and his family into cattle trucks that carried them east to Uzbekistan, deep in Soviet Central Asia:

We travelled 28 days. We were fed only once . . . the railcar was so full that I could not stretch my legs. The ones who died

on the journey were dumped along the road . . . When we
arrived at Samarkand, they gathered us at the stadium. They
gathered our belongings and piled them in a corner. They led
us, pushing and shoving with their rifles, to baths . . . They
were swearing and throwing on us boiling water with chemicals.
Some died of burns.

The deported Tatars were billeted in barns in scattered villages
on the steppe and forced into hard labour. In the first two years
30,000 died from hunger, disease and the rigours of a harsh desert
region so different from the sheltered Crimea. 'A woman and her
son were found eaten by jackals. We recognised the boy by his
shoes,' Arire Idrisli recalled.

Although tired, the new arrivals in Yalta took stock of their
surroundings. Roosevelt's daughter Anna noted gratefully how
Kathleen Harriman had made the Livadia Palace 'homely'. 'When
we arrived, fires were blazing merrily in all the downstairs rooms
– and were most welcome as we were pretty frozen after our
five hour drive.' Inspecting his three-room suite on the ground
floor, Roosevelt couldn't 'understand Winston's concern. This
place has all the comforts of home.' He was to sleep in a yellow-
satin panelled bedroom in a vast bed whose wooden frame was
inlaid with mythical beasts. Nicholas II's Tudor-style walnut-
ceilinged billiard room would be his private dining room and the
Tsar's red velvet-hung audience room his study. He also had a
newly built private bathroom with walls of sea blue – a colour
which had caused the Soviet decorators some anxiety and considerable repainting to achieve the right shade. Its lavatory had a
specially built-up seat.

Anna Boettiger's accommodation was more spartan – a
'cubicle-like room' with:

> a funny old iron bed in it, with a thin mattress which is a foot
> shorter than the springs, one round table and no chairs . . .
> Two rooms away is a big room housing a toilet and a basin with

cold running water and nothing else. This room has two doors and one has no lock.

With the nearest hot water some distance away, she decided that as her father's bathroom was closer, 'methinks I may use it'. She was surprised when a Soviet officer 'tried to pet me'. Her father described her molester as 'a most sinister-appearing pest' who reminded him of certain businessmen he had met.

Roosevelt's 'inner circle' of some two dozen, including Harry Hopkins, Averell Harriman and Edward Stettinius, also had their own rooms on the ground floor, with three bathrooms between them. Hopkins's room, in which he would spend much of the conference suffering from digestive problems, was next to Roosevelt's. Kathleen Harriman wrote to her friend Pamela Churchill, 'Harry arrived not very well & went straight to bed with dia (can't spell it) . . . The doctors ordered him to eat nothing but cereal & the fool had 2 huge helpings of caviar, cabbage soup with sour cream & and then his cereal.'

The large US military staff, billeted on the Livadia's first floor in rooms once occupied by the Tsarina and her four daughters, were, as Kathleen had anticipated, 'packed like patients in a ward'. Seven generals found themselves squeezed into one room and ten colonels into another. General George Marshall, Army Chief of Staff and leader of the US military delegation, was given the sole occupancy of the Tsarina's erstwhile bedroom. Fleet Admiral Ernest King, Commander-in-Chief, US Fleet, and a man whose own daughter said that he was 'the most even-tempered man in the Navy. He is always in a rage,' was allocated the Tsarina's boudoir – a cause of general mirth. Portal wrote, 'Ernie K. has the Empress's [boudoir] with a secret stair which Rasputin used to use. If his ghost walks up those stairs now, it is going to get one hell of a shock!'

King's quarters contained the only functioning lavatory in this part of the palace. King liked to read while sitting on the toilet, causing Marshall to hammer on the door, demanding his turn. King ignored him. With other senior military personnel also clamouring to use the lavatory, 'a time and motion system', as one colonel later joked, was eventually introduced. Some of the

American delegation felt the garden 'closely planted with thick shrubs and plants' might provide an alternative facility but soon found a Russian guard 'lurking' behind each tree:

> They understood no English, no gestures of urgency made by us and seemed to have no sympathy for the normal functioning of the human body. One night Admiral Brown was ordered then nudged back inside at a visibly unfortunate moment, protesting in the strongest English he knew against such treatment of a guest.

Major-General Kuter recalled that 'excepting only the war, the bathrooms were the most generally discussed subject'. During the breakneck redecoration programme directed by Lavrentii Beria, the Soviet teams had achieved a great deal, renovating forty-three rooms in the Livadia as well as a further forty-eight rooms in a nearby palace for more junior American personnel. They had installed electrical and heating systems in all the buildings and constructed a substantial bomb shelter in the Livadia's cellars for the President. Bathrooms, however, were, in Kathleen Harriman's words, 'practically nil'. Not that the Soviet leaders despised such bourgeois comforts. In May 1942 when Molotov was in England and Churchill invited him to Chequers, the Prime Minister's official country residence, Molotov grumbled, 'There was a bathroom but with no shower. I've been to Roosevelt's place. I've stayed overnight in the White House. Everything there was as it should be. He had a bathroom with a shower, too.'

Clerks and other junior personnel were squashed into the Livadia's top floor. Everyone became used to Russian chambermaids barging in without knocking and to encountering cleaners sweeping up with twig brooms or skimming barefoot over the polished floors on bundles of cleaning rags during the hours of darkness.

That first evening Roosevelt planned on mixing his usual cocktails but on learning there was no ice and that the Soviets had prepared their own version of cocktails decided on bourbon and water instead. The butler assigned to look after the President was the maître d'hôtel of the Moscow Metropol who, 'with many bows from the waist', continually addressed him as 'Your Excellency' – a courtesy about which Kuter thought 'The President did not seem to be displeased'. Under the maître d'hôtel's direction, black-coated waiters served dinner at an elaborately set table with five glasses for each guest. Kathleen Harriman told Anna Boettiger she had watched them practising setting and unsetting the table '3 or 4 times a day for the past week – experimenting with glass-ware and china effects'. Anna noticed during the meal that whenever anyone refused a dish 'the maitre d'hotel looked either like a thunder cloud or mortally wounded'.

Before going to bed Roosevelt asked Averell Harriman to visit the Soviet delegation at the nearby Yusupov Palace to discuss plans for the first meeting of the conference the next day, for which there was no agreed agenda. When Harriman had raised the issue with Molotov in Moscow two weeks earlier, the Russian had blandly replied, 'The Soviet government has not developed any agenda and would not suggest one . . . Marshal Stalin will be ready to discuss any questions the President may want to raise.' Harriman was also to ask whether Stalin would meet Roosevelt 'for a purely personal talk' before the conference formally opened.

Harriman's car encountered three Soviet security patrols along the dark road, including one with dogs, before he reached the Yusupov Palace where Molotov greeted him around midnight. When Harriman explained that the President wished the first discussion to cover military issues, Molotov agreed, saying Stalin too wanted to discuss the Allied advance into Germany, as well as related political issues. He also agreed that Stalin would visit the President at 4 p.m. before the conference convened at 5 p.m. and accepted an invitation for Stalin to mark the first day of the conference by dining with Roosevelt at the Livadia.

Churchill meanwhile was adjusting to the hundred-year-old Vorontsov Palace set in lush parkland among sub-tropical plants, magnolias and cypresses. Instead of finding it a 'hole', to his surprise he rather liked it:

The setting of our abode was impressive. Behind the villa, half Gothic and half Moorish in style, rose the mountains, covered in snow, culminating in the highest peak in the Crimea. Before us lay the dark expanse of the Black Sea, severe, but still agreeable and warm even at this time of year.

The palace had been built for Prince Mikhail Vorontsov, a hero of the Napoleonic Wars and later Governor of the Crimea, who had employed an English architect, Edward Blore. Perhaps strangely, Blore never visited the Crimea but he designed a building which Churchill's daughter Sarah thought 'fantastic! . . . a bit like a Scottish baronial hall inside and a Swiss Chalet plus Mosque outside!' Others were less impressed. Wren Maureen Stuart-Clark thought it 'quite the ugliest place I have ever seen'.

As with the Livadia, Lavrentii Beria had paid close personal attention to the renovations. Workers had made habitable twenty-two of the Vorontsov's high-ceilinged rooms though they had not constructed a subterranean bomb shelter for Churchill as they had for Roosevelt and Stalin at their residences. Churchill's accommodation consisted of three rooms, including a bedroom of Moorish exoticism with French windows opening onto a terrace overlooking the sea. In an adjacent room, naval Captain Richard Pim – an earlier arrival – had already set up Churchill's cherished Map Room that always accompanied him. In the run-up to the conference the British Embassy in Moscow had told the Russians that not only did Churchill want his Map Room to adjoin his living quarters at Yalta but placed 'so as to be accessible to President Roosevelt when wheeled in his chair'. Pim had first set up a Map Room for Churchill in 1939 when he took charge of the Admiralty. When Churchill became prime minister, the Map Room accompanied him to Downing Street. Churchill had taken it with him to the White House in December 1941 and showed the President how he used it to track the latest military and naval movements. Roosevelt was so impressed that he established one of his own on the ground floor of the White House.

Churchill's daughter Sarah Oliver and the grandees of the British delegation were also comfortable. 'Bowls of fruit and bottles of mineral water in every bedroom. Also a decanter of vodka!' Sir Alexander Cadogan, Permanent Under-Secretary at the Foreign Office, wrote in his diary. The palace lacked central heating – unlike the Livadia – but numerous fireplaces and tiled Russian stoves kept the rooms pleasantly warm. The electricity supply was, however, erratic:

> there is a system of 'remote control' of lighting which is some-what embarrassing. The lights . . . all turn on and off from a switchboard at the end of the passage! So that a Russian house-maid or a heavy-fingered Marine either plunge one in darkness or switch on the light at 6 a.m.!

Just as at the Livadia, the shortage of bathrooms and lavatories was a problem. Like Roosevelt, Churchill had the luxury of a private bathroom. So did Eden, which he offered to share with Cadogan. For the rest, it was first come, first served. 'If you were a spectator along the bedroom corridors here at about 7.30 in the morning, you would see 3 Field Marshals queuing for a bucket! And really some Field Marshals will not go in a bucket!' Sarah Oliver told her mother.

Conditions were better for the personnel living aboard the USS *Catoctin* which, following Russian insistence that Yalta's harbour was too heavily mined to be safe, had instead docked in Sebastopol eighty miles to the west, protected by two US mine-sweepers. From Sebastopol, messages to and from the President were either being couriered or transmitted along landlines laid by the US Signal Corps – vital communication links since, with White House couriers likely to take up to five days carrying mail to Yalta, the President would be at the absolute limit of the dis-tance he could travel while meeting his Constitutional obligation to respond to Congressional bills within ten days. The British Cunard liner *Franconia*, requisitioned as a troopship at the start of the war, was also anchored off Sebastopol, serving a similar function as a British headquarters and, as Churchill put it, a bolt hole 'in case accommodation on shore at Yalta broke down'. Her pre-war stock of wines had been removed from store and brought aboard and her best linen put back on the beds.

Soviet officials and marines kept a close eye on the movements of the signals teams sent ashore to set up communication lines with the delegations in Yalta. Sebastopol had been captured by the German army in late June 1942 only after a gruelling 250-day siege and retaken by the Red Army in May 1944. The scale of the devastation, with inhabitants subsisting in freezing conditions in hastily thrown-up shacks roofed with corrugated iron, shocked the visitors. 'Everything destroyed and the streets full of Romanian prisoners, pathetic sights, shovelling rubble', a British naval officer recalled.

Detailed briefing notes had warned the Americans and British in Yalta that they would not be able to move freely about: 'When a guard asks for your "documents", "propock", "passports" or "bumagy", show him your identification card without hesitation. If he challenges you for any reason whatsoever, produce your card. Do not try to bulldoze the guards – they have strict orders.' The warnings proved correct. At the Vorontsov Palace, Maureen Stuart-Clark found NKVD guards, 'very smart in their khaki uniforms with their high boots, red and blue caps, gold braid', omnipresent. She traded a threepenny bit for one of their red star cap badges, which she wore on her uniform tie. Despite the surveillance, Joan Evans, one of Churchill's cypher clerks, managed to explore a little, admiring the local people's well-tended, vine-hung gardens but shocked by the amount of war debris including 'a tin hat with part of a head in it'.

The large number of Russian soldiers and machine-gun-toting NKVD men patrolling the Livadia grounds disconcerted Anna Boettiger, who complained:

> we have to carry our identification cards everywhere. We were asked to produce them about every 25 feet . . . We found we could not go all the way to the beach. One excuse given us was that mines still wash up on the beach and sometimes explode – only an excuse is my guess, though I'm told it has happened.

*

In the hilltop Yusupov Palace at Koreiz, set in formal grounds of maples and oaks with gravel walks lined with statuary, Stalin prepared for the conference. The palace had once belonged to Prince Felix Yusupov, an Oxford-educated, reputedly bisexual officer who enjoyed roaming St Petersburg dressed in his mother's clothes and jewels and was married to the Tsar's niece Irina. In late December 1916, in his yet more splendid palace in St Petersburg, Yusupov had tried to poison Grigori Rasputin, the charismatic priest loathed on almost every side for his influence over the imperial family, with wine and cake laced with enough cyanide to kill several men instantly. When to Yusupov's amazement the poison failed to have any effect, he shot Rasputin with his revolver. However, even this failed to kill the priest who stumbled out into a courtyard to be shot again by the Prince's co-conspirators before finally collapsing. The assassins bound his body, wrapped it in a sheet, smashed a hole in the ice of the frozen Moika River and pushed Rasputin in. When his corpse was retrieved the next day, the ropes binding him were partially undone suggesting he was still alive when dumped in the river.

After the Revolution, Yusupov and his family took refuge in his Yalta palace. When two bloodstained Bolshevik sailors burst in, the Prince's status as Rasputin's assassin saved him: 'One of them asked me if I was really the man who had murdered Rasputin, and on receiving my reply they both drank to my health, declaring . . . neither my family nor I had anything to fear from them.' In April 1919 – nine months after the Bolsheviks murdered the Tsar and his immediate family in Ekaterinburg – the Yusupovs, together with surviving members of the Romanov family, including the Tsar's mother, sailed from Koreiz aboard a British dreadnought into exile.

Stalin's lodgings in the Yusupov Palace were modest – he occupied a large room partitioned in two for sleeping and working, both very plainly furnished. Though he enjoyed mocking the last Tsar's fears of assassination, he too was nervous of attack, preferring to slip into the palace through an inconspicuous side door rather than use the main entrance. The Yusupov Palace's newly built bomb shelter was even more robust than Roosevelt's at the

Livadia. Lavrentii Beria assured Stalin that not even a 500-kilogram bomb could shatter its roof of two metres of concrete and one metre of sand. He had had the palace's former billiard room converted into a cinema where Stalin could watch newsreels showing the latest fighting as well as his favourite films. He had also installed high-frequency telephone and telegraph systems to keep Stalin in touch with Moscow, the military fronts and any town across the Soviet Union as well as a separate telephone system linked to the American and British delegations, the cables well-guarded by NKVD units. In fact, Beria had turned Yalta effectively into a fortress with 244 Soviet aircraft on standby and anti-aircraft batteries equipped with 300 anti-aircraft and machine guns to protect its airspace.

With only himself to answer to as supreme leader, unchallenged in either the political or military spheres, as he contemplated the days ahead, Stalin was probably the best-prepared of the three leaders and certainly the clearest about his aims. Beyond the shared objective of defeating Germany as soon as possible and to that end showing a united front to discourage any attempt to split the Allies, he wanted to secure a cordon sanitaire of subordinate states around Russia, an aim which differed little from that of his Tsarist predecessors – indeed Eden called Stalin 'much more the heir of Peter the Great rather than of Lenin'.

Importantly, Stalin knew that in achieving his aims he would be vastly helped by his armies now occupying most of the territories in question. He was also determined to extract a high price for any agreement to join the war against Japan. Stalin remained particularly suspicious of Churchill and what he saw as his nation's historical perfidy. On the eve of D-Day he had told a senior Yugoslav Communist:

> Perhaps you think that just because we are the allies of the English we have forgotten who they are and who Churchill is. There's nothing they like better than to trick their allies. During the First World War they constantly tricked the Russians and the French. And Churchill? Churchill is the kind of man who will pick your pocket of a kopeck if you don't watch him! Yes,

pick your pocket of a kopeck! And Roosevelt? Roosevelt is not like that. He dips in his hand only for bigger coins. But Churchill? Churchill – will do it for a kopeck.

In some ways Stalin's view was right. Roosevelt concerned himself more with the reconciliation of broad views and the agreement of principles than with the difficulties of detail. However, Stalin failed to recognize that his own position had more similarities with Churchill's. Both were imperialists, although of very different kinds and from very different ends of the political spectrum: the Soviet Union's 'republics' were as diverse as Britain's colonies but had fewer personal freedoms. Rooted in European history, both men believed in political and military power blocs and spheres of influence. On the other hand – even if the US government came to a similar position in later years – Roosevelt was president of a country somewhat reluctantly emerging from isolationism and himself envisaged a more harmonious future world where US dominance would stem from economic and moral factors.

According to Roosevelt's wife, 'he was a good bargainer and a good poker player, and he loved the game of negotiation'. Indeed, in terms of the skill of any pocket-picking to be done, Stalin probably had more to fear from the subtleties of the enigmatic, more devious Roosevelt whom he had met only once, than from the more familiar, upfront, easier to read albeit temperamental Churchill whom he had met twice in Moscow as well as at Teheran.

One of Stalin's deepest concerns, perhaps fuelled by his inherently suspicious nature as well as the knowledge that he himself had made an expedient pact with the Nazis in 1939, continued to be that the US and UK might go further than gang up on him in negotiating the peace. His nagging anxiety, never fully grasped by either Roosevelt or Churchill, was that the two might attempt a separate peace deal with some elements within Germany and perhaps even turn their collective armies east against him. In an attempt to forestall any such prospect, throughout the conference Stalin would persistently stress the closeness of the alliance between the three powers. He would also ask repeated and pointed questions about the speed of the American and British advance into Germany to satisfy himself that the US and Britain were not holding back their troops in the hope of concluding a separate peace. To maintain moral pressure on his allies, Stalin would also frequently emphasize the blood debt they owed to the Soviet Union in terms of the massive loss of life, so much greater than that of their own countries, sustained by Soviet forces in pursuit of their common goal of defeating Hitler.

During the conference, Stalin's Foreign Minister, the moustached sixty-four-year-old – only five feet four inches tall – Vyacheslav Molotov would be almost permanently at his side, peering through pince-nez at the other delegates. Molotov's accommodation in the Yusupov Palace was grander than Stalin's. He had an elegant balcony from which to gaze over the sea and at his request a piano. His real name was Vyacheslav Scriabin but he had taken the name 'Molotov', 'hammer', on becoming a revolutionary. He was the ninth of ten children born to a woman whose brothers owned a prosperous general store where his father worked as a clerk. The young Molotov had been exiled twice in Tsarist times for revolutionary activities. After the Revolution for a while he edited *Pravda* and as a skilful and devoted party bureaucrat caught the eye of Lenin's wife Krupskaya, who promoted his rise. When Stalin took power, Molotov became his most loyal supporter.

Though he had a bare smattering of foreign languages and lacked experience in international diplomacy, in 1939 Stalin made Molotov the People's Commissar for Foreign Affairs. He replaced the respected Maxim Litvinov whose Jewish origins, Stalin thought, might make matters awkward in dealing with the Nazis, though Molotov's much-loved wife Polina was Jewish. Charles Bohlen, who would be Roosevelt's interpreter at Yalta as at Teheran, first met Molotov in Moscow and found him 'a careful, sober negotiator' but 'a man of mystery', hard to fathom. 'Although he was obviously trying to be affable, he had a hard time smiling, and his face remained impassive throughout most of the talks.' Eden recognized 'a confidence, even an intimacy, between Stalin and Molotov such as I have never seen between any other two Soviet leaders, as if Stalin knew that he had a valuable henchman and Molotov was confident because he was so regarded'.

Although Molotov's general demeanour was forbidding and dour, he was capable of occasional mordant wit. Taking cover with von Ribbentrop in Berlin during a British air raid in 1940 in the time of the Molotov–Ribbentrop Pact, he remarked, 'You say that England is defeated. So why are we sitting here now in this air raid shelter?' Churchill's view of Molotov reflected all these elements:

> A man of outstanding ability and cold-blooded ruthlessness . . . His cannonball head, black moustache, and comprehending eyes, his slab face, his verbal adroitness and imperturbable demeanour, were appropriate manifestations of his qualities and skill . . . I have never seen a human being who more perfectly represented the modern conception of a robot. And yet with all this there was an apparently reasonable and keenly polished diplomatist.*

Lavrentii Beria occupied the room next to Stalin's at the Yusupov. Like Stalin, the forty-five-year-old security chief was an 'outsider' from Georgia. During the 'Great Terror' of Stalin's 1937 political purges, as head of the Georgian Communist Party, Beria personally tortured prisoners, battering them with truncheons. The following year, Stalin appointed him head of the NKVD in charge of state security and some 1.7 million wretched slave labourers in the gulags, more than 900,000 of whom would die during the war. Later, as Soviet troops liberated regions occupied by the Nazis, Beria began deporting minorities he suspected of collusion with the Germans – such as the Chechen and Ingush populations of the North Caucasus and, in May 1944, the Crimean Tatars.

---

* In the last years of Stalin's life and rule when Molotov's wife Polina was arrested on trumped-up charges of sedition, Molotov duly and dutifully denounced and divorced her only for the couple to re-marry after she was released following Stalin's death.

Beria was physically unprepossessing: 'a rather short man' according to Yugoslav Milovan Djilas, who noticed that 'in Stalin's Politburo there was hardly anyone taller than himself'. Beria was also 'somewhat plump, greenish and pale, and with soft damp hands . . . square-cut mouth and bulging eyes behind his pince-nez'. He enjoyed what he considered practical jokes — placing tomatoes on people's chairs before they sat down, then roaring with laughter at their discomfiture. He was sexually voracious with a well-earned and sinister reputation as a rapist. Some women willingly prostituted themselves or their daughters to him for favours but his Caucasian bodyguards kidnapped others who caught his eye. Tatiana Okunevskaya, a film actress brought to Beria's house on his orders, recalled how:

> He undressed himself and rolled about in his luxurious bed, his eyes ogling me. He looked . . . not quite like a jellyfish, but like an ugly, shapeless toad. He said: 'Let's have supper. You are a long way from anywhere, so whether you scream or not doesn't matter. You are in my power now.'

During the conference Beria would read transcripts of American and British conversations prepared by his son Sergo and his bugging team. In them 'Roosevelt often spoke against the English' but Sergo wondered whether this might be a bluff intended to mislead any listening Soviets and win over Stalin as 'a friend to the U.S.' Both the British and the Americans were certainly well aware of Soviet capability to bug them wherever they were in the Soviet Union. Translator Hugh Lunghi recalled how whenever members of the British military mission in Moscow had anything particularly sensitive to discuss they would cram into a bathroom and turn the taps on full to drown out their conversations. Just after the war they would discover surveillance equipment beneath a parquet floor and call in an American team to debug the premises. They found 'every room was bugged — even our cipher room. And it was either bugged under the ventilators or in the skirting boards.' Newspapers wrapped round the equipment dated from the 1930s.

Neither the Americans nor the British, however, were aware that the Soviets had spies in their governments' services, transmitting information to Moscow and alerting Soviet authorities to their negotiating tactics and 'red lines'. The American delegation to Yalta actually included a Soviet agent, lanky Harvard graduate Alger Hiss who after the conference received special congratulations from a senior Soviet spymaster. Other prominent agents in the US administration included Gregory Silvermaster in the Board of Economic Warfare and Dexter White, at the time of Yalta newly promoted to Assistant Secretary of the Treasury at the request of Roosevelt's friend and Treasury Secretary Henry Morgenthau. White had also had a senior role in the discussions at Bretton Woods in New Hampshire in 1944 leading to the foundation of the International Monetary Fund. All were inspired by Soviet and Communist beliefs. Silvermaster – code-named initially 'PAL' and subsequently 'ROBERT' – who provided Moscow with, among other important information, details of the Morgenthau Plan as it was being formulated – had chronic asthma and did not think he would live long. He wrote, 'My time is strictly limited, and when I die I want to feel that at least I have had some part in building a decent life for those who come after me.'

The prime sources of information from the British side to the Soviets in the run up to Yalta were the 'Cambridge Five' group of agents – Donald MacLean, Guy Burgess, Kim Philby, John Cairncross and Anthony Blunt. Between them they provided much vital intelligence. However, both Beria and Stalin had in their own youth been double agents, at times spying on their revolutionary comrades. Both were therefore sufficiently wary – not to say paranoid – to suspect in the early 1940s that the five were double agents, and indeed contact was broken off with them for a good portion of 1940 and 1941. Part of the reason for their suspicion was the very quality of their information, which seemed too good to be true. Even more significantly in Soviet eyes, the five did not reveal any information about either British or American agents in the Soviet Union or about the conspiracy the Soviets were certain existed around the flight to Scotland in 1941 by Hitler's deputy Rudolf Hess, in what the Soviets believed was an attempt to make a separate peace. In fact neither the United States nor the United Kingdom had any agents in the Soviet Union during the Second World War and the British authorities simply imprisoned Hess, who on 4 February 1945 – the day the Yalta Conference opened – confined in Abergavenny in Wales, attempted suicide with a bread knife.

Not until the summer of 1944 did the Soviet 'spy residency' in London absolve the five of being double agents and allow their information to be given its due weight. In the first six months of 1945, for example, Guy Burgess provided 389 UK Foreign Office documents classified top secret to the Soviets. Donald MacLean, then a First Secretary in the British Embassy in Washington, provided much useful information on British and American negotiating strategies and on tensions between the two powers.

Meanwhile in the wider world, on the eve of the Yalta conference, Saturday 3 February, as part of the targeted heavy bombing campaign agreed by Kuter and Portal at Malta, 1,000 B-17 bombers of the US 8th Army Air Force, escorted by over 500 P-51 Mustang fighters, attacked Berlin. A bombardier recalled briefing officers telling the air crews:

> this was to be a demoralization mission to create confusion and break their morale . . . it was a maximum effort . . . every Bomb Group in the Eighth Air Force would be in it. We were . . . told to expect enemy fighters and heavy flak and we would probably lose many planes.

He wondered what his fate would be if he was shot down and captured since on his dog tag giving his name, rank and serial number was also 'H' for Hebrew.

The raid destroyed the Gestapo's headquarters on Prinz-Albrechtstrasse, set the German Air Ministry ablaze, killed more than 2,500, wounded some 20,000 and made over 100,000 homeless. Berlin journalist Ursula von Kardorff, who survived in a bunker, described wandering the shattered streets in the aftermath. 'Why does nobody shout, "enough, enough", why does no one go crazy? Why isn't there a revolution?' she wondered. 'Hold out to the end, what a stupid phrase. We're to hold out until we're all dead – as if there is no other salvation.' Among the fatalities was Roland Freisler, the notorious presiding judge at the still continuing trials of suspected conspirators in the July 1944 plot to kill Hitler. When a bomb hit the People's Court, a falling beam and other debris crushed him as he clutched the papers for the trial in progress that day. With the files destroyed, the tortured logic of the Nazis decreed that the trial could not continue. The three prisoners who had been about to be condemned to death but had been dragged manacled back to the cells when the raid began, survived. They were eventually released.

In Britain the V2s still fell. That day *The Times* reported how a soldier returning home on leave 'found his house a pile of debris. Earlier in the day a V bomb had hit his house . . . His wife was in hospital injured, and two of his four young children were killed.'

The same issue also reported the publication in London of a pamphlet entitled *Nil Desperandum* setting out 'a realistic and sensible plan for a final settlement of the Polish-Russian problem'. The authors were the Polish government in exile, waiting with mingled anxiety and hope to see whether the Yalta Conference would restore their country to them. That day they also wrote to Churchill and Roosevelt acknowledging that 'the fate of many nations rests in your hands' but reminding them that Poland 'has been fighting unflinchingly . . . at the side of the great American and British democracies' and pleading that 'you will not permit any decisions to be taken which might jeopardize the legitimate rights of Poland or her independence, and that you will not recognise any faits accomplis with regard to Poland'.

CHAPTER SIX

'Uncle Joe and Stone Arse'

Towards noon on Sunday 4 February – a 'wonderfully mild' day – Anthony Eden was driven to the Yusupov Palace for his own discussions with Molotov. Ever since they had first met on a chill night in December 1941 amid the pops and flashes of press cameras as the Soviet Foreign Minister greeted him at Moscow's railway station, Eden had found Molotov's truculence, incessant demands and 'repeated negatives' deeply exasperating. Like Harriman, Eden wanted to agree an agenda before the conference opened. He was content with Harriman's and Molotov's proposals for the military situation and the treatment of a defeated Nazi Germany to take priority but he also wanted delegates to discuss the plans for a United Nations and the future of Poland. Molotov agreed about the UN but said curtly that Poland had been liberated from the Nazis and should be left to manage its own affairs. Perhaps alerted by Soviet agents to the tensions between the British and the Americans on the matter, he also suggested how helpful it was that they had already consulted one another since this would speed the conference's business. A discomfited Eden denied any such collusion.

In fact, though Roosevelt had succeeded in sidestepping British attempts to agree common negotiating positions in Malta, Eden had not given up but had asked Harry Hopkins's help. The night before, Anna Boettiger had visited Hopkins to see how he was, only to find him 'in a stew':

He gave me a long song and dance that FDR <u>must</u> see Churchill in the morning for a long meeting to dope out how those two are going to map out the Conference; made a few insulting remarks to the effect that after all FDR had asked for this job and that now, whether he liked it or not, he had to do the work, and that it was imperative that FDR and Churchill have some prearrangements before the big Conference.

Anna – who cautioned that this might 'stir up some distrust among our Russian brethren' – wondered whether ill health was affecting Hopkins's judgement or whether it was simply that she had 'never quite realized how pro-British Harry is'.

Churchill's Foreign Secretary since December 1940, the forty-seven-year-old Eden had also held the office from 1935 until he resigned in 1938 in protest at then Prime Minister Neville Chamberlain's policy of appeasement of Hitler. Like so many British politicians then and now, he was educated at Eton public school and Oxford University – a dominance Roosevelt even then decried as 'too much Eton and Oxford'. Eden was the younger son of a landed baronet and the great-great-grandson of Sir Robert Eden, the last colonial governor of Maryland. During the First World War he had won the Military Cross for his courage in rescuing his wounded sergeant.

Languidly and elegantly handsome, he attracted taunts of vanity, even effeminacy, although he was an enthusiastic womanizer. 'Worth his weight in gold as a floorwalker in any West End store', was one jibe. His Cabinet colleague Rab Butler called the sensitive, highly strung Eden 'half mad baronet, half beautiful woman'. In Malta he had been pleased to be recognized by some British soldiers, writing, 'Nothing gives me more comfort than when a soldier's face lights up with pleasure when he recognises one. I suppose this is vanity, but I hope not entirely. The truth is that I like our people and to be with them.' Eden's chief adviser Alexander Cadogan recalled Eden's 'delight' at being recognized, but also how Churchill's arrival slightly earlier than anticipated in Malta had displeased Eden 'frightfully . . . taking the wind out of his sails' – not the only occasion when Eden was visibly piqued at being upstaged or outshone by Churchill.

Eden had visited Moscow several times after Soviet Russia entered the war. Andrei Gromyko wrote of 'his enchanting smile', saying 'Anthony Eden was exactly my typical Englishman . . . a living model of what a subject of the British empire should be. He had the enviable quality, in a politician, of being able to strike up a conversation on the smallest pretext.' Charles Bohlen agreed that Eden had 'diplomatic skills' and was 'very suave' in his handling of Molotov, something he achieved in part by cultivating 'the British attitude of indifference or even frivolity'. However, he showed a 'touch of petulance' when discussions did not go as he wished, particularly when Churchill disagreed with him. Bohlen judged the relations between the two Britons were 'not the most harmonious'.

Eden's approach towards the United States was and always had been more cautious and openly critical than Churchill's. He remarked of Roosevelt's desire for decolonization, 'it was a principle with him, not the less cherished for its possible advantages . . . He hoped that former territories once free of their masters would become politically and economically dependent on the United States.' In October 1941, concerned about Britain's growing dependence on the US for supplies, he had initiated planning on the post-war order in case Roosevelt tried to pre-empt Britain with his own proposals. After the US entered the war, one of Eden's staff described him as 'rather isolationist where Americans coming into Europe is concerned. He wants us, not them to be the predominant partner.'

Others in Britain shared Eden's views, even calling Churchill's attitude to America 'appeasement'. On 30 December 1944 *The Economist* lambasted Churchill's policy towards the United States 'which at [his] personal bidding, has been followed, with all the humiliation and abasements it has brought in its train, ever since Pearl Harbour removed the need for it'. Stettinius showed the piece to Roosevelt, commenting astutely that 'it represents what is in the minds of millions of Englishmen . . . the underlying cause is the emotional difficulty which . . . any Englishman has in adjusting himself to a secondary role after having always accepted a leading one as his national right.'

*

Stalin kept his word to call on Roosevelt at the Livadia for a private discussion before the conference opened, but first he visited Churchill at the Vorontsov – the fourth time the two had met. Churchill's interpreter Arthur Birse thought that, whatever their private opinions, on the surface at least 'both seemed glad to meet again, and they talked like old friends'. They discussed military, not political, issues. With the tide of Allied victory running high, Stalin was buoyant about 'the helpless situation in which the German army was now placed in Poland and East Prussia'. What interested Churchill was whether Stalin's eyes were on the prize of Berlin to the exclusion of all else. The Soviet armies were within fifty miles of the city but even when British and American troops crossed the Rhine they would still have nearly 400 miles to go – Berlin was Stalin's if he wanted it. To test Stalin, Churchill asked what he would do if Hitler fled Berlin. Stalin replied that wherever Hitler went, Soviet armies would hunt him down. He asked for a British and American offensive in the west to stop Hitler moving troops eastwards and in particular for an attack on the Ruhr which, now that the Russians had captured Silesia, would deny Germany access to its last remaining coal fields.

Churchill showed Stalin his Map Room and was chagrined when Stalin immediately pointed out that the position of the Russian front line was inaccurately marked. Churchill then asked Field Marshal Harold Alexander to join them to report on the latest position in the Mediterranean. Alexander's presentation, as he pointed to a detailed map of Italy, was 'the perfection of clarity and conciseness', Birse thought. Stalin too seemed impressed, looking at Alexander 'as if to say; "Well, you certainly know your job!"' However when Stalin suggested outflanking Nazi forces in the Apennines and sending Allied troops from Italy through northern Yugoslavia to rendezvous with Soviet forces near Vienna, Alexander told him he simply did not have enough men. As Stalin probably knew, Churchill had long advocated such a campaign but been unable to convince either his own military or the Americans. One American general damned his ideas as 'Churchill's eternal and infernal Balkan enterprises'. Realizing it was now too late, Churchill merely replied to Stalin, 'the Red Army may not give us time to complete the operation'.

Next Stalin set off in his heavily armour-plated black Packard limousine, with three-inch-thick glass windows capable of withstanding machine-gun fire, to see Roosevelt. As Stalin strode into the Livadia Palace, watched by NKVD guards stationed on the roof, Edward Stettinius was struck that with 'his powerful head and shoulders set on a stocky body, [he] radiated an impression of great strength'. The President, dressed in a pale suit and flowered tie, was waiting with Charles Bohlen to greet Stalin in his red velvet-lined study. Stalin, in a high-collared khaki tunic with a marshal's gold star embroidered on the shoulder straps, had brought Molotov and also Molotov's aide, Vladimir Pavlov, as his translator. Bohlen described how 'The two leaders greeted each other as old friends . . . Smiling broadly, the President grasped Stalin by the hand and shook it warmly. Stalin, his face cracked in one of his rare, if slight, smiles expressed pleasure at seeing the President again.'

Stalin's arrival took Harry Hopkins's son Robert, a US army combat photographer attached to the US delegation as its official photographer, by surprise: 'I scrambled downstairs with my Speed Graphic [camera] in time to photograph the President chatting with Stalin . . . They were seated on a plush couch with an inlaid table in front of them.' His picture captures a genial, relaxed-looking Stalin sitting with hands resting on his thighs, and the President's cigarettes and an ashtray lying within easy reach on the table. Hopkins watched the President repeat the ritual 'he regularly performed at the White House. He made a pitcher of dry martinis. As he passed a glass to Stalin, he said apologetically that a good martini should really have a twist of lemon.' Next day, a huge lemon tree flown in from Stalin's native Georgia and bowing under the weight of '200 pieces of fruit' appeared in the Livadia's entrance hall.

The courtesies continued. Roosevelt said that while crossing the Atlantic on the *Quincy* 'he had made a number of bets . . . that the Red Army would get to Berlin before the Americans got to Manila'. Stalin replied graciously that he was sure that the Americans would be in Manila before his troops reached Berlin, and was proved right when US soldiers entered the city the next day. Roosevelt also told Stalin that the sights he had seen on the road between Saki airfield and Yalta had made him more 'bloodthirsty in regard to the Germans than he had been a year ago'. Stalin replied that 'everyone was more bloodthirsty than they had been a year ago . . . the Germans were savages'. Once more cultivating Stalin and distancing himself from Churchill, Roosevelt recalled Stalin's comments at Teheran that had so greatly offended Churchill that 50,000 German officers should be executed, saying he hoped Stalin 'would again propose a toast to the execution of 50,000'.

Getting down to business, Stalin warned that much hard fighting remained to be done. As he had with Churchill, he pressed for a swift and emphatic advance into the Ruhr to precipitate Germany's economic collapse but did not seem perturbed when Roosevelt told him that, though Eisenhower was planning smaller-scale offensives on 8 and 12 February, the Allies would not make their major push across the Rhine until March. He readily agreed to the President's request to allow Eisenhower to communicate directly with the Soviet high command to improve military coordination.

Roosevelt then asked Stalin what he thought of de Gaulle, himself recalling the French leader's fondness for comparing himself to Joan of Arc as France's spiritual leader and to Georges Clemenceau as its political leader. Stalin dismissed de Gaulle as 'a very complicated person' whose expectations that his country be treated equally with Russia, the US and Britain were 'unrealistic' given that in 1940 France 'had not fought at all'. He asked Roosevelt whether France should have a zone of occupation in Germany, to which the President replied that while not a bad idea it should be 'only out of kindness'. Stalin agreed.

Roosevelt now said he would tell the Marshal 'something indiscreet, since he would not wish to say it in front of Prime Minister Churchill, namely that the British for two years have had the idea of building up France into a strong power which would have 200,000 troops on the eastern border of France to hold the line for the period required to assemble a strong British army' if another war broke out. 'The British were a peculiar people' who wanted to 'have their cake and eat it too'. They 'seemed to think that the Americans should restore order in France' and then hand political control back to them. He also said he was having 'a good deal of trouble with the British' about zones of occupation in a conquered Germany. Though Stalin made no comment, Roosevelt's remark about the British and their cake appears in the Russian record of the meeting.

Towards 5 p.m. the delegates gathered at the Livadia for the first plenary session. Robert Hopkins was no longer the only photographer present. 'By this time the entire American, British and Russian contingents of official photographers had arrived . . . 16 U.S. Army still photographers and motion-picture cameramen, 2 British photographers, and at least 30 Russians' but 'no civilian press photographers'. Also, by mutual agreement no journalists had been permitted to come to Yalta. Anna Boettiger had also set up her camera. Hopkins described chaotic scenes:

> The main entrance hall . . . was jammed; we were jostled from all sides . . . I managed to photograph the arrivals of Churchill and of Stalin and their greetings to the other notables present. Outnumbered as we were by Russian photographers, it seemed to me that every time I raised my camera to take a picture, one of them would pop up in front of me, blocking my view.

The cameramen were not allowed into the conference room itself 'and tried to shoulder one another out of the way as they struggled to get their pictures from the doorway'.

The Soviet delegation led by Stalin was the last to enter the Livadia's Grand Ballroom through the handsome, walnut double doors which attendants then closed behind them. The cavernous ballroom, also known as the 'White Hall', was more than 120 feet long with ceilings studded with elaborate plaster mouldings. Along one side, French doors opened onto a pretty Italianate courtyard while along the other side seven tall arched windows looked north towards the mountains. In the massive Renaissance-style white marble fireplace opposite the entrance doors a birchwood fire crackled as it must have done at the first official function held here – the ball given in November 1911 to mark the sixteenth birthday of the Tsar's eldest daughter Grand Duchess Olga. That world was long gone, the world of princes, grand-dukes and diamond-diademed matrons conversing in soft light while young women in pastel silks and chiffons in the words of the Tsar's secret police chief floated 'like butterflies' in the arms of their dancing partners. Yet Arthur Birse could not help conjuring the Livadia's ghosts – 'the splendour and sparkling life which those walls must have witnessed and the fate which had overtaken its Imperial occupants'.

The three leaders who, Admiral William Leahy wrote, together controlled 'the most powerful military force ever assembled' took their assigned places around the large round table covered by a dun-coloured tablecloth, set up near the fireplace. Stalin solicitously ensured that Roosevelt had the seat nearest the fire. On each leader's right sat his foreign affairs chief – Molotov, Eden and Stettinius. The other delegates, grouped by nationality, filled the gaps around the table or behind their leaders. Harry Hopkins, though too ill to attend this first session, would attend the rest, sitting close enough behind the President to pass him handwritten notes.

Throughout the conference, each leader would have his interpreter to his left who would translate his words, the belief being, Bohlen recalled, 'that the speaker's own interpreter would have a better understanding of what his man said than would the translator for the leader who was listening'. The interpreters' responsibility was tremendous. Stalin once said to Eden, 'We are completely in their hands.' To enable the translators to keep up, each speaker would say no more than a sentence or short paragraph at a time – a slow, painful process. Churchill's flights of oratory would prove a real challenge. Birse recalled struggling with such florid rhetorical questions as 'Will the families be reunited? Will the warrior come home? Will the shattered dwellings be rebuilt? Will the toiler see his home?' but still thought it easier than translating for the 'sphinx-like' Stalin. There would be no single official record of the meetings. Instead, each delegation kept its own private minutes, presenting a broadly similar account but unsurprisingly giving prominence to its own leader's utterances, placing different emphasis and nuance and only occasionally disagreeing. Neither would there be any voting. All decisions had to be unanimous.

As well as Harry Hopkins, another of the American delegation was absent from the first meeting. Roosevelt had informed James Byrnes, his Director of the Office of War Mobilization, that since the main discussion would be about military matters and Stalin might talk more freely with fewer civilians present, he would not be needed until conversation turned to politics. Told to be ready at 6 p.m., at which time he would be admitted, Byrnes waited at the set time outside the closed double doors for forty-five minutes but then, losing patience, stalked off 'to vent his piled up spleen' on 'Pa' Watson and others, Anna Boettiger wrote in her diary. The Russian, American and British military staffs, however, attended throughout, sitting in their gold-braided uniforms in an outer circle behind their respective leaders.

Stalin invited Roosevelt, as the only head of state present, to open the conference as he had at Teheran. Roosevelt gracefully accepted, realizing Stalin was thereby again making him the conference chairman. Throughout the conference, Stalin's tone towards the President would be far more deferential than towards Churchill. Harriman noticed that, 'Whenever Roosevelt spoke, Stalin sort of watched him with a certain awe. He was afraid of Roosevelt's influence in the world.'

A hush descended as everyone looked expectantly towards Roosevelt. A master of drama, he remained silent for some moments, scanning the faces of those around him. Then he said: 'they would cover the map of the world' while in Yalta, but the first item for discussion should be the latest military position and especially Soviet progress on the Eastern Front – an advance so dramatic 'that he doubted whether the jubilation of the Russian people over the Red Army's advance into Germany exceeded the joy of the American and British peoples'.

Churchill then asked if one of Stalin's staff officers could give the latest position. With Stalin's most senior commanders like Zhukov busy at the front, First Deputy Chief of the Red Army General Staff General Alexei Antonov was heading the Soviet military delegation and reported on the Russian advance launched on 12 January. In eighteen days, despite heavy fog which had hampered aircraft and artillery, Soviet troops had advanced 300 miles, destroyed forty-five German divisions and taken 100,000 prisoners. However the Soviets had themselves suffered 300,000 casualties and believed that the German high command were shifting a further thirty to thirty-five divisions to the east. To relieve the pressure upon them, the Russians wished the British and American armies to speed up their advance and to launch air strikes to hinder German troop movements to the east. Although not in the formal record, Hugh Lunghi of the British military mission in Moscow recalled that in addition to attacks on rail junctions in Berlin and Leipzig, Antonov particularly requested they bomb the Dresden railway junction because 'they didn't want reinforcements coming over from the Western front and from Norway, from Italy and so on' to impede their advance. According to Lunghi, the British and American chiefs agreed to such attacks.

Antonov's report, Field Marshal Alan Brooke noted, did not tell the Americans and British 'much we did not know'. In particular they learned nothing about the issue Churchill had tried to probe with Stalin: whether the Russian armies would halt at the Oder to regroup or continue hell for leather for Berlin. In truth, Stalin had not decided. On the eve of the conference Marshal Zhukov had asked Stalin for urgent assistance. His vanguard had crossed the frozen Oder on 30 January and established a bridgehead but his extended flanks were highly vulnerable to counter-attack. Zhukov requested Stalin to bring up reinforcements quickly but the troops he wanted were bogged down in East Prussia by fierce German resistance. Soviet troops had just taken Lansberg, but German forces had swiftly counter-attacked and were now besieging the city. The situation was so desperate that even Soviet nurses were fighting on the front line.

General Marshall next outlined the position in the west. The sixty-four-year-old Marshall was the first American to be given five-star army rank and had overseen the largest military expansion and modernization in American history. He had hoped to command the D-Day landings, but Roosevelt had appointed Eisenhower instead, telling Marshall, 'I didn't feel I could sleep at ease if you were out of Washington.'

Marshall reported that US and British fighter aircraft and light

bombers had 'destroyed a great deal of German transport' as well
as German oil supplies and that the opening of the port of Antwerp
was making it easier to bring up supplies though German troops
were still bombarding the port with 'robot bombs and rockets'
[V2s]. He also summarized the planned American and British
operations over the next few weeks and in particular the Allied
advance across the Rhine. Three or four suitable crossing sites
had been identified and troops would cross as soon as they reached
the river. However, ice floes churning about in the swift current
would make any crossings attempted before 1 March hazardous.
He also warned that the Germans 'were about to resume large-
scale submarine warfare' using their new schnorkel vessels.

Stalin, smoking Russian cigarettes and doodling on a piece of
paper – he liked to draw pictures of wolves, filling in the background with red pencil – quizzed Marshall closely about the
number of British and American tanks and divisions, pointing out
that in recent fighting the Russians had deployed 9,000 tanks.
According to Stettinius, 'He spoke in forceful language, and at
one point rose from his chair and emphasised his points with
dramatic gestures.' Churchill, dressed in colonel's uniform and
peering over the top of his horn-rimmed glasses, reassured him
the British and Americans had an overwhelming advantage over
German forces in both aircraft and armour though not in infantry.
Stalin simply asked what else his allies wanted him to do, to
which Churchill replied all they asked was 'that the Russians
continue to do as they are doing now'. He was particularly pleased
Russian troops were nearing Danzig, where about one third of
the Nazis' dangerous new schnorkel submarines were assembled.
He also proposed that next day the three leaders should discuss
'the future of Germany, if she had any'.

This first plenary session – a model of politeness and mutual
back-slapping – concluded shortly before 8 p.m. with agreement
that the Soviet, American and British military staffs at Yalta would
convene next day to discuss how best to coordinate action on the
Western and Eastern Fronts, while the Foreign Ministers would
also meet. This would be the pattern of the conference. Roosevelt,
Churchill and Stalin, who would meet daily, usually at 4 p.m. and

debate until early evening, would remit issues to their military chiefs and to their Foreign Ministers, who would discuss them next morning before reporting back to the afternoon plenary sessions.

This approach provided a useful way of defusing tensions. When the leaders' discussions turned difficult or acrimonious, they could easily shunt problems off to their military and political advisers who would spend long hours searching for common ground. The Foreign Ministers in particular – helped by Averell Harriman and Sir Archibald Clark Kerr, the US and British ambassadors to Moscow, and by Andrei Gromyko and Fedor Gusev, the Soviet ambassadors to Washington and London – would be the Yalta Conference's engine room. Each afternoon, their report would be the first item on the agenda for the three leaders.

As the delegates left the ballroom, the anxiety of the two NKVD guards assigned to Stalin amused Stettinius when they 'somehow lost him when he hurried to the washroom. There was a great scurrying and immense furore in the corridors until the Marshal reappeared.'

Stalin's appearance and demeanour had surprised those of the US and UK delegations who, like Kuter, had not met him before: 'It was known that he was not a man of large physical size, but it was surprising to find him so very small a man.' However,

he was so well proportioned that normal photographs of him and his shaggy head give the impression of someone physically very much bigger . . . It was also somewhat of a surprise to hear him speak in a very moderate volume, in a voice which, while not high, had no forceful tones and definitely did not indicate the source of his power and control. On the other hand he spoke with simple, unquestioned finality.

That night Roosevelt hosted the first of the three formal dinners the leaders would hold during the conference. James Byrnes, still angry about being excluded from the plenary session, at first refused to attend. Alerted by Dr Bruenn that Byrnes was 'having a tantrum', Anna Boettiger abandoned the task of checking the spelling of the names on the place cards on the dinner table and hurried to his room. As she wrote in her diary, 'A tantrum was putting it mildly! Fire was shooting from his eyes' as Byrnes raged that 'At home he could and did consult with the military, but here he was not considered important enough.' Averell Harriman arrived as Byrnes was 'storming that he had never been so insulted in his life and that he was going to order a plane to take him home'.

By now thoroughly exasperated, Anna felt like saying, 'Okay. Who cares anyhow if you do or don't go the dinner!' However, Harriman attempted to reason with Byrnes and when that didn't work told him sternly, 'If you go home, you'll be a busted man. The American people will look on you as a man who has behaved badly.' Anna finally suggested that having thirteen around the dinner table 'would give superstitious FDR ten fits!' Calmer, if unchastened, Byrnes duly appeared at the dinner. Harriman considered his behaviour 'an extreme case of conference fever . . . everyone wanting to go to every meeting because it made them feel important'.

Robert Hopkins photographed the guests around the dinner table. At the time a seat at the far end was empty because Churchill's interpreter Arthur Birse had not yet sat down. Hopkins learned later that the French magazine *Paris-Match* gave the photograph a full-page spread, captioned, 'The empty chair was General de Gaulle's' – 'reflecting French bitterness at his exclusion from the Yalta deliberations'.

Roosevelt's Filipino mess team had prepared a Russo-American fusion of caviar, sturgeon, chicken salad, meat pie and Southern-style fried chicken which the diners washed down with Russian champagne and vodka, accompanied by dozens of toasts in which everyone joined except for a secret service man among the Russian guests who was only drinking water and lemonade, saying nothing but 'listening to everyone'. Stettinius noticed Stalin watering down his vodka when he thought no one was looking and, unlike at the conference session, smoking the American cigarettes 'that he seemed to prefer'. Stalin had learned a few English expressions such as, 'What the hell goes on around here?' and 'You said it!' from the American films he enjoyed and now tried them out on his surprised visitors.

Towards the end of the dinner, in a spirit of bonhomie Roosevelt told Stalin, as he had at Teheran, that he and Churchill called him 'Uncle Joe' as a term of endearment. This time, however, Stalin appeared offended, causing Roosevelt to call hastily for more champagne and Byrnes to say mollifyingly to Stalin, 'After all, you do not mind talking about Uncle Sam, so why should Uncle Joe be so bad?' Whether Stalin was really offended – or as Molotov maintained 'just pulling your leg' – the mood had changed. When conversation turned to how best to preserve peace when it came, Stalin insisted that only those who had borne the brunt of the fighting should determine the peace. Giving an equal voice to a tiny country like Albania, for example, would be absurd. Roosevelt argued that the problem of dealing with the smaller powers was complex. 'We have, for instance, lots of Poles in America who are vitally interested in the future of Poland.' 'But of your seven million Poles, only seven thousand vote,' Stalin shot back.

Despite his agreement on spheres of influence with Stalin in Moscow, and invoking Shakespeare's *Titus Andronicus*, Churchill insisted the great powers had a moral responsibility to respect the rights of smaller nations: 'The eagle should permit the small birds to sing and care not wherefor they sang.' Perhaps feeling he had gone too far, Churchill proposed a toast to 'the proletarian masses of the world'. Talk around the table turned to people's rights to get rid of leaders they no longer supported. The Prime Minister pointed out – as he would do several times during the conference – that though he was constantly being 'beaten up' for being a reactionary, he alone of the three leaders present could be thrown out of office at any time. When Stalin suggested that Churchill seemed to be afraid of elections, he replied that, 'Far from fearing them, he was proud of the right enjoyed by the British people to change governments whenever they saw fit.'

Talking about the rights of the American people to express their opinions, Charles Bohlen clashed with Andrei Vyshinsky, Deputy People's Commissar for Foreign Affairs, who snapped that 'the American people should learn to obey their leaders and not question what they were told to do', to which Bohlen replied that he 'would like to see him go to the United States and tell that to the American people'. Vyshinsky had been the Chief Prosecutor during Stalin's merciless purges in the late 1930s – something Bohlen found hard to forget: 'Whenever I looked into those pale eyes, I saw the horrible spectacle of the prosecutor browbeating the defendants.' Vyshinsky was sensitive on the subject, on another occasion telling Arthur Birse, 'I know what you people abroad have been saying – that I was responsible for the death and exile of many innocent people. But do you realize that I saved the lives of thousands who might have been engulfed in the plot to undermine the safety of our State?' Hugh Lunghi overheard Stalin say of Vyshinsky at Yalta, 'I don't trust Vyshinsky but with him all things are possible. He'll jump whichever way we tell him.' Lunghi observed that, perhaps unsurprisingly, Vyshinsky acted 'like a frightened hound' before Stalin.

That night, a dispirited Anthony Eden wrote in his diary: 'Dinner with Americans; a terrible party . . . President vague and loose and ineffective. Winston, understanding that business was flagging, made desperate efforts and too long speeches to get things going again. Stalin's attitude to small countries struck me as grim, not to say sinister.' He did not mention that as the evening was ending he himself had argued with Churchill. Bohlen, who overheard them, described how when Churchill, reverting to his Moscow position, said that 'he rather agreed with Marshal Stalin that small nations' rights should be protected but that they should not have a voice in great matters', Eden replied that he disagreed and 'was prepared to go before the House of Commons at any time and put the matter to a vote'.

*

Meanwhile elsewhere that same day, 4 February 1945, near Brandscheid in south-western Germany, American troops broke through the outer defences of the Siegfried Line, also called the West Wall – a barrier intended to protect Germany from attack from the west. Constructed between 1938 and 1940, it extended nearly 400 miles from Germany's border with the Netherlands to the border with Switzerland and incorporated more than

18,000 bunkers, tank traps and tunnels. The previous August Hitler had ordered its reinforcement and 20,000 slave labourers had been put to work, helped by German civilians.*

Also that day, General Karl Wolff, the head of the SS in Italy, was in Berlin to discuss a secret plan – code-named 'Wool' – first conceived by members of the SS in November 1944. Its purpose was to contact the American and British ambassadors in Switzerland to probe their countries' attitude to concluding a separate peace with Germany on more favourable terms than the total and unconditional surrender the Allies were publicly demanding. Its genesis was the conviction that the bond between the Communist Soviet Union and the capitalist West was unnatural and could not endure and the hope was that, even if the approach failed, it might divide the Allies by fuelling suspicion between them.

Hitler, meanwhile, aware that the Big Three conference was under way, ranted against his adversaries. He lambasted Churchill in particular for not negotiating a peace deal with Germany in 1941 after Britain's 'success in North Africa had re-established her prestige', for denying Germany a free rein in Europe and for kowtowing to Stalin and Roosevelt:

> The crucial new factor is the existence of these two giants, the United States and Russia. Pitt's England [in the Napoleonic Wars] ensured the balance of world power . . . If fate had granted to an ageing and enfeebled Britain a new Pitt instead of this Jew-ridden, half-American drunkard, the new Pitt would at once have recognised that Britain's traditional policy of balance of power would now have to be applied on a different scale, and this time on a world scale. Instead of maintaining, creating and adding fuel to European rivalries, Britain ought to do her utmost to encourage and bring about a unification of Europe.

---

* The original Siegfried Line was a line of forts and tank defences built by the Imperial German Army in northern France during 1916–17.

CHAPTER SEVEN

'To Each According to his Deserts'

Monday 5 February, the conference's second day, dawned mild but grey: 'our bright sun had gone'. At 7.30 a.m. a courier from the White House arrived at the Livadia Palace – the first test of the complex arrangements to ensure Roosevelt could continue to deal with the ongoing affairs of his nation while in Yalta. The courier had left Washington on 31 January, flying in stages to Cairo and then on to Saki. The trip had taken five days but over the conference the average time would reduce to four days.

Anxious about her father's health, Anna Boettiger was watching over him 'very carefully', trying to keep 'unnecessary' people from bothering him. As Frances Perkins rightly observed, 'She had gone expressly as a kind of authoritative secretary who could reduce the number and length of exhausting conversations.' Some found her a little overpowering. Robert Meiklejohn, Harriman's aide, thought her 'an enormous woman much on the lines of her peripatetic mother' and endowed with 'the usual Roosevelt brass, tossing her weight around wherever she can'. 'Pa' Watson, however, knew Anna was one of the very few who could 'manage' Roosevelt. 'She can tell him, "You mustn't see people . . . You mustn't talk with them. It tires you out".'

Anna Boettiger was only just realizing the full extent of her father's frailty and how worried both Howard Bruenn and Ross

McIntire were about Roosevelt's 'old ticker trouble'. She wrote to her husband:

> I have found out thru' Bruenn (who won't let me tell Ross that I know) that this 'ticker' situation is far more serious than I ever knew. And the biggest difficulty in handling the situation here is that we can, of course, tell no one . . . It's truly worrisome – and there's not a helluva lot anyone can do about it.

She added, 'Better tear off and destroy this paragraph', advice her husband didn't follow. She was also distressed that her mother had not yet written to her father. 'That is a very sad situation, Honey, because the only times he has mentioned her to me on this trip have been times when he has griped about her attitudes towards things he's done and people he likes.'

By contrast, Clementine Churchill had asked Sarah to 'send me a little line everyday telling me about Papa' and throughout the conference Churchill found time to dash off affectionate notes to 'Mrs Kent' – Clementine's code name. That day, at the Vorontsov Palace Churchill woke late as he would do throughout the conference. His daughter wrote to her mother that his habit 'presents a certain problem . . . there isn't any time for breakfast and lunch . . . he has just orange juice when he is called and "brunch" at 11.30 – then nothing till 9 o'clock!' The juice and brunch were served to Churchill sitting up in the large double bed in which he worked and slept. Ever impatient for the latest news, that morning he waited for the British diplomatic pouch delivered daily during the conference by Mosquito aircraft to Saki and then brought to Yalta by road. Later in the conference, it would arrive around midnight but on 5 February it was delayed until midmorning. In a whimsical gesture to the conference's code name 'Argonaut', incoming messages to Churchill were entitled 'Fleece' and outbound messages 'Jason'. In case the Soviets intercepted the dispatches, no top secret ULTRA decrypts of Nazi secret messages were included while Churchill was in Yalta.

Among that morning's documents was a cable reporting that, despite Churchill's strenuous efforts to head off a Greek

Communist uprising, the Greek Communists were making fresh demands. In October 1944 British troops had landed in Greece as German forces hurriedly abandoned the country, harassed as they went by resistance fighters, many of whom had strong links with the Communist Party. Convinced that Britain must dominate the eastern Mediterranean to protect its interests in the Middle East, the Suez Canal and India, that same month while in Moscow Churchill had argued strongly to Stalin: 'Britain must be the leading Mediterranean power and he hoped Marshal Stalin would let him have the first say about Greece.' Stalin had agreed:

> Great Britain lost a great deal as a result of German seizure of the Mediterranean sea lanes . . . if the security of that route is not ensured, Great Britain will suffer a great loss. Greece is an important point for establishing [that] security . . . England should have the right to a deciding voice in Greece.

He consented in Churchill's 'naughty document' to 90 per cent British influence in that country.

However, in the first weeks following the British arrival, tensions between them and the Greek National Liberation Front (EAM) and its military wing, the Greek People's Liberation Army (ELAS), had grown. This was due to British support, at Churchill's behest, for the return of the Greek King and for the inclusion of more right-wing elements, including some suspected collaborators, in the hastily formed coalition government led by Georgios Papandreou, of which EAM was an uneasy member. Each side feared a coup by the other. The American ambassador complained about the British treatment of 'this fanatically freedom-loving country . . . as if it were composed of natives under the British Raj'. He too feared trouble.

The crisis came in early December when the EAM members walked out of the government. Greek police fired on demonstrators who had taken to the streets in protest. EAM supporters at once retaliated, setting up blockades and attacking government offices and police stations. The fighting intensified and Churchill sent in reinforcements, ordering British troops not to 'hesitate to act as if you were in a conquered city where a local rebellion is in progress . . . We have to hold and dominate Athens. It would be a great thing for you to succeed in this without bloodshed, if possible, but also with bloodshed if necessary.' British forces attacked using artillery and aircraft, causing considerable casualties.

There were protests in the US when Churchill's top secret order was leaked. The media spoke of the British 'giving an ugly twist to the word liberation' and that the issue 'boil[ed] down to whether the Allies are going to champion kings or republicans in Europe under the Atlantic Charter'. In the UK, Churchill overcame a no-confidence motion in the House of Commons. He decided to visit Athens. Gunfire broke out as, on Christmas Day 1944, he entered the British Embassy and a woman was shot in the street outside. So too were other people elsewhere in the city during his visit.

This was the last time in his life that Churchill came under fire. At a meeting with all sides, Churchill shook hands with everyone and a temporary truce was patched up. However, it soon collapsed and fighting broke out again from which, by the end of January 1945, right-wing elements emerged as victors intent on a bloody revenge on their opponents. Many of the ELAS members and their supporters, however, survived and would resume serious hostilities in 1946. This had been the only occasion during the Second World War when Western troops fought to prevent a Communist takeover in a European country and fired on opponents who had formerly been members of the anti-Nazi resistance. In line with his commitment in Moscow, Stalin had not intervened. However, one of Churchill's worries throughout the Yalta negotiations was that Stalin might yet shift his position, thus aggravating the tense situation in Greece.

Looking after Churchill as he ferreted through his papers, often tossing them to the floor, was a demanding task for his valet Frank Sawyers. 'All morning the P.M. has been losing things,' Moran wrote, describing his querulous calls of 'Sawyers, Sawyers, where are my glasses?' and demands to know where his hot-water bottle was – 'You are sitting on it, sir.' Churchill's mood did not improve when he learned that Stalin had sent 'a Russian colonel drenched in scent' to correct the inaccuracies on the Map Room charts Stalin had spotted the previous day. Marian Holmes and Churchill's other secretaries Jo Sturdee and Elizabeth Layton worked in an adjoining room separated from his bedroom by 'a sliding door . . . which is noisy and difficult to open and shut'. Holmes recalled how, after filling his fountain pen for him that morning, 'I returned, opened the door just a few inches and squeezed myself through. The PM burst out laughing and said that I looked like a lizard.'

Other members of the British delegation continued to adjust to their new surroundings. Conditions in the two former sanatoria where junior staff lodged were austere. 'No one seemed to mind,' Churchill noted blithely and probably incorrectly. Wren officer Maureen Stuart-Clark recalled 'tempers were fairly short'. She was finding things 'rather superficial and unreal', especially the mainly female 'hordes of interpreters from Moscow . . . who spoke excellent English although they had never left the country'. She was also a little embarrassed by the lengths the Russians had gone to for their guests. Russia was 'a hard, ruthless country . . . yet they had laid on the most terrific show' including:

> maids in caps, aprons and high heeled shoes which they had never worn before and consequently presented a ludicrous spectacle wobbling unsteadily around; interpreters in new suits and stockings so they would not be inferior to us; vodka, champagne, smoked salmon etc when the only ration they themselves are certain of getting is black bread . . . one thought they could have afforded to say, 'We've done jolly well on this so you ought to try it and jolly well like it.'

However, their hosts had done nothing about the water, which 'was unsafe to drink and the only liquid there was to swallow was the vodka, champagne etc. . . . we spent the whole time either very definitely muzzy or else parched with thirst.'

Strangest of all were the sanitary arrangements:

> In our place there was a bath and three showers all in a little hut together down the garden. There was a sweet peasant girl

in attendance who scrubbed your back vigorously, irrespective of your sex. In fact there was considerable trouble at first as they all bath and swim in the nude together and couldn't understand our reluctance to bath with Major Generals or Naval officers at the same time.

The sight of 'bigwigs half-stripped waiting for a bath' amused Gladys Adams, a shorthand writer billeted in a cabin in the sanatorium grounds. However, like the other British women, she was delighted that the Soviets had provided hairdressers and manicurists – a facility not on offer at the Livadia where Kathleen Harriman and Anna Boettiger were the only women among the American delegation.

As Churchill had predicted, bedbugs bothered everyone, wherever they were billeted. He had initially trusted in 'an adequate supply of whisky . . . good for typhus and deadly on lice which thrive in those parts', but nevertheless his feet were severely bitten. Sergo Beria and his eavesdropping team, listening in, were amused by his vociferous complaining. When Moran visited the sanatoria to see how their inmates were faring, he was horrified by 'the most elementary bedding arrangements, spread out on the floor, and bugs in all the bedding'.

Moran at once telephoned the American delegation at the Livadia to ask their help. Despite precautions, they too had problems. Harry Hopkins's son Robert had bagged a tiny room of his own under the eaves only to find himself sharing it with 'a horde of Russian bedbugs that emerged from under the torn wallpaper in battalions'. Despite their own difficulties, the Americans came to Moran's aid, sending over 'a couple of their sanitary squads and we began going round all the beds with an instrument which squirted D. D. T.' As for himself, he wrote, 'I haven't unpacked my suitcase, and I have no intention of doing so.'

At 10 a.m. the American and British Chiefs of Staff met to prepare for their meeting later that morning with their Russian counterparts. One key item discussed was Soviet participation in the war against Japan. With US military planners estimating it could take at least eighteen months after Germany's surrender to defeat such fanatical fighters as the Japanese troops, the US Chiefs considered Soviet help essential. Douglas MacArthur had told Roosevelt, 'I will not consider going into any part of the Japanese islands unless the Japanese armies in Manchuria are contained by the Russians.' On 23 January – the day Roosevelt had embarked on the *Quincy* – the chiefs had sent him a top secret memo urging that Russia's entry into the war as soon as possible was 'necessary to provide maximum assistance to our Pacific operations'. Paramount in their minds was the need to save young American lives. The chiefs estimated that US casualties could be reduced by 200,000 if the Soviet Union entered the war before they launched amphibious assaults on the Japanese home islands.

At Teheran, Stalin had announced, in the words of Andrei Gromyko, 'After Hitler's Germany has been destroyed, the Soviet Union will give the necessary help to the Allies in the war against Japan.' However, no agreement had yet been reached either on what this help would mean in practice or on the price Stalin would extract for giving it.

The US Chiefs proposed making a two-pronged approach to the Russians at Yalta. They themselves would write to the Russian Chiefs of Staff seeking a bilateral meeting to discuss planning and logistical issues associated with Soviet entry into the Pacific war, while the President should write to Stalin seeking answers to such specific military questions as whether the Russians would allow the US to establish air force bases in eastern Siberia. The British supported these suggestions, and the proposed memoranda to the Russians were dispatched that day.

At midday, the Soviet, American and British military chiefs gathered at the Yusupov Palace for their first tripartite meeting – an event that Stalin, without necessarily meaning a word of it, hailed as a sign of the mutual confidence between the Allies. The British arrived first and, 'after many examinations by sentries', were finally admitted. The Americans 'had lost themselves' and were half an hour late. The British took advantage of their absence, with Field Marshal Brooke able to get 'into a hug' with his opposite number Antonov, and Portal and Cunningham proceeding 'to break the ice and make friends' with their Russian counterparts. Once Marshall and Admirals Leahy and King and their teams arrived they too took stock of the Russians. Admiral Kuznetsov, the Soviet People's Commissar for the Navy, particularly impressed Leahy, who wrote of this 'great big man, dressed in a handsomely tailored Admiral's uniform', who spoke fluent French and seemed 'thoroughly informed'. Nevertheless Leahy doubted whether he was a very good naval commander, observing patronizingly, 'The Russians have never been good sailors.'

Invited by Antonov to take the chair, Brooke at once raised the question of coordinating the Soviet and Anglo-American offensives over the months ahead. He asked the Soviet army to maintain maximum pressure on German forces during March and April while American and British troops crossed the Rhine. Antonov said the Soviets would continue their offensive 'as long as the weather permitted' and in turn probed British and American commitment to hindering the German army from transferring troops to the Eastern Front, particularly from Italy. Brooke responded that some Allied divisions were being transferred from Italy to the Western Front since, with the vital death blows being dealt by the Soviet armies in the east, the correct place for the western death blow was in north-western Europe, but promised that the British and American forces remaining there would do all they could to obstruct German troop transfers from Italy.

Marshall sought to reassure an obviously uneasy Antonov about the strength of Anglo-American air superiority and quoted from a report he had just received about air operations. On 2 February the RAF had flown 2,400 sorties, hitting road and rail targets in Koblenz and east of Alsace; the same night 1,000 USAAF aircraft had attacked Wiesbaden and Karlsruhe. On 3 February Allied bombers had raided the railway yards at Marienberg and 1,000 bombers had attacked Berlin. A similar raid was planned on Leipzig, just behind the German lines in the east and an important communications and supply centre for the Eastern Front. Portal reminded Antonov that Britain and America had 14,000 aircraft on the Western and Italian Fronts and reported plans for strategic bombing raids on the enemy's oil supply – 'the best contribution which the air forces could make, both to the offensive on land and in the air' – and on German factories manufacturing jet-propelled fighter aircraft. They would also continue to target the enemy's rail communications and once the Anglo-American land offensive began would deploy 'everything in the air that could contribute to its success'. According to Hugh Lunghi who was interpreting, Antonov again made a point of saying, 'we want the Dresden railway junction bombed', and the British and Americans agreed.

Despite Brooke's efforts, discussions on improving communications between Russian, American and British commanders foundered. With the gap between the Western and Eastern Fronts narrowing daily, the British and Americans both wanted direct lines of communication between commanders on the ground. Antonov, however, insisted that 'no tactical coordination was required between Allied and Russian ground forces'; the priority was coordinating strategy between the respective air forces with all communications channelled through the Soviet General Staff in Moscow. When the Americans and British pressed for some means of day-to-day liaison to maximize opportunities 'to hit the Germans from the air', Antonov and his colleagues again resisted. As they well knew, Stalin made all the top military decisions in Moscow. He did not want his commanders in the field dealing directly with their American and British counterparts.

After three hours the meeting, which had not really satisfied anyone, broke up. That afternoon Brooke, a keen ornithologist, relaxed by going bird-watching, spotting 'cormorants, many gulls and other diving ducks'. But later as he contemplated the tasks and challenges that still lay ahead in the war he wrote in his diary, 'My God! how tired I am of it all!'

While the military chiefs debated at the Yusupov Palace, Molotov hosted a convivial lunch there for Foreign Ministers. With the conference barely under way, they had not yet assumed the task of conference workhorses, striving to tight deadlines to report back

on issues referred to them at the plenary sessions, and the mood
was relaxed. Molotov opened with 'a toast to the leaders of the
three countries'. When Averell Harriman announced 'the thrilling
news' that General MacArthur had that day entered Manila, Molotov
at once proposed a further toast. Sixteen more followed.

When Eden asked what issues the Soviets wished to raise at
that day's plenary session Molotov graciously replied, 'Any question the United Kingdom or the United States desired'. He added
that the Russians wanted to discuss German reparations and
returned to an issue he had previously raised with Harriman in
January – that the Soviet Union wanted the United States to
provide long-term credits for $6 billion at 2 per cent interest,
with repayment to begin in fifteen years and take thirty years to
complete. Bohlen had been amused by the Russian assertion that
'The funds would be used to purchase industrial goods in the
United States' and the underlying suggestion that this was 'less a
request for American help to the Soviet Union to rebuild after
the war than an offer of Soviet aid to the United States to relieve
its unemployment problem'. Stettinius assured Molotov that 'the
United States was willing to discuss the question anytime'.*

The lunch continued until around 3.30 p.m. when the party
climbed into their limousines to drive to the Livadia. Cadogan
grumbled, 'It's an awful bore our various Delegations being so
scattered.'

The day's plenary session began at 4.15 p.m. Photographers
captured Churchill's arrival at the Livadia Palace twenty minutes
earlier in a large fur hat, his coat concealing his army uniform
and double row of medals. A Soviet newsreel related, 'first the
huge cigar entered, which was followed by Winston Churchill,
accompanied by his adjutant and his daughter Sarah.' Stalin was
already there, waving to the photographers lining the hall, Robert
Hopkins among them. Roosevelt was still in his quarters,

* Talks were indeed held, but ultimately came to nothing.

consulting with Harry Hopkins who had dragged himself from his sickbed. Then the doors to Roosevelt's rooms opened and a valet wheeled the President out into the hall. The three leaders shook hands and made their way into the ballroom.

A weary-looking Roosevelt, suffering from a hacking cough, opened the meeting and proposed they discuss Allied zones of occupation in a conquered Germany. Almost immediately, Stalin butted in, throwing out a string of questions. How exactly should a conquered Germany be dismembered? How should they handle its surrender, especially if Hitler's power base collapsed? Suppose a group declared it had thrown out Hitler? Should they be prepared to deal with them? Should the Big Three set up a single unified German government or establish separate governments in their own areas? What should be the precise terms of Germany's unconditional surrender? What type of reparations should Germany pay and how much? 'Hasn't the time come for decision?' Stalin asked.

At Teheran, the three leaders had agreed that for occupation purposes Germany should be divided into three zones, one for each country, and subsequently decided the US would take the south-west, Britain the north-west and the Soviet Union the east. On Germany's longer-term future, they had broadly concluded that, to protect Europe's security, Germany should be dismembered into a number of individual states but had not decided how many. Roosevelt, with rose-tinted memories of the small German principalities he had visited in his youth, had proposed five. Stalin, determined on 'scattering the German tribes' to make Germany 'impotent ever again to plunge the world into war' but not especially concerned about the mathematics, had agreed. Churchill, believing that however they divided Germany up it would eventually 'reunite into one nation' and that 'the main thing is to keep Germany divided, if only for fifty years', had suggested separating Prussia – 'the root of evil in Germany' – from southern Germany 'which will not start a new war'. The following year in Moscow – at the time he had presented Stalin with his scribbled 'naughty document' proposing British and Russian spheres of influence in the Balkans – he had also suggested to Stalin placing the Ruhr and Westphalia under international control. However, no decision had yet been taken.

As the three leaders again debated the issue, Bohlen wondered whether Roosevelt's ill health was affecting his thinking:

> The President rambled on about the Germany he had known in 1886, when small, semi-autonomous states such as Darmstadt and Rothenburg thrived. The centralisation of Germany in the Berlin government was one of the causes . . . of the ills from which the world was suffering. Roosevelt's rambling and inconclusive statement didn't even hang together.

Bohlen also thought Roosevelt had anyway lost interest and 'was just giving lip service' to the idea of dismemberment. The Soviet delegation listened 'with polite indifference' and the British with 'slight signs of boredom', with Churchill fiddling with his cigar and Eden gazing off into the distance.

However, when Stalin insisted that they must take a decision Churchill became animated, arguing that the issues were far too complex historically, geographically and ethnographically to be resolved at once and must receive further detailed study. When Stalin proposed telling the German government that the unconditional surrender the Allies were demanding would entail Germany's dismemberment, he grew yet more heated. Though Churchill and his Cabinet had approved the policy of unconditional surrender, they had worried it might harden German resistance. Stalin's proposal revived those fears. Informing the German public that their country was to be carved up would 'make the Germans fight all the harder', Churchill argued. The Allies could order dismemberment any time they liked after the surrender and all the Germans need be told at this stage was, 'Await our decision as to your future'. Stalin, however, took the opposite view. Telling the German people in advance would force them to accept 'what was in store for them' and by giving them some certainty would make it more difficult for Goebbels to whip up their fear of the unknown to encourage them to keep fighting.

Sensing impasse, Hopkins scribbled Roosevelt a note:

Mr. President,
I would suggest that you say this is a very important and
urgent matter and that the three foreign ministers present
a proposal tomorrow as to the procedure by which a
determination as to dismemberment can be arrived at [at]
an early date.
      Harry

Roosevelt duly proposed this and Stalin and Churchill agreed.
However, when Stalin continued to insist a reference to dismemberment be included in the unconditional surrender terms,
Roosevelt sided with him and proposed that Foreign Ministers
also be asked to recommend how this could be achieved – something Churchill had to accept.

However, the real shock to Churchill that day was a casual
remark by Roosevelt, during discussion of whether France should
be allowed a zone of occupation in Germany, that 'he did not
believe that American troops would stay in Europe much more
than two years' because neither Congress nor American public
opinion would allow it. This was as much a surprise to Roosevelt's
advisers, with whom he had not discussed it. To Churchill it was
a 'momentous statement'. If the Americans indeed pulled out of
Europe, Britain would be left 'to occupy single-handed the entire
western portion of Germany . . . a task far beyond our strength'.

Fearing not only a renascent Germany but also Soviet intentions
in Europe, Churchill already realized that a war-weary, impoverished Britain needed help. In the absence of the US that could
only come from France. Supported by Eden, he began immediately
to argue not only for a French zone of occupation in Germany,
to be carved out of the British and American zones, but for France
to be a full member of the Allied Control Commission that would
administer a defeated Germany. Stalin, whose hand had just been
greatly strengthened by Roosevelt's remarks, demanded to know
why France – which, he said contemptuously, had 'opened the
gates to the enemy' – deserved a zone of occupation. Even if
France was given one – and he would not object so long as it
did not diminish the Soviet zone – it should not entitle it to a

role in the proposed control machinery. He ignored a comment by Churchill that if France had made mistakes, so had other countries, a dig at the Soviet Union's 1939 pact with Nazi Germany.

As Roosevelt had told Stalin at their private meeting, he did not object to allowing France its own zone. On the matter of permitting it a part in the control arrangements, he once more sided with Stalin, saying to do so would only encourage other countries to demand a role. Stalin finally ended the discussion, asserting that they had agreed that France should have a zone but not a role in the Control Commission. Foreign Ministers should consider the relationship of the French zone to the Control Commission. Stalin and Roosevelt had again frustrated Churchill. If Roosevelt wished to woo Stalin, Stettinius thought the reverse was equally true: 'All through this discussion, as well as during most of the Conference, Stalin showed an obvious desire to reach an agreement with Roosevelt', which was 'not so true' of Stalin's attitude towards Churchill.

The issue of German reparations sparked further friction. Andrei Gromyko noticed that though Churchill tried to conceal his feelings at such moments 'his cigars gave him away. He smoked far more of them when he was tense or excited. The number of his cigar stubs was in direct proportion to the stresses of the meeting.' Opening the discussion, Roosevelt told Stalin that neither the United States nor Britain wanted German 'reparations in manpower'. Stalin blandly avoided the issue, stating that he was not yet ready to talk about 'the use of German manpower'. Leahy assumed this was because the Russians were already 'using many thousands of prisoners in what was reported to be virtual slave camps [and so] had little to gain by discussing the matter'.

Stalin did, however, want to discuss reparations in kind and asked the scholarly looking, trim-bearded Ivan Maisky, a former Soviet ambassador to London, where he had been friendly with H. G. Wells and George Bernard Shaw, to present the Soviet demands. Maisky had been preparing for this moment: 'a big day!' he wrote in his diary. He spoke concisely and bluntly. Russia's estimates of its losses were 'quite astronomical' – they wanted at least $10 billion back, to be obtained in two ways. 'First, withdrawals from the national wealth of Germany. That means factories, land, machinery, machine tools, rolling stock of railways, investments in foreign enterprises, and so on.' Second, yearly payments in kind and drawn from current production would last ten years after the end of hostilities. Maisky also proposed confiscating and physically removing 80 per cent of Germany's iron and steel, engineering, metal and chemical industries and 100 per cent of its 'aviation plants, facilities for the production of synthetic oil and all other military enterprises'. He argued that retention of 20 per cent of its heavy industry would be quite enough to sustain Germany's economic life and to furnish the annual payments.

To Churchill such demands seemed excessive and, like the Morgenthau Plan, unnecessarily destructive. A fellow politician said of him with a degree of justice, 'He never sought to trample on a fallen foe, whether a political opponent or a defeated nation.' Relying now on practical rather than emotional arguments, he reminded Stalin where bleeding Germany after the First World War had led. Who, he asked, would pay for food for a phantom, starving Germany? Reparations should depend on what a defeated Germany could afford. 'If you wanted a horse to pull your wagon you had to give him some hay.' 'That's right, but care should be taken that the horse did not turn around and kick you,' Stalin replied, to which Churchill retorted, 'If you have a motor car, you must give it a certain amount of petrol to make it go.' Reluctant to allow the Prime Minister the last word, Stalin snapped that was a false analogy: 'The Germans were men and not machines.'

Roosevelt recalled that after the First World War the United States had loaned an impoverished Germany, struggling to pay reparations, billions of dollars and suffered great losses when Germany defaulted. He could not allow the same situation to arise again. He also said, 'America would not want any manpower, any factories, or any machinery,' but might seize Germany's modest assets in the United States, 'estimated not to exceed 200 million dollars'. However, in a nod to Stalin, he said 'he would willingly support any claims for Soviet reparations since he felt that the German standard of living should not be higher than that of the Soviet Union'. The maximum should be extracted from Germany so long as its people did not actually starve.

Alarmed by the direction of the discussion, Churchill suggested setting up a commission to evaluate the claims for reparations not only of the three major powers but of other countries which had suffered Nazi aggression. Stalin insisted that the three powers who had made the most sacrifices must have 'first claim on reparations'. France, for example, had suffered less than Belgium, Yugoslavia or Poland. He was unmoved by Churchill's reply that 'the Allies had done a great deal of the damage in France'. Yet again Foreign Ministers were tasked to resolve the detail – in this case to consider how a reparations commission, to sit in Moscow, would function and to report back. The Soviet records suggest that Stalin again had the last word. When Churchill, slyly quoting Marx, suggested the underlying principle of reparations should be 'each according to his needs', Stalin said 'he preferred another principle: to each according to his deserts'.

After what had been a gruelling four hours and after agreeing that the United Nations and Poland should top the next day's agenda, the meeting adjourned. Roosevelt dined early with his closest advisers and his daughter. Though he had presided formally over the discussions – something Kathleen Harriman thought he was 'getting a big kick out of' as the youngest of the three leaders – Stalin had been the one in the driving seat. Andrei Gromyko related how the chain-smoking Stalin had as usual 'missed nothing', working with 'no papers, no notes'. Unlike Roosevelt, who several times had to be corrected or reminded, his memory remained formidable.

American and British participants also admired Stalin's abilities. In his memoirs Eden wrote that at Yalta,

Marshal Stalin as a negotiator was the toughest proposition of all . . . if I had to pick a team for going into a conference room, Stalin would be my first choice. Of course the man was ruthless and of course he knew his purpose. He never wasted a word. He never stormed, he was seldom even irritated. Hooded, calm, never raising his voice, he avoided the repeated negatives of Molotov . . . By more subtle methods he got what he wanted without having seemed so obdurate.

By contrast, Churchill 'liked to talk, he did not like to listen, and he found it difficult to wait for, and seldom let pass, his turn to speak. The spoils in the diplomatic game do not necessarily go to the man most eager to debate. Stalin sometimes led him on'. Cadogan too had already concluded that 'Uncle Joe [is] much the most impressive of the three men. He is very quiet and restrained.' He admired how Stalin could sit for long periods,

> without saying a word [when] there was no call for him to do so. The President flapped about and the P.M. boomed, but Joe just sat taking it all in and being rather amused. When he did chip in, he never used a superfluous word, and spoke very much to the point. He's obviously got a very good sense of humour – and a rather quick temper.

Pondering Roosevelt's comment that American public opinion would demand the quick return home of US troops from Europe, Stalin reflected later to Lavrentii Beria that 'the weakness of the democracies lay in the fact that the people did not delegate permanent rights such as the Soviet government possessed'. Meanwhile, his stock with the American and British publics, whose political freedoms he disparaged, had never been higher. The cover image of the 5 February issue of *Time* magazine was of an avuncular but purposeful-looking Stalin. Inside, an article headed 'Russia: Historic Force' declared that 'Barring the possible existence on earth of undetected saints and major prophets, about the most important person in the world last week was Joseph Vissarionovitch Djugashvili' whose 'gigantic armies' were ripping the guts out of German forces in Poland and the Reich.

However, Stalin was not quite so confident himself that his armies would continue to storm triumphantly onward. Concerned about his troops' vulnerability to counter-attack particularly on their exposed flanks and their over-extended supply lines, that night he telephoned Marshal Zhukov to order him to halt his advance on Berlin. Instead he was to secure his position on the Oder and then to turn his forces north.

Worried about how the conference was progressing, Churchill that evening unburdened himself to his doctor. It perplexed him that Stalin saw France simply as a country that had capitulated and had no understanding of or reverence for its contribution to Western civilization. 'Do you suppose Stalin reads books? He talks of France as a country without a past. Does he not know her history?' he demanded. Moran, noting Churchill's words in his diary, added, 'He loves France like a woman. When Stalin said he did not know what France had done for civilization he felt bewildered. In Winston's eyes France is civilization.' Moran also wrote that day that, 'when the President's opinions flutter in the wind', Churchill looked to Harry Hopkins for help, even though, according to Moran, Hopkins appeared 'only half in this world', his skin just 'a yellow-white membrane stretched tight over his bones'. And Hopkins was indeed trying to help. Though he was too unwell to dine with Roosevelt, earlier that evening he tried to persuade Roosevelt not only that 'it was impossible to give France a zone in Germany without a seat on the Control Council' but that 'it was virtually a political impossibility to endeavor to administer Germany without the participation of France, her hereditary enemy and neighbor and our oldest friend'.

That night, the melancholia that had overcome Churchill in Malta again afflicted him. Before going to bed he told his daughter in similar words to those he had written to his wife from Malta, 'I do not suppose that at any moment in history has the agony of the world been so great or wide-spread. To-night the sun goes down on more suffering than ever before in the World.'

Again, his words reflected some truth. Though American troops had entered Manila that day, the battle for the city would last a month at great cost to MacArthur's men – 1,000 men killed and 5,000 injured – and to the civilian population who had already suffered so much. As advancing US forces had closed in on the city, Japanese troops had rounded up more than twenty Filipino women and over the past two days had been raping them repeatedly. When a US artillery shell landed on the building where they were being held some managed to escape. One, Esther Moras, would later testify at the Tokyo war crimes trials.

Also on this day, Vladimir Gelfand, a young Soviet lieutenant from central Ukraine, described in his diary how he and his comrades had captured a group of German women fighters near the Oder. The 'German female cats declared they were avenging their dead husbands. They must be destroyed without mercy. Our soldiers suggest stabbing them through their genitals but I would just execute them.' He did not record the method he used. Meanwhile in the 'execution alley' of Ravensbrück concentration camp, fifty miles north of Berlin, an SS soldier killed twenty-three-year-old British Special Operations Executive agent Violette Szabo by shooting her in the back of the head. Nazi troops had captured her in June 1944 on her second mission in occupied France after a fierce gun battle. She survived four days of interrogation and torture by the SS before eventually being sent to Ravensbrück. Killed with her on 5 February 1945 were her fellow SOE operatives Lilian Rolfe and Denise Bloch – both so weak they were carried to their deaths by stretcher.

The American, British and German press continued to ponder where the Big Three conference was being held and what was being discussed. On 5 February, New York State's *Middletown Times Herald* reported a rumour 'in Balkan diplomatic circles' that it was being held in Stalingrad. It also reported 'rants' on German radio that although at the conference 'The Big Three might call upon Germany to surrender' the German soldier would fight on 'without fear'. The *Syracuse Herald Journal* grumbled:

> Some official announcement on the place and meeting of the Big Three may be forthcoming later this week, but it looks today as if the Allied public is going to be grossly short-changed again on the real news of the proceedings . . . The fact is that nobody knows much of anything about the event which can be

said to be making history not only for our time, but for a long time to come.

An article by *The Times*'s diplomatic correspondent stated that 'Ribbentrop's official spokesmen in Berlin are busy suggesting the place of the conference . . . Clearly the Germans are "fishing".' The Nazis had apparently not gone to the same lengths as before Teheran, when Heinrich Himmler consulted German mystics and magicians about where and when the Big Three would meet. *The Times* itself speculated presciently on the issues: 'What, for example, is to be the part of France?'; what were the Big Three's proposals for preventing Germany from ever again being able 'to ravage Europe from end to end?'; what were the plans for 'a new League for international security?' and, above all, would 'the Polish problem' be resolved?

CHAPTER EIGHT

'The Monstrous Bastard of the Peace of Versailles'

On Tuesday 6 February, Churchill wrote to his wife, 'much heavy business. Probably five or six days more.' However, Sarah Oliver assured her mother, 'Papa is well and in good spirits and steady strength.' Like many of the British delegation used to strict rationing, the food continued to impress her. She ended her letter, 'You know whatever the material difficulties of this place our paws are well buttered here. Wow.'

Churchill's secretary Jo Sturdee was 'eating far too much . . . I wish I were a camel and could store some of the lovely creamy butter which we seem to get in half-pound pats for a quarter of a slice of toast.' She particularly enjoyed the 'lovely hot sweet rolls . . . cheese, tangerines and apples and chocolates' though the amount of vodka, champagne and wine constantly on offer was a challenge. 'You have to take darned good care that you are definitely steady on your feet and can walk in a straight line.'

The day was warm enough to go outside without a coat. Sarah spent part of the morning standing on the terrace of the Vorontsov watching 'an amazing sight. A great shoal of fishes . . . being attacked by air and sea. From the sea by a school of porpoises, from the air by hundreds of gulls – the poor silly fish just huddled together closer.' Almost as strange was the

spectacle of 'Peter Portal feeding the goldfish in the conserva-
tory with bluebottles he had caught in the library!!' The air
chief was already bored, recalling, 'At all previous conferences
the military element had been the *prima donna* occupying the
centre of the stage. At Yalta we hung about in the wings waiting
for calls that never came . . . my difficulty was to find sufficient
work to occupy my time.'

To pass the hours Portal, a skilled magician often called upon
in both Malta and Yalta 'to do all my party tricks with cards and
string', found his own solution to the daily competition for the
bathroom in the Vorontsov:

> I am very pleased with myself at having found out how to pick
> the lock of the . . . bathroom with a piece of wood. There are
> one or two anti-social people who didn't realize that it is a bad
> show to spend half an hour in the bath between 8 a.m. and
> 9 a.m. when (a) the only hot water for everyone's shaving water
> is over the bath, and (b) the best of the only two w/cs is through
> the bathroom. So now I pick the lock whenever necessary and
> just burst in on them. Yesterday it was Sawyers [Churchill's
> valet]! He hopped out of the bath and put on his pyjamas without
> drying himself, but I got my shaving water all right!

Later that day, Sarah Oliver joined Kathleen Harriman and
Anna Boettiger for a two-and-a-half-hour drive along tortuous
roads to Sebastopol, 'a terrible sight. I didn't see one house that
had not been shattered – yet still the people live there.'
'Bedraggled' Romanian prisoners were queuing for their lunch
– 'something out of a bucket brought on a cart by a tired thin
horse. One has seen similar queues of hopeless stunned humans
on the films – but in reality it is too terrible.' Their guide, a
Russian sailor, seemed oblivious, pointing out a square which was
'lovely in summer'. The three women 'gazed dumbfounded at a
devastated area – a square wilderness of broken trees and shell
holes'. Sarah realized the guide saw Sebastopol 'like someone
who really loves a person, still sees them, in spite of some terrible
physical tragedy, unchanged – unbroken'.

Foreign Ministers met that morning at the Livadia Palace. After further wrangling over what to say in the surrender terms about Germany's dismemberment, they drafted a press release responding to the mounting international speculation about the conference's location and purpose. In concise, spare language the statement said the three leaders were meeting 'in the Black Sea area' to concert plans 'for completing the defeat of the common enemy' and building foundations for a lasting peace. Discussions would include 'the occupation and control of Germany' and 'the earliest possible establishment of a permanent international organization to maintain Peace'. A further communiqué would be issued at the conference's end. British Foreign Office officials received a caution from their Yalta delegation that 'no local colour can be given' when releasing the statement to the press.

Churchill drove over to the Livadia for lunch with Roosevelt in the palace's sunroom. Concerned that Churchill should not exhaust her father, Anna Boettiger asked Harriman, who was attending, 'to shoo the PM out at 2.45' so her father could rest before the plenary and 'not have to work steadily thru from one o'clock lunch to 7.30 or 8 pm when the Conferences usually come to an end'. Cadogan, also present, thought the occasion, 'Quite agreeable and amusing but not awfully useful . . . The President has certainly aged.' To Cadogan the three leaders were barely beginning to grapple with the issues:

It's always the same with these Conferences; they take *days* to get on the rails. The Great Men don't know what they're talking about and have to be educated and made a bit more tidy in their methods. I think we're making some progress, but this place is still rather a madhouse.

Roosevelt himself brought the lunch to a close at 3 p.m. Knowing Churchill's liking for siestas, he suggested he nap in the Livadia before the plenary session. Harry Hopkins, who had risen from his sickbed to attend, hurried off to find him a ground-floor room. The one he chose, the Tsarevitch's former sitting room, was now shared by Vice-Admiral Wilson Brown and General 'Pa'

Watson, who was in bed at the time – Dr Bruenn had diagnosed heart and prostate problems. When Hopkins asked Watson to vacate the room Watson refused, protesting he was sick and the Prime Minister was not. When Hopkins insisted, a shouting match ensued, with Hopkins threatening to have Watson escorted from the room. Finally giving in, the usually equable 'Pa' got up, grabbed his clothes and stalked off. Hopkins then sent word that he had found a bed for Churchill who, oblivious to the mayhem he had caused, enjoyed a fortifying sleep in readiness for the discussions to come.

Each of the leaders knew that day they were about to address the most difficult and highly charged issue of the conference – Poland. It was also the one that would absorb the most time and generate the most words in the official records. Churchill would later recall it as 'the most urgent reason for the Yalta Conference' and 'the first of the great causes which led to the breakdown of the Grand Alliance'. Two questions dominated: who should govern Poland and what should its boundaries be?

Such considerations had long bedevilled a country whose history was the victim of its geography. Its situation in the narrowest, albeit 300-mile wide, area of the north European plain which stretched from the North Sea to the Ural mountains – the natural dividing line between Europe and Asia – meant its borders had rarely been settled for long. The country's strategic location made it a much-contested corridor through which invading armies had passed both east and west throughout its troubled history.

Poland first emerged as a recognizable entity early in the last millennium. In the fifteenth century, dynastic marriages united it with Lithuania. Together they ruled a large part of central Europe, including the Ukraine, Belorussia and other territories that later became part of Russia. Thereafter, a period of decline set in, during which in 1655 invading Swedes seized Poland's Baltic coast. Several wars against attacking Turks sapped more of the country's military and financial strength. Poland became so weak that three partitions of its territory – first in 1772, then in

1793 and again in 1795 – divided it between its three larger neighbours, Russia, Prussia and Austro-Hungary.

Though Poland ceased to exist as a state, Poles never gave up their sense of national identity or their struggle for independence. Many supported Napoleon, both in his campaigns against the three empires that had swallowed their country and in his creation of a Duchy of Warsaw. Some joined his Grand Army as it advanced through their territory in 1812 to attack Russia and seize Moscow, only for the army's starving, freezing survivors to struggle back through their lands during the winter of 1812/13.

Reabsorbed into the surrounding empires, Poles continued to rebel. In their attempts to crush Polish culture and resistance, Russia in 1863 and Prussia in 1872 imposed the use of their languages on the Poles for all public purposes including education. In adolescence Marie Curie, née Skłodowska, born in Russian Poland, risked prison or deportation to Siberia by studying and then teaching at the clandestine 'Floating University' in Warsaw – a radical Polish-language night school for young women. The university's aim was to develop a cadre of committed women capable in turn of educating Poland's poor and thereby equipping them to resist Russian oppression. During this period many Poles emigrated, particularly to North America. In discussions about Poland during the Second World War Roosevelt would often refer to the millions of Polish voters in the United States. Others left for Western Europe, including Marie Curie to France and the seaman and future novelist Joseph Conrad to Britain.

In the First World War, the Polish plains once more became a battleground, initially as Russian troops pushed west into Prussia, then – after Russian forces were defeated at Tannenberg – as German and Austro-Hungarian forces invaded Russia. Germany celebrated von Hindenburg's victory at Tannenberg with great passion as revenge for the defeat there by Polish-Lithuanian forces in 1410 of invading Teutonic Knights.

Poland regained its independence under the Versailles Treaty at the war's end, obtaining the return of a large portion of its western territory from Germany but initially nothing from Russia. Polish forces also seized the province of Galicia and its capital

Lvov from the collapsing Austro-Hungarian Empire.* In 1920, the Bolsheviks invaded the resurgent Poland in an attempt to extend their revolution westwards. Stalin was appointed as the political commissar of the south-west front army. His failure to authorize the timely transfer of units from his front to Mikhail Tukhachevsky, commanding the western army as its troops advanced on Warsaw, was a major contributor to the repulse of Bolshevik forces from the outskirts of Warsaw, known to the Poles as 'the Miracle of the Vistula'. So sensitive was Stalin to his failure to send reinforcements that in 1925 he attempted to conceal his role by removing relevant papers from the Kiev archives, and in 1937 he had Tukhachevsky killed in one of his purges.

The Treaty of Riga in 1921 handed eastern territory to the Poles from the new Soviet republics of Russia, Belorussia and the Ukraine, leaving Poland's eastern frontier corresponding roughly to that of the 1793 partition. This new border was considerably further east than that suggested by the British Foreign Secretary Lord Curzon in a rejected attempt to arbitrate between the two sides. Nevertheless, his 'Curzon Line', which ran just west of Lvov and was based on ethnographic considerations, would feature large in Second World War discussions on Poland's future eastern frontier.

During the interwar years Poland's economy grew but problems between minorities persisted. In 1939 Poland had a population of some 35 million of whom about 16 per cent were Ukrainian, 10 per cent Jewish, 6 per cent Belorussian and 3 per cent German, and the rest ethnic Poles, although in the eastern territories ceded by the Treaty of Riga the latter were in a minority. These diverse ethnicities and disputed post-First World War borders led Molotov, no fonder of Poles and Poland than Stalin, to call Poland 'the monstrous bastard of the Peace of Versailles.'

The Polish government had become increasingly concerned about the threat from the dictatorships on its borders, particularly

---

* Over the past century the city of Lvov – its Russian name – has also been known as Lemberg (Austro-Hungarian), Lwów (Polish) and Lviv (Ukrainian), reflecting the changes in boundaries.

Hitlerite Germany to the west. Following the Nazi occupation of Czechoslovakia in defiance of the 1938 Munich Agreement, on 31 March 1939 Britain guaranteed Polish borders and agreed that 'in the event of any action which clearly threatened Poland's independence . . . His Majesty's Government would feel themselves bound at once to lend the Polish Government all support in their power.' Further exchanges firmed up the British pledge to come to Poland's aid in the case of aggression but an unpublished protocol made clear that this applied only to aggression from Germany. In other cases the two countries would 'consult'. France, a much longer-standing ally of the Poles, had similar agreements with them.

As the Poles feared, Hitler had well-advanced plans to invade Poland to secure the return of West Prussia and other lands ceded by the Versailles Treaty as well as to grab further 'Lebensraum' for his German 'Volk'. However, he realized that any invasion would almost certainly provoke war with France and Britain. Therefore Hitler, although he was contemptuous of the 'Slavic races' and had previously called the Soviet leaders 'an uncivilised Jewish-Bolshevik international guild of criminals' and the Soviet Union itself 'the greatest danger for the culture and civilisation of mankind . . . since the collapse of the states of the ancient world', began to probe what the attitude of the Soviet Union might be to an alliance. The Soviet government responded cautiously and simultaneously put out feelers of its own about a possible alliance to the British and French governments, who responded coolly. Their attitude led Stalin to conclude that the best way to protect Soviet interests – if only temporarily – would be to proceed with the discussions with Germany. Any agreement with the Nazis also held out the possibility of acquiring, in yet another partition of Poland, new territory as a kind of defensive shield.

On the afternoon of 23 August 1939, the German Foreign Minister Joachim von Ribbentrop was driven in Stalin's personal vehicle into the Kremlin where not only Molotov but Stalin waited to greet him. They quickly got down to business. Von Ribbentrop said his Fuhrer proposed 'a non-aggression agreement between our two countries that will last for a hundred years'. Stalin responded, 'If we agree to a hundred years people will laugh at us for not being serious. I propose . . . ten years.' Discussion soon turned to 'spheres of influence' – a euphemism for acquisition of territory. Von Ribbentrop stated, 'the Fuhrer accepts that the eastern part of Poland and Bessarabia as well as Finland, Estonia and Latvia, up to the River Duena, will all fall within the Soviet sphere.' Stalin asked additionally for the whole of Latvia which, after consultation with Hitler, von Ribbentrop agreed. Throughout there was no open discussion of any aggression towards the territories concerned.

After further negotiation and a caviar, champagne and vodka-fuelled reception of the type with which the Allies would later become familiar, the Soviet Union and Nazi Germany signed a non-aggression pact in the early hours of 24 August 1939, and in a secret protocol outlined plans for a partition of Poland between them. As they relaxed afterwards, Stalin discussed the other European powers, telling von Ribbentrop:

> I dislike and distrust the British; they are skilful and stubborn opponents. But the British army is weak. If England is still ruling the world it is due to the stupidity of other countries which let themselves be cheated. It is ridiculous that only a few hundred British are still able to rule the vast Indian population.

Nine days later, on 1 September 1939, Germany invaded Poland. Britain and France declared war but could offer Poland little practical help. On 17 September, 600,000 Soviet troops entered and occupied eastern Poland, their commissars telling the soldiers they were liberating their ethnic cousins from exploitation by Polish capitalists.

With Russian and German spheres of influence in Poland transformed into zones of occupation, von Ribbentrop visited Moscow again in late September 1939 to discuss further 'spheres of influence' with Stalin, revealing Nazi plans to extend German power into the Balkans. That same day, elsewhere in the Kremlin, Molotov informed the Estonian Foreign Minister that 35,000 Russian troops were being sent 'to garrison' his country. Similar 'garrisons' were sent into Lithuania and Latvia, the first stages of the assimilation of the three Baltic states into the Soviet Union which was formally announced on 1 October 1940. As a Soviet republic Lithuania regained Vilnius (Polish Wilno), seized by the Poles after the First World War. At the banquet following their business meeting, Stalin introduced Lavrentii Beria to von Ribbentrop with the words, 'Look, this is our Himmler – he isn't bad [at his work] either.' He would use very similar words when introducing Beria at Yalta.

Britain and France protested furiously and extensively to Moscow at the Soviet invasions but took no other action. With Poland overrun, Polish soldiers, sailors and airmen began to make their way west to continue their fight. Polish pilots made a major contribution to the defeat of the Luftwaffe in the Battle of Britain in 1940, shooting down 203 enemy aircraft with the loss of thirty-nine pilots. One of the Polish squadrons became the most successful RAF Fighter Command unit in the battle, destroying 128 German aircraft in only forty-two days.

However, many members of Poland's forces were unable to escape and were interned by the Russians as well as the Germans. Soon Stalin and Beria began to act against 'undesirables' among them and others in the newly acquired territories in a series of deportations. The first to suffer were Polish veterans of the 1920 war with the Bolsheviks in which Stalin himself had been involved. Known as 'Osadniks', many had been settled with land grants near the Soviet border. Now they and their families were rounded up, together with what few possessions they could pack up in half an hour. Crammed into railway wagons, they were deported to the north of Russia and Siberia where they died in great numbers from cold and starvation. One survivor, Wiesława Saturnus recalled, 'the hunger was horrible . . . Real hunger damages a human being – a person becomes an animal.'

At least 130,000 Poles were deported at this time but an even worse fate was reserved for captured Polish officers and prominent citizens of eastern Poland. In response to an order signed by Stalin, the Soviet secret police, the NKVD, methodically murdered nearly 22,000 of them as 'counter-revolutionaries' in the spring of 1940.

The atrocity has become known by the name of one of the sites where it was carried out – the Katyn forest, some twelve miles from Smolensk in western Russia. A local farmer recalled, 'for approximately four to five weeks there were three to four lorries daily driving to the forest loaded with people . . . I could hear the shooting and screaming of men's voices . . . it was no secret the Poles were being shot by the NKVD.' The victims' families were deported to remote places such as Siberia and Kazakhstan. Wolves attacked them in the vehicles transporting them. Soviet officials warned Siberian and Kazakh villagers to keep away from the new arrivals and not to offer shelter as they shivered in the cold because they were 'Polish enemies of the people'. Many died. Others barely survived. One man who did recalled how he was put to work in and around a gold mine: '[An] orchestra very often played while the prisoners were at work. To the accompaniment of this music the guards would call out prisoners whose work was especially feeble and shoot them there and then.'

News of the deportations, though not yet of the Katyn massacres, reached the west. On 15 April 1940, the *New York Times* reported, 'The exiles got only fifteen minutes to leave their homes . . . even seriously ill persons were forced into the unheated emigration trains.' But only a wringing of hands followed from the American and British authorities.

Like the representatives of several other occupied countries, Poles who reached Britain established a government in exile in London. After the Soviet Union joined the Allies following the German invasion in 1941, the Soviet authorities released most of the Polish soldiers they still held in camps. Many travelled to the west. Under the command of General Władysław Anders they formed an efficient force as part of the British army. Then in April 1943 Radio Berlin announced that mass graves had been found in the Katyn forest containing the bodies of thousands of Polish officers. A number of Russian civilians were taken to witness the removal of the bodies. One, Dimitry Khudykh, described 'the black faces . . . the terrible stench'. Already by this stage of the war this witness was becoming immune to suffering: 'We were young, we were not particularly interested. We had seen death inflicted by the Germans. We had seen that Russian prisoners of war were dying in the camps.'

The Polish government in exile had often asked the Soviet authorities about the numerous officers they knew to be missing, only to be brushed off with the response that they had been released and that their whereabouts were unknown. Now they renewed their enquiries with greater vigour. Despite Stalin having signed the execution order himself, the Soviets placed the blame for Katyn on Germany and in *Pravda* suggested that the Polish government in exile was collaborating with the Nazis to blame the virtuous Soviet authorities – an accusation especially hurtful to the new Polish Prime Minister Stanisław Mikołajczyk whose wife Cecylia was in a Nazi concentration camp. To convince the world of their innocence, in January 1944 the Soviets invited a group of foreign journalists to Katyn. Kathleen Harriman and a junior diplomat from the US embassy in Moscow joined the carefully managed event. The party was given less than twenty-four hours to assess the evidence the Russians were prepared to let them see, on which basis Kathleen and her companion concluded that the German authorities were indeed guilty because of 'the methodical method of killing, each man having been executed by one shot to the base of the skull'. Despite considerable emerging evidence to the contrary neither the US nor UK governments publicly queried their Soviet ally's innocence.

When the London Poles continued to press for answers, Stalin broke off relations with them, maintaining to Churchill, 'The Soviet government are aware that this hostile campaign against the Soviet Union has been undertaken by the Polish government in order to exert pressure . . . for the purpose of wresting from them territorial concessions at the expense of the interests of the Soviet Ukraine, Soviet Belorussia and Soviet Lithuania.' The Polish government in exile in London would not concede it was wrong in suspecting the Soviet Union, leading to a permanent rupture with the Soviet government.*

* Polish suspicions were confirmed forty-seven years later when in 1990 President Mikhail Gorbachev formally accepted Soviet responsibility for the massacres.

In summer 1944 the Soviet authorities established a group of Poles prepared to accede to Soviet wishes for a friendly socialist nation on their borders and, most importantly, to accept the Curzon Line as the new eastern boundary of Poland, which the Polish government in exile would not. As Soviet forces advanced they based the group in Lublin in eastern Poland. Quickly becoming known as 'the Lublin Poles', they became the de facto government of Soviet-occupied areas of the new Poland, a status which the Soviet Union confirmed on 1 January 1945 by publicly recognizing the Lublin group as the legitimate Polish government.

Meanwhile the Polish divisions in the British army continued to fight valiantly. In May 1944, after weeks of continuous fighting, often hand-to-hand, Polish troops had raised their flag over the ruins of the hilltop Italian monastery of Monte Cassino whose German defenders had successfully resisted previous assaults, initially by Free French troops and then, after heavy bombing, by New Zealand, British and Indian soldiers. General Anders, who visited the battlefield, recalled, 'Corpses of German and Polish soldiers, sometimes entangled in a deathly embrace, lay everywhere, and the air was full of the stench of rotting bodies' lying over and in the innumerable craters pitting the sides of the hill.

The Polish government in exile in London had considerable but not complete control over the Polish home army, a large group of underground resistance fighters in their homeland. In summer 1944, 3,000 of its members helped the Red Army liberate Lvov, only to find their officers arrested and their units disarmed and disbanded in the aftermath. Soon afterwards, as the Red Army neared Warsaw, the government in exile told their commander in Warsaw, Tadeusz Bór-Komorowski, to rise to assist the Soviets when he thought the time was right. Encouraged by Soviet radio broadcasts urging partisans to assist, Bór-Komorowski gave the order for 'W Hour', the beginning of the rising, to be five o'clock on the afternoon of 1 August.

Stalin, however, held back his forces and refused to help 'the bunch of criminals', as he called the home army. He incorrectly accused them of collaborating with the Nazis but correctly claimed they had not informed him of their intention to rise – something which both Churchill and Eden had strongly urged them to do. He would not permit Allied aircraft to land at Soviet bases after dropping supplies to the partisans. Nevertheless Polish pilots in the British RAF made some flights from southern Italy to drop supplies, but these were suspended after heavy losses. Hugh Lunghi recorded continuing British attempts to persuade Stalin to help with air drops:

> I must have gone there with [the Chief of Staff] almost daily for the first two weeks and afterwards it became sort of hopeless. We realised they were not going to allow either us or the Americans to land on Soviet territory. And this seemed to us the most terrible betrayal, not only of the Poles but of the [Western] Allies.

Inside Warsaw the Poles fought bravely, though heavily outgunned. In Berlin Himmler rejoiced:

> from the historical point of view the action of the Poles is a blessing. We shall finish them off . . . Warsaw will be liquidated, and this city which is the intellectual capital of a sixteen to seventeen million strong nation that has blocked our path to the east for seven hundred years . . . will have ceased to exist. By the same token . . . the Poles themselves will cease to be a problem . . . for all who will follow us.

German troops treated both civilians and surrendering fighters with the utmost brutality. A German soldier recalled the SS entering a makeshift school. Three hundred children were making their way downstairs with their hands up, crying they were not partisans: 'The SS started to shoot. And then the commander said: "No ammunition – use the butt of the gun!". And the blood spilled down the stairs.' Elsewhere German troops, including members of a collaborating Cossack regiment, murdered, raped and pillaged at will. Despite pleas from the British, the Americans and the Polish government in exile in London, Stalin made only

the most token attempts to aid the rising before on 2 October
the Warsaw insurgents surrendered.

In a final broadcast from Warsaw, the Polish resistance told the
world:

> This is the stark truth. We were treated worse than Hitler's
> satellites, worse than Italy, Romania, Finland. May God, who
> is just, pass punishment on the terrible injustice suffered by the
> Polish Nation . . . Your heroes are the soldiers whose only
> weapons against tanks, planes and guns were their revolvers
> and bottles filled with petrol. Your heroes are the women who
> tended the wounded and carried messages under fire, who
> cooked in bombed and ruined cellars to feed children and
> adults, and who soothed and comforted the dying. Your heroes
> are the children who went on quietly playing among the smoul-
> dering ruins. These are the people of Warsaw . . . those who
> live will fight on, will conquer and again bear witness that
> Poland lives when the Poles live.

Some 220,000 Poles – 90 per cent of them civilians – were killed
during the rising. Afterwards German troops systematically
destroyed the city. The Soviet forces did not take the ruins of
Warsaw until two weeks before the Yalta Conference began.

When during the rising General Anders begged 'a deeply
moved' Churchill to do more, Churchill replied, 'I know that the
Germans and Russians are destroying all of your best elements,
especially intellectual spheres. I deeply sympathise. [But] you
should trust Great Britain who will never abandon you – never.'
The knowledge of the debt Britain owed to the valour of the
150,000 Poles fighting with the British forces at Monte Cassino,
in the Battle of Britain and elsewhere, a degree of guilt they had
not done more to help the Warsaw rising, and the fact that Britain
had gone to war in the first place to defend Polish sovereignty
were all constant factors in the mind not only of Churchill but
of many of his advisers in any discussions between the great
powers about Poland.

These had begun as early as when British Foreign Secretary

Anthony Eden visited Moscow in December 1941, a time when
German troops were less than fifty miles from the Russian capital.
Stalin immediately demanded that Poland's post-war eastern frontier should be that of 1941 after the 'Ribbentrop–Molotov' line
had partitioned Poland. This line had great similarities to the
Curzon Line. One argument Stalin liked to deploy in favour of
the Curzon Line was how could the Soviet Union accept less than
Curzon, the most aristocratic of British foreign secretaries, had
suggested in December 1919 in a supposedly disinterested attempt
at arbitration.

Stalin maintained his insistence on 'the Curzon Line' or 'the
old frontiers, the frontiers of 1941' – both names he preferred
to one evoking the Soviet Union's alliance with Germany – at
subsequent meetings. Though both Churchill and Roosevelt at
first expressed outrage that Stalin planned to keep the territory
he had invaded in 1939, at Teheran both gave in. Roosevelt told
Stalin and Molotov secretly during a private meeting that he
would accept shifting Poland west. At his own late-night meeting
with Stalin, Churchill suggested, using matchsticks to demonstrate
his meaning, 'Poland might move westwards after the war, like
soldiers at drill . . . If Poland trod on some German toes, that
could not be helped.'

When Eden told Prime Minister Mikołajczyk the British
expected him to accept the Curzon Line he protested that after
so much 'suffering and fighting' his people 'expected to emerge
from this war with . . . her eastern provinces intact'. The Nazi
propaganda machine tried to take advantage of the situation,
broadcasting from Rome to Polish soldiers fighting at Monte
Cassino, 'Your land has been delivered into Stalin's hands by
Churchill. You have no place to which to return when the war is
done.'

In October 1944, while in Moscow, Churchill persuaded Stalin
to invite Mikołajczyk to join them and to meet some of the Lublin
Poles while he was there. Averell Harriman was present when
Mikołajczyk met Stalin and Churchill in the Kremlin. Hoping to
act as mediator, Churchill spoke passionately about Poland's
suffering but argued that Poland must be 'friendly' to the Soviet

Union and that Russia's sacrifices to liberate Poland entitled it to territories behind the Curzon Line. When Mikołajczyk would not agree to partitioning his country, Molotov snapped that at Teheran (in November 1943), although he 'did not wish it published at the moment' Roosevelt had 'agreed to the Curzon Line'. Therefore 'the points of view of the Soviet Union, Britain and America were the same'. Since Roosevelt had assured him in the White House in June 1944 – seven months after the Teheran Conference – that he opposed the Curzon Line, Mikołajczyk was stunned. 'I looked at Churchill and Harriman, silently begging them to call this damnable deal a lie. Harriman looked down at the rug. Churchill looked straight back at me, "I confirm this", he said quietly.'

Next day, at a dacha outside Moscow, Churchill continued to pressure Mikołajczyk, telling him, 'We shall tell the world how unreasonable you are. You will start another war in which 25 million lives will be lost! But you don't care.' When the Polish leader continued to resist, Churchill said, 'You ought to be in a lunatic asylum! I don't know whether the British government will continue to recognise you.'

Back in London, Mikołajczyk wrote to Roosevelt of his 'shocked surprise' that he had accepted the Curzon Line at Teheran. However, by now Roosevelt, always more pragmatic on the Polish question than Churchill, had been re-elected and had less reason to worry about Polish sentiment within or outside the US. On 24 November Mikołajczyk resigned as prime minister. If he thought Churchill and Roosevelt were letting Poland down, Churchill blamed the London Poles for their stubbornness, telling Parliament that if they had reached agreement with Stalin, 'Poland might now have taken full place in the ranks of the nations contending against Germany'. Although the British and US governments continued to recognize the London Poles under their new leader Tomasz Arciszewski, relations were strained.

Mikołajczyk still hoped to salvage something. In January 1945, he told Charles Bohlen, in London with Harry Hopkins, that 'almost any compromise would be better than a flat failure to reach an agreement' at Yalta, which would only result in the Soviet

Union's 'domination of Poland'. He asked the Western Allies to propose a provisional government 'consisting of a number of prominent Poles who had stayed in Poland and a number who had fled' until free elections could be held. In Yalta, Hopkins and Bohlen reported Mikołajczyk's wishes to Roosevelt, who agreed to support them, as did Churchill. As Bohlen later wrote, the Western leaders' goal at Yalta was 'absurdly simple – the right of the Poles to govern themselves, even if they chose a Communist government'.

When the plenary session opened at 4 p.m. on 6 February, Poland was not the first item debated. Stettinius reported briefly on the Foreign Ministers' discussions that morning about the surrender terms to be put to Germany. Churchill then renewed his demands for a strong France which – when American troops went home – 'alone could deny the rocket sites on her Channel coast and build up an army large and strong enough to contain the Germans'. Backtracking a little from his remarks of the previous day, Roosevelt said that, though US public opinion at present wanted American troops home quickly, the establishment of a world organization to preserve the peace might alter their attitude to maintaining US forces in Europe.

Roosevelt thus neatly turned the conversation to the United Nations. At his request, Stettinius set out somewhat verbosely the United States' proposed formula for voting in the Security Council which had not been resolved at Dumbarton Oaks. Each of the eleven council members would have one vote. On procedural matters no motion could be carried unless seven members voted for it. On all other issues – admitting or expelling countries from the organization, suppressing or settling disputes, regulating armaments and sending troops to trouble spots – once again, the support of seven members would be needed but these seven had to include all five permanent members, the Soviet Union, the United States, Britain, China and France. Thus each of the five had an effective veto by refusing their support. Roosevelt had sent Churchill and Stalin a note outlining these proposals two months earlier, on 5 December, but as Stettinius continued fulsomely to expound the detail, Stalin looked increasingly puzzled. Harry Hopkins decided he had not bothered to read the President's note and that 'That guy can't be much interested in this peace organization.' It did not help that the interpreters, struggling to convey Stettinius's nuances and complexities, sometimes themselves became confused.

Stalin asked Stettinius whether his proposals contained anything new not in the President's note. 'A minor drafting change,' he replied, raising Stalin's suspicions, according to Stettinius, that 'we were trying to slip something over on them'. Stalin said the proposals seemed 'not altogether clear' and he must study them further. Churchill weighed in, assuring Stalin that the British government had studied them carefully and that they were acceptable. Although 'in the last resort world peace depended on the friendship and cooperation of the three Governments' present at Yalta, he believed the current proposals protected the position of the great powers while also allowing smaller countries a forum in which to state and debate their grievances. The latter was only just since otherwise it might look 'as though the Three Great Powers were trying to rule the world whereas our desires are to save the world and save it from a repetition of the horrors of this war'. To illustrate his point Churchill said that if China were to demand the return of Hong Kong, China would have the perfect right to state its case but in the final analysis Britain could protect its position by exercising its right of veto. Similarly Britain could veto any request by Egypt for the return of the Suez Canal.

Stalin, however, remained sceptical not only that the proposed arrangements provided adequate safeguards for the great powers but also that smaller countries would be content with the mere opportunity of stating their opinions and grievances. To him the greatest danger was 'conflict among ourselves'. Russia, America and Britain were currently allies but who knew what might happen in ten years' time when there might be a new generation of leaders? The system had to be robust enough to 'secure peace for at least fifty years' and preserve the great powers' unity and thus prevent 'the renewal of German aggression'.

When Churchill and Stettinius argued that under the US proposals the United Nations could never direct its power of action against a permanent member, Stalin reminded them how in December 1939, during the Russo-Finnish War, Britain and France had succeeded in having the Soviet Union expelled from the League of Nations and had even 'talked of a crusade against Russia'. Roosevelt tried to calm the discussion. There would always be differences between the great powers but allowing them to be debated openly in the Security Council would 'show the confidence which we all had in each other, and in our ability to solve such problems. This would strengthen our unity, not weaken it.' Stalin grudgingly agreed to study the proposals and continue the discussion next day.

Then came Poland. Opening the debate, Roosevelt said, somewhat disingenuously, that coming from the United States he had 'a distant view on the Polish question'. The 5 or 6 million Poles in America tended to favour the Curzon Line as the eastern boundary so long as Poland was compensated with German territory to the west. Just as he had at Teheran, Roosevelt suggested that convincing home opinion would be easier if the Soviet Union would make some concessions to the Poles on the new eastern frontier, such as allowing them the city of Lvov and the oil deposits in the region, though he did not insist on it. The Poles, he suggested, were 'like the Chinese . . . always worried about "losing face"'.

Stalin pounced, asking which Poles Roosevelt meant – 'the real ones or the émigrés? The real Poles lived in Poland'. Taken aback, the President said he meant 'all Poles'. Moving swiftly on, Roosevelt said, 'the most important matter is that of a permanent Government for Poland'. US public opinion opposed recognizing the Soviet-backed Lublin government because people believed it represented only a small section of the Polish people. What the Polish people wanted was a 'representative government' and he suggested establishing a Presidential Council of Polish leaders to create such a government, composed of the chiefs of the five main Polish political parties.

Churchill spoke next, saying that despite criticism in Parliament his support for the Curzon Line as Poland's eastern border remained unwavering. 'After the agonies Russia had suffered in defending herself against the Germans, and her great deeds in driving them back and liberating Poland, her claim was founded not on force but on right.' However, he repeated the President's plea for territorial concessions in the east as 'a gesture of magnanimity to a much weaker Power'. Again echoing Roosevelt, he argued that Poland's freedom and independence mattered more than territorial boundaries. That was why Britain had gone to war against Germany, taking a terrible risk that 'had nearly cost us our life'. Britain could never accept a settlement that did not leave Poland 'mistress in her own house and captain of her own soul'. At present Poland had two governments – the Lublin and London groups. The world would criticize the three great powers, Churchill declared, if they allowed these rival groups to divide them. Surely, here at Yalta they could create a representative government for Poland, pending full and free elections.

At Stalin's request, the session adjourned for ten minutes. When discussions resumed, a 'blunt, stubborn' Stalin gave his response. Rising theatrically to his feet, he marched up and down behind his chair while expounding his points – the only time during the entire conference that he displayed such passion or spoke at such length. If Poland was a point of honour for the British, for Russia it was 'a matter of life and death'. Twice in the past thirty years Poland had been the corridor through which German troops had marched to attack Russia. They had been able to do so because Poland was weak. Unlike Tsarist Russia which had sought to annex Poland, Soviet Russia wanted it not only to be free and independent but powerful enough to keep invaders out.

Stalin reminded Roosevelt and Churchill that the Curzon Line was not a Russian invention and that Lenin himself had opposed it. By accepting it, he had already retreated from Lenin's position. To take even less by offering territorial concessions 'would be shameful' in the eyes of his countrymen. Did the Americans and the British want 'the Soviet leaders to be less Russian than Curzon . . . ?' If Poland wanted more land it must come at Germany's expense in the west. He reminded Roosevelt and

Churchill that while in Moscow the previous October, Mikołajczyk had been 'very pleased' when Stalin said that Poland's western border would be the River Neisse. He wished to clarify what he had meant. There were two rivers of that name, one by Breslau, the other farther west. 'It was the Western Neisse he had in mind.' Would Roosevelt and Churchill support him? What Stalin did not say was that in fact, and unknown to the Western leaders, Molotov had already signed a Memorandum of Understanding with the head of the Lublin Poles committing the Soviet government to supporting both the Curzon Line and the Western Neisse as Poland's new borders.

Stalin derided Churchill's suggestion that they should establish a new provisional Polish government while in Yalta. He hoped Churchill had made 'a slip of the tongue'. After all, how could such a thing be done without the Poles' participation? 'I am called a dictator and not a democrat, but I have enough democratic feeling to refuse to create a Polish government without the Poles being consulted.' He reminded Roosevelt and Churchill that agreement could have been reached during Mikołajczyk's visit to Moscow with Churchill in October 1944 when there had appeared to be some common ground. However, the London Poles had subsequently refused all dealings with the Lublin group, labelling them 'bandits and criminals'. The Lublin Poles had responded in kind, denouncing the London Poles as 'traitors and turncoats'. He claimed that he did not know how to reconcile them but would try anything to achieve a solution and offered to invite to Yalta some of the Lublin Poles whose democratic base was 'equal at least to that of de Gaulle'.

Finally, Stalin claimed that as a military man he wanted only one thing of the government of a country recently liberated by the Red Army: that his soldiers 'should not be shot at from behind'. He accused the London Poles of supporting anti-Communist partisans who even now were attacking his troops. They had already killed 212 Russian soldiers and raided supply dumps for munitions. By contrast the Lublin government was being very helpful and could be trusted to 'keep the peace in Poland and stop civil war and attacks on the Red Army'.

A clearly fatigued Roosevelt suggested adjourning until the next day, but Churchill had more to say. He told Stalin his own information on Poland was quite different, suggesting only one third of the population supported the Lublin Poles. The Western Allies greatly feared a conflict between Polish partisans and the Lublin government and the ensuing 'bitterness, bloodshed, arrests, and deportations' this might lead to. That was why they were so anxious to see a single, more representative government established.

Stalin said nothing more. Roosevelt, determined to wind up the session, commented that 'Poland has been a source of trouble for over five hundred years'. Churchill replied, 'All the more must we do what we can to put an end to these troubles.' With that the most difficult session of the conference so far ended.

Both the Americans and the British were depressed by what Eden called Stalin's 'very dusty' response on Poland. After the meeting, Churchill told Maisky:

I am very distressed. Stalin is too unyielding. In my last speech I tried to be as delicate and careful as I could. I spoke of 'different information' . . . But to speak frankly, every day we receive many reports that cast the internal situation in Poland in an extremely murky light: the Lublin government is unpopular: many detest it; all dissidents are being arrested and exiled to Siberia en masse; everything rests on your bayonets.

However, as he and Eden knew, the reality was that 'the Red Army held most of the country; Stalin had the power to enforce his will'. That evening over dinner, Eden and Churchill – who three days earlier had told Moran, 'We can't agree that Poland shall be a mere puppet state of Russia, where the people who don't agree with Stalin are bumped off' – discussed briefly and inconclusively what more they could do.

Tired though he was, Roosevelt was also thinking about Poland that evening. A massage and a short rest restored him a little before dinner but he complained to Byrnes, who dropped in to see him, that 'the long meetings are really Winston's fault because he makes too many speeches'. During a quiet dinner, Roosevelt asked his daughter and Kathleen Harriman about their visit to Sebastopol but as soon as the meal was over, with Charles Bohlen's help, drafted a letter to Stalin about Poland which he asked Harriman to take at once to the Vorontsov Palace to show Churchill.

The letter was, as Harriman wrote, 'shrewdly couched in terms of an appeal for the preservation of Allied unity'. It told the Marshal that Roosevelt was 'greatly disturbed' that the three powers could not agree 'about the political set-up in Poland'. That Stalin supported one group and his allies supported another suggested to the watching world that there was a breach between them. The President wished to pursue Stalin's suggestion of bringing to Yalta members of the Lublin group but also 'other elements of the Polish people'. He listed five including the Archbishop of Kraków. If Stalin would agree, both he and Churchill would be willing to explore circumstances in which they could disassociate themselves from the London government and transfer their support to a new broad-based provisional government which pledged to hold free elections as soon as possible. 'If we cannot get a meeting of minds when our armies are converging on the common enemy, how can we get an understanding on even more vital things in the future?' Roosevelt asked.

Churchill and Eden thought the US draft 'on the right lines but not quite stiff enough'. They suggested adding Mikołajczyk and two other London Poles to the list of non-Lublin Poles to be invited to Yalta. Harriman took the amendments back to the President who accepted the changes and the letter was delivered to the Yusupov Palace that night. In the early hours of 7 February Churchill sent a message to Clement Attlee, 'We are having a hard time here. Poland will be very difficult.'

Once again, Stalin was the only one of the Big Three who was content. Sergo Beria's father Lavrentii came into his room that night to boast, 'On Poland Iosif Vissarionovich has not moved one inch.' Gleaning what he could about the day's discussions, Moran contrasted Stalin and Roosevelt in his diary: 'Stalin can see no point in vague sentiments and misty aspirations for the freedom of certain small nations . . . Roosevelt would like to prescribe for the world. Stalin is content to make clear what the Soviet Union will swallow.'

Meanwhile, that night in Berlin Eva Braun celebrated her thirty-third – and last – birthday with a party in Hitler's bomb-proof bunker complex beneath the Old Chancellery Gardens. There was dancing and Hitler himself was 'radiant', still hopeful that the Big Three would yet fall out: 'these states are at loggerheads. He who, like a spider sitting in the middle of his web, can watch developments, observes how these antagonisms grow stronger and stronger from hour to hour.'

Further east, on 6 February, Soviet commanders in already occupied German territory ordered the round-up of all German males between the ages of seventeen and fifty to be sent as forced labourers to the Soviet Union.

In Manila, Japanese troops were still putting up fierce resistance, causing American newspapers to run banner headlines such as 'Japs Burn Manila'. In Burma, the British 14th Army had crossed the Irrawaddy and was preparing to advance on Mandalay. A young British soldier, George MacDonald Fraser, who later wrote the Flashman novels, was out on patrol when a Japanese soldier appeared over the top of a gully just a few yards away. Just as MacDonald Fraser fired at him, the Japanese soldier exploded 'and I was blinded by an enormous flash . . . I rolled away, deafened and then debris came raining down – earth and stones and bits of Jap . . .' The soldier had been a suicide bomber.

CHAPTER NINE

'The Riviera of Hades'

By the fourth day of the conference, 7 February, the novelty of life in the Crimea was fading and some aspects becoming irksome. While Anna Boettiger was out for a stroll with Kathleen Harriman and Robert Hopkins they gave chocolate to a child but a Soviet soldier forced them to take it back, saying curtly, 'Russian children aren't in need of food.'

NKVD agents had previously warned ordinary citizens to keep out of the foreigners' way and not to accept gifts. The summer before a Soviet official had lectured an American diplomat:

We must teach our people to assume that every foreigner is a spy. It is only in this way that we can train them to exercise the self-control which they should exercise as citizens of a great power . . . We cannot permit you to associate closely with them. You will tell them all sorts of things about your countries, about your higher standard of living . . . You will confuse them. You will weaken their loyalty to their own system.

Robert Hopkins, like many others, was starting to tire of the lavish food. 'There was an abundance of beluga caviar at the Livadia Palace. In fact, a heaping saucer of caviar for each person was the first course at breakfast every day followed by herring, bread, fruit and tea. The menu never varied. I longed for orange juice, fried eggs, toast and coffee.' He usually breakfasted with his father Harry in his bedroom where a pair of unsmiling waiters from the Hotel Metropol served them. Hopkins senior was amused as his son 'vainly tried with gestures and sketches to describe to the waiters the breakfast I preferred'. Several days passed before 'they triumphantly brought me a platter of one dozen fried pullet eggs'. Robert ate his other meals with US secret service and naval staff. That menu never varied either: 'caviar, followed by roast pheasant, string beans, cabbage, and potatoes, all accompanied by excellent Georgian wine'. White House naval aide William Rigdon recalled, 'when some of us asked for eggs we got them, so soft boiled that they seemed to have been dipped into hot water, then lifted right out again. Almost raw but warm.'

General Marshall was having more serious problems with the food, especially the Black Sea turbot, bass, shrimp, squid and crayfish so often on the menu as he hated fish and was allergic to shellfish, which made him sick. During the conference he relied on a stack of jumbo-size Hershey bars he had brought with him to keep him going. Yet, whether they liked the food or not, delegates realized how privileged they were. British cypher clerk Joan Evans was at first charmed by the foot-high bears sculpted from butter placed on the dining tables but noticed how on their return to the kitchen the elderly waiters – relics of Tsarist times, she thought – 'hurriedly ate anything we had left on our plates – so we left as much as we could'.

Joan was also adapting to strict security procedures to keep British secrets from Sergo Beria and his team. Some obvious Soviet surveillance in the Vorontsov had already caused amusement. Two days after Portal 'admired a large glass tank with plants growing in it, and remarked that it contained no fish', the goldfish he had taken to feeding with flies had arrived. A British security officer searched the office Joan Evans and her colleagues were initially allocated for listening devices, which intrigued her 'as the idea of bugs was new to me'. Deeming the room too vulnerable, the officer moved the cypher clerks and their equipment to another room. 'There was a sailor with us 24/7. Normally when two people are working on a cypher a lot of the work is verbal but we were told to be completely silent and all scrap paper was put into bags to be taken back to the ship [the *Franconia* in Sebastopol]. We covered 24 hours a day – two on during the day and one at night.' The security officer warned Joan that the many 'young men idly pushing brooms around' in the corridors were 'probably spies'.

However, she and her friends enjoyed some lighter moments. One night members of the British naval delegation from the military mission in Moscow, 'not having seen a British girl for a long time', invited them to a riotous party which ended with the men drinking champagne out of their shoes. At the Livadia US 'intelligence men' warned Anna Boettiger, Dr Bruenn and others who often enjoyed a convivial meal together 'to assume that every room was wired for sound and so to be careful how we talked'.

The daily routines were becoming well established. Morning and evening in his study at the Yusupov Palace Stalin reviewed progress with his advisers. He always found time to talk with those who, 'because of their position', were able 'to express a judgement or maintain contact with the Americans and British', Gromyko recalled. Stalin also hosted late-night parties for all fifty-three members of the Soviet delegation, making sure 'he exchanged a few words with each'.

Every morning Churchill and Roosevelt dealt with the paperwork that arrived by daily courier from Downing Street and the White House and then prepared with their advisers for that day's plenary session. Alexander Cadogan wrote to his wife that 'one day is very like another'. The Foreign Ministers met around midday to tackle their heavy agendas, while the military chiefs, whose meetings were briefer, sometimes had time to spare. Members of the US delegation were offered trips to Sebastopol though they did not sound enticing: 'This is a 3-hour trip over an extremely winding and mountainous road. There are no restaurants or hotels . . . The drive should be attempted only in daylight.' The British Administrative Office, operating in the hall of the Vorontsov, offered tours to such local attractions as Chekhov's house, botanical gardens and beauty spots and to Massandra, 'where one of the famous local wines is brewed'.

Field Marshal Brooke and other British commanders decided that day on a longer excursion to the battlefields of Balaclava, scene of the disastrous charge of the British Light Brigade in 1854 during the Crimean War. The site was still a place of death. With so much debris from recent fighting scattered on the ground, Brooke needed the detailed sketches of the 1854 campaign he had brought to reconstruct the action. He was still puzzling events out when 'someone discovered a complete human skeleton within 5 yards of us'. Poking at the skull, they wondered whether the remains were Russian or German. Although Brooke recognized 'the mud, the storms, the frightful difficulties, the awful sufferings' of British soldiers nearly a century before, what moved him most – 'as if this small corner of the world had not witnessed sufficient human suffering' – were the 'ample signs of the vast recent conflicts to capture Sebastopol and then to free it! A grave beside a wrecked aeroplane here, a broken down tank there, rows upon rows of shell and bomb craters . . . odd graves, and the usual rubbish of a battlefield. It is very strange how history can repeat itself under a different guise.'

Meanwhile in Yalta that day, American Chiefs of Staff endorsed the bomb line separating those areas which the British and American air forces would attack from those their rapidly advancing Soviet allies would assault. The line, drawn up jointly by the American, British and Russian air staffs, would run through Berlin, Dresden and Vienna to Zagreb; its purpose would be to avoid any accidental Anglo-American bombing of Soviet troops. On the political front, that morning Harry Hopkins and James Byrnes impressed on Edward Stettinius the importance of Soviet acceptance of the American plan for voting in the UN Security Council and urged him to raise it at the Foreign Ministers' meeting due to start at the Yusupov Palace at midday. Stettinius duly tried, but Molotov, who was presiding, said firmly that 'he was not prepared to go into this subject at the present time'.

Roosevelt lunched quietly with his daughter and 'Pa' Watson, the latter's health seemingly recovered after being evicted from his room by Hopkins for Churchill's siesta. Sarah Oliver drove with her father to the Livadia for that day's plenary session in brilliant sunshine that 'tried hard to warm the granite peaks [and] shone so hard on the sea that the reflection made one blink. Papa and I looked stolidly out on the scene and presently he said "The Riviera of Hades"!' Earlier that day, she had walked down to the shore for 'a closer inspection of the Black Sea . . . a vivid angry blue flecked white', swirling and hissing among gigantic boulders.

The plenary opened shortly after 4 p.m. According to Stettinius, the British had got wind that the Russians were about to concede on the UN voting procedures. Sitting down next to the President for a few moments, Churchill said in a low voice, 'Uncle Joe will take Dumbarton Oaks.' However, in his opening remarks as chairman Roosevelt raised Poland rather than the UN as the first major topic of the day, reprising his argument of the previous day that 'the problem of the Polish Government' was more important than issues about Polish borders. He was not worried about achieving continuity of government in Poland – after all there had not really been a Polish government since 1939 – but he wanted the Big Three to act boldly and decisively to agree a provisional government. 'We want something new and drastic – like a breath of fresh air.'

However, before discussion could turn to Poland, protocol required the delegates listen to Molotov's report on that morning's meeting of Foreign Ministers. Pince-nez balanced on the bridge of his nose, Molotov said their work continued both on how best to incorporate a reference to Germany's dismemberment into the unconditional surrender terms and on the division of Germany. Though ministers had agreed France should have a zone of occupation, they could not agree on whether France should be admitted to the Control Commission. He and Stettinius favoured deferring a decision to the European Advisory Commission set up by the three powers in 1943 to consider 'European questions connected with the termination of hostilities'. Eden, however, was pressing for a place for France on the Control Commission and for the matter to be resolved at Yalta. On German reparations, Molotov reaffirmed that the new committee to consider this would meet in Moscow and that its priority would be to agree fundamental issues such as how much Germany was to pay and in what manner.

Roosevelt and Churchill acknowledged the Foreign Ministers' work with the usual courtesies but immediately began sparring about France. Churchill argued fiercely that giving France an occupation zone without a voice on the Control Commission was both illogical and unworkable, while Roosevelt continued to insist that a decision be deferred. Their ill-tempered exchange ended with a bland comment from Stalin that 'the three Governments had been able to settle a good many things by correspondence' – surely France's position could be one of them?

Leaving the issue unresolved, Roosevelt suggested they move on to Poland, expecting a response to the letter he had agreed with Churchill and dispatched to Stalin the night before. Stalin claimed to have received it 'only about an hour and a half before'. He had tried to reach the leaders of the Lublin Poles by telephone only to discover that they were away in Kraków and Łódź. As for the other Poles identified in the letter, 'he was not sure that they could be found in time to come to the Crimea'. Molotov had proposals 'which to a certain extent met the President's ideas' but since these had not yet been translated into English, he suggested they first discuss the United Nations – a clever move by Stalin who well knew the issue was close to Roosevelt's heart.

Alerted by Churchill that the Russians had concessions to offer, Roosevelt readily agreed. At Stalin's invitation, Molotov set out the Soviet position. Having considered Stettinius's report on the UN voting formula and Churchill's clarifications, 'the Soviet Government felt that these proposals fully guaranteed the unity of the Great Powers in the matter of preservation of peace' and were 'entirely acceptable'. The relief of the American and British delegations was palpable, with 'smiles on many lips', Ivan Maisky wrote in his diary. However, he disliked what he considered the sanctimonious tone the Western Allies had adopted when pressing their case: 'England and the USA fancied themselves as Almighty God, with a mission to judge the remainder of the sinful world, including my own country.'

If Stalin wished to generate goodwill, he had succeeded. Sergo Beria wrote:

> in his dealing with the Allies, Stalin always sought to give the impression that he was a man of his word. He even made small concessions in order to succeed in this . . . But each of his gestures of goodwill was carefully weighed and measured out in advance. Unlike Roosevelt, Stalin never yielded to an impulse.

In this case, he had calculated he could afford a sting in the tail in the guise of a further concession. Molotov reminded his audience that the admission of the sixteen Soviet republics as UN members had been raised but not resolved at Dumbarton Oaks. The Soviet Union was no longer pressing for membership for all but 'would be satisfied with the admission of three or at least two'. Candidates were the Ukraine, Belorussia and Lithuania – the republics which 'had borne the greatest sacrifices in the war and were the first to be invaded by the enemy' and which were surely as worthy of membership as British Dominions such as Australia and Canada.

Roosevelt, who had told his cabinet and Congressional leaders in Washington that if the Soviets insisted on extra seats, 'he would demand forty-eight votes for the United States', remained opposed. While Molotov was still speaking he slid Stettinius a note: 'This is not so good.'

When Molotov finished, the President sought to avoid giving a straight answer. After clarifying that the Soviets meant membership of the General Assembly not the Security Council, he said that Molotov's suggestion deserved closer study, but cautioned that 'if the larger nations were given more than one vote it might prejudice the thesis of one vote for each member'. He then spoke at length – at times confusingly – about the difficulties that could arise if that policy were to be abandoned. For example, some countries were large geographically but had small populations and vice versa. What should their rights be? The immediate priority, he urged, was to hold a conference at the end of March or even earlier to discuss how the UN should be set up. A key question was which countries should be invited to attend? Obviously those which had fought against Hitler, but what about others like Paraguay, Peru, Uruguay, Chile, Egypt and Iceland, which had merely severed relations with Germany but not declared war?

With Stalin starting to look restless Hopkins passed Roosevelt a note:

Mr President
I think you should try to get this referred to foreign ministers before there is trouble.
Harry

Roosevelt took the advice and proposed that Foreign Ministers be asked to recommend where and when the conference should take place, which nations should be invited and also to consider the Soviet proposals for membership of their republics.

Before this could be agreed, Churchill intervened. Conscious of the possible implications of 'one nation, one vote' for the British Empire, he expounded on the right of Britain's four self-governing Dominions – Canada, Australia, New Zealand and South Africa, which had all been members of the League of Nations – to seats in the United Nations. They had not been forced to fight. Their governments had entered the war of their own accord and Britain 'could never agree to any system which excluded them'. By analogy he had 'profound sympathy' with the aspirations of the Soviet Union with its 180 million citizens and could understand why it 'might well look with a questioning eye at the constitutional arrangements of the British Commonwealth, which resulted in our having more than one voice in the Assembly'. He had no personal authority to accept the Soviet proposal without consulting his War Cabinet but would perhaps send a telegram to London that night.

Churchill's comments did not surprise the Americans, who knew he wanted to protect the position of the Dominions and even 'to get India into the United Nations', Bohlen wrote. They were, however, surprised when Churchill next opposed holding a UN conference as early as March, arguing this would be very difficult since 'The battle would be at its height and more soldiers would be involved than at any time of the war.' Furthermore, some nations 'would still be under the German yoke . . . Other countries would be starving and in misery, such as Holland.' Therefore it was hardly a suitable time to 'undertake the immense task of the future organization of the world'.

Churchill's comments also startled his British colleagues. Eden thought the Americans 'not unnaturally' resented his remarks 'since we had long ago agreed to such a meeting' and considered them 'another example of the Prime Minister's reluctance to see any energies diverted to peacetime tasks'. Cadogan was less guarded: 'The PM got rather off the rails. Silly old man – without a word of warning to Anthony [Eden] or me, he plunged into a long harangue about [the] World Organisation, knowing nothing whatever of what he was talking about and making complete nonsense of the whole thing.' In a scribbled note to Roosevelt, Hopkins warned: 'There is something behind this talk that we do not know of its basis. Perhaps we better to wait till later tonight [to find out] what is on his mind.'

Roosevelt scribbled underneath: '*All this is rot*', then crossed out '*rot*' and substituted '*local politics*'. Hopkins responded: 'I am quite sure now he is thinking about the next election in Britain.'

Roosevelt doggedly repeated his proposal that Foreign Ministers consider the location and timing of the conference – as early as possible, as agreed at Dumbarton Oaks – the nations to be invited and the Soviet request for membership for its republics. Churchill gave in, though cautioning that the conference's timing was no mere technical issue but a point 'of great decision'. Stalin, who as so often had sat quietly through the spat between President and Prime Minister, said soothingly that Foreign Ministers were not being asked to decide anything – merely to report back.

Churchill proposed they next discuss Persia – as he still liked to call Iran though it had changed its name in 1935 – where Britain and Russia had contended for influence since the days of the 'Great Game'. In 1907 they had agreed on spheres of influence with Russia dominating the north and Britain the south of the country. The following year British prospectors found oil and formed what would become the British Petroleum Company (BP) to exploit it. In the 1930s, worried about British and Soviet ambitions, the Shah of Iran sought the friendship of Hitler's Germany as a counter-balance. However, in August 1941 Britain and the Soviet Union, now allied, jointly invaded the country, as they claimed, to protect their access to its oil refineries. Iran's Shah appealed to Roosevelt 'to take efficacious and urgent human- itarian steps to put an end to these acts of aggression', but the President declined to intervene. Within a month of the invasion the Shah abdicated in favour of his more compliant son Mohammed Reza Pahlavi, who would remain on the Peacock Throne until displaced in 1979 by Ayatollah Khomeini. After the United States entered the war, American troops and advisers also arrived in Iran where they established and ran a Lend-Lease supply route north from the Persian Gulf through to Soviet Azerbaijan.

At the Teheran Conference in 1943, the Big Three – all now firmly ensconced in the country – signed a declaration guaran- teeing Iran's sovereignty, independence and territorial integrity, undertaking to withdraw their troops within six months of the war's end and promising financial aid. Suspecting that, despite their lofty words, the Russians and the British would be hard to dislodge, the new Shah courted the United States. Roosevelt publicly promised to pursue an 'unselfish American policy' in Iran but according to his then Secretary of State Cordell Hull privately and vigorously 'support[ed] the efforts of American companies to obtain petroleum concessions' in Iran. By late 1944, this dual approach was proving successful in establishing the United States as the dominant foreign power in Iran both financially and politically.

Churchill had noted this with dismay. However, he did not want rivalries over oil to sour Anglo-American relations and, despite the misgivings of some of his Cabinet, in August 1944 supported an Anglo-American agreement on access to Middle Eastern oil. Its ostensible purpose was to develop oil production and make it available to 'all peaceable countries at fair prices and on a non-discriminatory basis' but the real aim was to protect British and American interests. Beria urged Stalin to seek membership of this Anglo-American 'oil club' and also a Soviet–Iranian agreement on oil concessions in northern Iran. Stalin ignored the former advice but agreed to the latter, only to be frustrated when the Iranians – with American and British encouragement – resisted Soviet pressure and in late 1944 passed a decree prohibiting the granting of further new oil concessions until the war was over. Meanwhile, the British were pressing for an even earlier withdrawal of troops from Iran than announced at Teheran – a move, the Soviets suspected, that would allow them to resume their petroleum business in southern Iran undistracted and unthreatened by foreign rivals.

Iran was therefore a sore point for Stalin at Yalta. However, on 7 February discussion was brief, with Roosevelt merely remarking that he 'had never seen a poorer country than Persia was at the present time' but that he hoped the UN would help such undeveloped countries contribute to the expansion of world trade. According to Ivan Maisky, while Churchill politely listened to the President's pious statement, 'Stalin remained silent and drew figures in his notebook' throughout the inconclusive exchange.

Finally, with the Soviet proposals now translated and brought into the ballroom for distribution, discussion again turned to Poland with Molotov setting out the Soviet position. The Curzon Line should be Poland's eastern border, with minor digressions of a few kilometres in favour of Poland, and the western border should be the Oder and Western Neisse Rivers. It would be desirable to add to the Polish provisional (Lublin) government 'some democratic leaders from Polish émigré circles' and for the Allied governments to recognize the enlarged government, which would hold elections 'as soon as possible'. After returning to Moscow, Molotov said that he, Harriman and the British ambassador Sir Archibald Clark Kerr should submit detailed proposals to the three governments on how the Polish provisional government should be expanded. Putting his piece of paper down, Molotov repeated Stalin's claim that it had been impossible to reach anyone in Poland by telephone but that the Soviet proposals 'went far toward meeting the President's wishes'. Bohlen later wrote that they became 'the basis for the final agreement on Poland'. However, the debate was by no means yet over.

Neither Roosevelt nor Churchill questioned the ridiculous fiction that it had been impossible to contact the Lublin Poles or others to invite them to Yalta. Nor did they challenge the fact that the Russian proposals assumed the retention of the Lublin group as the core of Poland's provisional government, rather than the establishment of an entirely new body as they had previously required. Roosevelt merely objected that the proposals only referred to including Polish 'émigrés' in the government, suggesting that surely 'Poles in Poland' could also be found, and asked for more time to study the proposals with Stettinius. Churchill too challenged the use of the word émigrés but for different somewhat pedantic reasons. In Britain it meant people driven out of their own country by their fellow countrymen – like refugees in the French Revolution. However on this occasion, Poles had left because of 'brutal German attack'. He suggested the term 'Poles temporarily abroad' be substituted and Stalin agreed.

Next, Churchill said he had always favoured a westward shift of Polish borders but not more than the Poles could handle, arguing, 'It would be a great pity to stuff the Polish goose so full of German food it died of indigestion.' Also, the British public would be 'frankly shocked' at the idea of transferring so many millions of Germans westward by force. When Stalin suggested quietly that this was not a problem since 'most Germans in those areas had already run away from the Red Army', Churchill acknowledged that made matters easier: 'Moreover, 6 or 7 million Germans had already been killed, and at least 1 or 1.5 million more would probably be killed before the end of the war,' which would create more space. Nevertheless, he cautioned that the transfer of such huge numbers of people must be considered in the context of 'the capacity of the Poles to handle it and the capability of the Germans to receive them' and asked for time 'to sleep on this problem'. And with that – it was now 8 p.m. – the day's plenary session adjourned.

Churchill had a 'cheerful' dinner that night with his daughter, Eden and Cadogan. Later he telegraphed Attlee and the War Cabinet that 'Today has been much better. All the American proposals for the Dumbarton Oaks constitution were accepted by the Russians' who had limited their demands for membership of the UN Assembly for their republics. Roosevelt 'obviously visualised difficulties from the American standpoint' but Britain's position, Churchill suggested, was 'somewhat different'. Britain was asking 'a great deal' in having places in the Assembly for Canada, Australia, South Africa, New Zealand and perhaps India, as well as for itself. It was 'not much to ask' that Russia should have seats for two of its republics and it would help shield Britain from criticism if the British Empire was not 'the only multiple voter in the field'. Furthermore, making 'a friendly gesture to Russia' might be expedient 'in view of other important concessions by them which are achieved or pending'. He asked for approval to tell the Russians that when the issue of their republics came up for decision, whether at Yalta or later, Britain would support them. It would be 'in the nature of a gentlemen's agreement'.

Churchill's optimism spilled into a little vignette of Yalta for his Cabinet colleagues. 'In spite of our gloomy warnings and forebodings, Yalta has turned out very well so far. It is a sheltered strip of austere Riviera, with winding Corniche roads. The villas and palaces . . . are of an extinct imperialism and nobility. In these we squat on furniture carried with extraordinary effort from Moscow.'

He also perceived a glimmer of hope over Poland, telegraphing Attlee that night, 'It is our plan to fight hard for a government in Poland which we and the United States can recognize and to which we can attract the recognition of all the United Nations.' In return, Britain would require 'real substantial and effective representation' from the London Poles, especially Mikołajczyk, as well as from Poles still in Poland 'whom the Americans have listed'. It would be expedient to recognize such a government at once so 'we could then get ambassadors and missions into Poland, and find out at least to some extent what is happening there and whether the foundations can be laid for the free, fair, and unfettered election which alone can give life and being to a Polish Government'.

Cadogan also thought they were finally making progress: 'Uncle Joe showed signs of being accommodating' over both the UN and Poland. Eden, though, was less optimistic, recording that on Poland the 'Russians again made some concessions which give hope though we are still far from where we want to be'. To try and narrow the gap that night he and his team produced a revised version of the Soviet proposals for discussion next day.

The President was in a good mood that evening but, as Stettinius discovered when he visited him, preoccupied with the Russian request for extra seats in the UN General Assembly which he spent some time analysing. 'From the standpoint of geography and population he did not believe there was anything preposterous about the Russian proposal for two extra votes,' he told Stettinius, especially as the real power would rest in the Security Council, and each country in this body, large or small, would have only one vote. Furthermore, he knew Stalin thought 'a vote for the Ukraine was essential . . . for Soviet Unity'. Roosevelt also reflected, 'The British were in too embarrassing a situation from the standpoint of the make-up of the British Empire to oppose the Russian request. India was not self-governing – and Churchill had made it clear earlier that he did not favor Indian independence – and yet India was to have a vote.'

Late that night at the Yusupov Palace, Antonov made his customary military report to Stalin. Around midnight, Stalin and his military commanders sat down to eat. Stalin asked Admiral Kuznetsov about the state of the Soviet Pacific Fleet. Kuznetsov, who was eager to join the war on Japan, reminded Stalin that at the start of the conference he had asked his permission to discuss with Admiral King the transfer of some US vessels to the Soviet fleet. Stalin had told him to wait but now promised him, 'I shall speak with Roosevelt.'

*

That day, 7 February 1945, in cold, wet drizzle, US infantry divisions were crossing the Sauer River from Luxembourg into Germany. An infantryman recalled:

> In front of us was the famous Siegfried Line of fortifications, manned by an elite cadre from an SS officers' school, no sixteen- or sixty-five-year-old Volksturm troops hastily thrown into combat by Hitler. Our job was to cross the river in assault rowboats and climb up a very steep, very muddy hill, taking three steps up and sliding back two. Concrete bunkers bristling with machine guns dotted the hill. . . . All that night, courtesy of General Patton, every available piece, augmented by tanks and even anti aircraft guns, ceaselessly pounded the hill and beyond. The sky was streaked by tracers and it sounded like an endless freight train howling overhead . . . It was our turn now. The artillery barrage was to continue till the last possible moment. Concrete bunkers are immune to artillery shells, their only weakness is the steel door on the side or rear. Their occupants must have been dazed, though, because we made it up that slimy hill.

Also that day, after forty-eight hours' heavy fighting, the 2nd Ukrainian Front captured the southern railway station in Buda – the western part of the Hungarian capital of Budapest across the Danube from Pest. The entire city fell to the Red Army shortly afterwards following a siege that had lasted six weeks and taken a heavy toll on civilians. A survivor recalled it as:

> a God-awful time. I was a young teenager . . . and remember spending most of the siege deep in our cellar lit by candles amid food stocks and coal while the city shook itself apart. At night a young German soldier named Gunther – he was just a few years older than I – would come and stay with us. My mother tried to console him as he wept about missing his family and that he didn't want to die alone in Budapest. One day he didn't come back.

Meanwhile in Germany that day, in the Ruhr Valley German engineers blew up floodgates of dams in a desperate bid to frustrate the Allied advance by turning the area west of Cologne into a lake; in East Prussia naval gunfire from the German cruisers *Scheer* and *Lützow* was hampering Soviet attacks north of Königsberg.

Across the Atlantic, Paraguay – one of the countries singled out by Roosevelt as holding back – and Argentina finally declared war on Germany and Japan.

The British and North American publics could scarcely keep up with the good news, with papers running such headlines as 'Oder River Line Sagging After Strong Red Attacks', 'Grand Assault on Berlin Beginning', 'Trapped Japs Put Torch to Manila' and, optimistically, '"Big Three" Reach Complete Agreement for Wind-Up of War Against Germany'. The latter was pure speculation since the terse press release drafted by Foreign Ministers and outlining the conference's objectives was only released that day and made no such claims.

CHAPTER TEN

'The Broad Sunlit Plains of Peace and Happiness'

As the fifth day of the conference, Thursday 8 February, began, Sarah Oliver wrote to her mother: 'Papa is bearing up very well — despite the strain of getting through so much in really so short a time, and the accompanying patience and toil that a million complexities call for . . . He has been sleeping well without any little pink pills.' She and Sawyers, his valet, had had 'a wonderful idea' for keeping her father sustained at the long plenary sessions — 'We are going to send him over some chicken soup in a thermos — and when they break for a few minutes for tea — he could have his chicken soup! If he doesn't have a whisky and soda!'

With a cold wind blowing from the east, Moran and Cadogan visited Chekhov's small, neat house perched above Yalta, as had Kathleen Harriman a few days earlier when she had met the writer's sister, 'a grand old lady of 83, thrilled to meet some Americans'. Moran thought the dining room with its piano, large photograph of the playwright, 'and a life-size painting by Chekhov's brother of a young woman sitting distractedly trailing a very shapeless hand' rather 'grim'. He preferred the homelier sitting room with its window overlooking the valley, bronze bust of Tolstoy and, lying on a table, the small wooden stethoscope belonging to the consumptive Chekhov, a fellow physician who had only reluctantly ceased practising on his own doctor's advice.

Moran also called in at the Livadia to visit Hopkins. He 'looked ghastly' though he soon 'began to talk with all his old verve' about the Soviet request for two additional votes in the UN General Assembly. He complained, 'The President seems to have no mind of his own. He came to Yalta apparently determined to oppose any country having more than one vote, but when the P.M. came out strongly in favour of Stalin's proposal Roosevelt said he, too, would support Stalin.' Some in the US team – himself and Byrnes included – remained strongly opposed to the Soviet demand, and State Department official Alger Hiss had that morning circulated a memo entitled 'Arguments Against the Inclusion of Any of the Soviet Republics Among the Initial Members'. One can only wonder if he had also passed copies to his Russian handlers. At noon Roosevelt conferred with Hopkins, Harriman, Byrnes and Bohlen about the issue.

Meanwhile Stettinius set out by car for the Vorontsov Palace where Eden was chairing that day's Foreign Ministers' meeting, at which the major issues for discussion would be the time and place of the inaugural UN conference and, of course, the Soviet request for additional seats. Negotiating the precipitous hairpin bends, Stettinius was struck afresh by the burned-out shells of villas where the Tsarist aristocracy had once passed balmy summers, dotted ghostlike on the hillsides.

The Foreign Ministers quickly agreed a date for the conference – 25 April – and accepted Stettinius's invitation for it to convene in the US. Discussions on the Soviet demand for extra seats proved more difficult. Although Roosevelt had told Stettinius the night before that the Russian request 'was all right' and appeared to be leaning towards making some concessions, Stettinius wanted to reserve the US position until he could speak to the President again and be certain he had reached 'a definite conclusion'. He therefore tried to steer a middle course, telling Molotov the Soviet request would receive 'sympathetic consideration' at the April conference. Unmoved and with support from Eden, Molotov battled for the immediate granting of extra Soviet seats. When Stettinius objected that this would conflict with the principle of 'one nation, one vote' agreed at Dumbarton Oaks, Molotov reminded him that Australia and Canada had individual membership despite being part of the British Empire. He then began ridiculing other aspects of the UN proposals, observing that some countries to be invited did not have diplomatic relations with the Soviet Union and questioning which Polish government was to attend. He also suggested that if the powers failed to agree on UN membership, this should be made public.

Realizing that any exposure of disagreement between the Allies would compromise the new organization before it was even established, Stettinius said hastily that he was seeking a way of satisfying the Soviet request before the UN conference met. When Eden suggested placing the admission of the Soviet republics as original members on the UN conference agenda, Molotov pressed for 'an amendment' to Eden's plan, a statement that at Yalta Foreign Ministers had 'agreed that it would be advisable to grant admission to the Assembly to two or three Soviet Republics'. Stettinius said he was 'favorably impressed' but had to consult the President. He expected that 'the United States would be able to give a favorable reply before the end of the day'.

When the meeting ended, Stettinius hastened back to the Livadia to report to Roosevelt, leaving a drafting committee to produce the report that Eden would present to that day's plenary session. Stettinius told the President the British and Russians were united in pressing for membership of the UN for at least two additional Soviet republics but that he had 'reserved the American position'. At that moment, 3.30 p.m., as Roosevelt replied that 'somehow we would now have to accept the proposal', the study doors opened and Bohlen ushered in Stalin. Roosevelt immediately told him the Foreign Ministers had met and reached agreement on their report to the day's plenary meeting. When Stalin asked whether this agreement included the admission of additional Soviet republics the President simply said, 'Yes.'

The reason for Stalin's private visit to the President was the issue raised in Roosevelt's memorandum to him of 5 February

– the Soviet Union's entry into the war on Japan. The parallel approach of the US Chiefs of Staff to their Soviet counterparts had also borne fruit. Somewhat to their surprise, the Russian Chiefs had agreed to meet the Americans at the Yusupov Palace at 3 p.m. that same afternoon – 'a good omen', General Marshall thought. While Roosevelt was welcoming Stalin at the Livadia, the two sides were already sitting down together for the first time in the war without the British present. Leahy and Marshall were detailing the support they wanted from the Soviet Union. Antonov was being encouraging, calling the American proposals 'excellent', but saying he could not agree anything without the permission of his Commander-in-Chief – Stalin.

Roosevelt now set about winning the commitments his military chiefs wanted so badly. He told Stalin that with the fall of Manila the Pacific war had entered a new phase. Given that Japan had 4 million soldiers, he would only invade the Japanese home islands if absolutely necessary but hoped 'by intensive bombing to be able to destroy Japan and its army and thus save American lives'. To achieve this he needed new air bases in the Far East.

Stalin said he would not object to the US establishing bases on the Amur River – the border between the Russian Far East and north-eastern China – but setting up US bases on the Kamchatka Peninsula would be 'difficult': a Japanese consul based there could not but help notice the military build-up. However, he agreed that Soviet military staff should begin detailed planning talks with their American counterparts. Knowing Roosevelt was the suitor and he the one being wooed, Stalin then queried whether after the war the US might sell some of its surplus shipping to the Soviet Union as Stettinius had suggested to Molotov. Roosevelt said it should be possible for both America and Great Britain to supply vessels on interest-free credit, adding that although 'the British had never sold anything without [charging] commercial interest . . . he had different ideas'. When Stalin praised the President's approach and lauded Lend-Lease as 'a remarkable invention without which victory would have been delayed', Roosevelt told him the idea had originally come to him while sailing his yacht.

Stalin then set out his terms for joining the war against Japan. They were not entirely new to Roosevelt. In mid-December 1944 in Moscow, Stalin had presented Harriman with a list of demands which he now restated. First, he asked for the southern half of Sakhalin Island, north of Japan, and the largely uninhabited Kuriles, a chain of thirty-two islands extending from ten miles beyond the northernmost Japanese home island of Hokkaido 800 miles northwards to the Russian Kamchatka Peninsula. Believing that Japan had seized all these territories after its victory over Tsarist Russia in the 1904/5 Russo-Japanese War, Roosevelt assured him, 'there would be no difficulty whatsoever' about restoring them to Russia. In fact, Japan had acquired only southern Sakhalin at that time. Tsarist Russia had ceded the Kuriles to Japan earlier – in the second half of the nineteenth century. Bohlen later wrote, 'If the President had done his homework, or if any of us had been more familiar with Far Eastern history, the United States might not have given all the Kuriles to Stalin so easily.'

Unprompted, Roosevelt next reminded Stalin of the latter's request at the Teheran Conference for access to warm-water ports in Manchuria which Russia had lost as a result of the 1904 war, and his own suggestion of Dairen at the end of the Chinese-owned Manchurian railway as a solution. Acknowledging he had yet to discuss this with his ally, the Chinese Nationalist leader Chiang Kai-shek, he suggested either establishing Dairen as an international free port or that the Soviet Union lease it from China. Personally he preferred the former because of the issue of Hong Kong, which he hoped the British would return to China after the war to function as an internationalized port, though 'he knew Mr Churchill would have strong objections'.

Stalin said he would not object to Dairen becoming an international port, then continued his demands, which included access to the Manchurian railways, pointing out that the tsars had made use of the lines. Roosevelt suggested Russia and China could operate the railway jointly or even that Russia might lease the railway direct but again commented that he had not consulted Chiang Kai-shek.

Stalin did not share Roosevelt's reservations, however mildly expressed. Privately he considered the Chinese Nationalist leader a nonentity and did not intend to allow squeamishness about consulting him to pose an obstacle. He told Roosevelt that unless all his conditions were met he would find it hard to explain to the Supreme Soviet why their country was going to war against Japan, a country that, unlike Germany, had not attacked it and with which he had signed a non-aggression pact. However, if his demands were met, the Supreme Soviet – and the Russian people – would understand that the national interest was involved. As Bohlen realized, invoking the Supreme Soviet as 'the pre-eminent arbiter in the country' was a favoured Stalin ploy. Although it fooled few, it often signalled issues on which the Marshal was determined to have his way. Stalin, in turn, suspected that the President often played a similar game, telling Molotov:

> Roosevelt . . . thinks I will believe that he is truly afraid of Congress, and that is why he is unable to make concessions to us. He just does not want to do it and is using Congress as an excuse. It is all nonsense! . . . But he won't take me in.

Roosevelt repeated for the third time that he had not yet been able to discuss matters with the Chinese Nationalists, but made the excuse for not doing so that their security was so poor that anything said to them was known to the whole world within twenty-four hours. Useful expedient though this was, there was a genuine point behind it. If Japan did get wind of a US–Soviet pact against it, their forces might attack Siberia before Russia was ready to send troops to the region. Stalin agreed that nothing could be announced publicly and suggested there was no need to speak to Chiang Kai-shek until he had moved Soviet divisions eastwards. Shrewdly he also suggested 'it would be well to leave here with these conditions set forth in writing agreed to by the three powers'. Roosevelt agreed that Molotov should draft a secret agreement.

If Chiang Kai-shek was being sidelined, so too to an extent was Churchill, who was disconcerted to learn, on arriving at the Livadia for the plenary session, that Stalin was privately with Roosevelt; the President had not told him about the meeting. Stettinius sent in an aide with a message that the British Prime Minister had arrived, to which Roosevelt wrote back 'Let him wait.'

Churchill would also have been displeased had he known that Roosevelt and Stalin had discussed trusteeships in the Far East. Roosevelt proposed that after the war Korea – occupied by the Japanese since 1910 – be administered by a joint Soviet, American and Chinese trusteeship body to prepare the country for eventual self-government but, he suggested, one issue was 'delicate'. Though he personally saw no need to invite British participation, 'they might resent this'. Openly amused, Stalin replied they must certainly be invited or the 'Prime Minister might kill us'. When he queried whether foreign troops would be stationed in Korea, Roosevelt said no. The President also suggested a trusteeship would be suitable for Indochina, whose people were 'of small stature and . . . not warlike' but, in a further poke at Churchill, said the British would oppose this since they wanted Indochina returned to France so as not to raise questions about their own rule over Burma.

With that, the President and Stalin moved the short distance to the ballroom where the assembled delegates were waiting for them. Both must have felt reasonably content. In a meeting lasting barely half an hour, Roosevelt had secured Soviet agreement to enter the war against Japan while Stalin had obtained his objective of territorial acquisitions at Japan's expense and a Soviet foothold in north-east China at the expense of an unconsulted major American ally.

At 4.15 p.m. Roosevelt opened the fifth plenary session with a buoyant announcement that the Foreign Ministers had achieved 'complete success' in their discussions and invited Eden to present their report. Eden duly said that the ministers recommended that the UN conference be held on 25 April 1945 in the United States, that only those countries which had declared war on Germany and signed the UN Declaration by a specified date in February should be invited and that the conference itself should decide who should be the organization's original members. At that stage the delegates from the US and UK would support the proposal to admit two Soviet republics as initial members.

While the latter statement was no surprise to Roosevelt after his brief conversation with Stettinius, it shocked some of his delegation. Alger Hiss, one of those who had drafted the Foreign Ministers' report which the British had then had typed up, knew the original text had not referred to US support for extra UN votes for the Soviet republics. The first he knew of it was when Eden handed him a copy of the report just as the plenary was about to open. Though as a Soviet agent the revised wording would have pleased him, in his guise of dedicated State Department man he joined his colleagues in accusing the British of exceeding their authority. He challenged Eden, who snapped back, 'You don't know what has taken place.' What had actually happened remains unclear. The British insisted Stettinius – presumably after his brief meeting with the President – had sanctioned the wording. Stettinius later claimed it was the President himself after 'a private talk' with the British.

Whatever the case, Stalin was still far from satisfied with the UN proposals. As Molotov had done, he pounced on the illogicality that the list of states which met the proposed criteria for UN membership included ten which had no diplomatic relations with the Soviet Union. How could the Soviet government be expected 'to attempt to build future world security' with such countries? Roosevelt suggested that most of those countries would like to have relations with Russia 'but had just not gotten around to doing anything about it' and in the case of others blamed the influence of the Catholic Church, which was hostile to the Soviet Union. He also reminded Stalin that earlier in the war the Soviet Union had sat down with such nations. The best way of encouraging them to establish relations was surely to invite them to the conference.

Unconvinced, Stalin also challenged why nations which 'had wavered and speculated on being on the winning side' and were now rushing to declare war on Germany should be treated the same as nations 'who had really waged war and had suffered'. Churchill said he sympathized with Stalin's points but felt that 'having a whole new group of nations declare war on Germany' would help puncture German morale. He also said the British government felt a special responsibility towards Egypt, which it had twice dissuaded from declaring war on Germany and Italy in order to preserve its neutrality, more useful to Britain than if Egypt had joined the fight. Roosevelt said it had been his personal idea that only those nations which had declared war on Germany should be invited to join the UN. He proposed 1 March 1945 as a cut-off date for them to do so, which Stalin and Churchill accepted.

After further wrangling and sniping over which countries had behaved well in the war and which had not – Stalin agreed Turkey should be invited to the UN conference provided it declared war by 1 March but queried whether Denmark, which 'had let the Germans in', need yet be admitted – discussions finally turned to the position of the Soviet republics. Stalin asked that the Foreign Ministers' report specifically name the Ukraine and Belorussia as the Soviet republics for which he was seeking UN membership. Molotov asked whether it would smooth their admission if these republics signed the United Nations Declaration by 1 March and Stalin suggested that, although the Big Three had agreed to recommend their admission, the fact that they had not signed the Declaration might be used as a pretext for excluding them. Roosevelt and Stettinius rushed to assure him this would not happen. However, as he had the previous day, Churchill weighed in on the Soviet's side, suggesting it was 'not entirely logical' to invite to the UN conference, as he himself wished, 'small countries which had done next to nothing for victory and had declared war only at that last moment' while failing to reward 'the martyrdom and sufferings' of the Ukraine and Belorussia with an invitation. The two republics, he said, should sign the UN Declaration and attend the conference.

Claiming he did not wish to 'embarrass' the President, Stalin asked him to explain his specific difficulties over the Soviet republics. Flushed into the open, Roosevelt said that 'giving one of the Great Powers three votes instead of one' in the General Assembly was so significant it must be put before the forthcoming conference itself. When Stalin proposed that the Ukraine and Belorussia at least be allowed to sign the UN Declaration, Roosevelt again resisted, saying it would not overcome his difficulty, and Stalin withdrew his proposal.

After these uneasy exchanges, the Big Three again 'wrestled

with the problem of Poland', as Harriman put it. The American delegation had prepared a response to Molotov's proposals of the previous day, which they had circulated that morning and which Roosevelt now read out, claiming it was 'very close' to Molotov's proposals. It accepted the Curzon Line, with minor modifications, as Poland's eastern border but stated there was little justification for extending Poland's western frontier as far as the Western Neisse River.

On Poland's government, the President proposed that Molotov, Harriman and Clark Kerr meet in Moscow to oversee the appointment of the presidential council he had suggested two days earlier. Composed of perhaps three men it would 'represent the Presidential office of the Polish Republic' and in turn form a new 'Polish Government of National Unity' comprising 'representative leaders from the present Polish provisional government in Warsaw; from other democratic elements inside Poland, and from Polish democratic leaders abroad'. This government would need to pledge to hold free elections as soon as a new Polish constitution was in place. Molotov at once sought assurance that on recognizing the new Government of National Unity the US and UK would no longer recognize the London government. Roosevelt and Churchill confirmed this.

However, if the British and American delegations hoped the Polish question was about to be resolved, they were disappointed, as what Andrei Gromyko recalled as 'a sharp confrontation' ensued. After a short adjournment, Molotov launched a barrage of objections. He accused both the Americans and the British of ignoring 'the existence of the present government in Poland', which had 'great authority'. The Polish people 'would never agree to anything which would greatly change the Provisional Government'. The only viable course was to enlarge the existing provisional government and the only debate was the number and identity of the additional Poles to be invited to join it. He added that the government in Warsaw would not accept Mikołajczyk as one of the Poles to be invited to Moscow to take part in the discussions. Molotov also claimed he had not 'the slightest doubt' that the Poles themselves desired their western frontier to be along the Western Neisse.

When he had finally finished, Churchill spoke. Guessing what was coming, Roosevelt scribbled a note to Stettinius: 'Now we're in for 1/2 hour of it.'

Peering over his half-moon glasses, Churchill said that they had reached 'the crucial point of the Conference'. If they left Yalta while still recognizing different Polish governments, 'the whole world will see that fundamental differences between us still exist. The consequences will be most lamentable and will stamp our meeting with the seal of failure.' He had seen no evidence that the overwhelming mass of the Polish people supported the Lublin Poles – in fact quite to the contrary. 'If the Conference is to brush aside the existing London government and lend all its weight to the Lublin Government there will be a world outcry.' Furthermore 150,000 Poles had fought bravely for the Allied cause. Those soldiers would regard it as a betrayal if the British government abandoned the Polish government in London to which they had looked since the war began. He himself had no special regard for the London Poles. They 'had been foolish at every stage' but the provisional government formed by the Lublin Poles had been in place only a year.

Building to his finale, Churchill said the only way to avoid a situation highly destructive to Allied unity was to demonstrate that 'a new government, representative of the Polish people, had been created, pledged to an election on the basis of universal suffrage by secret ballot . . . When such elections were held in Poland . . . Great Britain would salute the government which emerges without regard for the Polish government in London.'

Ignoring the previous charade over inviting Polish leaders to Yalta, Molotov said blandly that it was very hard to resolve the Polish question without the participation of the Poles themselves. Roosevelt sought to move things on by suggesting that, since all were agreed on the need for free elections, the only remaining issue was how Poland should be governed until then. Stalin, who had listened in silence to these exchanges, now spoke at greater length than usual, making clear his own rejection of the US proposals by stating, 'Molotov is right'. He insisted the situation was by no means as 'tragic' as Churchill had made out. The British and Americans could send their own observers to Poland where they would discover that the popularity of the provisional government – admittedly not composed of 'geniuses' – was 'truly tremendous'.

Stalin spoke of the psychology of the Poles whose sympathies lay with those who had stayed in the country and suffered with them under a brutal occupation, rather than with those who had left. He also claimed that the Red Army's advance into Poland had transformed the age-old hostility of the Poles to the Russians into tremendous goodwill. They viewed their liberation from the Nazis as 'a great national festival in their history'. Clearly implying that the Americans and the British were being hypocritical, he compared the legitimacy of the Lublin government with that of the unelected de Gaulle, asking, 'who is more popular?' and pointing out that the two had concluded treaties with the French leader. 'Why was more to be demanded of Poland than of France?' he asked, then came to the crux. The way to achieve agreement at Yalta was to focus on reconstructing the existing provisional government in Warsaw – not to attempt to set up a new one.

Roosevelt tried to shift the debate back to holding elections in Poland, saying his main concern was early elections and asking how soon they could be held. 'In about one month unless there is a catastrophe on the front and the Germans defeat us,' Stalin said, adding with a smile, 'I do not think this will happen.' Churchill conceded the holding of free elections would settle the worries of the British government and Roosevelt suggested deferring further discussions until the following day to allow Foreign Ministers to reconsider the issues, prompting rare jocularity from Molotov who said, laughing, 'The other two will outvote me.'

After briefly discussing the obstacles to forming a unified government in liberated areas of Yugoslavia and the current situation in Greece, where Stalin assured Churchill he had no desire to intervene but merely to know the facts, and Churchill reciprocated by saying that he was 'very much obliged to Marshal Stalin for not having taken too great an interest in Greek affairs', the meeting finally broke up at 7.40 p.m. Stalin again had conceded nothing. On Poland's government, he had told Lavrentii Beria,

'We shall allow one or two émigrés in, for decorative purposes, but no more,' and true to his word he had not budged. A depressed Eden wrote in his diary, 'February 8th: Not such a good day. Stuck again over Poland.'

Roosevelt was exhausted. Howard Bruenn recalled how the President emerged from an 'arduous' and 'emotionally disturbing' meeting 'worried and upset' about Poland and looking even more worn than the day he had arrived in Yalta. His complexion was grey. When Bruenn took his blood pressure he discovered for the first time that the President was suffering from 'pulsus alternans' − a condition in which strong heartbeats alternate with weak ones and a sure indication of an overtaxed heart. Bruenn had already done what he could to restrict his patient's working hours. Again taking Anna Boettiger into his confidence about her father's condition, he sought her help in restricting them further and ensuring that the President received no visitors until noon.

However, Roosevelt had less than an hour to rest and change his clothes before departing for the grand dinner Stalin was hosting that night at the Yusupov Palace. Tropical plants fringed the double doors though which the guests entered the fifty-foot-long, twenty-five-foot-high dining room which had a large half-moon window high in one wall and an elegant Moorish-style fireplace. The table was laid with the very best china and crystal the Moscow hotels had produced. Cadogan rejoiced he had not been invited. Some of the thirty guests who had, anticipated little enjoyment. Brooke feared it would be 'one of those late nights with many toasts and much vodka'. He was right. They would have to sit through twenty courses and forty-five toasts, with people moving endlessly up and down the long table to clink glasses with the person being toasted. Leahy recalled how 'All the people who had any sense watered their liquor and managed to stay alert.' He also remembered voracious mosquitoes buzzing beneath the table 'that worked very successfully on my ankles'.

Stalin himself, well pleased with what he called 'the good, very good' agreement with Roosevelt on Soviet entry into the war against Japan, was in 'excellent humour and even in high spirits', teasing Gusev, the Soviet ambassador to London, 'for always being glum and serious and for never cracking a smile'. The 'regular giant of a man wearing a black alpaca jacket' who stood behind the Soviet leader's chair and 'occasionally helped with the waiting and sometimes advised the great man what to eat and drink' intrigued the British and Americans. British naval chief Andrew Cunningham wondered whether he was Stalin's personal body-guard but next day saw the same man, 'unless my eyes deceived me . . . in a General's uniform'.

Stettinius was observing Lavrentii Beria, who was among the guests and whom he had not seen before at Yalta. 'I had been informed that he was one of the strong men in the Politburo, and he impressed me that evening as being hard, forceful and extremely alert.' Cunningham, sitting beside Stettinius, noted Beria's 'satur-nine' expression and how 'he listened very carefully to all that was said, and drank all the toasts in lemonade or mineral water'. Beria also intrigued Roosevelt, who asked who he was. A grinning Stalin, speaking loudly so Beria could hear, said – just as he had once told Ribbentrop – 'Ah, that one, that's our Himmler,' a comparison Beria resented deeply, as Stalin very well knew.

Despite the frequent moments of 'irritation and bitterness' in recent days, Charles Bohlen was struck by the generally benev-olent mood that night. So was Churchill, who recalled that 'even Molotov was in genial mood'. One reason, perhaps, was the knowledge that for better or worse, the conference with its strains and stresses, would soon be over. Writing to his wife that day Cadogan predicted the conference would end on Sunday 11 February or Monday at the latest and that he would be home by the middle of the month, which would be a relief: 'caviare [sic] and mince pies for breakfast are all very well once in a way, but they pall after a bit.'

The inevitable toasts began. Stalin first proposed the health of Churchill – 'the bravest governmental figure in the world'. He lauded Britain for standing alone 'when the rest of Europe was falling flat on its face before Hitler' and claimed he could think of few other instances when one man's bravery had been so crucial 'to the future history of the world'. Churchill was 'his fighting friend and a brave man' and he laughingly quoted Ribbentrop who in 1939 had assured him 'the British and Americans were only merchants and would never fight'. Stalin's passion convinced Clark Kerr that 'Stalin has got an impression of the P.M. as a broth of a boy, full of guts and determination'. Not to be outdone in fulsome rhetoric, Churchill hailed Stalin as 'the mighty leader of a mighty country which had taken the full shock of the German war machine, had broken its back and had driven the tyrants from her soil'.

Stalin next toasted Roosevelt. He himself and Churchill 'had had relatively simple decisions'. They had been fighting for their countries' 'very existence against Hitlerite Germany'. Roosevelt's position had been very different. Though his country had not seriously faced invasion, the President 'had been the chief forger of the instruments which had led to the mobilization of the world against Hitler' and Stalin again singled out the Lend-Lease programme as one of the President's 'most remarkable and vital achievements'. Roosevelt replied graciously, likening the atmosphere that night to 'that of a family' and claimed that the Big Three had met in Yalta 'to give to every man, woman and child on this earth the possibility of security and wellbeing'.

Stalin, at his most genial, also said:

> I am talking as an old man; that is why I am talking so much. But I want to drink to our alliance, that it should not lose its character of intimacy, of its free expression of views. In the history of diplomacy I know of no such close alliance of three Great Powers as this, when allies had the opportunity of so frankly expressing their views.

However, he struck the most realistic note that night when in toasting the alliance between the Big Three, he observed that maintaining unity in wartime when there was a common enemy to defeat was 'not so difficult'. The harder challenge would come after the war when differing interests might divide the Allies, but he expressed himself confident that they would withstand the test. It would be the three leaders' duty to ensure their relations in peacetime were 'as strong as they had been in wartime'.

Shortly before the dinner broke up, Churchill – perhaps under the influence of 'buckets of Caucasian champagne which would undermine the health of any ordinary man', as Cadogan observed of Churchill's consumption at Yalta, or of the Armenian brandy on offer – proposed yet another toast. They 'were all standing on the crest of a hill . . . with the glories of future possibilities stretching before us'. A leader's duty was:

> to lead the people out from the forests into the broad sunlit plains of peace and happiness. This prize . . . was nearer our grasp than at any time before in history, and it would be a tragedy for which history would never forgive us if we let this prize slip from our grasp through inertia or carelessness.

For the translators it was a hard night after a long, hard day. Charles Bohlen always enjoyed Churchill's 'extraordinarily impressive oratory', noting how carefully he crafted and practised apparently extemporary remarks. However, he considered that his speeches suffered 'a great deal from translation':

> While I suppose serious hours of work might have produced a Russian equivalent to Churchill's masterly use of English, the immediate responsibility of the interpreter did not permit this and they largely came out relatively colourless, relatively flat. But sometimes the passion and feeling in his voice would be transmitted to Stalin. It is a question at international conferences working through interpreters whether eloquence is ever worth the trouble it costs to produce.

However, the translators had their reward. To their amazement during the dinner Stalin 'got up, glass in hand and said':

> Tonight, and on other occasions, we three leaders have got together. We talk, we eat and drink, and we enjoy ourselves. But meanwhile our three interpreters . . . have to work, and their work is not easy. They have no time to eat or drink. We rely on them to transmit our ideas to each other. I propose a toast to our interpreters.

Arthur Birse recalled, 'Stalin then walked around the table, clinking glasses with each one of us.' Churchill raised his glass, exclaiming: 'Interpreters of the world unite! You have nothing to lose but your audience!' This parody of the Communist slogan 'so tickled Stalin's sense of humour that it was some minutes before he could stop laughing'.

Watching and listening with fascination were the 'Little Three' as the leaders called them – Sarah Oliver, Anna Boettiger and Kathleen Harriman – whom Stalin had invited. Sarah wrote to her mother, 'The "Bear" as host was in terrific form.' The three women were the subject of frequent toasts. Warned by her father 'that the price of my meal ticket would be a toast in Russian' and coached on what to say by Bohlen, sitting to one side of her, and General Antonov sitting on the other, Kathleen Harriman stood and thanked their hosts for all they had done 'to make everyone so comfortable'. 'Jesus, I was scared,' she wrote home afterwards.

Before the meal began, Sarah Oliver, helped by the normally austere and distant Ivan Maisky – 'very friendly' she thought – had recited to Beria the five Russian sentences she had mastered, including, 'Can I have a hot water bottle please,' to which the security chief leerily replied, 'I cannot believe that you need one! Surely there is enough fire in you.' Kathleen Harriman was amused when during the dinner the somewhat tipsy Archibald Clark Kerr, whom she knew well from Moscow, toasted Beria as the 'man who looks after our bodies', writing to her sister, 'Archie always seems to get an obscene touch to his toast.'

Churchill wasn't pleased to have his eccentric ambassador toast Beria with such an inept innuendo. He walked round to Clark Kerr and instead of clinking glasses shook his finger at him and warned, 'None of that. Be careful, Archie, be careful.' Nevertheless, Clark Kerr and Beria were soon enthusiastically debating the sex life of fish.

The stocky, Australian-born British ambassador, who wrote his diplomatic dispatches with goose quills plucked from a flock of geese he kept especially for that purpose, indeed had a lewd sense of humour. He famously wrote from Moscow to a friend during the war:

In these dark days man tends to look for little shafts of light that spill from Heaven . . . So I propose to share with you a tiny flash that has illuminated my sombre life and tell you that God has given me a new Turkish colleague whose card tells me that he is called Mustapha Kunt. We all feel like that, Reggie, now and then, especially when Spring is upon us, but few of us would care to put it on our cards.

The dinner finally broke up well after midnight. Churchill returned with his daughter to the Vorontsov, 'sentimental and emotional', Moran wrote. Secretary Marian Holmes, waiting up for him in the little office adjoining his bedroom, knew he had returned when she heard him singing 'The Glory Song', a boisterous Evangelical hymn. He told her gleefully that he had persuaded Stalin to drink the King's health – something he had previously declined to do.

Others were merely relieved the evening was over. Writing to Pamela Churchill 'while letting the vodka settle', Peter Portal told her it had been:

a very trying meal . . . FDR was very wet indeed, and just blathered. U.J. in marvellous form and so was big W, but as usual he ran away from the interpreter & was untranslatable . . . Honestly, FDR spoke more tripe to the minute than I have ever heard before, sentimental twaddle without a spark of real wit.

Brooke took an even dimmer view. 'Stalin was in the very best of form, and was full of fun and good humour apparently thoroughly enjoying himself', but 'the standard of the speeches was remarkably low and most consisted of insincere slimy sort of slush! I became more and more bored, and more and more sleepy, and on and on it dragged.'

Stettinius went to bed that night with the UN still very much on his mind. He woke suddenly in the early hours,

with a clear picture in my mind of San Francisco playing host to the United Nations. My mind raced with enthusiasm and freshness. I saw Nob Hill, the Opera House . . . the Fairmont and the St. Francis Hotel, each filling its purpose. I saw the golden sunshine, and as I lay there on the shores of the Black Sea in the Crimea, I could almost feel the fresh and invigorating air from the Pacific.

The Allied advance continued that day. Montgomery launched his new offensive, Operation Veritable, aimed at driving south from Nijmegen to clear German troops from the area between the Rhine and Maas Rivers as part of Eisenhower's 'broad front' strategy to secure the west bank of the Rhine. In cold, grey, miserable weather Veritable began with a five-hour barrage by 1,034 guns – the heaviest of the war in the West – followed by an advance along an eight-mile front of five British and Canadian infantry divisions and three armoured brigades. Lieutenant-General Brian Horrocks found the sight 'awe-inspiring. All across the front shells were exploding. We had arranged for a barrage, a curtain of fire, to move forward at a rate of 300 yards every twelve minutes, or 100 yards every four minutes, in front of the troops.' To signal when the guns would increase their range 'they all fired a round of yellow smoke . . . I could see small scattered groups of men and tanks all moving slowly forward'. 'All our thoughts are with you and your splendid troops,' Churchill found time to telegraph Montgomery that day. 'Strike hard for victory in the West.'

In a slave labour camp at Peenemünde, on a Baltic island where the German scientists and engineers led by Werner von Braun researched and produced their V2 ballistic missiles, a Russian prisoner, fighter pilot Mikhail Petrovich Devyataev, knew that unless he got away he would soon be dead either of starvation or at the hands of his brutal guards who considered him and his compatriots as 'Untermensch', subhuman. His solution on 8 February was to steal the camp commandant's plane. Persuading the nine other members of his work gang to join him, they killed a guard with a crowbar and stole his uniform so one of them could impersonate him. Then, 'escorted' by the fake guard, they

marched a mile to the airfield where the commandant's Heinkel
111 was standing. It took time to start the twin engines and
Luftwaffe mechanics were already at work on other aircraft nearby
by the time they were ready to take off. However, no one challenged them and as the Heinkel raced along the runway and rose
into the sky, they broke into the Communist Internationale.*

Disaster nearly followed. Devyataev had never flown this type
of plane before and didn't know how to raise the undercarriage.
The aircraft went into a sharp nosedive. He struggled with the
lever controlling the flaps to level out the plane but, by now
emaciated and weighing only ninety pounds, he lacked the
strength. Only when others entered the cockpit and added their
efforts to his did he manage to pull back the lever and fly on
along the Baltic coast to attempt a crash-landing in snow behind
the Soviet lines. As the Heinkel touched the ground its undercarriage collapsed. The first Red Army soldiers to reach the shaken
escapers greeted them as heroes. But they were followed by
members of Beria's NKVD who refused to believe their story
and alleged, 'This is obviously a German plot.' Devyataev's
companions were sent to penal battalions and five were killed in
the subsequent weeks crossing German minefields. He himself
was locked up in solitary confinement and only released a year
after the war ended. He later said, 'the sun began to shine for
me again only when Stalin died'.

While Stalin feasted his guests at the Yusupov, in Berlin Hitler
studied a grandiose architectural model for the post-war reconstruction of his birthplace of Linz in Austria, destroyed by Allied
bombing, which he wished to rise phoenix-like as one of five
'Fuhrer Cities' of the Third Reich. As they viewed the model he
told an SS general worried about the state of the German people's
morale, 'Do you imagine I could talk like this about my plans for
the future if I did not believe deep down that we really are going
to win this war at the end.'

* Werner von Braun later became one of the heads of the NASA Space Programme.

CHAPTER ELEVEN

'Quite a Decent Arrangement
About Poland'

Next morning, Friday 9 February, despite Dr Bruenn's banning of visitors before midday, after he had bathed and breakfasted, Roosevelt had a private meeting with Stettinius. The Secretary of State was full of excitement about his idea of holding the UN Conference in San Francisco, which he had cleared even earlier that morning with Marshall and King. However, the President did not respond as positively as he had hoped, saying, 'It sounds most interesting, Ed, but we have called off all unnecessary movements of people, conventions, and so forth. What about transporting these people two or three thousand miles unnecessarily?' He asked Stettinius to discuss it with Byrnes.

Roosevelt's lack of enthusiasm on a subject he cared so much about was perhaps a sign of extreme weariness. At around this time, hearing that the President was feeling unwell, Stalin visited him, accompanied by Molotov and Gromyko. In his memoirs the latter wrote,

The President was delighted to see us, as he was confined to his bed and had hardly any visitors. He was clearly tired and drained, though he tried not to show it. We sat with him for maybe twenty minutes, while he and Stalin exchanged polite remarks about health, the weather and the beauties of the Crimea. We left him when it seemed that Roosevelt had become detached, strangely remote, as if he could see us, yet was gazing somewhere into the distance.

Outside the room, halting to pack his pipe with tobacco, Stalin said quietly, 'Why did nature have to punish him so? Is he any worse than other people?' Roosevelt's frail condition also struck Fenya, an elderly Russian chambermaid from Moscow's Metropol Hotel who, on her return from Yalta, said of him, 'Such a sweet and kind man, but so terribly, terribly ill.' Anna Boettiger worried about the strain her father was under while so many aides had nothing to do but 'sit on their fannies and play gin rummy' or watch the latest films shown every night in an upstairs conference room.

Roosevelt, though, had not given up. With the conference nearing its close and having achieved his objectives of Soviet agreement to enter the war with Japan and to his plans for the UN, he was particularly anxious to settle the matter of Poland. That morning he impressed on Stettinius how hard it would be to convince the American people that participating in 'a world organization for peace and security' would be worthwhile if the Polish question could not be settled. To move things along he instructed Stettinius to withdraw the US proposal for a presidential committee to oversee the establishment of a new Polish government and to prepare a revised statement on Poland.

Churchill was also feeling the strain. That morning Sarah Oliver wrote to her mother that 'Papa's eyes are sore and are bothering him quite a bit. Charles [Moran] thinks he should see another eye-man when he gets back.' At noon, Churchill joined Roosevelt to receive the final report of their Combined Chiefs of Staff detailing plans to ensure 'at the earliest possible date the unconditional surrender of Germany and Japan'. Their recommended planning dates for the defeat of Nazi Germany were 1 July 1945 at the earliest and 31 December 1945 at the latest, and for Japan some eighteen months later.

Roosevelt and Churchill accepted their report without amendment but during brief discussions Churchill suggested inviting

the Soviet Union to join the US, Britain and China in issuing a
four-power ultimatum to Japan 'to surrender unconditionally' or
face 'the overwhelming weight of all the forces of the four powers'.
Even if Japan sought some 'mitigation of the full rigour of unconditional surrender' this might be worth considering if it led to
'the saving of a year or a year and a half of a war in which so
much blood and treasure would be poured out'. Roosevelt thought
the idea worth mentioning to Stalin but doubted whether an
ultimatum 'would have much effect on the Japanese, who did not
seem to realize what was going on in the world outside . . . They
would be unlikely to wake up to the true state of affairs until all
of their islands had felt the full weight of air attack.' Brooke
characteristically dismissed the debate as a waste of time,
complaining in his diary that for a fruitless forty-five minutes the
two leaders 'meandered about amongst their thoughts and failed
to produce any suggestions worthy of the long delay'.

With military issues largely settled, the Chiefs of Staff would
leave Yalta shortly but the Foreign Ministers, gathered in the
Livadia's white ballroom under Stettinius's chairmanship that day,
faced a longer haul. Poland again topped the agenda. As Roosevelt
had instructed, Stettinius announced that the US would no longer
push for a presidential committee and suggested the Big Three
were not, after all, so far apart. Any disagreements were largely
about semantics and he had a new 'formula' to propose.

Reading from a prepared statement, Stettinius suggested that
the existing Lublin government 'be reorganized' into a fully representative government including democratic leaders from within
Poland and abroad. Molotov, Clark Kerr and Harriman should
be authorized to consult all the relevant parties on how to achieve
this. Once the 'reorganized' government was in place, as soon as
practicable it had to hold elections which 'The Ambassadors of
the three powers in Warsaw . . . would be charged with the
responsibility of observing and reporting to their respective
Governments on the carrying out of the pledge in regard to free
and unfettered elections.'

Molotov said before responding in detail he needed to study a
Russian translation of Stettinius's statement. Eden, who recognized

that the reference to a 'reorganized' government implied a retreat from the demand for a 'new' government, reiterated that 'hardly anyone in Great Britain' believed the Lublin government represented the Polish people. Only a new government, particularly one with Mikołajczyk as a member, would convince British political and public opinion. Molotov at once battened on to the divide between the Americans and the British, arguing – as had Roosevelt the previous day – that holding elections quickly was what mattered, rather than the composition of the interim government. As regards Mikołajczyk, his inclusion in the government would be for the Poles to decide. According to his memoirs, Eden lost his temper with the Russians: 'I fairly let them have it, told them something of British opinion, said I would far rather go back without a text than be a party to the sort of thing they wanted.'

A pause followed while a hastily prepared Russian translation of Stettinius's statement was handed to Molotov, who said he could give no definitive answer without consulting Stalin which he hoped to do before the plenary session opened. Nevertheless, he suggested two points of principle. First, the existing Lublin government should be the basis of any new Polish government. Second, though ambassadors could 'of course' observe and report on the elections as they saw fit, no reference to this should be included in the formal statement for fear of offending the Poles by suggesting 'they were under the control of foreign diplomatic representatives'. With no agreement, Stettinius said they would have to report to the plenary session that their discussions remained deadlocked.

The Foreign Ministers then moved on to debate German reparations. The Soviet delegation had earlier circulated a paper setting out their views, to which Stettinius now presented counter-proposals which were close to Stalin's demands four days before. The nations which had sacrificed most in the war should be first in the queue for compensation. Germany should pay in two ways – first by surrendering items such as equipment, rolling stock, machine tools, ships and overseas investments to ensure its military and economic disarmament, secondly through annual deliveries of commodities for the next ten years. The issue of using German forced labour as a form of reparations should be deferred 'for the moment'. In deciding the total reparations to be extracted from Germany, the special commission set up in Moscow would bear in mind the Soviet Union's suggested total of $20 billion.

Ivan Maisky, Stalin's reparations 'expert', said the Soviet Union agreed the US proposals for the type of reparations Germany was to pay. However he cautioned that a total of $20 billion should only be used for planning purposes, since the final sum 'might be a little more or less'. Returning to Stalin's earlier demands, Molotov sought a commitment that $10 billion would go to Russia. Stettinius countered that the best solution would be to agree that the Soviet Union would receive 50 per cent of the total, to which Molotov grudgingly agreed. Eden, who adamantly opposed specifying any total figure until the Moscow commission had ascertained how much wealth Germany still possessed, found himself isolated and said he must discuss this with his government colleagues.

On the forthcoming UN conference, Stettinius said the United States intended to consult both China and France as the UN's fourth and fifth sponsoring powers about UN matters discussed at Yalta before issuing invitations to nations to attend, and Eden and Molotov agreed. The three ministers also agreed that the topics outlined in the invitations should not include territorial trusteeships – a subject which should be left to the five permanent members of the Security Council to explore through diplomatic channels before the conference opened.

When the meeting adjourned, Foreign Ministers were free to prepare for that day's plenary session since they had given up holding official lunches after their midday meetings. 'Thank Goodness . . . It's a most tiresome and distracting habit. Molotov proposes a toast immediately the meal has begun. Someone has to reply and propose another. And so it goes on. One is always rising to one's feet and having to devise some silly remarks,' Cadogan wrote to his wife with relief. He particularly resented having to toast Vyshinsky – 'a great villain' about whose health 'I don't care tuppence'.

Roosevelt lunched that day with his daughter Anna, Harriman and his daughter Kathleen, Churchill and Sarah Oliver and Leahy and Byrnes. During the meal, served by the President's Filipino mess team, conversation centred on the UN with Churchill agreeing the US, Britain and the Soviet Union should have equal voting power in the General Assembly. Roosevelt, at Byrnes's prodding, agreed to write to Stalin requesting additional seats in the Assembly for the US.

At 3.30 p.m. US Chiefs of Staff again met their Russian counterparts to thrash out the Soviet Union's needs in the Pacific for war with Japan. Having consulted Stalin, Antonov said that since the enemy might disrupt the operation of the Trans-Siberian railway, the Russians could not rely on it to support their forces. They therefore needed secure sea and air supply routes to be kept open across the Pacific, particularly for the shipment of fuel and food. Antonov also said that the USAAF would be permitted to establish air bases in eastern Siberia large enough to accommodate B-29 Superfortresses and that US assistance in defending the large Kamchatka Peninsula would be 'very useful'. The only jarring note, in a meeting conducted, according to the US record 'in a friendly tone', occurred when Antonov complained that persistent US requests for assurance that joint US–USSR military planning in Moscow would be 'vigorously pursued' implied that the Americans doubted his and the Soviet Union's good faith. Marshall hastily assured Antonov this was not so.

Shortly before 4 p.m. the three leaders gathered for a photo call in the rug-strewn colonnaded courtyard of the Livadia where three chairs stood ready. Roosevelt, enveloped in his favourite dark cape, was helped to the middle chair. Churchill, wearing a Russian fur hat to the amusement of Roosevelt and Stalin and swaddled in a buff-coloured army greatcoat sat, cigar clamped between his jaws, to his right. Stalin, in a grey-green red-flashed army greatcoat with gold epaulettes and wearing a military cap, sat to his left. Their diplomatic and military staffs waited in the background. Robert Hopkins, present among the photographers and movie cameramen, recalled 'a kind of euphoria among the principals and members of all three delegations for what had been accomplished during the conference. Their faces reflected relief from the strain of negotiations, and there was laughter and good-natured banter.'

Gesturing Hopkins over, Roosevelt asked, 'How do you want to handle this, Robert?' The young man positioned each of the Foreign Ministers – the patrician Eden, the silver-haired Stettinius, both in dark suits, and the short, squat, overcoated Molotov in a high-crowned hat – behind his respective leader. Once these pictures had been taken, Hopkins motioned the military chiefs and others forward to ensure a comprehensive photographic record of the conference. His father was, however, not among them because 'Dad was too ill to attend and remained in bed.'

While Robert Hopkins was photographing Stalin and Molotov, posing side by side beneath an arch, Stalin motioned him over and smilingly shook his hand. Through an interpreter, Stalin, who had met him before, asked what Robert had been doing recently to which he replied he had been filming action on the German front. When Stalin asked what he wanted to do next, Hopkins told him, 'Well, I want to be the first American photographer in Berlin, but this seems unlikely, since your troops are on the outskirts of the city, and we're 125 [sic] miles away.' 'How would you like to be attached to the Red Army?' Stalin asked. Overlooking the fact that the Marshal could do whatever he wanted, an astonished Hopkins blurted out, 'Could you arrange that?' 'You take care of it from your end, and I'll take care of it from ours,' was the reply.

However, when an excited Robert hurried to his father's sickroom with the news of Stalin's offer, Hopkins senior told him flatly, 'You can't go.' Even when Robert complained about missing 'the biggest story of the war!' he would not budge. Neither would he advise his son on what to say to Stalin, snapping, 'That's your problem.' When Robert awkwardly informed Stalin he had to decline his offer the Soviet leader 'merely shrugged'.

Robert Hopkins's woes that afternoon were nothing compared with those of twenty-nine-year-old Samary Gurary, a captain in the Red Army and a professional photographer formerly employed by the Soviet paper *Izvestiia*. In his haste after the shoot Gurary opened his camera before rewinding the film. Immediately he snapped it shut but was sure he had exposed the film and ruined it. Gurary knew Stalin personally vetted official photos of himself and would take a particular interest in pictures of such a signif-icant event as the Yalta Conference. 'During the ten minutes that it took to develop the film, my life hung by a thread,' Gurary recalled. Luckily for him his shots of the three leaders were undamaged and appeared in the most prestigious Soviet organ of all, *Pravda*.

Despite the smiles and camaraderie during the photo session, the sixth plenary session, when it convened soon after in the ballroom, warmed as usual by a log fire, would be one of the most gruelling of the conference. When Stettinius reported that the Foreign Ministers still could not agree on Poland, discussions on the subject once again went round in circles. Molotov, who had by now discussed the latest US proposals with Stalin, announced that the Soviet Union was 'very anxious' to reach agreement for which the US proposals provided a suitable foun-dation, subject to 'certain amendments'. The statement on Poland should read: 'The present Provisional Government of Poland should be reorganised on a wider democratic basis with the inclusion of democratic leaders from Poland itself and from those living abroad' and be called 'the National Provisional Government of Poland'. References to 'democratic parties' should be qualified by the addition of 'non-Fascist and anti-Fascist'. Finally, references to ambassadors observing and reporting on the elections 'should be eliminated' as offensive to the Poles.

Then, in a clumsy attempt to deflect discussion, Molotov tried to raise the delay in establishing a new government in Yugoslavia, for which the Russians blamed the British. Churchill was having none of it. Stating that the Yugoslavian situation was nearly resolved, he insisted on returning to 'the urgent, immediate and painful problem of Poland'. He cautioned against taking decisions in a rush just because 'there remained only 48 hours for their meetings' and everyone was eager 'to put foot in the stirrup and be off', especially since, if they failed to settle the Polish question, 'the whole Conference would be regarded as a failure'. When

Churchill asked for time to study the latest proposals, Roosevelt suggested that Stettinius complete his report of the Foreign Ministers' meeting, after which they should break for half an hour.

Stettinius's report went relatively smoothly until he reached the proposal that the five permanent members of the Security Council should discuss the subject of territorial trusteeships before the UN conference opened. Churchill erupted. Even the restrained Soviet official note of the discussions recorded his 'great agitation'. He shouted that he did not agree. Under no circumstances 'would he ever consent to forty or fifty nations thrusting interfering fingers into the life's existence of the British Empire. As long as he was [Prime] Minister he would never yield one scrap of their heritage.' Eden, who was attempting to calm Churchill, thought Stalin was positively enjoying his outburst. He 'got up from his chair, walked up and down, beamed, and at intervals broke into applause'.

Roosevelt and Stettinius assured Churchill that the trusteeships in question concerned not the British Empire but dependent areas to be taken from enemy hands, such as 'the Japanese islands in the Pacific'. However, some time passed before Churchill, aquiver with rage and repeating 'never, never, never', could be persuaded to listen. Calming down a little, he said he had no objection to enemy territory coming under trusteeship, but demanded it be explicitly stated that trusteeships had no relevance to the British Empire. Then he 'dramatically turned to Stalin' to ask how he would feel 'if an international organisation had offered to place the Crimea under international control as an international holiday resort'. Stalin dulcetly assured him he 'would willingly make the Crimea available for Three-Power conferences'. The irony remained that the Soviet Union, with its vast expanses inhabited by diverse peoples, was as much an empire as the British one.

After the recess to allow scrutiny of Molotov's latest Polish formula, Roosevelt suggested hopefully that the three powers were 'now very near agreement and it was only a matter of drafting'. For example, governments like his own which still recognized the London government, had difficulty with the Lublin group being described in Molotov's document as the 'Provisional Government' and would prefer the substitution of the words 'The Government now operating in Poland'. He also asked that the reference to foreign ambassadors observing and reporting on the Polish elections be reinstated and suggested that perhaps a little more work by the three Foreign Ministers that evening might settle what was 'only a matter of words and details'.

Churchill agreed politely that good progress had been made on Poland and that Foreign Ministers should consider outstanding points further, but his next words made clear his continuing concerns. He repeated Eden's arguments earlier that day that the Western Allies knew very little about events inside Poland and what they were hearing was alarming: for example that the Lublin government intended 'to try as traitors the members of the Polish Home Army and the underground forces', a situation in which, if true, he asked Stalin to intervene with his 'usual patience and kindness'. Stalin made no response.

Turning to allowing ambassadors to observe the elections, Churchill pointed out that in Yugoslavia Tito had agreed that Russian, American and British observers could attend the elections there. Similarly the British government would welcome foreign observers in Greece and Italy. Roosevelt agreed, telling Stalin that if impartial observers were present it would help him convince the 'six million Poles in the United States' that the elections were fair.

Shifting tack a little, Churchill continued to fight for the London Poles. Though asserting that personally he did 'not care much about Poles', he said it would help him convince the House of Commons that the elections in Poland were free and fair if Mikołajczyk was allowed to participate. Stalin, who had been listening quietly and saying little, replied that as Mikołajczyk's Peasant Party was not Fascist he could, but that this was really a matter for the Poles. 'We shall have to hear what the Poles have to say . . . There are some very good people among them. They are good fighters, and they have had some good scientists and musicians, but they are very quarrelsome.' He also suggested that there were still Fascist elements in Poland. That was why it was so important to qualify the term 'democratic parties' by prefixing it with 'non-Fascist'. Churchill replied that he 'did not much like the division between Fascists and non-Fascists, on the grounds that anybody could call anybody else anything'. All he wanted was for 'all sides to get a fair hearing'.

With the debate on Poland again bogged down, Stalin switched discussion to the 'Joint Declaration on Liberated Europe'. Drafted by the US State Department and approved by the Foreign Ministers, the page-and-a-half-long statement of high-flown ideals was intended for release to the world once the conference ended. It spoke of re-establishing order in a liberated Europe and of rebuilding national economic life to allow 'liberated peoples to destroy the last vestiges of Nazism and Fascism and to create democratic institutions of their own choice'. It also reiterated a key element of the Atlantic Charter – 'the right of all peoples to choose the form of government under which they will live' – and promised that the three great powers would assist the liberated peoples to foster the conditions in which they could exercise these rights. It concluded loftily, 'By this declaration we reaffirm our faith in the principles of the Atlantic Charter . . . and our determination to build, in co-operation with other peace-loving nations, a world order under law, dedicated to peace, security, freedom and general well-being of all mankind.' On first seeing the Declaration, Molotov had told Stalin, 'This is going too far!' to which the Marshal replied, 'Don't worry, work it out. We can deal with it in our own way later. The point is the correlation of forces.'

At the plenary Stalin praised the wording about eradicating Fascism and said that, subject to 'one small change' – stating that support would particularly be given 'to the political leaders of those countries who have taken an active part in the struggle against the German invaders' – he could accept it. He suggested mischievously that Churchill 'need have no anxiety that the proposed Russian amendment applied to Greece' and that he had 'complete confidence in British policy in Greece'.

Roosevelt pointed out that the Joint Declaration would apply 'to any areas or countries where it was needed', including Poland, where the elections would be seen as the first test of the Declaration in practice. That was why, 'like Caesar's wife', they must be 'above suspicion'. 'Caesar's wife only had that kind of reputation. Actually, she wasn't all that lily-white,' Stalin retorted.

Churchill said he could accept the Declaration provided it was clearly understood that the reference to the Atlantic Charter did not embrace the British Empire since the principles it embodied 'already applied' to British territories – a point he had made plain in a statement to Parliament at the time of the Atlantic Charter. He added that he had given a copy of his parliamentary statement to US politician Wendell Wilkie during the latter's visit to London. Roosevelt raised smiles round the table by asking whether 'that was what had killed Mr. Wilkie'; Wilkie had died from a heart attack soon after his visit.

Roosevelt also observed that though France had been mentioned as a sponsor of the Declaration in earlier drafts, the reference had been dropped since France was not represented at Yalta. Perhaps the President's reason for pointing this out was that Harry Hopkins had been working hard to convince him not to marginalize France. Hopkins 'has the good sense to see that a stable Europe is impossible without a strong and virile France', Moran wrote in his diary, adding that Hopkins was a valuable British ally, especially,

> now, when the President's opinions flutter in the wind. He knows the President's moods like a wife watching the domestic climate. He will sit patiently for hours, blinking like a cat, waiting for the right moment to put his point; and if it never comes, he is content to leave it to another time.

'Three powers are better than four,' Stalin immediately responded. However, when Churchill – ever keen to improve France's status – suggested France be asked to associate itself with the Declaration, Roosevelt, pulling back somewhat, proposed adding the topic to the lengthening agenda of the Foreign Ministers' meeting later that evening.

With the hour drawing on, Churchill raised the treatment of German war criminals, calling the subject 'an egg I have laid myself'. In 1943, Molotov, Eden and the then US Secretary of State Cordell Hull had issued the 'Moscow Declaration' on war crimes. Authored largely by Churchill, it called for Germans suspected of atrocities to be 'sent back to the countries in which their abominable deeds were done' and for major war criminals guilty of crimes in more than one country to be tried by the Allies. Churchill now suggested that while they were still in Yalta they should compile a list of the 'grand criminals'.

Stalin asked Churchill what should happen to Rudolf Hess, Hitler's deputy who had parachuted into Britain in 1941 hoping to contact elements in the country sympathetic to concluding peace with Germany. Would prisoners of war like him be considered war criminals? Events would catch up with Hess, Churchill replied, and war criminals – including prisoners of war suspected of crimes – should be given a judicial trial. However, quickly realizing the potential complexities, he dropped his suggestion of drawing up a list of war criminals at Yalta and urged that 'nothing should be published on the subject to prevent the chief criminals from revenging themselves on Allied prisoners of war'. The task of resolving the detail was again left to Foreign Ministers.

As the plenary session drew to a close, Stalin asked whether the Allied offensive in the West had begun. Churchill told him that 100,000 British and Canadian soldiers had launched the attack at dawn the previous day in the Nijmegen area – Montgomery's Operation Veritable. They had already advanced some distance, taking seven towns and villages and 1,800 prisoners. A second wave, made up of the US 9th Army, would push forward the following day as the offensive intensified.

The session finally over, Roosevelt was wheeled back to his rooms where that day's mail from the White House had arrived twenty minutes earlier. By now the courier's journey time from Washington to Yalta had reduced to only three days. Roosevelt was receiving the alcoholic rubdown and light massage in his bedroom that McIntire had ordered for him every evening before dinner when McIntire himself arrived to ask how the conference was going. He found the President buoyant. 'It was with his old smile that he announced, "I've got everything I came for, and not at too high a price".' Stalin had 'agreed to full participation' in the UN. Furthermore, the Soviet Union 'would enter the war against Japan at an early date'. As for China, the situation was 'more than satisfactory'. The Soviet Union would negotiate a treaty of friendship and alliance with Chiang Kai-shek. The only fly in the ointment was Poland, where the situation 'left a good deal to be desired'.

Churchill dined that evening with Brooke, Marshall and Alexander. Brooke found his companions profoundly dull with 'Marshall's never ending accounts about details connected with his life and work, Winston's wanderings on useless strategy, and Alex displaying the smallness of his vision and conception of war in its more complicated aspects of higher direction'.

Like Roosevelt, Churchill remained concerned about Poland. That night he cabled Attlee in London that he was continuing to press on Poland – the key issues were that the elections should be observed and 'informing ourselves properly about what is going on in Poland. All the reality in this business depends on this point', which would 'be fought out' next day.

Meanwhile Moran, hearing of the 'sad scene' a few hours earlier on trusteeships, reflected how, whenever the British Empire was mentioned, Churchill indulged 'in histrionics which do no good' and would do better 'if only he would listen occasionally!' However, he thought the President and Hopkins also seemed to lose their balance when colonies were discussed: 'they might be back in the War of Independence, fighting their English oppressors at Yorktown.' Although the President understood Churchill's sensitivity, 'he cannot leave the Empire alone . . . though he never turns a hair when a great chunk of Europe falls into the clutches of the Soviet Union. I don't think he has ever grasped that Russia is a Police State.'

At 10.30 p.m. that night the Foreign Ministers gathered yet again at the Yusupov Palace where they would work into the early hours. Once more the chief topic – and the chief obstacle – was Poland. Earlier that evening Eden had received a strongly worded cable from the War Cabinet in London instructing him to hold out for the creation of a new government and insisting that ambassadors be allowed to observe the elections. He had accordingly prepared a 'British Revised Formula'. Although Eden fought hard, during ill-tempered discussions he failed to convince Molotov, who suggested that the British proposals were not new but merely a revamped version of the earlier American ones.

The Foreign Ministers finally produced a draft stating that the Lublin government would be 'reorganised on a broader democratic basis with the inclusion of democratic leaders from Poland itself and from those living abroad'. However, despite strenuous efforts by Eden and Stettinius, Molotov refused to allow any reference to the ambassadors of the three powers observing the election and 'the question was finally left for the Prime Minister, the Marshal, and the President to handle at their meeting next day'. Eden was disappointed. Cadogan was more optimistic, writing to his wife that they were close to securing 'quite a decent arrangement about Poland' which he hoped they would be able to 'get over the last hurdle' since if they couldn't 'none of our other high-falutin plans for World Organisation and suchlike would make much sense'.

Turning to the Declaration on Liberated Europe, Stettinius and Eden refused to accept Stalin's proposed amendment that particular 'support should be given to the political leaders of those countries who took an active part in the struggle against the German invaders', knowing it could be used as an excuse to exclude the London Poles from the political process in Poland. This subject, too, was referred back to the three leaders.

However, only limited time remained to resolve outstanding issues and many were already looking beyond the conference. That day, Cadogan wrote to his wife:

We leave here the 11th or 12th. I think Anthony [Eden] and I go to Athens for 24 hours. He's delighted at the prospect of a little trip on his own, without the P.M. who will proceed to Alexandria, where we may join him for a day or two. P.M. has told Attlee that he expects to be back on the 18th.

*

1. Roosevelt, Stalin and Churchill and the US, Soviet and British delegations at the 1943 Teheran Conference – the first meeting of 'The Big Three', as the newspapers called them.

2. The destruction caused in Chiswick, west London, by the first Nazi V2 rocket – a ballistic missile – to hit Britain, which fell on 8 September 1944.

3. The armour-plated *Ferdinand Magellan* railcar that, in late January 1945, carried Roosevelt on the first phase of his journey a third of the way round the world from Washington to Yalta.

4. Roosevelt and Churchill aboard the USS *Quincy*, Valetta Harbour, Malta, on 2 February 1945, eve of the Yalta Conference.

5. Roosevelt and Churchill on arrival at Saki airfield in the Crimea on 3 February 1945. Molotov is to the left of Churchill.

6. Roosevelt aboard the USS *Quincy* in Malta with, from left to right, Leahy, King, Marshall and Kuter.

7. The Italianate Livadia Palace built by the last Tsar where Roosevelt stayed
and the plenary sessions of the Yalta Conference convened.

8. Soviet women working to prepare the Livadia Palace.

9. & 10. The Vorontsov Palace – 'part Scottish castle, part Moorish fantasy' – where Churchill stayed during the conference.

11. One of the lions of the Vorontsov Palace: Churchill admired one so much he wanted to buy it.

12. The Yusupov Palace at Koreiz, once owned by Rasputin's assassin Prince Felix Yusupov, where Stalin stayed during the conference.

13. Photo call for Churchill, Roosevelt and Stalin during the Yalta Conference with their respective foreign ministers, Eden, Stettinius and Molotov, behind them.

D I N N E R

10. Downing Street,
Whitehall.

Caviare
Pies

White and Red Salmon
Shamaya
Salted Herrings
Sturgeon in Aspic

Swiss Cheese
Game
Sausage
Sucking Pig, horse-radish sauce
—
Vol-au-Vent of Game
—
Game Bouillon
Cream of Chicken
—
White Fish, Champagne Sauce
Baked Kefal
—
Shashlik of Mutton
Wild Goat from the Steppes
Pilau of Mutton
—
Roast Turkey
Roast Quails
Roast Partridge
Green Peas
—
Ice Cream
Fruit
Petits Fours
Roasted Almonds
—
Coffee

VORONTSOV VILLA.   FEBRUARY 10th, 1945.

14. The menu of the dinner hosted by Churchill at the Vorontsov Palace on the night of 10 February 1945.

15. Stalin in Moscow, August 1945, with, to his left, Malenkov, Beria and Molotov, and to his immediate right his eventual successor Khruschev.

16. Stanisław Mikołajczyk, Prime Minister of the Polish Government in exile in London during most of the war and briefly postwar deputy Prime Minister.

17. Cadogan and Eden during the Teheran Conference, 1943.

18. Churchill's daughter Sarah, Roosevelt's daughter Anna and Harriman's daughter Kathleen at Yalta where they were known as 'The Little Three'.

19. General Charles de Gaulle, leader of the Free French, who was not invited to Yalta.

20. Roosevelt and Churchill with Chinese Nationalist leader Chiang Kai-shek at their Pre-Teheran meeting in Cairo. Chiang Kai-shek was not invited to Yalta.

21. Roosevelt's meeting with King Ibn Saud of Saudi Arabia on 14 February 1945 aboard the USS *Quincy*, moored in the Great Bitter Lake in the Suez Canal.

22. German refugees forcibly expelled in the latter stages of the war from Eastern Europe.

23. The results of the RAF/USAAF bombing raids on Dresden in mid-February 1945 carried out in fulfilment of commitments made to the Soviets at Yalta.

24. A staged photograph of the capture of Berlin by the Soviet Red Army.

25. Delegates at the first meeting of the United Nations, San Francisco, 25 April 1945.

26. Churchill, Truman and Stalin at the Potsdam Conference held in Allied-occupied Germany between 17 July and 2 August 1945. Attlee would replace Churchill as prime minister during the conference following his victory in the British general election.

27. The atomic bomb 'Little Boy' exploding over Hiroshima, 6 August 1945.

That day, Royal Navy submarine HMS *Venturer* sank the German U-boat *U-864* – the first and only known example of one submarine intentionally sinking another in combat while both were submerged at periscope depth. *Venturer* had been dispatched to hunt for *U-864* after British ULTRA code-breakers decrypted a message suggesting she was off Norway's south-east coast on her way to Japan with valuable equipment for the Japanese military: engine parts and design drawings for Messerschmitt Me 262 jet fighters and over 1,800 canisters of scarce mercury for use in manufacturing explosives. When *Venturer*'s hydrophone operator picked up an unusual sound he could not identify, the commander, twenty-five-year-old Lieutenant Jimmy Launders, decided to track it. Then the officer of the watch spotted through his periscope what he thought was another periscope above the surface of the water. More likely it was one of the new schnorkels which allowed German U-boats to run their diesel engines while submerged. Realizing he had probably located *U-864*, Launders continued to follow her. When she failed to surface he decided to attack anyway, before *Venturer*'s batteries ran down. Hastily making what calculations he could, he ordered the firing of the torpedoes in each of the four bow torpedo tubes. The fourth torpedo hit the pressurized hull of *U-864* which immediately imploded, destroying the vessel with the loss of all seventy-three crewmen aboard.

Also that day, in an operation that survivors would call 'Black Friday', a wave of heavily armed Bristol Beaufighters escorted by Mustang Mk III fighters of RAF No. 65 Squadron attacked the German destroyer *Z33* and her escorting vessels in a Norwegian fjord. Targeted both by Luftwaffe fighters and fierce anti-aircraft fire, nine Beaufighters and one Mustang were lost. On the German side, several ships were damaged and four or five fighters shot down.

For the first time, soldiers of the Russian Liberation Army – Soviet prisoners of war recruited by the Germans – went into action against their own compatriots, attacking a Soviet bridgehead on the right bank of the Oder less than forty-five miles from Berlin. The Liberation Army battalion fought so courageously that four of its members received the Iron Cross.

German tank-busting Stuka pilot Hans-Ulrich Rudel, decorated by Hitler on New Year's Day, was again in action on 9 February, despite the Fuhrer's offer to remove him from front-line duty. He had already destroyed twelve Russian tanks when, diving towards the thirteenth, flak exploded in his cockpit, hitting him in his right leg and temporarily blinding him. His navigator/air gunner guided him to crash-land behind German lines. Rudel's leg was amputated below the knee but he was back in action by the end of March, destroying a further twenty-six enemy tanks before the war's end.[*]

Meanwhile, in his underground bunker, Hitler was reading the nineteenth-century Scottish writer Thomas Carlyle's biography of Frederick the Great of Prussia, the historical figure he most revered. The book had been a gift from Goebbels. In 1762, the persistent and resourceful Frederick had, against all odds, triumphed after a grand coalition against him including the Russian Empire and France collapsed. Hitler clung to the hope that the alliance between the Soviet Union, the US and Britain – currently debating his Reich's future in Yalta – might similarly disintegrate.

Conversely the delegates at Yalta were increasingly cheered by news coming in from the front – 'one can't help wondering how much longer the Germans can stand it', Cadogan wrote that night.

---

[*] Rudel survived the war and emigrated to Argentina where he helped Nazi fugitives from justice and founded a local branch of the Nazi Party before returning to West Germany.

CHAPTER TWELVE

'Judge Roosevelt Approves'

Churchill's eyes still troubled him as he worked in bed next morning, Saturday 10 February, receiving a stream of visitors. Marian Holmes wrote in her diary, 'P.M. a bit irate. Bothered about the sun shining in his eyes. A lot of fuss and bother about fixing the curtain. "Down a little. No, that's too much. A little higher".' 'Have been very hard pressed these last few days', Churchill cabled his wife.

Roosevelt, however, seemed a little revived. Dr Bruenn noted, 'Spirits are much better. Is eating well – delights in Russian food and cooking. *Pulsus alternans* has disappeared. No cough.' Perhaps knowing the conference was almost over was revitalizing him. He was certainly eager to be off, telling Stettinius that morning, 'do everything humanly possible to speed up the conclusion of the Conference'. He wanted to see 'the three kings', as he called Ibn Saud of Saudi Arabia, Haile Selassie of Ethiopia and Farouk of Egypt, on his way back but if the conference dragged on 'interminably', he would be unable to. In the same spirit, he told Stettinius that to reach final agreement on Poland that day he would drop his insistence on a formal statement about ambassadors observing and reporting on the Polish elections, though 'the Russians . . . must understand our firm determination that the ambassadors will observe and report on the elections in any case'.

Stettinius joined the other Foreign Ministers for their meeting at noon at the Vorontsov Palace and duly reported the change in the US position. Eden objected immediately and also sent a note out of the meeting to Churchill informing him and complaining: 'Americans gave us no warning.' From his bed Churchill instructed: 'Certainly do not agree.'

Meanwhile, Molotov proposed his own amendment to the draft agreement. Instead of calling for the US and British governments to recognize the Polish Provisional Government of National Unity, it would instead require them to recognize 'the Polish Government as has been done by the Soviet Union'. This time, however, Eden and Stettinius were as one, objecting that their governments must be seen to be recognizing 'a new Polish Government', something all three powers – including the Soviet Union – had to do in unison. Faced by this opposition, Molotov proposed they simply report to the plenary session where discussions had reached.

Stettinius was also firm with Molotov on the draft Declaration on Liberated Europe, again rejecting his proposal the previous day to add that the strongest support would be given to those 'who took an active part in the struggle against German occupation'. Molotov dropped his suggestion but pressed for another amendment. Instead of requiring the signatories to establish 'appropriate machinery' to uphold the Declaration's democratic principles in newly liberated countries or former Axis satellite states, the Declaration should only require them to undertake 'mutual consultation' when problems arose. Stettinius agreed to this considerable weakening of the Declaration as did Eden, who proposed his own change reflecting Britain's wish to bring the French into the new arrangements: that the Declaration express the hope that France would associate itself with it. Stettinius agreed but Molotov, saying he wished to consider it further, asked for it to be referred to the plenary session.

The most difficult topic was reparations from Germany. Eden said the British wanted the agreed reparations commission in Moscow to start work as soon as possible. However, he could not support the previously discussed US proposals for reparations and circulated a redraft. As Molotov and Maisky spotted at once, Eden's text omitted any reference to $20 billion as a possible total. When Maisky protested that without a figure the commission 'would have no basis, no directives for its work', Eden argued that the Soviets were pursuing two near-irreconcilable objectives – depleting German manufacturing capacity and ensuring Germany's ability to make large payments at a later date. Britain, on the other hand, wished to avoid having to finance and feed Germany because of over-harsh reparations and believed no figure should be specified until the commission had studied the question. Britain also considered that reparations should be paid for five years not ten.

Maisky retorted that the British wanted 'to take from Germany as little as possible'. The US proposals did not commit the Allies to an exact figure – $20 billion was for planning purposes only – and the British 'could easily agree' if they wanted to. Eden insisted that Russian expectations of reparations were wholly unrealistic. Having reached an ill-tempered impasse, the issue was deferred to the plenary session.

After briefly discussing the conference's joint final communiqué, the last item considered was Iran. The British delegation had drafted a joint statement that, given the 'remarkable progress' in the war against Germany, Allied troops should begin gradually withdrawing from Iran before hostilities ended. Allied governments should not press 'suggestions for further oil concessions upon the Persian Government' while the withdrawal was under way. Afterwards, however, individual governments would be free to discuss the future exploitation of Iranian oil reserves with the Iranian authorities.

Though Molotov did not challenge the content of the document, despite pressure from Eden and Stettinius he resolutely opposed making any public statement on Iran. The US record of the discussion showed why Molotov had earned his nickname 'stone arse':

Mr. Eden inquired whether Mr. Molotov had considered the British document on Iran.

Mr. Molotov stated that he had nothing to add to what he had said several days ago on the subject.

Mr. Eden inquired whether it would not be advisable to issue a communiqué on Iran.

Mr. Molotov stated that this would be inadvisable.

Mr. Stettinius urged that some reference be made that Iranian problems had been discussed and clarified during the Crimean Conference.

Mr. Molotov stated that he opposed this idea.

Mr. Eden suggested that it be stated that [a previous] declaration on Iran had been reaffirmed and re-examined during the present meeting.

Mr. Molotov opposed this suggestion.

In the early afternoon of this hectic day Molotov and Harriman met at the Yusupov Palace to finalize the secret agreement on Soviet terms for entering the war against Japan. As Harriman quickly realized, Stalin's demands now went beyond those he had sought from Roosevelt two days earlier. Instead of just one port, the draft presented by Molotov referred to the Soviet Union's 'possession' not only of Dairen, as previously discussed, but also of Port Arthur, a neighbouring port in the north-east of China and a Russian naval base from 1898 until lost to the Japanese in 1905 after a heroic defence. Molotov's draft additionally referred to sole Soviet control over the Manchurian railway.

Harriman said he believed the President would require certain amendments – specifically Stalin's agreement that Port Arthur and Dairen should be free ports, that the Manchurian railway should be operated jointly by a Chinese–Soviet commission and that 'the concurrence of Generalissimo Chiang Kai-shek' should be sought. Telling Molotov he must consult Roosevelt, Harriman hurried back to the Livadia Palace where Roosevelt agreed Harriman's suggested changes and asked him to resubmit an amended text to the Soviets.

An unusually large number of black limousines negotiated the hairpin bends of the cliff-top roads that day. Alarmed by that morning's discussion about Poland at the Foreign Ministers' meeting, Churchill drove with Eden to the Yusupov Palace to do battle with Stalin and Molotov at a private meeting. In obdurate mood, Churchill again stressed the backlash he would face from Parliament unless it was clear that a British ambassador would be allowed into Poland to report on what was happening. An evasive Stalin said that as soon as Britain recognized the new Polish government it would, of course, be free to send an ambassador to Warsaw. He, personally, would guarantee that the Red Army would not inhibit the ambassador's movement but added, 'you will have to make your own arrangements with the Polish Government'.

Eden and Churchill had, however, come prepared. They suggested adding to the agreement on Poland a sentence stating that recognition of the new Polish government 'would entail an exchange of Ambassadors, by whose reports the respective Governments would be informed about the situation in Poland', to which, to their relief, Stalin agreed. Although by no means the full-blooded commitment Eden and Churchill had spent hours arguing for, it was something. In his memoirs Churchill called it 'the best I could get'.

Churchill also raised the question of the repatriation of prisoners of war. Concerned to get their men home, the British and Americans had for some months been pushing the Soviet government to cooperate and hoped to use the momentum of the conference to conclude a formal agreement. On 8 February, the US and UK Combined Chiefs of Staff had approved a draft text 'Concerning Liberated Prisoners of War and Civilians' which, in line with Soviet wishes, provided for all Soviet citizens freed by the Western Allies to be returned to the Soviet Union, including soldiers captured fighting for the Nazis. Some within the State Department had argued that the latter could claim protection under the Geneva Convention and that any agreement should say so but Stettinius had overruled them. The first tripartite meeting to discuss the agreement was scheduled for the following day and to avoid any last-minute hitches Eden wanted Churchill to raise it personally with Stalin.

When Churchill did so, asking Stalin what he wished to be done with the large number of Russian prisoners of war the British were holding, he confirmed that they should all be returned 'as quickly as possible' to Russia where those who had fought for the Nazis 'could be dealt with'. Among Stalin's requests were that 'there should be no attempt to induce any of them to refuse repatriation'. Churchill promised his government's full cooperation in meeting Stalin's wishes. In turn, the Prime Minister asked how many British prisoners of war the Red Army had liberated during their advance and 'begged for good treatment for them: every mother in England was anxious about the fate of her prisoner sons'. Stalin replied not entirely accurately that the Red Army had freed 'very few' but acknowledged that as Soviet troops pushed deeper into Germany they might find more and, to Churchill's satisfaction, said the British could send liaison officers behind Red Army lines to oversee their care.

With that, leaving the detail to their subordinates, Churchill and Stalin turned to reparations. Just as Eden had told Molotov, Churchill cautioned Stalin that the enormous sum the Soviet Union was seeking 'would be impossible'. However, he sought to convince Stalin that Britain indeed believed the Soviet Union deserved compensation. He suggested that by removing German factories and equipment from Germany, Russia would be doing Britain a favour by putting an end to German exports which could then be replaced by British ones. As for Britain, it did not want German labour. Neither did it want manufactured goods since this would only create unemployment at home. However, Britain might want raw materials such as potash and timber.

Still unaware of the proposed secret agreement between the US and the Soviet Union, Churchill probed Russian wishes in the Far East. When Stalin said he wanted a naval base such as Port Arthur, Churchill assured him that the British would 'welcome the appearance of Russian ships in the Pacific, and were in favour of Russia's losses in the Russo-Japanese War being made good'.

Finally, Stalin raised the Montreux Convention which in 1936

had awarded Turkey control over the passage of warships between
the Black Sea and Aegean through the Dardanelles, complaining
it was 'intolerable' for Russia to have to beg Turkey for the right
to send ships through the Turkish straits. Churchill promised to
support a Soviet request for changes to the convention's terms.

Meanwhile with their business concluded, most of the UK and
US military chiefs had packed their bags, received farewell parcels
of Russian delicacies from their Soviet counterparts and were on
the bumpy road to Saki airfield. So was Byrnes, whom Roosevelt
was dispatching early back to Washington by air to be his mouth-
piece when the Conference Communiqué was issued. Those who
remained were thinking about their own departure. That afternoon, in spitting rain, Churchill's valet Sawyers took souvenir
photographs of Jo Sturdee and her secretarial colleagues on the
porch of the Vorontsov Palace and on its grand terrace overlooking
the sea.

At 4 p.m. at the Livadia Palace, Roosevelt presented specially
engraved Fourth-Term Inaugural Medallions to Churchill, Stalin,
Eden and Molotov. He also had a particular present for the Russian
leader – a photograph book, 'Target Germany', illustrating the
heavy damage US bombers had inflicted. He and Stalin then
withdrew to his study – their last-ever private meeting – to confer
again about Soviet terms for entering the Pacific war. Stalin agreed
that Dairen should operate as a free port but argued that since
Port Arthur would be a Russian naval base the Soviet Union
wished to lease it. Roosevelt made no objection. In turn, Stalin
accepted that Chiang Kai-shek's agreement would need to be
sought but not immediately due to the need to preserve secrecy.
Stalin would suggest to Roosevelt when he thought the time was
right for the President to do so. The meeting ended after just
twenty minutes.

Shortly afterwards, Roosevelt was wheeled into the Livadia's
ballroom to join the advisers already gathered around the great
circular table. Churchill arrived next. Apologizing to Roosevelt for
his lateness, he added, 'I believe that I have succeeded in retrieving
the situation' – a reference to his recent discussion on Poland with
Stalin at the Yusupov Palace. Stalin arrived five minutes later.

At Roosevelt's invitation, Eden presented the revised draft agreement on Poland which now included the wording Churchill had agreed with Stalin that the UK and US governments 'will establish diplomatic relations with the new Polish Provisional Government of National Unity, and will exchange Ambassadors by whose reports the respective Governments will be kept informed about the situation in Poland'. Roosevelt passed Leahy a copy of the statement. Handing it back, Leahy whispered, 'Mr. President, this is so elastic that the Russians can stretch it all the way from Yalta to Washington without ever technically breaking it.' Roosevelt replied, 'I know, Bill, I know it. But it's the best I can do for Poland at this time.'

Although Roosevelt might have thought the discussion on Poland was over, Churchill pointed out that the text was silent on Poland's future borders. Something had to be said 'otherwise the whole world would wonder what had been decided'. All were agreed on Poland's eastern frontier – that it would follow the Curzon Line with some minor digressions in favour of Poland, though Poland would not gain Lvov.

As for the west, Churchill was prepared to announce that Poland would be compensated 'up to the line of the Oder if the Poles so desired' but did not believe his War Cabinet would accept the line of the Western Neisse. Roosevelt said he would prefer to say nothing about the western border, arguing that the Polish government must be consulted first. However, with Molotov suggesting that something not too specific should be said and Churchill pointing out that he himself was already on record as saying Poland should receive 'a good slice of territory in the North and in the West', Roosevelt gave way and proposed that Churchill should draft some suitable words.

Discussions on the Declaration on Liberated Europe went more smoothly. The leaders approved the revised text and accepted Eden's proposal to attach a note that the three powers hoped France would associate itself with it. At this point Roosevelt, on whom Hopkins's arguments about not marginalizing France had had their effect, announced he had changed his mind about French participation in the Control Commission for Germany. He now agreed with Churchill that allowing France to administer a zone of Germany but not to sit on the commission was illogical. According to Bohlen, a jovial Stalin 'raised his arms above his head and said, "Sdaiyous" – "I surrender!"' In fact, it was no surprise. Harriman had already told Stalin of Roosevelt's change of heart and he had agreed not to oppose it. The three leaders agreed to send de Gaulle a telegram informing him of their decisions.

However, discussion on reparations again quickly turned acrimonious. Churchill read from what he called 'a very severe telegram' from his War Cabinet instructing him not to agree to any specific figure and stating that $20 billion was, in any case, 'far too great. It is roughly the equivalent of Germany's pre-war gross exports,' and beyond the capacity of a 'bombed, defeated, perhaps dismembered' Germany to pay. As Churchill enlarged on his Cabinet's objections, Stettinius admired his eloquence, 'The beautiful phrases just roll out as water in a running stream.'

Hoping to move things on, Roosevelt suggested nothing need be said publicly 'about amounts of money' which should be left to the reparations commission to study. However Stalin was so angry that he rose from his chair. Gripping its back so tightly 'that his brown hands went white at the knuckles', he 'spat out his words as if they burnt his mouth. Great stretches of his country had been laid waste and the peasants put to the sword. Reparations should be paid to the countries that had suffered most.' He then reminded Churchill and Roosevelt that, as they had previously agreed, it was not reparations in money but in goods he sought. 'Was it the wish of the Conference that the Russians should not receive any reparations at all?'

Churchill hastily responded, 'Not at all, on the contrary.' Nevertheless, like Roosevelt, he urged leaving the detail on reparations to the commission in Moscow. Stalin pointed out that the Big Three had not yet formally agreed 'even the principles of levying reparations' and that the US had accepted the Soviet suggestion of a figure of $20 billion for planning purposes. Hopkins scribbled a note to Roosevelt:

Mr. President,
The Russians have given in so much at this conference
that I don't think we should let them down. Let the
British disagree if they want to.

However, Roosevelt continued to urge that 'the whole matter be
left to the Commission in Moscow' while Churchill refused to
budge on mentioning a specific figure.

Finally, grudgingly, Stalin proposed new wording that the Big
Three had agreed that Germany must compensate the Allied
nations for the damage it had caused them during the war and
would instruct the Moscow commission to consider the amount
of reparations. Churchill agreed, then asked the President what
he thought, to which he replied 'Judge Roosevelt approves and
the document is accepted' – an insight into how Roosevelt had
viewed his role in recent days, that of a judge mediating between
two contending parties. According to the Soviet official record,
Stalin enquired 'ironically', 'You will not go back on this
tomorrow?'

After a fifteen-minute pause for tea served in eight-ounce
glasses in silver holders, the session resumed. Stalin raised the
Montreux Convention which gave Turkey control over the
passage of warships from the Black Sea to the Mediterranean,
claiming it was outmoded and that it was impossible to accept
a situation in which Turkey 'had a hand on Russia's throat'. With
a rueful smile Churchill reminded the conference of the 1915
Dardanelles/Gallipoli campaign which had almost ended his
political career: 'I tried some time ago to get through the
Dardanelles and the former Russian government had two army
corps ready to help me at the other end. However, we did not
succeed in joining hands. I consequently have some feeling on
this question.' Stalin attempted to console him, suggesting the
British Empire forces had withdrawn too soon. Churchill
responded, 'I had nothing to do with that decision. I was already
out of the government.'

Rambling a little, Roosevelt said that,

he did not like fortifications between nations . . . Canada and
the United States had had for over a hundred years an unarmed
frontier stretching over three thousand miles . . . It was his
hope . . . that other frontiers in the world would eventually
be without forts or armed forces on any part of their national
boundaries.

Churchill – as he had promised Stalin earlier that day – confirmed
Britain would support a change to the convention, provided Turkey
was assured that neither its sovereignty nor its territorial integrity
would be damaged.

The final act of that day's plenary session was to consider the
re-drafted text on Poland's borders that the British had now
produced following the earlier discussion. Roosevelt accepted it
subject to minor amendment including the substitution of 'the
Heads of the Three Governments' for 'the Three Governments',
explaining that if he committed the US government, rather than
himself as president, he would be obliged to seek the approval
of Congress. Molotov suggested adding that Poland's 'ancient
frontiers in East Prussia and on the Oder' would be returned to
it – a clear reference to a massive extension of Poland's western
boundaries. Roosevelt asked shrewdly 'how long ago these lands
had been Polish'. When Molotov admitted 'very long ago',
Roosevelt joked that 'this might lead the British to ask for the
return of the United States to Great Britain'. Molotov withdrew
his amendment.

After some further debate the leaders finally agreed a less
definitive statement that the heads of government 'considered'
Poland's eastern frontier should follow the Curzon Line, 'with
minor digressions'. The statement went on to recognize that
Poland must receive 'substantial accessions of territory in the
North and the West' but that the leaders 'felt' that the views of
the Polish Provisional Government of National Unity should be
sought and that the final delineation of the western border should
await the eventual peace conference. The subject that had gener-
ated 18,000 words of discussion in the official records was closed
for the remainder of the conference at least.

Then to both Stalin's and Churchill's amazement, Roosevelt announced his intention to leave next day at 3 p.m. Churchill argued that the remaining tasks, including agreeing the Conference Communiqué, might not be accomplished in time and were too important to rush. Stalin suggested cancelling the dinner that Churchill was hosting that evening so they could work on. Instead, after hurried discussion, the three agreed that a communiqué-drafting committee should set to work that night.

At 8 p.m. the plenary finally broke up with everyone, Leahy thought, looking 'thoroughly tired'. Weary though he was, back in his study Roosevelt wrote what would be his last letters of the conference: one to Stalin and one to Churchill. Citing the political difficulties he might face if, alone of the three powers, the US had only a single vote in the UN General Assembly, he sought assurance that, if he requested additional votes to ensure parity with the Soviet Union and Britain, they would support him. Task done, Roosevelt prepared for the last formal banquet.

Churchill had put considerable thought into his dinner at the Vorontsov Palace that night for the three leaders and their Foreign Ministers, with Bohlen, Birse and Pavlov to translate. Applying what Stettinius called his 'great sense of showmanship and appreciation of military pomp', Churchill had summoned a detachment of Royal Marines from the *Franconia* to provide an honour guard as his guests arrived. He personally checked the seating plan and the menu, which was printed with two addresses – 10, Downing Street, Whitehall and the Vorontsov. Marian Holmes noted in her diary that Churchill decided to cut some courses, saying that 'what they would lose in pleasure they would gain in business'. Nevertheless the menu, as at all the Yalta banquets, was extensive. The first course included caviar, salmon, sturgeon and suckling pig with horseradish sauce. Next came vol-au-vent of game, then a choice of two soups, followed by white fish in champagne sauce, then mutton shashlik and pilau and 'wild goat from the steppes', then roast turkey, quails and partridge with green peas, and finally ice cream, fruit, petits fours, roasted almonds and coffee. Abundant quantities of wine, vodka and champagne stood ready.

Numerous Soviet staff had taken an interest in the preparations. Marian Holmes noted 'hordes of Russians working on decorations, fussing with the table' and 'Red Army personnel all over the Palace' checking the security arrangements. Churchill himself recalled, 'They locked the doors on either side of the reception rooms which were to be used for dinner. Guards were posted and no one was allowed to enter. They then searched everywhere – under the tables and behind the walls.'

Jo Sturdee, Marian Holmes, Elizabeth Layton and Joan Bright with other junior British staff 'all massed . . . in the tremendous entrance hall' to watch the guests arrive. Shortly before 9 p.m. Churchill appeared dressed, Marian Holmes noted, 'in his tropical drill Colonel's uniform. He sat in a chair eyeing the Russian soldiery. At two minutes past nine, the entrance doors opened and President Roosevelt was wheeled in.' He was 'surrounded by a posse of behatted and bulldog-jawed Secret Service men' whose 'dark looks of suspicion' amused Elizabeth Layton. 'The P.M. greeted him and the President said in a deep, loud voice "Sorry I'm late. I couldn't get something done up".' His 'dreadfully ill' appearance shocked Joan Bright.

Stalin arrived 'hard on the heels of the President'. Jo Sturdee and others 'happened to be standing near the hat stand (!) and there was old Marshal Stalin positively almost standing on our toes . . . With the Royal Marines, and numerous colourful uniforms of this country – and us – it was a gay sight.' Joan Bright noted that Stalin insisted on taking off his own coat and how 'he and Mr. Churchill had the same tussle together in hanging it up as they had had at Teheran'. Stalin 'remained a little in the background' until Churchill asked courteously, 'may I escort you' and led the Marshal into a reception room where drinks were being served.

While the guests were still grouped around a glowing fire consuming pre-dinner drinks and caviar, Molotov edged up to Stettinius to ask, 'can you not tell us where the [UN] conference is to be held?' Stettinius immediately went to Roosevelt, sitting in his wheelchair, and leaning down said 'Molotov is pressing me on a decision as to a place for the conference. Are you ready to say San Francisco?' 'Go ahead, Ed; San Francisco it is,' Roosevelt replied. Stettinius hurried back to Molotov who, after hearing the news, beckoned Eden over. Together the three Foreign Ministers toasted the success of the forthcoming conference, just ten weeks away.

Churchill described the dinner that followed as convivial, but it had moments of tension. Stalin proposed the King's health but, Churchill recalled, 'in a manner . . . not to my liking', saying he had 'always been against kings, and that he was on the side of the people'. During the meal Stalin made clear his continuing resentment over what had been agreed on reparations, complaining he would have to 'tell the Soviet people they were not going to get any reparations because the British were opposed to it'. To mollify him Churchill and Roosevelt agreed that the Conference Communiqué would mention that Germany was to compensate the Allied nations 'for the damage it had caused' and that the conference protocol, which would not be published, would state that the US and USSR – but not the UK – accepted $20 billion as the basis for planning, of which half would go to Russia.

Churchill then tried a charm offensive. Toasting Stalin's health, he said,

> There was a time when the Marshal was not so kindly towards us, and I remember that I said a few rude things about him, but our common dangers and common loyalties have wiped all that out. The fire of war has burnt up the misunderstandings of the past. We feel we have a friend whom we can trust, and I hope he will continue to feel the same about us.

He went on to envisage 'a Russia which had already been glorious in war as a happy and smiling nation in times of peace'.

Roosevelt told a slightly strange story about a meeting in the American South with a Ku Klux Klan member, an Italian man and a Jewish man. Knowing the anti-Catholic, anti-Semitic bias of the Klan, Roosevelt asked the Klansman whether the other two were also members. The man answered yes – 'they were considered all right since everyone in the community knew them . . . it was a good illustration of how difficult it was to have any prejudices – racial, religious or otherwise – if you really knew people.'

Churchill took Stalin and Roosevelt to his Map Room –'the zenith of the Map Room's career', he later called it – where Captain Pim gave them the latest news: the capture by Canadian troops of the German town of Cleves. Pim recalled Churchill gleefully recounting the tale of King Henry VIII's rejection of his plain fourth wife Anne of Cleves. Then in reference to the great offensive 'which in the course of the next few weeks was to push the Allied forces up to the western bank of the Rhine', Churchill began singing the First World War song, 'When We've Wound up the Watch on the Rhine'. When Stalin suggested that perhaps 'the British wished to make an earlier armistice than the Russians', according to Pim, 'The Prime Minster looked hurt and in a corner of the Map Room, with his hand in his pockets, gave us a few lines of his favourite song, "Keep Right on to the End of the Road".' Stalin looked extremely puzzled. Grinning broadly, Roosevelt told Pavlov, 'Tell your Chief that this singing by the Prime Minister is Britain's secret weapon.'

Back in the dining room for a final drink and smoke, conversation turned to British politics. Stalin expressed scepticism that the Labour Party would ever succeed in forming a government in England. Less encouragingly, Roosevelt commented that Churchill had been in and out of government for many years and had perhaps been 'of even greater service when he was not in the government since he had forced people to think'. Churchill admitted he faced difficult elections shortly since 'he did not know what the Left would do', telling Stalin he had a much easier political task 'since he had only one party to deal with'. As previously, Stalin replied with doubtless sincerity that 'experience had shown one party was of great convenience to a leader of state'. Roosevelt gave Churchill some advice on dealing with socialism and the left, saying that 'any leader of a people must take care of their primary needs'. When he first became president, 'the United States was close to revolution because the people lacked food, clothing and shelter'. He had agreed to provide all that and been elected; 'since then there was little problem in regard to social disorder in the United States'. Later in the wide-ranging conversation about politics, Churchill told Stalin that 'British opposition to Communism was not based on any attachment to private property but to the old question of the individual versus the state', but 'in war the individual of necessity is subordinate to the state'.

As the hour grew late, Stalin tried to persuade Roosevelt to stay longer in Yalta. When Roosevelt told him 'he had three Kings waiting for him in the Near East', including Ibn Saud of Saudi Arabia, conversation turned to the subject of a Jewish homeland. Roosevelt said he was a Zionist and asked whether Stalin was. Stalin said, yes, in principle, but that he 'recognised the difficulty'; the Soviet Union had attempted to establish a national home for Jewish people in Birobidzhan (in Russia's far east) but after two or three years they had dispersed back to the cities. Bohlen recalled him deriding Jewish people as 'middlemen, profiteers and parasites'. When Stalin asked Roosevelt what present he planned to make Ibn Saud, he replied his only concession might be to give him the 6 million Jews living in the US.

Churchill again appealed to Roosevelt to stay longer: 'But, Franklin, you cannot go. We have within reach a very great prize'. Roosevelt replied 'in a firm tone' that he had commitments and had to depart the next day. However, as the evening was about to break up, Stalin again pressed Roosevelt. This time he gave way, saying if necessary he would even delay his departure until Monday 12 February. They agreed to hold an additional plenary session at noon next day, after which the three leaders would lunch together.

Jo Sturdee was again in the hall as Roosevelt and Stalin departed, writing home, 'They broke it up at about 12.30 and as the Marshal was leaving the dear old P.M. led us in three cheers. I have kept a copy of the menu of the dinner. You will be staggered.' She had dined with some of her British colleagues, including Churchill's valet Sawyers, and five of Roosevelt's bodyguards:

> I might tell you the President has thousands of these so-called body guards. They are now affectionately termed 'The Crazy Gang' and the 'Thugs' . . . Anyway, it proved to be the most

hilarious evening of the whole Conference as far as we were concerned. You know what the Yanks are – they were all positively throwing back their heads, bellowing with laughter and thumping you on the back. But, out of it all, we have been promised some lipstick and some silk stockings. I wonder if we shall ever see them. I doubt if they will even remember – if the amount of champagne consumed is anything to do with it! Anyway they sure made the party go.

So did Sawyers, who, Elizabeth Layton recalled:

we managed to get on the go . . . he entertained the company with reports of our various trips, the different beds in which Mr. Churchill had slept and so on . . . Perhaps what Sawyers said was never so funny, but his mannerisms, giggle, lisp and rolling eyes made him at times what one might call 'a perfect scream'.

That day, the Soviet submarine *S-13* commanded by Captain Alexander Marinesko, which had sunk the *Wilhelm Gustloff* ten days before, torpedoed another German transport, the former passenger liner *General von Steuben,* also engaged in Operation Hannibal. The *General von Steuben* had sailed on 9 February from Pillau near Königsberg with some 4,000 people aboard, including about 2,800 wounded German soldiers and some 1,000 civilians and refugees. Hit just before midnight by two of *S-13*'s torpedoes, the *Steuben* sank in twenty minutes. Accompanying craft picked up only 600 survivors. Marinesko was the Soviet Union's most successful submarine commander. However, at this time he was facing a court martial ostensibly for drinking problems but actually connected to his 'unsound' reactionary views. Despite his achievements he was downgraded to the rank of lieutenant and in October 1945 given a dishonourable discharge.*

---

* Marinesko was reinstated in his rank of captain just before he died in 1963. In 1990 Mikhail Gorbachev posthumously honoured him as a Hero of the Soviet Union. The Submarine Museum in St Petersburg is now named after him.

Also on 10 February, as Captain Pim of the Map Room noted in his diary, 'the Soviet forces were only 38 miles from Berlin on the river Oder and the British and Canadians were storming their way to the banks of the Rhine. In Luzon the US forces had captured Manila after a wonderfully swift campaign.' In Berlin Reich officials were making final arrangements to evacuate Nazi Germany's gold reserves – some 100 tons – next day to salt mines near Eisenach in Thuringia.

Edith van Hessen, a Dutch Holocaust survivor, waiting anxiously for news of loved ones wrote that day, 'Just heard over the radio that 300 Dutch people have arrived safe in Switzerland, inmates of a Jewish concentration camp in Theresienstadt . . . Mother?'

British prisoner of war Ron Jones, captured in North Africa and forced to labour in an I. G. Farben synthetic petrol plant adjacent to Auschwitz, was enduring the fifth week of a seventeen-week death march across Poland, Germany and into Austria in sub-zero temperatures and with sacking for footwear. Of the 280 prisoners of war who set out, Jones would be one of the 150 survivors and live to be over 100, selling poppies for the British Legion in his local supermarket.

CHAPTER THIRTEEN

'A Landmark in Human History'

Cadogan and his American colleagues stayed up till 1.30 a.m. on 11 February working on the draft Conference Communiqué, which still needed Soviet approval before being formally blessed at the plenary session. Writing to his wife, Cadogan, whose admiration for Stalin's abilities had not waned, reflected, 'Joe has been extremely good. He *is* a great man, and shows up very impressively against the background of the other two ageing statesmen. The President in particular is very woolly and wobbly. Lord Moran says there's no doubt which of the three will go first.'

While officials laboured into the small hours at Yalta, Operation Veritable pressed on. A British artillery officer recorded in his war diary for 11 February: 'INTO GERMANY! We moved forward at 02.30 hours through Kranenburg to a position approximately one mile south east of Nutterden.' There they occupied a 'bunker of the famous Siegfried Line – a luxurious place of steel and concrete. There was very little firing . . . but an endless stream of traffic passed by, all going into Germany.'

Churchill was in a bad mood that day. When Moran visited him after breakfast the Prime Minister gave him 'a sour look' and complained, 'The President is behaving very badly. He won't take any interest in what we are trying to do.' Moran thought Churchill was 'impatient with the President's apathy and indifference' because 'he did not seem to realize that Roosevelt was a very sick man'. He also thought the Prime Minister increasingly 'conscious of his own impotence'.

Of particular concern to Churchill was Roosevelt's plan to meet the rulers of Egypt, Saudi Arabia and Ethiopia, since he jealously guarded the Middle East as a specifically British sphere of influence. Though he gave Hopkins the impression when they met that day that he had not known of Roosevelt's intention and was 'flabbergasted', Churchill already knew of the planned visit. A top secret Foreign Office telegram of 5 February to Eden reported:

> Ibn Saud . . . has received invitation from Mr Roosevelt to meet him . . . Roosevelt states that he is also meeting the Emperor of Abyssinia . . . Ibn Saud would like to meet Roosevelt but will not accept his invitation unless His Majesty's Government approve of meeting . . . Ibn Saud has expressed strong desire to see Mr. Churchill.

On 9 February Churchill had himself telegraphed Ibn Saud: 'My dear friend, I greatly desire you to meet the President of the United States who is also one of my most cherished friends. I am coming to Egypt especially to see you after you have had your talks with him,' and had begun to put in place arrangements for his visit.

Under the pretence of being surprised about Roosevelt's proposed visit, on 11 February Churchill quizzed Hopkins closely about the President's intentions. Hopkins sought to reassure him that the visit was 'in the main a lot of horseplay and that the President was going to thoroughly enjoy the colorful panoply of the sovereigns of this part of the world'. The only serious business the President would discuss with Ibn Saud was Palestine. However, Hopkins realized that Churchill 'thought we had some deep laid plot to undermine the British Empire in these areas'. Churchill told Hopkins that he too would visit the three sovereigns, perhaps after the brief visit to Greece he was contemplating.

A genuine surprise was in store for Churchill when later that morning Roosevelt showed him and Eden the secret agreement setting out Stalin's conditions for entering the war against Japan and asked him to sign it. Eden was horrified that Roosevelt had 'found time to negotiate in secret, and without informing his British colleague or his Chinese ally, an agreement with Stalin to cover the Far East'. In particular, he thought it 'unjust to take decisions affecting the future of China without consulting her'. To him the agreement was 'a discreditable by-product of the Conference' and he advised Churchill not to sign. When asked for his view, Cadogan, who had been UK ambassador to China, sided with Eden. However, as Eden wrote, Churchill 'felt that whether we liked it or not, our authority in the Far East would suffer if we were not signatories, and therefore not parties to any later discussions'.

In his memoirs Churchill claimed that the agreement was 'an American affair, and was certainly of prime interest to their military operations . . . To us the problem was remote and secondary.' However, Sergo Beria, listening to recordings made through his concealed microphones, thought the Prime Minister was offended Roosevelt had not told him earlier, writing, 'The British leader did not conceal his resentment.' Whatever the case, Churchill duly signed the document which was then held 'in the closest secrecy'. On the US side, Bohlen, Harriman and Stettinius were the only State Department representatives who knew of its existence and it was entrusted to Admiral Leahy to lock away with his secret papers at the White House.

Neither Churchill nor Roosevelt, who had had considerably more time to scrutinize the agreement, queried the statement that 'the Heads of the three Great Powers have agreed that these claims of the Soviet Union shall be unquestionably fulfilled after Japan had been defeated.' These words made it absolutely clear that, whatever view Chiang Kai-shek took when eventually informed, the US and the UK would ensure that the Soviet Union received its promised rewards for its entry into the war against Japan.

Roosevelt's morning was easier than Churchill's. A brief note from Stalin and a more fulsome letter from Churchill ending 'I need hardly assure you that I should do everything possible to assist you' informed him they would both support any US request for extra votes in the UN General Assembly. Half an hour before the plenary session, accompanied by his daughter, Roosevelt took a jeep ride through the grounds of the Livadia. The weather was pleasant, as it had been during most of the conference – some Russians present called it 'Roosevelt weather'. On his return, the President inspected a guard of US navy sailors drawn up outside the palace.

The eighth and final plenary session opened at midday with an exchange of pleasantries. Roosevelt described his farewell tour of the Livadia grounds, and Stalin said that after the conference the Livadia and also the Vorontsov and Yusupov Palaces would be turned into spas – in fact they became resorts for Beria's NKVD staff.

As they got down to business for the last time, the main topic was the Conference Communiqué – 'this bloody thing', Churchill called it. The communiqué detailed what lay in store for Germany: unconditional surrender, disarmament, the removal or destruction of any industries with military applications, the trial of war criminals, the levying of reparations, and the imposition of Allied zones of occupation, including one for France. However, the word 'dismemberment' was omitted for fear of increasing German resistance. The communiqué also covered the forthcoming UN Conference in San Francisco, giving no specifics of the voting procedure in the Security Council, and quoted the full text of the Declaration on Liberated Europe.

As they worked through the draft communiqué, Churchill objected to the frequent use of the word 'joint' because to him it conjured in the British mind 'the Sunday family roast of mutton'. The text was amended to pander to his whimsy. Thus 'our joint purpose to destroy German militarism and Nazism' became 'our inflexible purpose'. Roosevelt and Stalin continued in lighthearted mood, experimenting with each other's languages with Stalin saying 'OK' and Roosevelt nodding '*Khorosho*', 'Good', as they approved point after point. One of Eden's staff thought the President was 'clearly in a hurry to get off'. The only brief sticking point was over the UN, where Molotov again sought unsuccessfully for Belorussia and the Ukraine to be invited as founder members to the San Francisco conference. When they came to Poland, Churchill predicted that the London Poles would 'raise a dreadful outcry' and that he would face fierce criticism at home 'on the grounds that we had yielded completely to the Russian view'. However, he assured Stalin he would defend the agreement on Poland 'to the best of my ability'.

A mere fifty minutes later the session ended. Roosevelt, Churchill, Stalin, Eden, Molotov, Stettinius, Cadogan and a handful of others withdrew to the Tsar's billiard room for lunch, leaving Vyshinsky to produce the final text of the communiqué – 'he is not interested in lunch', a grinning Stalin said. Robert Hopkins, ready with his camera, took a picture of the lunch that would appear in *Life* magazine with the commentary:

> Together they represent a large part of the world's population. One is a cobbler's son, another an aristocrat, the third a descendant of thrifty Dutch settlers. In character and temperament one could hardly find three more different men. Their debates are now over – and the hopes are high for a peaceful world. Look at them! Churchill is taking a large spoonful of the caviar and is out for more; Stalin's helping is a moderate one; FDR passes it up. Does it have any significance?

Charles Bohlen recalled the conversation during that final lunch as 'general and personal' except for a pointed comment by Stalin, clearly referring to Iran, that 'any nation which kept its oil in the ground and would not let it be exploited was, in fact, "Working against peace"'. 'Not too many toasts', Cadogan wrote, though at one point he felt a dig in the back. Turning, he found Stalin, tumbler of brandy in each hand, wanting to raise a final glass with him.

Towards the end of the meal, the final communiqué was brought in for signature. Roosevelt suggested that, as 'such a wonderful host', Stalin should sign first, but he objected that this might give the 'sharp-tongued press' in America the impression that he 'had

had the President and the Prime Minister on a lead'. Instead he proposed they sign in alphabetical order which, following the Cyrillic alphabet, would mean first Roosevelt, then Stalin, and finally Churchill. Churchill immediately pointed out that in the English alphabet, his name came before Roosevelt's and that he was also the eldest. The others courteously agreed he should sign first, then the President and finally Stalin. The three also decided that the text of the communiqué should be broadcast simultaneously in Moscow, London and Washington at 11.30 p.m. Moscow time the following day, 12 February.

Since final versions of other conference documents would not be ready before they left, the three leaders also signed blank sheets of paper on which the text would be completed by the hard-working Foreign Ministers and their teams who were remaining behind for a few hours to tie up loose ends. Then at 3.45 p.m. the lunch – and the conference – formally ended with, Sarah Oliver thought, 'everyone in the highest spirits'. Roosevelt gave Stalin eight Legion of Merit decorations for members of the Russian military delegation, and told him, 'We will meet again soon – in Berlin!' Stettinius asked Molotov if he could have a painting of a wintry scene hanging on the wall behind the President's chair as a souvenir and Molotov agreed. Arthur Birse, the British interpreter, gave his Soviet counterpart Pavlov a complete set of the works of Charles Dickens.

Churchill fared less well. He had particularly admired the three pairs of white marble lions guarding the flight of stairs descending to the terraced gardens of the Vorontsov. The first pair lay slumped, sleepy heads resting on their paws, the second pair sat heads raised and alert, while the third were sitting up and growling. Deciding that one of the slumped lions was 'Like me, only without the cigar', he had offered to buy it, but his Soviet hosts had refused on the grounds it was the property of the Soviet people.

After final handshakes and farewells, at 3.55 p.m. Stalin left the Livadia to board his armoured train to return to Moscow. Five minutes later Roosevelt, his daughter Anna and the Harrimans left for Sebastopol and the *Catoctin*. Packed into their limousine were last-minute Soviet gifts of vodka, wine from Stalin's native

Georgia, champagne, caviar, butter, oranges and tangerines. Watching the President depart, Leahy thought he 'looked fatigued . . . but so did we all. It was one of the most strenuous weeks I had ever had.'

After remarking glumly to Eden that 'the only bond of the victors is their common hate', Churchill set off with his daughter back to the Vorontsov Palace which he had planned to leave next day. However, as Sarah wrote, 'having said goodbye to everyone, [he] suddenly felt lonely I think. "Why do we stay here? Why don't we go tonight – I see no reason to stay here a minute longer – we're off!"' As they drew up outside the Vorontsov, Churchill

sprang out of the car and whirling into the Private office announced: 'I don't know about you – but I'm off! I leave in 50 minutes!' After a second's stunned silence, everyone was galvanized into activity. Trunks and large mysterious paper parcels given to us by the Russians – whoopee – filled the hall. Laundry arrived back clean but damp. Naturally 50 minutes gave us time to change our minds six more times! 'We will spend the night here after all and leave tomorrow lunchtime – We will fly – We will leave tonight and go by sea – We will go to Athens – Alexandria – Cairo – Constantinople – We will not go to any of them – We will stay on board and read the newspapers! Where is the pouch? Why hasn't it arrived'.

His valet Sawyers, 'tears in his eyes, surrounded by half-packed suitcases, beat his breast and said: "They can't do this to me!"' Meanwhile Churchill, 'genial and sprightly like a boy out of school, his homework done, walked from room to room saying: "Come on, come on!"'

Caught up in the general whirlwind, Moran noted how 'The P.M., who has been in a vile mood throughout the Conference, irritable and bad-tempered, is now in tearing spirits,' exulting that it would be 'grand to get back to English fare after the suckling-pig and the cold fatty approaches to all their meals'. Jo Sturdee and her colleagues, swept along in the rush, felt 'in a peculiar sort of way . . . very sorry to leave'. Although 'we are still getting bitten regularly by the dear little bed bugs, and still washing in the communal washroom we have all had a jolly good time.'

As Churchill was about to depart, the Vorontsov's Soviet staff lined up in the hall. Joan Bright watched in some embarrassment as 'Mr. Churchill shook hands and thanked each one in turn' because 'unfortunately there were no presents to give'. She had requested what a London colleague called 'the whole of Dunhill's quota for a month' to be flown out to the Crimea — 'two silver cigarette-boxes, four cigarette lighters, a silver powder-compact, six silver propelling pencils and four leather powder-compacts' — and on their arrival in Yalta had put the items in a desk drawer. However, when she went to retrieve them, 'they had disappeared. It was very awkward. I could not ask the Russians; if I did, to save their face they would have probably accused, rightly or wrongly, some wretched domestic. So I said nothing — and they got nothing.'

Then Churchill was off. 'Believe it or not, 1 hour and 20 minutes later, about 5.30 saw a cavalcade of cars groaning with bulging suitcases winding its way to Sebastopol,' Sarah Oliver wrote. Marian Holmes, bringing up the rear with Sawyers 'in a comfortable car, followed by two lorry loads of luggage', peered into the twilight as they set off along the 'winding and dangerous-looking mountain road'. With Roosevelt already on the road and Stalin having disappeared, 'like some genie', Sarah Oliver thought, 'three hours after the last hand-shake, Yalta was deserted, except for those who always have to tidy up after a party'.

The Foreign Ministers, tasked with that 'tidying up', and their teams convened for the last time at 4.20 p.m. Their main job was to agree the lengthy and detailed confidential protocol summarizing the conference decisions that the ministers them-selves would sign, but a host of other documents also required their attention. The closing hours of Yalta, wrote Bohlen, bought 'great confusion and a good deal of irritation and squabbling' even within his own delegation. He and the other interpreters were hard-pressed translating from Russian to English and back again, including the text of bilateral agreements between the US and the USSR and the UK and the USSR on the repatriation of liberated prisoners of war and civilians, the details of which had only been finalized that day following the discussions between their leaders. These stipulated that each party would provide details of the other's citizens it was holding, separate them from enemy prisoners of war and allow access to them until they could be handed over.

Eden attempted at the eleventh hour to add Britain's long-time ally Saudi Arabia to the countries to be invited to the UN conference, arguing that the country had wanted to declare war on Germany and only the Allies' discouragement had prevented it and that 'It would be good to have a Moslem or two.' It would also be a tactful diplomatic move given that Ibn Saud would shortly be 'having a cup of coffee with the President'. Stettinius liked the idea but Molotov resisted with his usual stubbornness and Eden withdrew the suggestion.

By the time the last documents had been signed, darkness had fallen. Strolling into the hall of the Livadia, Molotov suggested that Eden and Stettinius each take a branch of the lemon tree that had appeared there so suddenly after Roosevelt had lamented the lack of lemons for martinis. Others quickly joined in stripping the tree until all that was left was those bits that 'could [only] be sawed or chopped with an axe'. Eden and his staff returned to the Vorontsov, from which they would depart next day, while Molotov went back to the Yusupov Palace. Meanwhile, once the last details of the various agreements had been transmitted through to Washington, Stettinius ordered the connection between the now-deserted Livadia and the *Catoctin* to be cut and, after a late supper, set out on the road to the railhead at Simferopol. As his car crested the mountains separating Yalta from the western Crimea, he stopped for 'a last view of the site of this historic Conference' visible in the moonlight.

Next day, 12 February, Joan Bright was among the last of the British delegation to leave the Vorontsov. She lunched with her old acquaintance from Moscow, Nina Alexandrovna, then visited the sanatoria where some British staff had lodged, to thank those looking after them. A Russian major ran up to her, hand held behind his back. 'With a bow and a kiss on my cheek he swept it at me and thrust a huge bunch of snowdrops into my hand.' Another officer told Joan the major had gone specially up the mountainside to pick them for her. Once she and the final members of the British team had gone, the Vorontsov's staff began rolling up carpets, packing up china, silverware and the double bed Churchill had insisted on, ready to be sent back to the denuded Moscow hotels and checking each item against an inventory, just as was happening at the Livadia. Briefing notes to the US delegation had requested, 'Please do not pilfer room and dining services for souvenirs. Supply in Russia is very short . . . any typical American souvenir collecting will leave a very unfortunate impression with our hosts.'

The local people, who had seen the constant comings and goings along the coastal roads but been warned by the NKVD to avoid the foreigners, finally learned something of what had been going on in their midst when later that evening, 12 February, the Conference Communiqué was broadcast to the world. Mike Reilly had noted, while making security checks on peasant huts near the Livadia, that 'every house, no matter how poverty-ridden, had a radio . . . They were odd-looking radios to these American eyes, as they had no knobs or dialling apparatus of any kind. It seemed that they were built to receive only one frequency, which was that of the powerful Moscow government-controlled station.'

In the US, Byrnes, newly arrived back in Washington, immediately called a press conference. Praising Roosevelt's leadership at the conference he focused his remarks on the agreement on the structure of the new United Nations and the holding of an inaugural conference. He also lauded the Declaration on Liberated Europe as an event 'of the greatest importance' and an unequivocal commitment to the holding of free, democratic elections in newly liberated countries including those occupied by the Red Army. Poland, he suggested, would be the first demonstration of the Declaration's principles in action.

Byrnes did his job well and the American press greeted the

Conference Communiqué enthusiastically, in some cases almost euphorically. Roosevelt's son-in-law John Boettiger cabled Roosevelt from the White House, 'All our hats are off to you . . . a world of orchids to you. Never have I seen such overwhelming praise for anything as for your achievements at Yalta.' The *Washington Post* proclaimed, 'The President is to be congratulated on his part in this all-encompassing achievement.' The *New York Times* predicted that the Yalta agreements pointed the way to 'a secure peace, and to a brighter world'. The *New York Herald Tribune* thought 'the conference has produced another great proof of allied unity, strength and power of decision'. To *Time* magazine 'All doubts about the Big Three's ability to cooperate in peace as well as in war seem now to have been swept away.' William Shirer, broadcasting on CBS, called the conference 'a landmark in human history'. The *Detroit News's* considered and percipient response was: 'The overwhelming significance of the Crimean Conference – far more important than its specific conclusions – is that the two new colossuses of the world, economically and militarily, one capitalist and the other communist have achieved a wide measure of agreement for the after-war future.' Although Britain had been the third nation represented at the conference, according to the *Detroit News*, it was broke, in decline and 'worn out'.

In Britain the welcome afforded to the communiqué was only slightly more restrained. Churchill's Minister of Information cabled him: 'The whole British press acclaim the results.' The left-wing *Tribune* magazine was in a small minority when it argued that despite his 'romantic strutting and political exhibitionism' Churchill was no longer 'influential'.

In Russia, to underline the achievements at Yalta, the Soviet news agency TASS published a dramatic poster showing Allied rifle butts pushing Hitler and his colleagues into a cage. The caption beneath read: 'An inevitable date. War Criminals. A realization of the unshakeable decisions of the Allied conference in the Crimea. The din of battle is growing ever louder in Germany – the organizers of Fascist crimes are approaching their end.' *Pravda* devoted an issue solely to the conference, hailing the decisions as showing that 'the alliance of the Three Big Powers possessed not only an historic yesterday but also a great tomorrow'. *Izvestiia* believed the conference 'the greatest political event of the present day'.

In Germany, where on 12 February all German women between the ages of sixteen and sixty were called up for service in the People's Army, the Volkssturm, Foreign Minister von Ribbentrop told the Japanese ambassador that Churchill had betrayed Europe to Bolshevism. It was understandable if America 'let Europe be trampled down . . . American capitalism could swagger about the world like a lord, but what future Britain saw for herself in a situation which was merely Bolshevising Europe and increasing her own dependence on America he could not for the life of him understand.'

On the evening of 13 February, in fulfilment of commitments made to the Soviets at Yalta to attack rail and communication centres in eastern Germany close to the line of the Soviet army's advance, nearly 800 RAF Lancaster heavy bombers raided Dresden, the Baroque city some called the 'Florence of the Elbe'. In the words of the target information issued to the RAF crews:

> Dresden is the seventh largest city in Germany . . . and is also by far the largest unbombed area the enemy has got . . . At one time well-known for its china, Dresden has developed into an industrial city of first class importance . . . the intentions of the attack are to hit the enemy where he will feel it most behind an already partially collapsed front . . . and incidentally to show the Russians when they arrive what Bomber Command can do.

The information also highlighted the need to deprive 'refugees pouring westward . . . workers and troops alike of roofs . . . in the midst of winter'.

The first Lancasters opened their bomb doors just before 10.15 p.m. and over the next hours RAF planes dropped more than 14,000 tons of high explosive and more than 1,100 tons of incendiaries, creating a great firestorm which reached 1,800° F. The next day, grotesquely appropriately Ash Wednesday, USAAF bombers added to the carnage by dropping nearly 1,000 tons of high explosive and nearly 300 tons of incendiaries. With at least 100,000 refugees in the city, casualty numbers are not certain. Estimates vary from 30,000 to more than 100,000 with the likely figure towards the lower end. The inscription on one of the mass graves reads:

How many died?
Who knows the number?

An RAF bomb aimer approaching the city when it was already alight recalled:

other Lancasters were clearly visible; their silhouettes black in the rosy glow. The streets . . . were a fantastic latticework of fire. It was as though one was looking down at the fiery outlines of a crossword puzzle, blazing streets stretched from east to west, from north to south, in a gigantic saturation of flame. I was completely awed by the spectacle.

One survivor recalled how 'our mother covered us with wet blankets and coats she found in a water tub'. As they ran through the burning streets, 'we saw terrible things; cremated adults shrunk to the size of small children, pieces of arms and legs . . . whole families burnt to death, burning people ran to and fro'.

A British prisoner of war, Victor Gregg, was ordered to help in the clear-up. It took his work party seven hours to get into one air-raid shelter in the old town designed to hold 1,000 people. Inside they found not bodies, 'only bones and scorched articles of clothing matted together on the floor and stuck together by a sort of jelly. There was no flesh visible, just a glutinous mass of solidified fat and bones inches thick.' American writer Kurt Vonnegut, also a prisoner of war in the city, described bodies dissolved in 'the semi-liquid way that dust actually turns to dust'.

Six weeks later Churchill, perhaps unsettled by the public unease expressed in the British press and Parliament about terror bombing when news of the destruction came out, wrote:

It seems to me that the moment has come when the question of bombing of German cities simply for the sake of increasing the terror, although under other pretexts, should be reviewed. Otherwise we shall come into control of an utterly ruined land . . . The destruction of Dresden remains a serious query against the conduct of Allied bombing . . . [I] feel the need for more precise concentration upon military objectives such as oil and communications behind the immediate battle zone, rather than on mere acts of terror and wanton destruction, however impressive.

PART FOUR

An Alliance Under Pressure, February to August 1945

'This issue of a settlement with Russia before our strength has gone seems to me to dwarf all others.'

Churchill to Truman, May 1945

CHAPTER FOURTEEN

Elephants in the Room

As the delegations dispersed there was time for reflection. Shortly before leaving the Livadia, Roosevelt had written to his wife, 'We have wound up the conference – successfully I think.' He thought that during Stalin's training as a priest in his youth 'something entered into his nature of the way in which a Christian gentleman should behave'.

The immediate reactions among Roosevelt's team were also largely positive. Harry Hopkins recalled a mood of exultation among the American delegates:

> We really believed in our hearts that this was the dawn of the new day we had all been praying for and talking about for so many years. We were absolutely certain that we had won the first great victory of the peace – and, by 'we', I mean all of us, the whole civilized human race. The Russians had proved that they could be reasonable and farseeing.

However, he worried 'what the results would be if anything should happen to Stalin. We felt sure that we could count on him to be reasonable and sensible and understanding – but we never could be sure who or what might be in back of him there in the Kremlin'.

Bohlen thought that despite a 'sense of frustration and some bitterness in regard to Poland, the general mood was one of satisfaction'. A particular source of that satisfaction was the Soviet agreement to participate in the Pacific war. Kathleen Harriman remembered how, 'When the Russians said at Yalta that they would fight Japan', a jubilant Admiral King said, 'We've just saved two million Americans.'

On the British side, Churchill wrote to his wife, much as Roosevelt had to his, 'We have covered a great amount of ground and I am very pleased with the decisions we have gained.' Cadogan was similarly upbeat when writing home:

> I think the Conference has been quite successful. We have got an agreement on Poland which may heal differences, for some time at least, and assure some degree of independence to the Poles. We have agreed the Dumbarton Oaks [UN] plan, and we have got a number of other things settled, including an important agreement with the Russians about the treatment of our prisoners whom they liberate. I hope the world will be impressed!

Stalin's apparent reasonableness had not convinced everyone. Unlike Hopkins and others, Admiral Leahy did not believe his claim that he was subservient to the Politburo and had no illusions about the extent of his personal power. To him, Stalin was not a trustworthy partner but the true victor of Yalta. The very day the conference broke up, Leahy predicted in his diary that the decisions taken there would 'make Russia the dominant power in Europe, which in itself carries a certainty of future international disagreements and the prospects of another war'.

Eden shared Leahy's pessimism about future relations with the Soviet Union. Roosevelt had suggested several times during the conference that the differences between the Western Allies and the Russians 'were largely a matter of the use of words'. Eden thought he 'was deluding himself'. What lay between the Western Allies and the Russians was not a difference of wording but a 'difference of intention'.

Stalin himself was indeed content with the conference's outcome. While it had still been underway, Lavrentii Beria had told his son Sergo, 'Everything is going well,' and the Soviets were winning agreement to what they wanted. Yet just as the Western Allies worried what might happen if Stalin died or was supplanted, so he was concerned about what might occur if Roosevelt, so obviously very ill, should die, commenting a few days later to the Politburo, 'Let's hope nothing happens to him. We shall never do business again with anyone like him.'

The true test of the Yalta agreements would be in their delivery, especially with regard to Poland. The day the Yalta Conference ended, Kiev Radio broadcast extracts from a letter from Colonel Marian Spychalski, appointed Mayor of Warsaw by the Lublin Poles, to Nikita Khrushchev, then First Secretary of the Communist Party of the Ukraine. The letter denounced Mikołajczyk and other London Poles as 'traitors', promising they 'will receive the punishment they deserve. We will deal with them as you deal with the Ukrainian nationalists, Hitler's mercenaries.'

When they departed from Yalta, the three leaders had, whatever their views of the conference's outcome, intentionally left undiscussed three issues that, looking back, they might have been expected to address explicitly: the atomic bomb, the Jewish genocide and the fate of the three Baltic republics of Estonia, Latvia and Lithuania.

Although all three leaders were aware of the explosive elephant in the room – the atomic bomb – no one raised the topic. When from the 1890s researchers such as Marie Curie and Ernest Rutherford began to unlock the secrets of the atom, they published their discoveries openly. The leading researchers, including the Dane Niels Bohr and Werner Heisenberg, the German father of quantum mechanics, knew each other both professionally and personally.

In 1932, Englishman James Chadwick made the key discovery of the neutron. Further discoveries and innovations such as particle accelerators to bombard and break up atoms quickly followed. When Hitler came to power many German scientists, mainly from a Jewish background but also including Communist sympathizers, were forced to emigrate. Two who remained – Otto Hahn and Fritz Strassmann – in 1938 achieved the splitting or fission of the uranium nucleus, although they needed the advice of their former colleague Lise Meitner, exiled in Sweden, and her nephew Otto Frisch to interpret their findings for them.

Scientists began to realize that splitting the uranium atom could release immense energy to power a city or produce a devastating weapon. However, many such as Bohr believed that to produce enough of the key isotope U-235 so much industrial effort would be required that, in Bohr's words, 'you would need to turn the entire country into a factory'. Nevertheless, some of his colleagues lobbied largely successfully to keep work on fission secret to hinder the world's dictatorships from using it as a weapon.

As the Second World War began, British physicists concentrated on war projects, in particular radar. However, many refugee scientists settled in Britain could not, as aliens, work on such classified areas. Among them was Otto Frisch who had joined another refugee physicist, Rudolf Peierls, at Birmingham University. Hunched over a small gas fire for warmth in the extremely cold winter of 1939/40, he and Peierls pondered how much pure U-235 would be needed to make a bomb. They calculated, using a formula worked out by Peierls for finding the 'critical mass', the amount of fissionable material needed to be brought together to release sufficient neutrons to start a self-sustaining chain reaction. The result amazed them. Others who had tried to calculate the critical mass had, according to Frisch, 'tended to come out with tons'. Their estimate was 'about a pound'. Using a thermal diffusion method of isotopic separation, Frisch thought he could produce such a quantity in weeks.

Scribbling literally on the back of an envelope, Frisch and Peierls calculated that the uranium would fissure, releasing energy equivalent to 'thousands of tons of ordinary explosive'. As Peierls recalled, 'an atomic bomb was possible at least in principle! As a weapon it would be so devastating that, from a military point of view, it would be worth setting up a plant to separate the isotopes.' Together they composed a three-page memorandum to the British government dealing with scientific, strategic and ethical issues. It suggested 'about 1 kg [of uranium] as a suitable size for the bomb' and described a mechanism to force two pieces of uranium, constituting the critical mass, together at tremendous speed to produce an explosion.

The blast would probably destroy 'the centre of a big city' and the subsequent radiation would be 'fatal to living beings, even a long time after the explosion'. Frisch and Peierls suggested that the probable very high civilian casualties, 'may make it unsuitable as a weapon for use by this country' [the UK] but pointed out that Germany might be working on a bomb. As the only defence was the threat of retaliation with the same weapon, it would be worth developing one as a deterrent, 'even if it is not intended to use the bomb as a means of attack'.

The British government created the high-powered Maud Committee to review the document, with James Chadwick, discoverer of the neutron, as a leading scientific adviser. The discovery in 1941 of plutonium in a cyclotron in the United States made Chadwick and his colleagues think that this, too, might be a possible bomb fuel. The Maud Committee's final report in summer 1941 recommended that Britain proceed with an atomic bomb project. Churchill approved it, writing, 'although personally I am quite content with the existing explosives, I feel we must not stand in the way of improvement'.

Even before the British scientists submitted their final report to their own government, they had sent copies to colleagues in the still-neutral US to encourage the US to advance its own programme. President Roosevelt, on the basis of subsequent advice from his own scientists, approved the creation of an American project. On Saturday 6 December 1941 – the day before Pearl Harbor and the day Hitler accepted that Moscow would not fall quickly – a high-level US committee allocated key tasks in what became the Manhattan A-Bomb Project.

Entirely unknown, of course, to the United States and British governments, the USSR had three months earlier acquired a copy of the Maud report, almost certainly through their British agent John Cairncross, the 'fifth man' of the notorious Cambridge University Five. With Russian forces retreating everywhere, the Soviet authorities took little action until, bolstered by indications from their agents that America was indeed working on an atomic bomb, they decided in autumn 1942 as the battle for Stalingrad intensified, to launch a nuclear project and to step up their quest for information about the US and UK projects.

In this they were substantially aided by Klaus Fuchs, a Communist physicist who had fled Germany in 1932 and who transmitted information to his Soviet controllers while working on atomic research in Britain and subsequently at Los Alamos in the United States as part of the Manhattan Project. Other important Soviet agents included David Greenglass, an American engineer at Los Alamos, and a nineteen-year-old Harvard physicist Theodore (Ted) Hall. By November 1944 the Russian authorities had obtained 1,167 documents on the bomb project, for which the Soviet code name was 'Enormoz', ('Enormous'), of which eighty-eight from the US and seventy-nine from the UK were deemed of special importance.

Thus by the time of Yalta the Soviets were well informed about the Manhattan A-Bomb Project, its U-235 and plutonium fuels, the bomb designs, and the likelihood of a test firing within a few months. Soviet spy chief Pavel Sudoplatov, who had overseen the project for the assassination of Trotsky in 1940 and was now responsible for gathering atomic intelligence, alleged after the fall of the Soviet Union in 1991 that among other informants had been Robert Oppenheimer, the scientific head of the Manhattan Project who is known to have associated with Communist sympathizers and whose security clearance was suspended on these grounds by the US authorities in December 1953. However, this claim is uncorroborated. Much more likely is that Oppenheimer, like so many of his colleagues used to sharing information freely, may have made unguarded comments which reached Moscow.

With it seeming very unlikely that Nazi Germany could produce an atomic bomb, some prominent scientists certainly believed information on the atomic project should be shared internationally. Chief among them was Niels Bohr. After successfully resisting being pumped for information by his former colleague and friend Werner Heisenberg – by then working on the German atomic bomb project – at their infamous Copenhagen meeting, he had escaped to Sweden and then been conveyed to

Britain, semi-conscious through lack of oxygen in the bomb-bay of a British Mosquito fighter-bomber. Bohr believed passionately that the United States, Britain and the Soviet Union had to agree on how atomic energy should be applied and controlled internationally before the bomb was completed and deployed. This meant telling the Russians about the Manhattan Project at once.

While in the United States, Bohr secured a meeting with one of Roosevelt's advisers to promote his message. The adviser passed his views to the President who suggested Bohr should go to London to discuss his beliefs with Churchill. Their meeting in May 1944 was not a success. At one point Churchill demanded of Lord Cherwell, his chief scientific adviser, 'What is he really talking about? Politics or physics?' To Bohr there was no difference. To Churchill politics was strictly his and Roosevelt's business. Bohr's advocacy of openness appalled Churchill. Bohr 'ought to be confined or at any rate made to see that he is very near the edge of mortal crimes'. Churchill's attitude in turn shocked Bohr: 'It was terrible. He scolded us [Bohr and Cherwell] like two schoolboys.'

Churchill and Roosevelt had at their 1943 Quebec meeting agreed formally to collaborate on the atomic project. The treaty they signed provided for their two countries to pool their nuclear research but crucially stipulated that the work would be kept secret and neither nation would pass information to a third party without the other's consent nor deploy the atomic bomb without the other's agreement. In line with this agreement, neither Roosevelt nor Churchill made any comments about the atomic project at the Yalta Conference and naturally Stalin did not reveal the success of his espionage. The failure of Roosevelt and Churchill to say anything can only have confirmed the sometimes paranoid Stalin's suspicion that despite Roosevelt's apparent distancing of himself from Churchill, the UK and the US were caballing against him. He later complained, 'Roosevelt clearly felt no need to put us in the picture. He could have done it at Yalta. He could have told me that the atomic bomb was going through its experimental stages. We were supposed to be allies.'

*

Although in the conference margins, Roosevelt and Stalin had had a brief almost jocular discussion about a homeland for Jewish people sparked by Roosevelt's planned visit to Egypt to meet that country's king and the King of Saudi Arabia, just as at Teheran neither the genocide of the Jewish people nor that of the Gypsies was raised at Yalta.* Russian forces had liberated Auschwitz on 27 January 1945, a few days before the conference began. However, very little information had yet reached the Western Allies. The first press reports were brief and based on equally brief Soviet newspaper reports. For example, on 29 January under the head-line 'Russian Front Week-End Advances' the *Manchester Guardian* reported, 'Marshal Koniev reached the Oder at several places north-west of Breslau. Still further south Oświęcim, site of the concentration camp which became notorious for the cruelties inflicted on its inmates, was one of the places captured.'

The *New York Times* on 2 February had two paragraphs:

> *Pravda* reported today that the Red Army had saved several thousand tortured emaciated inmates of the Germans' greatest 'murder factory' at Oświęcim in south-west Poland.
>
> *Pravda*'s correspondent said fragmentary reports indicated that at least 1,500,000 persons were slaughtered at Oświęcim . . . five trains arrived daily . . . with Russians, Poles, Jews, Czechs, French and Yugoslavs jammed in sealed cars.†

On the basis of these brief reports the British ambassador in Moscow Archibald Clark Kerr on his return from Yalta made enquiries of the Soviet government in mid-February. Despite promptings, the embassy did not receive a reply until nearly the end of April and then only a very brief one that it had been 'found from investigations from the Oświęcim group of concentration

---

* The term 'the Holocaust' to describe the Jewish genocide only came into use in the 1950s.

† The Russian reports were using Oświęcim, the Polish name, rather than the German Auschwitz.

camps that more than four million citizens of various European countries were destroyed by the Germans . . . No British were found among the survivors.' Like many other Soviet reports the communication did not refer specifically to Jewish people.

The reason, however, that the horrors of the genocide and the punishment of its perpetrators were not discussed at Yalta cannot have been that the existence of Auschwitz and other camps was unknown to the Western governments. As early as 1942 the future leader of the Polish government in exile Stanisław Mikołajczyk sent 'photographic evidence of the dead, stacked like cordwood' to the British and American press. They would not, he recalled, 'print the pictures. They could not believe them until their own men pressed into Dachau and Belsen.' Mikołajczyk also undoubtedly informed the two governments.

When Roosevelt first heard of the killings in September 1942 he didn't believe it. Deported Jews, he concluded, were simply being taken to build defences on the Soviet border. State Department officials initially suppressed such reports because of their 'fantastic nature', considering them similar to false First World War propaganda about German atrocities such as the alleged raping of nuns or crucifixion of captured soldiers. The American secret service initially called the reports 'a wild rumor inspired by Jewish fears'. In December 1942, Jewish leaders sent Roosevelt a twenty-page report on Nazi extermination plans. Roosevelt promised action but some of his advisers were concerned that action 'might lend color to the charges of Hitler that we were fighting this war on account of and at the instigation and direction of our Jewish citizens'.

In June 1944, Jewish leaders well aware of the ongoing mass deportation of Hungary's Jews to Auschwitz suggested to both British and US governments the bombing of the railway lines to the camp. Anthony Eden queried whether the camp itself should be bombed. 'Get everything out of the air force you can and invoke me if necessary,' Churchill responded. 'There is no doubt that is probably the greatest and most horrible crime ever committed in the whole history of the world and it has been done by scientific machinery, by nominally civilised men in the name of a great state and one of the leading races in Europe.'

The British air force commanders suggested that American bombers raiding in daylight were better suited to the precision task than Britain's night bombing force. When the proposal was put to the American War Department, assistant secretary John McCloy recalled some thirty years later that he took the prospect to Roosevelt who said,

> bombing Auschwitz wouldn't have done any good . . . we would have been accused of destroying Auschwitz by bombing these innocent people . . . Why, the idea! They'll say we bombed these people and they'll only move it [the camp] down the road a little way and we'll bomb them all the more . . . I won't have anything to do with it. We'll be accused of participating in this horrible business.

No other evidence of the conversation exists and several historians have suggested that McCloy himself took the decision. Whatever the case, no bombing ever took place of either the railway lines leading to the camp or of the camp itself.

More information about the concentration camps emerged in late July 1944 with the capture by advancing Red Army soldiers of the first camp to be liberated, Majdanek near Lublin. A *New York Times* reporter who visited the camp that August described it as 'The most terrible place on the face of the earth'. Little attention was paid to the revelation, partly perhaps because the camp was behind Soviet lines with very restricted access to Westerners and also because no film records were made. As Mikołajczyk recalled, it was only with the entrance of British and American troops accompanied by photojournalists to camps such as Belsen in Western Europe that the full horrors became widely known and believed.

The liberating Russian soldiers appear to have considered the atrocities in the camps simply to be part of the more general horrors inflicted by the Nazis in their ravages of the lands and people of Eastern Europe, including those of Russia itself.

Lieutenant Ivan Martynushkin, one of the first Russian officers to enter Auschwitz, took this view, explaining, 'I had [already] seen towns destroyed . . . seen destruction of villages. I had seen the suffering of our own people. I had seen small children maimed. There was not one village which had not experienced this horror, this tragedy, these sufferings.' To him, already numbed by his previous experiences, Auschwitz seemed just one more horror among so many others.

Given their own actions against other ethnic groups such as the Cossacks and Tatars, it certainly suited the Soviet authorities not to highlight at Yalta and elsewhere the racial nature of the killings in the camps but to portray them as they did in their press statements and propaganda as one further aspect of the general hell the Nazis created in Eastern Europe.

Winston Churchill had been a great supporter of the three Baltic states in their bid to retain the freedom newly bestowed on them by the Versailles Treaty after the First World War, advocating the sending of British naval forces to defend them against the Bolsheviks. However, neither he nor Roosevelt at Yalta or elsewhere attempted to resist their incorporation into the Soviet Union following their occupation by Soviet forces in 1940. The secret briefing document for the US delegation to Yalta by a senior State Department official summed up the US position to which that of the UK was identical:

> We know that the three Baltic states have been reincorporated into the Soviet Union and that nothing which we can do can alter this. It is not a question of whether we like it; I personally don't . . . The point is it had been done and nothing which it is within the power of the United States government to do can undo it.

Neither the US nor the UK delegation at Yalta raised the issue of the Baltic states' freedom. Nor did the Soviet delegation seek a formal acceptance of their absorption into the Soviet Union by the US and the UK, and none was ever given in the over forty years before the disintegration of the Soviet Union led to the re-emergence of the three states as sovereign nations. At Yalta both sides simply preferred to ignore the issue on the basis of a tacit but never explicit understanding by the Americans and the British – as the State Department document acknowledged – that there was nothing they could do about it.

CHAPTER FIFTEEN

'A Fraudulent Prospectus'

Roosevelt headed directly for Sebastopol from Yalta – an uncomfortable journey that took three hours. Dusk was falling by the time the presidential convoy arrived. Nevertheless, before boarding USS *Catoctin* the President insisted on being driven through the ruined city where the stark destruction seemed even worse than in Yalta.

According to the presidential log, that night 'The *Catoctin* served a delicious steak dinner to us which was a real treat for us after eight days of Russian fare.' Roosevelt, though, slept badly. Next morning, as he was leaving for Saki airfield, several Russian naval officers approached but he asked his interpreter, a former White Russian officer, Count Stroganoff-Scherbatoff, to tell them, 'I appreciate everything they've done, but I am very, very tired and I am too exhausted to talk anymore and to answer any questions.' At the airfield Roosevelt was reunited with some of his closest advisers, including Hopkins and Stettinius who had travelled overnight from Simferopol in a train once used by the tsars.

From Saki, Roosevelt flew in the 'Sacred Cow' to Ismailia in Egypt where he once more boarded USS *Quincy*, moored in the Great Bitter Lake in the middle of the British-controlled Suez Canal. There, as planned, he met King Farouk, the pleasure-loving ruler of Egypt under the British Protectorate established at the beginning of the century, Emperor Haile Selassie of Ethiopia and

King Ibn Saud of Saudi Arabia. The discussions with the first two involved little more than diplomatic pleasantries and the exchange of gifts. Those with Ibn Saud were more substantive.

The American navy had sent a destroyer, USS *Murphy*, to Jeddah to pick up the King and his extensive entourage. They numbered some fifty people and included, according to Bohlen, 'the royal astrologer, a coffee server, and nine miscellaneous slaves, cooks, porters and scullions'. The King, who refused to go below decks, asked for a large tent to be put up on the forecastle in which he and his courtiers could eat and pray away from prying eyes. Additionally he brought with him a small herd of goats also to be housed on deck. When a mealtime approached one would be hung from the rigging and slaughtered according to Islamic religious custom.

On Valentine's Day 1945, after a two-day voyage of more than 800 miles from Jeddah, USS *Murphy* approached USS *Quincy*. Roosevelt, who had dispatched his daughter Anna ashore to avoid any chance of giving offence to the King by the appearance of a woman participating in the meeting, watched as the *Murphy* came nearer with Ibn Saud sitting on a large gilded Louis Quinze chair on the destroyer's rug-strewn deck. The King's Nubian bodyguards were standing to attention at the ship's rails with drawn scimitars. The majesty of the *Murphy*'s approach was somewhat spoiled when the destroyer bumped against the *Quincy* as she attempted to come alongside and had to try again. Ibn Saud was quickly brought aboard the *Quincy* and the crew of the *Murphy* began telling their colleagues on the *Quincy* how the King's cooks had burned holes in the *Murphy*'s wooden decking as they barbecued the King's food and tried to make coffee in braziers set up, according to Bohlen, 'next to the ready ammunition hoist'.

Roosevelt, who later wrote to his cousin Daisy Suckley, 'whole party a scream', had determined to observe punctiliously his guest's religious scruples and therefore neither to smoke nor drink alcohol in his presence. He did, however, stop the lift in which he was descending to meet the King for long enough to smoke two cigarettes hurriedly before he greeted Ibn Saud. They lunched on rice, lamb stew and grapefruit. The King had second helpings of the latter two. After an exchange of courtesies, Roosevelt raised the question of Jewish immigration to Palestine, suggesting that 10,000 displaced Jewish people from Germany and Eastern Europe should be allowed to emigrate there. Ibn Saud objected. According to Bohlen:

> He denied that there had ever been any conflict between the two branches of the Semitic race in the Middle East. What changed the whole picture was the immigration of people from Eastern Europe who were technically and culturally on a higher level than the Arabs. As a result . . . the Arabs had great diffi-culty in surviving economically . . . That these energetic Europeans were Jewish was not the cause of the trouble, it was their superior skills and culture.

Roosevelt argued the case that Jewish people had suffered much under Hitler. According to Bohlen, Ibn Saud 'gravely replied that he did not see why the Arabs had to expiate the sins of Adolf Hitler when there were other countries in a much better position to help. Arabs would choose to die rather than yield their land to Jews. Amends should be made by the criminal, not by the innocent bystander.' The King suggested, 'Give the Jews and their descendants the choicest lands and homes of the Germans who oppressed them.'

The King's explicit refusal brought a speedy end to the polit-ical conversation after Roosevelt had assured Ibn Saud 'he would make no move hostile to the Arab people'. Roosevelt did, however, secure agreement from Ibn Saud to permit a US base on his territory to help move supplies and troops from Europe to Japan. In the exchange of gifts which followed Roosevelt presented to Ibn Saud who, Bohlen related, walked 'with a pronounced limp apparently from a wound received in internecine warfare in Arabia', his spare wheelchair as well as some of the penicillin the King had requested – according to some American accounts for use against venereal disease. William Rigdon, one of Roosevelt's naval aides, wrote that the President tactfully refused another request from the King, who said that 'the meal was the first he had eaten in a long time that was not followed by digestive disturbance and he would like, if the President would be so generous, to have the cook as a gift'.

Later, after the King had left, again according to Bohlen, Admiral Leahy remarked to Roosevelt over drinks, '"The King sure told you, didn't he?" "What do you mean, Bill?", Roosevelt responded. "If you put any more kikes in Palestine, he is going to kill them," Leahy said. Roosevelt smiled.'

Churchill boarded the Cunard liner *Franconia* in Sebastopol harbour on the evening of 11 February, the same evening Roosevelt joined the *Catoctin*. The next day, according to Cadogan, after he and the Prime Minister enjoyed 'a terrific lunch – dressed crab, roast beef, apple pie, washed down with excellent Liebfraumilch, and gorgonzola and port!' Churchill visited the Crimean War battlefields. In his memoirs Churchill related that the Russians did not realize he wished to inspect the nineteenth-century Crimean War battleground rather than the relics of the more recent conflict. However, when he suggested this, 'Our host gave no sign of comprehension, but seemed perfectly satisfied. So all passed off very pleasantly' as an English officer pointed out the valley down which the Light Brigade had charged. Back aboard the *Franconia*, where he stayed for the nights of 12 and 13 February, Churchill demanded that his Yalta clothing should be deloused.

His daughter Sarah Oliver was in more reflective mood. After all the destruction and hardship she had seen she wrote to her mother of the local people:

> how one wondered where or how they lived? Well, at night one discovers. From nearly every ruin wherever four walls of one room still stand, from behind boards that fill gaps, from basements, from piles of stones even, shafts and specks of lights shine and twinkle. It is incredible! They are incredible!

She went on to tell her mother how the churches which Stalin had allowed to reopen to improve wartime morale were a great comfort to the people, who were no different to any other human beings. 'It's no use saying "they're used to suffering. They're built differently from us. They don't expect much." Why are the churches so full, then? Of course they hope for more. Of course they dream in their darkened churches.' The scale of the devastation also struck Churchill's principal private secretary, John Martin, who wrote to his wife, 'No wonder if they talk about reparations.'

On 14 February, after much changing of his mind, Churchill decided he would accompany Eden to Athens, rather than allow the Foreign Secretary to go alone. The truce between the right-wing government forces and the Communists was holding for the present. In Constitution Square Churchill gave an open-air address to around 40,000 people, telling them 'Let right prevail. Let party hatreds die. Let there be unity, let there be resolute comradeship. Greece forever! Greece for all!' According to Marian Holmes who was present, 'the ovation was terrific. A Greek band played "God Save the King" and the Greek national anthem. The P.M. didn't recognise this latter and continued walking along until he noticed that General Scobie [the British commander in Greece] had stopped and was standing smartly to attention.' Cadogan wrote to his wife that the sea of faces looking up at Churchill had resembled 'one great stippled pink surface' and that Churchill enjoyed it all 'enormously', adding, 'Poor Anthony! All this would have been his if the P.M. hadn't butted in.' Coping with both the Prime Minister and the Foreign Secretary was, he thought, like having two prima donnas in one opera company.

Next morning, Churchill flew to Alexandria and was taken out by boat to the *Quincy* which had now moved out from the Suez Canal into the Mediterranean on its homeward journey. During a short visit a brief discussion about Anglo-American nuclear cooperation was followed by lunch. With the benefit of hindsight Churchill wrote in his memoirs, 'The President seemed placid and frail. I felt that he had a slender contact with life. I was not to see him again. We bade affectionate farewells.'

On 17 February Churchill met Ibn Saud in a hotel at an oasis in the Egyptian desert. Churchill wrote:

My admiration for [the King] was deep because of his unfailing loyalty to us. He was now over seventy but had lost none of his warrior vigour. He still lived the existence of a patriarchal king of the Arabian desert, with his forty living sons and the seventy ladies of his harem and three of the four official wives as prescribed by the Prophet.

However, perhaps because of his innate Victorian belief in Anglo-Saxon and Christian superiority, Churchill did not extend the courtesy that Roosevelt had of following the King's religious customs, writing,

> As I was the host at luncheon . . . I said to the interpreter that if it was the religion of His Majesty to deprive himself of smoking and alcohol I must point out that my rule of life prescribed as an absolute sacred right smoking cigars and also the drinking of alcohol before, after, and if need be during all meals and in the intervals between them. The King graciously accepted the position. His own cupbearer from Mecca offered me a glass of water from its sacred well, the most delicious that I had ever tasted.

Churchill's main interest was, like Roosevelt's, to maintain and improve relations to secure continuing access to Arabian oil. He did, however, raise the question of Jewish emigration to Palestine but received the same negative response as Roosevelt.

Later that day Churchill also met King Farouk of Egypt whom he admonished 'to concentrate on good works and, in particular, on improving the condition of the Fellaheen [the common people], for while Egypt at the moment was a country of great wealth, the differences between the level of living of the various social classes was more marked than ever before'. Before departing by air for London, Churchill also fitted in a meeting with Haile Selassie, whom he did not find as grateful as he expected for the successful British efforts to free Ethiopia of occupying Italian troops in 1940/1.

*

Minutes after Churchill had departed, the USS *Quincy* set sail from Alexandria westwards through the Mediterranean. Soon after leaving, 'Pa' Watson, Roosevelt's friend and aide who was already in the sickbay suffering from heart problems, had a cerebral haemorrhage and became semi-conscious. As they headed to Algiers, Roosevelt considered his response to a message that de Gaulle had cancelled their planned meeting there, as everyone assumed, out of pique at not being invited to Yalta. The French leader had already broadcast to the French people during the conference that France would not be bound by the conference's decisions but would pursue an independent line. Roosevelt himself drafted a most undiplomatic note to the French leader. Only with great difficulty did Hopkins and Bohlen, who told Roosevelt, 'we can all admit de Gaulle is one of the biggest sons of bitches who ever straddled a pot', persuade the President to allow them to draft and dispatch a stern if less positively 'insulting' alternative.

Hopkins, who according to Bohlen had lost eighteen pounds in weight in Yalta because of his gastric problems, told Roosevelt that he was too ill to make the sea voyage and wished to leave the *Quincy* at Algiers to recuperate in Marrakech before flying back to the United States. Roosevelt was not at all pleased. He had wanted Hopkins to help him draft his speech to Congress, reporting on Yalta, during the voyage and tried hard to persuade Hopkins to stay. Hopkins was resolute and eventually after some 'not very amiable discussions' Roosevelt agreed to his departure, together with Bohlen. According to his son Robert, a 'grouchy' Hopkins forgot to say goodbye to Roosevelt as he departed. Like Churchill, he would not see the President alive again.

To help him draft his speech during the transatlantic crossing Roosevelt summoned to Algiers Sam Rosenman, an aide, speech writer and former New York Supreme Court Justice. Soon after the *Quincy* passed through the Straits of Gibraltar 'Pa' Watson died, leaving Roosevelt, according to Rosenman, 'deeply depressed'.

For most of the crossing the President paid little attention to his speech, spending the daytime reading or gazing out to sea from the deck and the evenings, after as usual mixing cocktails, watching films. He did find time to give interviews to three carefully selected American journalists invited to make the crossing with him. One of their questions was whether Churchill wanted the British Empire's territories 'all back just the way they were'. Roosevelt responded accurately if uncharitably, 'Yes, he is mid-Victorian on all things like that.' Rosenman recalled that even though 'he had a real deep affection and admiration for Churchill', the President told him that:

> Dear old Winston was quite loquacious in these conferences . . . sometimes going into irrelevancies; that he quite obviously irritated Stalin by these long discourses and that at times he, Roosevelt, had to get Churchill back to the subject . . . Now that the time was drawing near for carrying out some of the tough principles contained in the Atlantic Charter the President was beginning to feel that the traditions of British imperialism were playing too heavy a part in Churchill's thinking.

The President also told Rosenman he was 'worried about what would happen if Stalin should die or be stripped of his power. But there was no doubt in his mind that if the Soviet leaders would back Stalin, a new era in world peace was at hand.' His remark again illustrated the common, entirely erroneous but persistent naive belief in the UK, and more particularly in the US administration, that Stalin was trustworthy but had to contend with powerful more extreme rivals within the Kremlin who were responsible for Soviet breaches of trust.

On the last day before the *Quincy* arrived Roosevelt finally worked hard on the draft of his speech which he gave to Congress three days later on Wednesday 1 March. For the first time the obviously frail, thin Roosevelt allowed secret service men to push him in his usual armless wheelchair to the mahogany table covered with broadcasters' microphones behind which he sat on a red plush chair to deliver his speech.

Roosevelt began:

> I hope that you will pardon me for an unusual posture of sitting down during the presentation . . . but I know that you will

realize that it makes it a lot easier for me in not having to carry about ten pounds of steel round on the bottom of my legs; and also because of the fact I have just completed a fourteen-thousand-mile trip.

Congress burst into applause before he went on to say, 'I come from the Crimea Conference with a firm belief that we have made a good start on the road to a world of peace', and then outlined the decisions taken at Yalta. The conference, he said, 'spells – it ought to spell – the end of the system of unilateral action, the exclusive alliances, the spheres of influence, the balances of power and all the other expedients that have been tried for centuries – and have always failed'.

Throughout Roosevelt's voice was low, he had difficulty turning the pages of his speech and sometimes seemed to lose his place in his text, resorting to much more ad libbing than usual, as those who had been given advance copies noticed. The poet Archibald MacLeish, an assistant secretary at the State Department, noted 'the cold spring light on his face and death in his eyes'. Nevertheless Roosevelt's speech seemed to convince both Congress and the wider public. US opinion polls showed a large rise to an all-time high in public satisfaction with Big Three cooperation and a belief in the success of the conference.

On his arrival back in London on 19 February after three weeks away from Britain, Churchill had a harder time. He reported that same day to the War Cabinet whom he told that he was 'quite sure' Stalin 'meant well to the world and to Poland' and he did not believe there would be 'any resentment on the part of Russia about the arrangements that had been made for free and fair elections in that country'.

As Churchill had predicted, the Polish government in London had already damned the Yalta terms 'as a fifth partition of Poland, now accomplished by her allies'. On 21 February Churchill had a two-and-a-half-hour meeting with the Polish Commander-in-Chief General Władysław Anders conducted 'in French of a kind' to avoid the need for an interpreter. According to Cadogan, who was present, 'Both men lost their tempers at first.' Anders believed that the Yalta agreements were 'a great calamity' for Poland which must become a Soviet republic. He asked how could he persuade his men to go on fighting. Churchill snapped back, 'We have never guaranteed your eastern frontiers. We have enough troops today, and we do not need your help. You can take away your divisions. We shall do without them.' Later, though, both 'calmed down' and Cadogan thought 'the meeting may have done some good', with Churchill promising that whatever happened members of the Polish forces would be free to settle in the UK if they did not wish to return to their homeland.

On 23 February Churchill told more junior members of his administration, 'Poor Neville Chamberlain believed he could trust Hitler. He was wrong. But I don't think I'm wrong about Stalin.'

Members of the British public sympathized with the Poles. Edie Rutherford, a housewife contributing to the government's Mass-Observation project launched in 1937 to provide insights into British people's thinking, wrote, 'So the Poles are NOT satisfied with the Big Three's arrangements. Well, I don't really blame them, as it isn't right for outsiders with the whip hand to sit down and make decisions which vitally affect others and only secondarily themselves.'

On 27 February, Churchill reported on the conference to the House of Commons. In a speech lasting nearly two hours, he told members, 'Most solemn declarations have been made by Marshal Stalin and the Soviet State that the sovereign independence of Poland is to be maintained' in agreement with Britain and the United States.

> The impression I brought back from the Crimea, and from all my other contacts, is that Marshal Stalin and the Soviet leaders wish to live in honourable friendship and equality with the Western democracies. I feel also that their word is their bond. I know of no government which stands to its obligations, even in its own despite, more solemnly than the Russian Soviet Government . . . I trust the House will feel that hope has been powerfully strengthened by our meeting . . . The ties that bind the three Great Powers together and their mutual comprehension

of each other have grown. The United States has entered deeply and constructively into the life and salvation of Europe. We have all three set our hands to far-reaching engagements at once practical and solemn . . . United we have the unchallengeable power to lead the world to prosperity, freedom and happiness. The Great Powers must seek to serve and not to rule.

Some Conservative MPs quickly moved an amendment regretting the failure of the Yalta agreements 'to ensure to those nations which had been liberated from German oppression the full right to choose their own Government free from the influence of any other power'. The motion was defeated by 396 votes to 25. The behaviour of the rebel Conservative MPs brought an outburst from Cadogan: 'How I hate Members of Parliament. They embody everything that my training has taught me to eschew – ambition, prejudice, dishonesty, self-seeking, light-hearted irresponsibility, black-hearted mendacity.'

Nevertheless Jock Colville, one of Churchill's private secretaries, thought Churchill 'in his heart . . . is worried about Poland and not convinced of the strength of our moral position'. Churchill's unease came through in a personal letter to the New Zealand Prime Minister when he wrote:

Great Britain and the British Commonwealth are very much weaker militarily than Soviet Russia and have no means, short of another general war, of enforcing their point of view. Nor can we ignore the position of the United States. We cannot go further in helping Poland than the United States is willing or can be persuaded to go. We have therefore to do the best we can . . . The proof of the pudding is in the eating.

Roosevelt expressed similar unease, telling an old friend who questioned the soundness of the agreement on Poland, as he had told Leahy at Yalta, that if not perfect the outcome was the best he could achieve.

By the beginning of March events were starting to justify the two leaders' misgivings. This first became evident in Romania, which, with the support of its young King, Michael, had in September 1944 switched sides from the Axis to the Allies and where the new government was led by a right-wing general, Nicolae Radescu, imprisoned under the previous Nazi regime. On 27 February, following clashes between government and Communist supporters, Stalin sent Andrei Vyshinsky to Bucharest. The next day he marched into King Michael's apartments. Banging his fist on the table, he delivered an ultimatum to the twenty-three-year-old ruler. He must dismiss Radescu immediately and appoint a Communist-dominated government or face the conse-quences. At the same time Russian tanks appeared on the streets of Bucharest and Russian soldiers disarmed Romanian troops. The King had no choice but to cave in to an arrangement which did not leave the choice of government to the Romanian people, as the Yalta Declaration on Liberated Europe required.

News of the coup reached London in what Jock Colville called 'sinister telegrams'. He described his subsequent conversation with Churchill:

> I spoke to him of the position and he said he feared he could do nothing. Russia had let us go our way in Greece; she would insist on imposing her will in Romania and Bulgaria. But as regards Poland we would have our say. As we went to bed, after 2 a.m. the P.M. said to me, 'I have not the slightest intention of being cheated over Poland, not even if we go to the verge of war with Russia'.

In an exchange with Churchill over the following days, Roosevelt agreed that 'the Russians have installed a minority government of their own choosing', but like Churchill, who must have had his 'naughty document' in mind, he did not think Romania was 'a good place for a test case' of the Yalta agreement since 'the Russians have been in undisputed control from the beginning and with Romania lying athwart the Russian lines of communications' he found it 'difficult to contest the plea of mili-tary necessity and security which they are using to justify their action'. Roosevelt was in any case concerned to retain Soviet support for the United Nations and, equally important, Soviet participation in the expected hard fight to capture the Japanese homeland. On reaching the White House from the *Quincy* he had gasped audibly when told of heavy American casualties in the invasion of the island of Iwo Jima which had not yet been secured.

Churchill, though, was heartened by how well the war in the West was going. On 3 March he found time to visit the Allied troops who had breached the Siegfried Line. There, together with Montgomery, Brooke, American Lieutenant-General William Simpson as the Allied commander in the area, their staffs and other officers, he indulged in a mass urination on the Siegfried Line after telling accompanying photographers, 'this is one of the operations connected with this great war which must not be reproduced graphically' and to turn away. That night Churchill went alone to the Rhine itself, whose opposite bank German troops still held, and urinated into the river. 'Most satisfactory', he proclaimed as he rebuttoned his flies.

Roosevelt's frailty was becoming increasingly clear to all those around him. Anna Boettiger was redoubling her efforts to restrict her father's visitors to the minimum consistent with the conduct of government business. Byrnes and Leahy were now drafting many of his telegrams and minutes for him. Eleanor Roosevelt was beginning to realize her husband no longer had the appetite for the political debate that had been a continuing mainstay of their unique marriage which reached its fortieth anniversary on 17 March, St Patrick's Day. After she had argued 'heatedly' with him about peacetime conscription she recalled:

I suddenly realised he was upset. I had forgotten that Franklin was no longer the calm and imperturbable person who, in the past, had always goaded me on to vehement arguments when questions of policy came up. It was just another indication of the change which we were all so unwilling to acknowledge.

Dr Bruenn noted that after such exchanges with his wife the President's blood pressure rose greatly. Anna Boettiger summed up her parents' debates. Her mother:

pressed more strongly and perhaps with less tact than in the past. The nerves of both of them were raw . . . Although she knew the doctors had said he should have his half hour of relaxation – no business, just sitting around, maybe a drink, she would come in more and more frequently with an enormous bundle of letters which she wished to discuss with him immediately and have a decision on . . . She could pester the hell out of him.

Roosevelt not only had such domestic debates to contend with but also what was becoming a barrage of messages from Churchill about the deteriorating situation in Poland; the Soviets were arresting and deporting those they considered their opponents, and Molotov was refusing to implement the Yalta agreement on the creation of a unity government and the holding of free elections in the country. Churchill wrote to Roosevelt in March that Poland was 'the test case between us and the Russians of the meaning which is to be attached to such terms as Democracy, Sovereignty, Independence, Representative Government and free and unfettered elections'. In his view Molotov wanted to make:

a farce of consultations with the 'Non-Lublin' Poles – which means that the new government in Poland would be merely the present one dressed up to look more respectable to the ignorant and also wants to prevent us from seeing the liquidations and deportations that are going on and all the rest of the game of setting up a totalitarian regime before elections are held and even before a new government is set up . . . if we do not get things right now, it will soon be seen by the world that you and I by putting our signatures to the Crimea settlement, have under-written a fraudulent prospectus.

Roosevelt's reply was that their only differences were about tactics. He did not wish to elevate the matter to the highest level (Stalin) before all other routes had been exhausted. This did not satisfy Churchill who in a further message complained that 'Poland has lost her frontier. Is she now to lose her freedom?' Churchill's own relatively mild protests to Stalin were brushed aside and his requests to allow British and American ambassadors to visit Poland ignored. On 27 March, the day the one thousand and fiftieth and last V2 rocket hit Britain, Churchill told Roosevelt it was 'plain as a pike staff' that Molotov's tactics were 'to drag the business out while the Lublin Committee consolidate their power . . . Surely we must not be manoeuvred into becoming parties to imposing on Poland, and on how much more of Eastern Europe, the Russian version of democracy?'

When, after these urgings, backed up by a telegram from Harriman in Moscow stating, 'We must come clearly to realise that the Soviet programme is the establishment of totalitarianism ending personal liberty and democracy as we know it,' on 31 March Roosevelt did indeed protest to Stalin. The Soviet leader was unmoved. He wanted a friendly government on his borders:

> The Soviet Government insists on this because of the blood of the Soviet troops abundantly shed for the liberation of Poland and the fact that in the course of the last 30 years the territory of Poland has been used by the enemy twice for attack upon Russia – all this obliges the Soviet Government to strive that the relations between the Soviet Union and Poland be friendly.

Soon afterwards news reached London that the fifteen leaders of the Polish home army, including leaders of the Warsaw rising, who had accepted an invitation to discussions with the Russians had disappeared. They had in fact been kidnapped and taken to Moscow's Lubyanka prison.

Other issues were disrupting relations between the Soviet Union and the West. The American and British authorities were becoming increasingly concerned about the treatment of the thousands of their prisoners of war released from German captivity in Eastern Europe by the Russians about whom, despite the agreement at Yalta, they had little information and less access.

For his part, Stalin was incensed to discover that SS General Karl Wolff had met UK and US representatives in Berne, Switzerland, to discuss the possible surrender to them of German forces in Italy. The story threatened to drive a wedge between Stalin – with his long-held fears of a separate peace between the two Western Allies and Germany and even of their combining with Germany to attack Russia – and the US and the UK. Molotov first protested to British ambassador Archibald Clark Kerr that negotiations were going on 'behind the backs of the Soviet Union'. Clark Kerr replied accurately that an attempt was merely being made to test Wolff's credentials and the seriousness of his approach. Molotov in turn responded that the Soviet Union saw this 'not as a misunderstanding but something worse'. Still unsatisfied, towards the end of March Stalin wrote to Roosevelt saying he understood his two allies were about to offer easier peace terms to Germany to allow their own troops to advance east unopposed. Why had he not been told and why had Russian participation in the meeting not been invited?

Roosevelt, who had heard little of Wolff's approach, after informing himself reiterated in a message to Stalin that this was indeed a misunderstanding. Only preliminary talks – not negotiations – were involved and there were 'no political implications whatever and no violation of our agreed principle of unconditional surrender'. An angry Stalin repeated his allegations and retorted he could only assume that the President had not been 'fully informed' by his military advisers. Roosevelt responded that he had told the truth and that 'it would be one of the great tragedies of history if at the very moment of victory now within our grasp, such distrust, such lack of faith should prejudice the entire undertaking after the colossal losses of life, materiel and treasure involved'. The message concluded, 'Frankly I cannot avoid a feeling of bitter resentment toward your informers, whoever they are, for such vile misrepresentations of my actions or those of my trusted subordinates.' Stalin sent a more emollient reply that he was not questioning the President's honour and the exchange fizzled out, as did the Wolff approach, which came to nothing.

On 29 March Roosevelt set out for Warm Springs in the hope of recuperating his strength during an extended Easter break. As he did so, the Allied war in Europe was fast approaching its victorious conclusion. On the morning of 7 March, American troops had captured intact the railway bridge over the Rhine at Remagen and established a bridgehead on its eastern bank – the first invaders to cross the Rhine into German territory since Napoleon's time. Backed up by tactical bombing offensives against road and rail communications, the Allies made several further crossings in the course of March and by the end of the month were pressing deep into the Ruhr with 15,000–20,000 prisoners being taken most days. The Soviet army had, by the month's end, Gdynia, Danzig and Königsberg all under siege and were less than seventy-five miles from Vienna. Allied bombing raids continued against ever-diminishing resistance from German aircraft. Many of Germany's new jet planes were shot down as they attacked the Allied bridgeheads across the Rhine or destroyed on the ground in bombing raids.

In the Pacific, on 9 March the USAAF undertook the most destructive conventional bombing raid in history against Tokyo. Three hundred and thirty-four bombers flying from Tinian Island dropped 2,000 tons of incendiaries, some for the first time containing a new American invention, 'sticky fire' – napalm – and producing a firestorm among the mostly wooden dwellings of the city which burned out sixteen square miles of Tokyo and killed more than 80,000 people. Further devastating raids followed on other Japanese cities. The US army and marines continued to capture further Philippine islands and, after concluding the conquest of Iwo Jima with heavy casualties, on the morning of 1 April landed on Okinawa. In the battle for the island more than 20,000 US servicemen would die, 4,900 of them on naval ships hit by kamikazes, while some 108,000 Japanese troops and 150,000 civilians were also killed.

In late March Churchill again visited the Western Front, making a two-day tour that included flying over the Rhine east of the River Meuse as Allied artillery thundered out further east. Then, after landing, he crossed the Rhine himself to make a one-and-a-half-hour visit to its eastern side, declaring, 'A beaten army, not long ago master of Europe, retreats before its pursuers. The goal is not long to be denied to those who have come so far and fought so well under proud and faithful leadership. Forward all on wings of flame to final Victory.' Returning with Churchill, Brooke recorded in his diary:

> It was a relief to get Winston home safely. I know that he longed to get into the most exposed position possible. I honestly believe that he would really have liked to be killed on the front at this moment of success. He had often told me that the way to die is to pass out fighting when your blood is up and you feel nothing.

Both because of his distance from the action and his frailty, Roosevelt was unable to visit the battlefronts. On his arrival at Warm Springs, where white and yellow azaleas were in bloom, his head of security Mike Reilly found the President unusually an 'absolutely dead weight' as he lifted him from his car. As well as dealing with essential correspondence, including the conclusion of his exchanges with Stalin on the Wolff approach, Roosevelt spent his time relaxing in the company of his two adoring cousins Daisy Suckley and Laura Delano – the latter, an enthusiastic user of exotic hair dyes, sporting 'bright blue hair' for the occasion – and looking over his stamp collection. He was particularly interested in some stamps the Japanese issued during their occupation of the Philippines which had recently been sent to him. He was looking forward to attending the opening session of the United Nations Conference in San Francisco on 25 April and sketched a design of a commemorative stamp to mark the event. On 5 April, he was delighted to learn that Moscow had repudiated its non-aggression pact with Japan, noting that this meant business.

On 9 April Lucy Mercer Rutherfurd joined the party at Warm Springs. His renewed acquaintance with her was well known to Roosevelt's cousins and his daughter Anna – absent on this occasion – but certainly not to Eleanor. Both Anna and his cousins realized how Lucy helped the President to relax. Anna recalled, 'She was a wonderful listener . . . an intelligent listener in that she knew the right questions while mother would get in there and say "I think you are wrong, Franklin".' Even if Daisy Suckley, perhaps a little jealous, complained in her diary after Lucy's arrival, 'Lucy is such a lovely person but she seems so very immature' and was bringing '*so* many problems and difficulties' to put on the President's shoulders, Roosevelt's pleasure at seeing Lucy, whom he had driven out to meet, was clear to all.

Lucy was accompanied by her friend Elizabeth Shoumatoff, a portrait painter whom she had commissioned to paint the President, together with a photographer to take pictures on which to base her work. Over the next two days Lucy talked to Roosevelt as Shoumatoff arranged the photographer's shots. In the late afternoon of 10 April, accompanied by his dog Fala, Roosevelt himself drove Lucy in his car, which had controls specially adapted to be used by hand, alone to a hilltop to view the sunset. On their return Daisy Suckley noticed Roosevelt's colour had improved to a much more healthy pink.

Next day, Roosevelt himself composed a message to Churchill in response to his oft-expressed worries about deteriorating relations with the Soviet Union: 'I would minimize the general Soviet problem as much as possible because these problems, in one form or another, seem to arise every day and most of them straighten out . . . We must be firm, however, and our course thus far is correct.' That evening Roosevelt's old friend Treasury Secretary Henry Morgenthau visited en route to Florida. Morgenthau recalled how Roosevelt's hands shook when he started to mix cocktails 'so that he started to knock the glasses over, and I had to hold each glass as he poured out the cocktail . . . I noticed that he took two cocktails and then seemed to feel a little bit better. I found his memory bad, and he was constantly confusing names.' Nevertheless, Roosevelt produced a large tin of caviar given to him by Stalin at Yalta, ate well, and spent a pleasant evening with Morgenthau, 'recalling different amusing and entertaining incidents about Churchill'. After Morgenthau had left, Roosevelt and the women were sitting around the fire telling ghost stories when Dr Bruenn entered to tell Roosevelt it was his bedtime. According to Shoumatoff he pleaded 'like a little boy to stay up longer' but then meekly retired to his bedroom.

The President rose late on the morning of 12 April after reading in bed press reports containing among other things news of the fall of both Königsberg and Vienna to the Russians and Allied successes around Bologna in Italy. Wearing a grey double-breasted suit and a crimson tie, he was installed at a card table in the wood-panelled living room, worked on some of his papers with his aide William Hassett, signed some Congressional bills, then allowed Elizabeth Shoumatoff to set up her easel to work on his portrait. He continued to study papers but, according to Hassett, was interrupted 'constantly' by Shoumatoff taking facial measurements to further her work, wanting 'the Boss to turn this way and that' as if 'nothing mattered but her whims'. A Filipino steward brought in a bowl of the nutritious gruel served to Roosevelt to improve his strength and the President took some spoonfuls before returning to his correspondence, telling his companions, 'We have got just about fifteen minutes more to work.'

A few minutes later, after Hassett had left, Daisy Suckley, who had been crocheting, saw Roosevelt's head fall forward onto his chest and his hands shake violently. She rushed towards him. 'Have you dropped your cigarette?' she asked. He 'looked at me with his forehead furrowed in pain and tried to smile. He put his left hand up to the back of his head and said, "I have a terrific pain in the back of my head!"' She quickly summoned Dr Bruenn and loosened the President's collar and tie. Lucy Rutherfurd tried to rouse him by placing camphor under his nose but Roosevelt was soon entirely unconscious. By 2.30 p.m. Lucy, concerned for propriety, and Elizabeth Shoumatoff had left Warm Springs. Despite all the efforts of Bruenn and a hastily summoned colleague, which included an injection of amyl nitrate, Roosevelt, whose face had turned bluish-purple, stopped breathing at 3.31 p.m. Bruenn's colleague injected adrenaline directly into the President's heart to no avail. At 3.35 p.m. Bruenn pronounced Franklin Delano Roosevelt dead.

CHAPTER SIXTEEN

'I Liked the Little Son of a Bitch'

Harry Truman, Vice-President for only eleven weeks, was called to the White House just after 5 p.m. and shown into Eleanor Roosevelt's study where she put her arm around his shoulder and told him, 'the President is dead'. Roosevelt had kept Truman out of all major decisions on the war and of relations with Churchill and Stalin. In fact, the sixty-year-old Truman had only been abroad once when he fought for seven months as an artillery officer in France in the First World War. He returned home from the White House 'very much shocked', to contemplate his new responsibilities as thirty-third President of the United States.*

Partly because of the difference in time zones, the news of Roosevelt's death did not reach Churchill until midnight London time. Churchill, who had already received the bad news that day of the death in action of one of his wife Clementine's cousins and of another close family friend, immediately informed Clementine, then visiting the Soviet Union on behalf of the Red Cross, and the King, of the President's death. He next telegraphed Lord Halifax, the British ambassador in Washington, asking him to find out if he would be welcome at the funeral. The reply was

---

* Truman was only the thirty-second person to hold the office but as Grover Cleveland held it on two separate occasions the Truman presidency is normally considered the thirty-third.

that he certainly would and that Truman would appreciate the opportunity to meet him and 'perhaps have two or three days talks with him'. Churchill began to make preparations to attend but with the plane ready to take off with the British party at 8.30 p.m. on 13 April, Churchill dithered. By 7.45 p.m. according to Cadogan he had still not made up his mind: 'PM said he would decide at the airport.' In the end he did not board the aircraft, leaving Eden to represent him.

Churchill's stated reason for not attending was the pressure of business, with many other ministers abroad. This cannot have been the prime reason – when Churchill wanted to do something he did it. There is no doubt about the real warmth of his friendship with Roosevelt despite their more recent frictions, and his staff and colleagues could see his evident distress at the news. He told his daughter Mary, 'You know how this will hit me.' He was undoubtedly sincere in his message to Eleanor Roosevelt, 'I feel so deeply for you all . . . I have lost a dear and cherished friendship which was forged in the fire of war', and when he told Hopkins, 'I feel a very painful personal loss, quite apart from the ties of public action which bound us so closely together. I had a true affection for Franklin.'

Perhaps knowing himself, Churchill simply feared becoming too emotional at the funeral and in so doing distracting attention from the mourning for Roosevelt. Perhaps Roosevelt's death, a sign of his own mortality, had brought on one of his moods of 'black dog' depression. Perhaps depression exacerbated a feeling that he was just too exhausted – that month he was spending even more time in bed and often had to be carried upstairs in a chair, lacking the energy or will to scale them himself. Others have suggested that Churchill, having long been the suitor, the client who always travelled to meet Roosevelt, now wished to be the one visited in London and wooed by Truman, showing the world that Britain and its empire remained a great power. No one will ever know.

Churchill gave an emotional eulogy for the President to the House of Commons on 17 April which ended: 'in Franklin Roosevelt there died the greatest American friend we have ever known, and the greatest champion of freedom who has ever brought help and comfort from the new world to the old'. Churchill was later sorry he had not accepted Truman's invitation and gone to Washington, writing in his memoirs:

> I regret that I did not adopt the new President's suggestion. I had never met him and I feel that there were many points on which personal talks would have been the greatest value, especially if they . . . were not hurried or formalised. It seemed to me extraordinary, especially during those last few months, that Roosevelt had not made his deputy and potential successor thoroughly acquainted with the whole story and brought him into the decisions which were being taken. This proved a grave disadvantage to our affairs.

Harriman learned of Roosevelt's death at 1 a.m. Moscow time on 13 April and immediately arranged through Molotov to see Stalin, which he did that evening in his office at the Kremlin. He remembered that Stalin held 'his hand for perhaps thirty seconds' and 'appeared deeply distressed'. The Russian leader, whose troops had that day reached Vienna, asked many questions about Truman whom, like Churchill, he had never met and about whom he knew little. He accepted Harriman's suggestion that Molotov should attend the San Francisco United Nations Conference and visit Washington to meet Truman. Later Stalin would convince himself that Roosevelt had been poisoned partly because there was no post mortem on the President (Eleanor Roosevelt had refused one on the grounds that it was not family custom to allow them), and the Soviet ambassador in Washington, Andrei Gromyko, had not been allowed to view the corpse. Mainly, however, his existing and worsening paranoia that he himself might easily be poisoned led him to believe that other leaders could suffer a similar fate.

In Berlin, already under attack by the Red Army and where on the day Roosevelt died the Berlin Philharmonic Orchestra had given what turned out to be its last concert of the war, culminating in the finale of Wagner's *Götterdämmerung*, Goebbels told

Hitler, 'My Fuhrer, I congratulate you! Roosevelt is dead. It is written in the stars that the second half of April will be the turning point for us. This is Friday 13 April. It is the turning point.' Hitler's verdict was, 'Fate has removed the greatest war criminal of all time.'

As Truman became acquainted with the international situation, to Churchill's relief he proved willing to take a stronger line than Roosevelt with the Soviet Union over issues such as Poland. After Truman had been in power for just a week Churchill telegraphed Eden, 'My appreciation is that the new man is not to be bullied by the Soviets. Seeking as I do a lasting friendship with the Russian people I am sure this can only be founded on the recognition of Anglo-American strength.'

When Truman met Molotov in Washington during the latter's visit to the United States for the UN conference, he first, at Molotov's request, confirmed his support for the Yalta deal on the terms for Soviet entry into the war against Japan. Then he grew stern with his visitor, telling him, 'An agreement has been reached on Poland and it only remains for Marshal Stalin to carry it out in accordance with his word,' and produced a letter for Molotov to take to Stalin insisting some non-Communist, non-Lublin, Poles should be appointed to the new Polish government. Bohlen, who was translating as usual, 'enjoyed' the President's approach – 'probably the first sharp words uttered during the war by an American President to a high Soviet official'. Truman later said, 'I gave it to him straight. I let him have it. It was a straight one-two to the jaw.'

On 11 April US forces had entered Buchenwald concentration camp in Germany. The next day Ed Murrow of CBS described how in one room 'there were two rows of bodies stacked up like cordwood. They were thin and very white. Some of the bodies were terribly bruised though there seemed to be little flesh to bruise. Some had been shot through the head, but they bled but little.' On 15 April British soldiers reached Belsen. One British soldier who was guarding the milk store they had established 'and doling the milk out to children' told his officer he was horrified when a woman came up to him 'and begged for milk for her baby. [He] took the baby and saw that it had been dead for days, black in the face and shrivelled up. The woman went on begging for milk. So he poured some on the dead lips. The mother then started to croon with joy and carried the baby off in triumph. She stumbled and fell dead in a few yards.' The revelations about the camps and in particular the photographs and films of emaciated survivors and corpses hardened British and American public opinion against Germany and in favour of the harshest punishment of war criminals.

In the late afternoon of 25 April, the day the San Francisco conference opened and that Truman was first told about the Manhattan Project, US and Soviet troops met on the River Elbe near Turgau. The war in Europe was going so well that Churchill had already sought and been given assurances that British breweries had produced sufficient beer to fuel the victory celebrations which could not now be long delayed. On 29 April Churchill made a final appeal to Stalin on Poland, telling him, 'This British flame burns still among all classes and parties . . . they can never feel this war will have ended rightly unless Poland has a fair deal in the full sense of sovereignty, independence and freedom on the basis of friendship with Russia . . . that I thought we had agreed at Yalta.' Next day, Hitler shot himself in his bunker deep beneath Berlin and that same day Russian troops flew the Red Flag from the roof of the Reichstag in the city.

As the Soviet soldiers, who had lost 80,000 of their comrades in the campaign for Berlin, including 25,000 in the fighting within it, gradually assumed control they indulged in an orgy of looting and raping. Soviet troops shot and killed a Berlin lawyer who had protected his wife who was Jewish from the Nazis throughout the war, when he attempted to save her from rape. Then they raped her anyway. Estimates suggest between 1 and 2 million German women were raped in those parts of Germany occupied by the Red Army over the next few months. On 7 May the German Chief of Staff General Alfred Jodl signed an unconditional surrender and the Western Allies celebrated 'VE' – 'Victory in Europe' on 8 May. The Soviet Union celebrated the following day.

Churchill continued to be perturbed by Soviet intransigence on Poland and the Western Allies' inability to find out what was happening there. On 12 May, he telegraphed Truman, 'An iron curtain is drawn down upon their front. We do not know what is going on behind . . . This issue of a settlement with Russia before our strength has gone seems to me to dwarf all others.'*

Ten days later Churchill received a report responding to his request, motivated by such concerns, to his generals to consider the feasibility of a war to impose on the Soviet Union the will of the UK and US governments. Their formal view was pessimistic if non-committal. Brooke in his diary was more forthright:

> This evening I went carefully through the Planners' report on the possibility of taking on Russia should trouble arise in our future discussions with her. We were instructed to carry out this investigation. The idea is of course fantastic and the chances of success quite impossible. There is no doubt that from now onwards Russia is all powerful in Europe.

Work on the atomic bomb – the weapon which would throw into doubt Brooke's conclusion – was now going well. On 10 and 11 May, the Targeting Committee, which had British as well as American representatives, met at Los Alamos in the office of Robert Oppenheimer, the scientific head of the Manhattan Project, and agreed criteria for target selection. Among these was 'that psychological factors in the target's selection were of great import-ance. Two aspects of this are, (1) obtaining the greatest psychological effect against Japan and (2) making the initial use sufficiently spectacular for the importance of the weapon to be internationally recognised when publicity on it is released.' The

* The term 'iron curtain' had previously been used as a metaphor to indicate an end to an era or a division between opposing countries or beliefs. Goebbels had used it on 25 February 1945 in an article in *Das Reich* railing against the Yalta deci-sions. Churchill's most famous use of the phrase would be in his 'Sinews of Peace' speech in Fulton, Missouri, in March 1946.

latter was a clear reference to the need to impress the Soviet Union. Five possible targets were selected including Hiroshima and Kyoto. Later, the long-serving Secretary of War Henry Stimson deleted the latter because of its historical and cultural importance.

In late May, Truman sent Harry Hopkins to Moscow to meet Stalin and in particular to remonstrate with him about the continued lack of progress on the Polish question and especially the composition of the future Polish government. In bruising discussions stretching over seven meetings and two weeks, Stalin lectured Hopkins on the Soviet need for friendly states on its borders and insisted that any attempt to use Lend-Lease as a bargaining tool 'to soften up the Russians' would be 'a fundamental mistake'. He suggested that Hopkins should have the courage to speak more frankly and not attempt to use US public opinion as a cover for the administration's own views: 'Despite the fact they were simple people the Russians should not be regarded as fools which was a mistake the West frequently made'.

In the end, Hopkins and subsequently the US and UK governments reluctantly agreed that five Poles from outside the Lublin government should simply be added to that body rather than the entire body being reconstituted. They would then recognize the government, which they did in early July. Mikołajczyk was one of the newly appointed Poles and served as deputy prime minister until ousted and forced into exile in spring 1947.

Hopkins did, however, win important agreements from Stalin. One was a provisional date of 8 August for Soviet entry into the war against Japan. Another was that the UN could go ahead on the basis of the agreement at Yalta about voting and the Security Council veto. This latter was a considerable concession since even after Yalta the subject had remained of continuing concern to the Soviet side who had wanted to restrict small countries' rights even to raise complaints against the veto holders. The agreement allowed all parties to sign the UN Charter on 26 June in San Francisco.*

* As foreshadowed at Yalta, Belorussia and the Ukraine, as well as the Soviet Union, were founding members.

In response to pressure from Hopkins about the Poles who had disappeared on their way to discussions with the Soviets, Stalin said that they had been imprisoned and would have to be tried for their anti-Soviet activities but he would support leniency for them. (In the event, most received sentences of five to eight years. Several were re-arrested on their release.) Finally, Hopkins agreed with Stalin that, with a number of important issues still to be settled, the time was right for the Big Three to meet again. Berlin and mid-July were the agreed venue and time.

The prospect of such a meeting, originally proposed by Churchill for mid-June, had already caused tension between Britain and the US. Truman, adopting Roosevelt's position that the US should not be seen to be ganging up with the UK against the Soviet Union, had rejected Churchill's offer of a pre-conference meeting in London to agree joint approaches. Even worse from Churchill's point of view, and again in line with Roosevelt's thinking about the major role resting with the US, Truman suggested that he should meet Stalin first and that Churchill should join them a few days later. Churchill's hurt and angry response was that he would 'not be prepared to attend a meeting which was a continuation of a conference between yourself and Marshal Stalin . . . we should meet simultaneously and on equal terms'. Truman thereupon accepted that the Prime Minister should attend from the start. Conscious that the Manhattan Project was progressing well, Truman insisted the conference should be postponed for a month to mid-July – the time he knew an atomic bomb test was likely.

Truman and Churchill arrived in Berlin before Stalin. Truman crossed the Atlantic to Antwerp on the heavy cruiser USS *Augusta* in which Roosevelt had travelled to Placentia Bay to meet Churchill in August 1941. Aboard ship Truman found time to play poker, his favourite game. On 15 July 1945, he flew on in the '*Sacred Cow*' to Berlin, before continuing by road to the conference venue of Potsdam, eighteen miles from the city centre.

The delegation Truman brought to the conference (usually known as the Potsdam Conference after its precise venue) was considerably changed from Roosevelt's at Yalta. On his return from Moscow in June, Harry Hopkins had resigned from the administration – he died only a few months later in January 1946. Truman had replaced Stettinius as Secretary of State with James Byrnes who played a prominent role at Potsdam. Although Morgenthau had not been at Yalta, he asked Truman to allow him to accompany him to Potsdam. When Truman refused, he offered his resignation, which Truman accepted. The President told Stimson, who was to attend, 'None of the Jew boys will be going to Potsdam.' Harriman did attend, as did Bohlen in his continuing role as interpreter. Harriman found working with Byrnes difficult, often disparaging his views, and sent Truman his resignation six weeks after Potsdam, finally leaving the Moscow Embassy in January 1946. Bohlen regretted that his duties were now mainly confined to interpreting whereas Roosevelt had often sought his advice.

Truman's lodgings, which quickly became known as the 'Little White House', were in a three-storey yellow stucco building beside Lake Griebnitz in whose waters Russian troops had reputedly drowned wounded Germans soldiers. Although Truman was told by the Russians that the house had belonged to a German film executive now serving in a labour battalion somewhere in the Soviet Union, the son of the real former owner – a German publisher – later told him the actual history of the 'Little White House':

> In the beginning of May the Russians arrived. Ten weeks before you entered this house, its tenants were living in constant fright and fear. By day and by night plundering Russian soldiers went in and out, raping my sisters before their own parents and children, beating up my old parents. All furniture, wardrobes and trunks etc were smashed with bayonets and rifle butts, their contents . . . destroyed in an indescribable manner.

Churchill came to Potsdam fresh from a painting holiday in Biarritz in the south-west of France and was housed in a lakeside villa not far from Truman. The British general election had been held on 5 July but because of the need to transport and count

votes from military personnel overseas the result would not be
known until during the conference. Consequently, Churchill
brought with him Clement Attlee, his calm, faithful, pipe-smoking
deputy in the now dissolved wartime coalition and the leader of
the opposition Labour Party. Among those from Yalta accompanying Churchill were Eden, Cadogan and Brooke.

Churchill and Truman met for the first time on 16 July at
10.30 a.m. – an hour Truman was surprised to discover was
reputedly the earliest the Prime Minister had risen for ten years.
Truman found Churchill 'charming and very clever' although
inclined to 'soft-soap'. Churchill told his daughter Mary, accompanying him on this occasion rather than Sarah, he 'liked the
President immensely – they talk[ed] the same language'.

As he settled in, Truman had been experiencing insect problems, not as Roosevelt had at Yalta from bedbugs but, because of
a lack of screened windows, from lakeside mosquitoes. The
President's log also recorded that 'like most European homes,
the bathroom and bathing facilities were wholly inadequate'.

That day both Churchill and Truman drove separately into the
ruined centre of Berlin. Although Truman did not leave his
open-top car as his cavalcade passed the Reichstag and the Reich's
Chancellery, Churchill, travelling with Eden in a jeep, got down
and with an escort of Russian soldiers passed through burned-out
tanks and armoured cars to inspect the Chancellery building itself.
Then in the garden he descended the seven flights of steps into
Hitler's bunker, which reeked of death and decay. According to
Cadogan, who secured a couple of iron crosses as souvenirs,
'unfortunately the lighting system was out of order, and by the
light of a single torch it was not easy to get a good view'. But
they were shown the spot where allegedly Hitler's corpse had
been burned. Churchill reflected that if Britain had been defeated
that would have been his own fate.

More junior arrivals witnessed continuing Russian looting.
Harriman's aide Robert Meiklejohn saw

a long train with flat cars, gondola cars and box cars all filled
with loot, except for a few flatcars carrying Soviet tanks . . .

one gondola car completely filled with chairs thrown on helter-skelter. Others were loaded with large wardrobes and other furniture. Flat cars had machine tools and airplane engines . . . Every car had its complement of hilarious men (civilians and troops) and women, waving gaily and making themselves comfortable in the 'requisitioned' furniture. It was about as convincing a picture as one could want of how the Soviets are looting the countryside.

Meiklejohn called it 'reparations à la carte'. He also recorded continuing rapes: 'a couple of sergeants at our billet told us of having rescued a fifteen year old German girl who had been raped by a Russian . . . She was found bleeding and half-naked in the woods at the edge of the road.'

Stalin arrived in Potsdam on 16 July in an eleven-coach armoured train, himself occupying four green carriages previously used by the tsars and removed from a museum for the occasion. The vast security operation surrounding him involved nearly 20,000 men with six sentries per kilometre of track in Russia, ten in Poland and fifteen in Germany. Three aircraft were kept in a constant state of readiness to evacuate him if necessary. Stalin, who had by now heard of his elder son Yakov's death in a German prison camp, went straight to his accommodation in a villa which was the former home of General Ludendorff, one of the leading German commanders in the First World War, refusing a suggestion that he should visit the ruins of Berlin.

Also on 16 July, the atomic bomb was successfully tested in New Mexico. Robert Oppenheimer, the project's scientific head, felt a surge of relief though he was 'a little scared of what we had made'. A line from the Bhagavad Gita raced through his brain, 'I am become Death, the destroyer of worlds.' Rudolph Peierls, who in a small room in Birmingham in England had first calculated a bomb was possible, recalled, 'The brilliant and blinding flash . . . told us we had done our job.' Others, who even in the final moments before the test had been nervously recalculating whether the explosion could ignite the earth's atmosphere, were simply relieved.

The news reached Truman in Potsdam that day in the following cryptic terms: 'Operated on this morning. Diagnosis not yet complete but results seem satisfactory and already exceed expectations.' That night Truman wrote in his diary, 'I hope for some sort of peace, but I fear that machines are ahead of mortals by some centuries, and when mortals catch up perhaps there'll be no reason for any of it.'

The next day Stimson handed Churchill a note, 'babies are satisfactorily born', which the Prime Minister failed to understand. Stimson then told him explicitly. His diary recorded Churchill's reaction: '"Now I know what happened to Truman yesterday. I couldn't understand it. When he got to the meeting after having read this report he was a changed man. He told the Russians just where they got on and off and generally bossed the whole meeting." Churchill said he now understood how this pepping up had taken place and that he felt the same way.' According to Brooke, Churchill was

> completely carried away. It was now no longer necessary for the Russians to come into the Japanese war; the new explosive was sufficient to settle the matter. Furthermore we now had something in our hands which would redress the balance with the Russians. The secret of this explosive and the power to use it would completely alter the diplomatic equilibrium which was adrift since the defeat of Germany.

A note from Churchill to Eden confirmed that his elation and disdain for Russia were shared by his American counterparts: 'It is quite clear that the United States do not at the present time desire Russian participation in the war against Japan.'

At midday on 17 July, Stalin did venture out to visit Truman in the 'Little White House' in another of the bilateral meetings which were to prove a greater feature of Potsdam than Yalta. Stalin found Truman 'couldn't be compared' to Roosevelt, being 'neither educated nor clever'. Truman felt he 'could deal with Stalin. He is honest – but smart as hell'. He 'looked you in the eye as he talked to you'. For some reason, perhaps his paranoia, Stalin insisted – as he had done to Hopkins in Moscow – that Hitler was still probably alive 'either in Spain or Argentina' even though he well knew a Soviet post mortem had confirmed that he had shot himself in his bunker.

The first plenary session of the conference – code-named 'Terminal' at Churchill's suggestion – took place later that day in the last Crown Prince of Germany's mock-Tudor palace, the Cecilienhof. It had only been completed in 1917, less than two years before the imperial family went into exile in Holland. Bohlen remembered how the Russians 'had planted a twenty-four-foot star of red geraniums in the garden'. Stalin dismissed the building as 'nothing much. The Russian Tsars built themselves something much more solid.' Whenever Britons and Americans wandered out into the grounds, as at Yalta they were immediately confronted by sub-machine-gun wielding NKVD security guards.

Once proceedings got under way Churchill's attitude towards Stalin seemed to soften. According to Eden, himself deep in sorrow at the death in action in Burma of one his sons, 'he is again under Stalin's spell. He kept repeating "I like that man". I am full of admiration of Stalin's handling of him.' Eden also admired Truman's 'business-like approach which was in contrast to his predecessor's practice of playing it by ear'. According to Cadogan:

> The P.M., since he left London, has refused to do any work or read anything. That is probably quite right, but then he can't have it both ways; if he knows nothing about the subject under discussion he should keep quiet . . . Instead of that he butts in . . . and talks the most irrelevant rubbish, and risks giving away our case at every point.

Stalin and Churchill appointed Truman as chairman in succession to Roosevelt. He did not relish his task, writing to his mother that 'Churchill talks all the time and Stalin just grunts but you know what he means'. Truman announced that he didn't 'want just to discuss, I want to decide.' Churchill somewhat unctuously responded, 'You want something in the bag each day.' Truman insisted that an early topic for discussion should be the holding of free elections in Soviet-occupied Eastern Europe, in particular Romania, Bulgaria and Hungary, to which Churchill predictably immediately added Poland. Stalin agreed only in as far as he wanted the latter's western border discussed. His own list of priorities included reparations, the division of captured German naval ships then in British hands and the removal of Franco from Spain.

In response to criticism of Soviet policies in Eastern Europe, Stalin suggested that they were an improvement on Western conduct in Italy where no elections at all were being held. Churchill retorted that they soon would be and that Soviet officials were free to go anywhere in that country whereas their British counterparts in Bucharest and elsewhere were 'penned up with a closeness approaching internment'. In fact, 'an iron fence has come down around them'. Stalin would 'be amazed to read the long list of incidents which have occurred'. 'All fairy tales,' Stalin responded. 'Statesmen may call one another's statements fairy tales if they wish,' was Churchill's peevish reply. Stalin reminded Churchill pointedly that he had not interfered in Greece.

On the question of German naval surface ships, of which there were only some thirty, the largest being three cruisers and the remainder destroyers and torpedo boats, Churchill seemed to favour destroying them. Stalin suggested dividing them between the three powers and letting each deal with them as they wished. He claimed that the forty-five German U-boats captured by the Russians in Danzig were too badly damaged to enter into the equation.

In discussions on reparations and loans, Truman tried to limit calls on US funds, writing to his wife,

I have to make it perfectly plain to them [Churchill and Stalin] at least once a day that so far as this President is concerned Santa Claus is dead and that my first interest is U.S.A., then I want the Jap War won and I want 'em both in it. Then I want peace – world peace and will do what can be done by us to get it. But certainly am not going to set up another [govt] here in Europe, pay reparations, feed the world, and get nothing for it but a nose thumbing.

He was already 'sick of the whole business'.

Bolstered by the news of the successful atomic bomb test, Truman pressed further on the Polish border question, saying that the Western Neisse had not been agreed at Yalta as the western border but simply that Poland should be compensated in the west for loss of territory in the east. If the Western Neisse was agreed, it would be like giving Poland an occupation zone of Germany. Stalin insisted, as he had at Yalta, that there were no Germans left in the disputed area – 'they had all run away'. When Churchill suggested they might return, Stalin responded that the Poles would 'hang them' if they did. Unlike at Yalta where he had claimed it was impossible to summon any Poles to the conference, Stalin produced two Communist members of the new Polish government to back up his thesis.

Discussions about a scheme to internationalize Europe's main waterways and rivers, suggested by Truman who believed that knowing they could trade freely along them would make European powers less likely to go to war; about Stalin's pleas for access to and perhaps a base on the Dardanelles first inconclusively raised at Yalta; about his ambitions in regard to Italy's pre-war African colonies as well as about the removal of Franco from power in Spain all came to nought.

The conference did, however, find it easier to agree on the creation of a Council of Foreign Ministers in an expansion of arrangements agreed at Yalta. The council would consist of the Big Three powers with the addition in due course of China and France and would oversee the preparation of peace treaties and undertake any other tasks allocated to them by the leaders. Stalin also conceded the right of the Western powers to take up their agreed zones of occupation in Austria, something he had been delaying in practice until then.

At the end of the day's plenary session on 24 July, in agreement with Churchill, Truman sauntered over to Stalin and 'casually mentioned . . . that we had a new weapon of unusual destructive force. The Russian premier showed no special interest. All he said was that he was glad to hear it and hoped we would make "good use of it against the Japanese".' Their mutual nonchalance concealed not only Truman's understanding of the bomb's potential, but also Stalin's prior knowledge of the bomb from his spies. Stalin was already pressing his generals to hasten their plans for Soviet entry into the war. Nikita Khrushchev later wrote, 'Stalin had his doubts about whether the Americans would keep their word . . . What if Japan capitulated before we entered the war? The Americans might say, "we don't owe you anything".'

Without consulting Stalin, on 26 July the American and British governments, together with Chiang Kai-shek's Nationalist Chinese government, issued what became known as the Potsdam Declaration. The text to which Chiang Kai-shek telegraphed his agreement had been drafted over the previous few days with Byrnes playing a leading role, resisting any suggestion from Stimson and Leahy that there should be a softening of the unconditional surrender terms in regard to the Emperor's position. It offered Japan 'an opportunity to end the war' on the basis of 'unconditional surrender' and ended, 'the alternative for Japan is complete and utter destruction'. Two days later the Japanese Prime Minister rejected the Potsdam offer, stating that his government would ignore it and press forward resolutely for the successful conclusion of the war. The Tokyo newspaper *Mainnichi* dismissed the Declaration as 'laughable'.

On 25 July, Churchill had flown back to Britain with Eden, whom Truman by now considered 'much overrated', and Attlee to hear the British election results, only to find that the domestic issues to which he habitually paid so little attention during the war had produced a landslide for the Labour Party. Clement Attlee, the new prime minister, and his Foreign Secretary Ernest Bevin, returned to Potsdam for the resumption of the conference. By the end of July Truman felt the talks on reparations and the Polish border were at an impasse. Eventually Byrnes and Molotov worked out a deal subsequently agreed by the three leaders, under which the Western powers recognized the Western Neisse as Poland's temporary border while awaiting the decision of a final peace conference, which never took place. The Soviet Union would take appropriate reparations from its areas of occupation, as well as being entitled to some industrial equipment from the western zones in return for the supply of essential foodstuffs from eastern to western zones. The latter provisions were, however, never put fully into practice.

The conference concluded on 2 August by which time the no-nonsense, 'speak as you find' Truman, like Churchill and Roosevelt before him, had come to 'like Stalin'. Even years later he repeated, 'I liked the little son of a bitch.' As only to be expected, the Potsdam Communiqué issued that day reflected unity and unanimity. The conference had 'strengthened the ties between the three governments' and 'renewed confidence that their governments and peoples, together with the United Nations, will ensure the creation of a just and enduring peace'.

Meanwhile, on 26 July, the heavy cruiser USS *Indianapolis* had reached Tinian at the end of its ten-day voyage from San Francisco with the components of the atomic bomb.* In the early hours of 6 August Paul Tibbetts pulled back the joystick and the modified B-29 Superfortress, named '*Enola Gay*' after his mother and newly blessed by the squadron's chaplain, rose slowly from the Tinian runway with the 9,700-pound Little Boy atomic bomb in its bomb-bay and disappeared into the velvet northern sky. After a six-and-a-half-hour flight, bombardier Tom Ferebee released the bomb at 9.15 a.m. Tinian time over Hiroshima. According to one of the crew, Bob Caron, as the bomb exploded the scene was 'beautifully horrible'. There was a mushroom cloud 'like a mass of bubbling molasses'.

In Hiroshima a fleeing survivor, Futaba Kitayama, approached a bridge. In the water 'corpses were floating by like dead dogs

---

* On its return voyage, the cruiser was torpedoed with the loss of 821 US sailors, the greatest loss at sea in US naval history.

and cats, their shreds of clothing dangling like rags. In the shoals . . . I saw a woman floating face up, her chest gouged out and gushing blood. Could such terrifying sights be of this world?' After crossing the bridge she saw 'all around me, junior high school girls and boys writhing on the ground. They seemed crazed, crying "mother, mother". As my eyes took in the cruel sight of their burns and gaping wounds . . . I couldn't bear to look at them.'

Before first light on 9 August, in an operation code-named 'August Storm', more than 1.5 million Soviet troops crossed into China behind massive artillery and rocket barrages. Advancing quickly, they pushed the Japanese forces before them. 'They're jumping the gun aren't they?' Truman, now less pleased about the Soviet intervention, asked Leahy. Crossing the Atlantic to Potsdam, Leahy had told Bohlen, 'the longhairs [scientists] were gypping the American government out of some $5 billion because the bomb would turn out to be no better than cordite, a simple smokeless powder'. Now he replied to Truman, 'the bomb did it. They want to get in before it's all over.' That same day, the USAAF dropped a second atomic bomb which obliterated Nagasaki. On 14 August Japan surrendered. The Second World War had ended.

Estimates of total war dead vary considerably, ranging from around 60 million to more than 70 million. Just under 420,000 Americans died. Britain lost some 450,000, both civilians and military, roughly the same as Italy; France lost some 500,000; nearly 300,000 Dutch lives were lost and some 500,000 Greeks died – the latter out of a pre-war population of 7 million. Some 6 million Polish citizens perished out of a pre-war population of 35 million. German losses were 6–8 million, at least a quarter of them civilians, and Japanese were some 3 million. All these numbers are dwarfed in absolute terms by the 14–28 million Chinese, and the more than 25 million Soviet citizens who died, of whom perhaps 7 million were Ukrainian. The number of Soviet soldiers severely wounded is suggested by an American report of Soviet attempts during 1944 to buy 2 million artificial legs from the United States.

By the time Japan surrendered, Soviet forces advancing through Manchuria had reached the thirty-eighth parallel, just north of Seoul on the Korean Peninsula. There, in agreement with a hastily formulated American proposal, made only on 10 August, they halted. According to Byrnes, the arrangement was for 'military convenience' and not intended to establish a permanent border. Soviet troops were also already ashore in both the Kurile Islands and Sakhalin. American troops needed nearly a month to occupy the area of the Korean Peninsula beneath the thirty-eighth parallel. If Stalin had wished, Soviet forces could have occupied the whole of Korea, which would have dramatically changed the politics of the peninsula and quite possibly had a profound and long-lasting effect on the Far East as a whole. The Korean War might never have taken place. Japan would have been an outpost against Communism and the relationship between China and the Soviet Union might have developed differently.

PART FIVE

Aftermath

'Whoever occupies a territory also imposes
on it his own social system.'

Stalin, April 1945

CHAPTER SEVENTEEN

The Iron Curtain Descends

Even by the time of Potsdam, the decisions on Eastern Europe taken at Yalta, and the related discussions with their emphasis on relocation of people by ethnicity, were adding to the waves of desperate displaced persons, liberated concentration camp survivors, prisoners of war, and forced labourers washing over Europe. Many were trying to reach home in devastated areas, some no longer containing the same mix of ethnicities and others now in different countries. Estimates suggest that up to 40 million people may have been displaced in total and that as the war ended 17 million of them were in Germany, including 8 million forced labourers, freed Allied prisoners of war of whom British and American prisoners accounted for some 275,000, as well as unknown numbers liberated from concentration camps and German refugees from the east.

The heavily changed borders of Poland, effectively moved some 200 miles to the west, were responsible for many of these displacements. The new boundaries between Poland and the Soviet Union and in particular the Ukraine, where Polish resistance fighters and Ukrainian Nazi collaborators had already clashed during the war, witnessed forced deportations and violence on both sides as the frontiers became ethnic as well as national boundaries. The Soviet and Lublin Polish governments authorized the deportations and condoned the violence. One example of the inhumanities practised mutually was a massacre of Ukrainians by Polish troops in the village of Zawadka Morochowska in south-eastern Poland. A survivor recalled, 'Whenever they captured a man he was killed instantly; where they could not find a man, they beat the women and children.' Many corpses were mutilated with eyes gouged out, noses and tongues removed and women's breasts sliced off. Later the surviving inhabitants were forced over the border into the Ukraine. The Poles expelled nearly half a million Ukrainians and any who remained were subject to severe discrimination.

In turn, between 1944 and 1946 some 750,000 Poles were expelled from the Ukraine, most forcibly, as were 160,000 Polish people from Lithuania and more than 230,000 from Belorussia, making a total of some 1.2 million expelled by the Soviets. Even these numbers were dwarfed by the Soviet and Lublin government-backed expulsion of Germans from what had been pre-war German territory but was now Polish. More than 7 million Germans fled or were expelled. Some were given only thirty minutes to pack and leave just as in previous Russian and German deportations. The displaced people were forced onto long treks on foot without food. A survivor, Anna Kientopf, recalled, 'people got ill. Small children under one year almost all died. I often saw people lying at the side of the highway blue in the face, and struggling for breath and others who had collapsed from fatigue, and never got on to their feet again.' Women were raped and everyone looted. Sometimes Soviet troops or local militias stopped the columns to extract fitter people of either sex for forced labour. Troops and police crammed other deportees so tightly into trains that when they crossed Germany's new eastern border those who opened the doors saw that 'out of one wagon alone ten corpses were taken . . . Several persons had become deranged . . . The people were covered in excrement . . . They were squeezed together so tightly there was no longer any possi-bility for them to relieve themselves at a designated place.'

As part of the rush to ethnic cleansing, 3 million Germans were expelled from Czechoslovakia, mostly from the Sudetenland, by the newly established government – a coalition between 'demo-crats' and 'Communists'. In other countries, former concentration and prisoner of war camps were used to contain those about to be deported but the Czechs went beyond the use of the former Nazi concentration camp at Theresienstadt for this purpose. They forced Germans still at liberty to wear cloth patches on their left breast with the initial 'N', standing for 'Nemec', the Czech for 'German'. They faced an 8 p.m. curfew, were not allowed to use public transport or public parks and had to remove hats and caps when approaching Czech or Russian officers, whom they had to pass at an appropriate and respectful distance.

In Yugoslavia, already riven by internal conflict among ethnic and religious groups during the war, Serbian partisan units massacred up to 70,000 fighters from a Croatian group – the Ustashas – that had fought with the Nazis and which, in attempting to 'ethnically cleanse' Croatia, had killed up to 500,000 Serbs, Muslims and Jews. Some of the Ustashas had been returned to Yugoslavia by the British, to whom they had surrendered in Austria, on the grounds that enemy fighters should surrender to those against whom they had fought, their fellow Yugoslavs.

The agreement at Yalta by Churchill and Roosevelt to repatriate all Soviet prisoners of war, together with any Soviet citizens captured fighting for Germany, which was motivated by the Western governments' concern to secure early access to their own prisoners of war liberated by the Soviets, was to have dire consequences.

Three million of the 5 million Soviet military personnel captured by the Nazis had died in German prison camps. On their return, the survivors faced interrogation and then, for many, arrest and confinement in the gulags and in some cases execution. A Canadian report described the fate of some returned by an Allied ship:

> The prisoner who had attempted suicide was very roughly handled and his wound opened up . . . He was . . . marched behind a packing case on the docks; a shot was then heard but nothing more was seen. The other thirty-two prisoners were

marched or dragged into a warehouse fifty yards from the ship
and after a lapse of fifteen minutes automatic fire was heard
coming from the warehouse; twenty minutes later a covered
lorry drove out of the warehouse and headed towards the town.
Later I had a chance to glance into the warehouse . . . and
found the cobbled floor stained dark in several places . . . and
the walls badly chipped for about five feet up.

The most notorious case was that of thousands of anti-
Communist Cossacks – many of whom had left the Soviet Union
after fighting for the White Russians against the Bolsheviks and
then fought for Germany – whom the British handed over to the
Soviets in Austria. In one incident in June 1945 a group of
Cossacks, some with their wives and children, struggled with
British troops trying to load them onto trucks. Some in despair,
knowing the fate that awaited them at Soviet hands, committed
suicide. Many were hurt as they resisted the rifle-butt wielding
soldiers. Other Cossacks were crushed in the melee and altars
at which their priests were offering prayers were knocked over.
As one of the British soldiers' chaplains later remembered, his
men 'could not believe that this was what they had been fighting
the war for. They were repulsed by the whole business.' A British
medical officer denounced the proceedings as 'inhuman'.

Within two years of Yalta, the British Empire that Churchill had
succeeded in protecting there was beginning the long process of
dissolution. In February 1947, the Attlee government appointed
Lord Louis Mountbatten, the former Allied Commander in South-
East Asia, Viceroy of India with the remit of overseeing a speedy
transition to independence. The aim was achieved at midnight on
14 August that year when India and Pakistan became separate and
independent countries. Some million lives were lost when, as in
Eastern Europe, those caught on the wrong side of frontiers,
drawn up on this occasion on religious grounds, were expelled
or fled and suffered violence as they did so.

Churchill's wish to protect the sea route to the east would be disappointed when in July 1956 President Gamal Abdel Nasser of Egypt – who had come to power following a coup in 1952 leading to the dissolution of the British Protectorate and the exile of King Farouk – nationalized the Suez Canal, leading Anthony Eden, then prime minister, to undertake a failed military intervention. The Suez Crisis was a major factor in his resignation as prime minister not long afterwards.

In upholding the British Empire, Churchill, as a corollary, supported the restoration of the French and Dutch South-East Asian Empires. In Vietnam, a Communist-led insurgency almost at once began to fight against French forces for independence. Following the complete defeat of the French in 1954, at a conference in Geneva the country was partitioned on what was intended to be a temporary basis between a Communist north led by Ho Chi Minh and an American-backed south. The partition was at a military demarcation line between the forces of the two opposing Vietnamese factions at the seventeenth parallel north, which was in turn surrounded by a demilitarized zone several miles deep. Three-quarters of a million people fled either way across the line. In particular, Christians, fearing Communist persecution, left the north for the south. In the subsequent Vietnam War lasting two decades, the Vietnamese, dismissed by President Roosevelt as 'of small stature . . . and not warlike', as members of the Viet Cong proved formidable opponents for US forces. In Indonesia, the returning Dutch also faced an insurgency which led to the country's independence under the presidency of Sukarno, one of the insurgency's leaders, in 1949.

In China, by late 1949 Chiang Kai-shek and his Nationalist forces, in whom the United States had placed so much confidence and supported with so much money and materiel, had been totally defeated by Mao Zedong, who proclaimed the People's Republic of China. Chiang Kai-shek, his wife Meiling and 2 million of his soldiers and supporters fled to Taiwan (Formosa), Chiang taking with him nearly all China's gold reserves and many of its ancient treasures. Shortly afterwards President Truman instituted an American naval blockade to prevent a Communist assault on the island and continued to recognize Chiang's government as the legitimate ruler of China.

In Korea, where all thoughts of trusteeships discussed at Yalta had been put aside, tensions had been building between the south, backed by the United States, and the Communist north, now ruled by Kim Il-Sung, the Soviet-supported premier elected in 1948 and grandfather of North Korea's present ruler. Emboldened by Communist success in China, in June 1950 Kim ordered the invasion of the south. Because the Soviet Union was at the time boycotting the Security Council in protest at the refusal to transfer the Chinese seat on the council from Chiang Kai-shek's to Mao Zedong's administration, the United States won UN support for its troops and those of its allies, landed to confront the invasion, being designated a UN force. A war of wildly fluctuating fortunes in which the Chinese government aided the north with their troops ended three years later with the opposing armies back at the thirty-eighth parallel, whereupon the two sides signed an armistice at Panmunjun. No peace treaty has yet been signed.

After the Potsdam Conference even the superficial unanimity between America, Britain and the Soviet Union boasted of by the Potsdam Communiqué slowly disappeared, metamorphosing over the course of the next two years or so into the Cold War. The actual phrase 'the Cold War' was first used by George Orwell in an article in *Tribune* in October 1945 in reference to a future nuclear stalemate 'between two or three monstrous superstates, each possessed of a weapon by which millions of people can be wiped out in a few seconds'. Possession of the bomb would make a country undefeatable, leading to 'an epoch as horribly stable as the slave empires of antiquity . . . a peace that is no peace', all of which would produce a permanent state 'of cold war'. The meeting of Foreign Ministers in London in 1945, upon which so many tasks had been loaded at Potsdam, ended in a decisionless impasse. The Soviet Union continued to impose its own concept of 'democracy' upon those Eastern European countries it occupied despite ineffectual Western protests that this was not in keeping with Stalin's statements at Yalta and the unanimous agreement there of the Declaration on Liberated Europe.

Thwarted at Yalta and elsewhere in his bid to ensure adequate access to Iranian oil supplies, and committed by the other powers to withdraw, like them, his forces from the country, within six months of the end of the war Stalin began to foment and arm a separatist movement among Azeries in northern Iran. With Soviet backing, at the end of 1945 his Azerie protégés proclaimed an autonomous republic – the prelude, Stalin hoped, to the annexation of the region to the Soviet Republic of Azerbaijan. In early January 1946, Truman wrote to Byrnes, 'Unless Russia is faced with an iron fist and strong language another war is in the making . . . I do not think we should play compromise any longer . . . we should let our position on Iran be known in no uncertain terms . . . I'm tired of babying the Soviets.'

In a February 1946 speech Stalin proclaimed Capitalism and Communism to be incompatible. At almost the same time the Soviet spy rings in the Manhattan Project were exposed. At the month's end Byrnes announced that the US government would treat the Soviet Union with 'both patience and firmness', would 'defend the UN Charter' and 'resist aggression', by force if necessary. He told his audience, 'If we are to be a great power we must act as a great power not only in order to secure our own security but in order to preserve the peace of the world.'

On 5 March 1946, Churchill delivered his famous 'Iron Curtain' speech in Fulton, Missouri. Although out of office he had consulted Truman and Byrnes about the text in Washington and travelled by train to Missouri with Truman aboard the *Ferdinand Magellan* that had carried Roosevelt on the first stage of his journey to Yalta. Truman introduced Churchill. In his oration the former Prime Minister condemned the Soviet Union's policies in Europe: 'From Stettin in the Baltic to Trieste in the Adriatic an Iron Curtain has descended across Europe' behind which the Soviet Union was 'increasing its control over its neighbours'. He denounced 'Communist fifth columns' operating in Western and Southern Europe. He warned against appeasement of the Soviet Union, comparing it to the pre-war appeasement of Hitler and suggested that the Soviets admired nothing 'so much as strength and there is nothing for which they have less respect than for military weakness'. He called for 'a special relationship' – a phrase he brought into common usage – between the US and the UK as the leaders of the English-speaking world.

This speech a year after Yalta marked a hardening of attitudes. In an interview in *Pravda*, Stalin condemned Churchill's speech as 'a dangerous act' and 'an insult', accusing him of racism in suggesting the superiority of the English-speaking peoples and arguing that there was nothing wrong in 'the Soviet Union anxious for its future safety' trying to ensure 'governments loyal to the Soviet Union in Eastern Europe'. Nevertheless, responding to a seemingly new militancy among the Western powers as well as realizing there was a degree of overstretch among his forces, Stalin withdrew his troops from northern Iran only a few months later than the Yalta agreement would have provided, leading the nascent Azeri autonomous republic to collapse.

With tensions rising over the next year as Stalin continued to ignore the provisions of the Yalta Declaration on Liberated Europe, on 12 March 1947 Truman urged Congress that 'it must be the policy of the United States to support free peoples who are resisting attempts of subjugation by armed minorities or by outside pressure . . . we must assist free people to work out their own destinies in their own way.' In this speech, indeed in these few sentences in which he laid out the 'Truman Doctrine', he condemned both Communist-inspired armed uprisings and Soviet influence on so-called independent countries and pledged US support against them – keystones of US policy for many subsequent years in Vietnam, Central America and elsewhere.

The first example of practical US support came almost immediately in spring 1947 in aid given to Greece where the civil war between the Communists and the right-wing government had renewed itself after Yalta with great brutality on both sides. Stalin had kept his promise to Churchill not to intervene but the presence of Soviet forces on the country's borders held an implicit threat. In supplying aid to the right-wing government, the US took over from the near-bankrupt British, whose Labour government under Clement Attlee had announced it could no longer afford such financial or other commitments. The Greek civil war ended in 1949 with the defeat of the left. Also in 1947, soon after giving support to Greece, the US again took over from Britain, giving aid to Turkey, which was facing pressure from Soviet troops massing on its borders.

The US government had ceased Lend-Lease to both the UK and the USSR ten days after the Japanese surrender. In June 1947, the US authorities, already underwriting post-war recovery in Japan, announced the Marshall Plan. Overseen by former US Chief of Army Staff George Marshall, by now Secretary of State in succession to Byrnes, it was designed to assist post-war recovery in any European country, including both Germany and the USSR. Stalin rejected the offer – which Molotov on his behalf called 'dollar imperialism' – and compelled Eastern European countries to do likewise, fearing that acceptance would provide a foothold in them for the US and a consequent loss of Soviet control. In response to the plan Stalin brought together the leaders of the Eastern European countries in Poland and created Cominform (the Communist Information Bureau) – in effect formally establishing an Eastern bloc. He reinforced these measures by forcing each country to agree exclusive trade treaties with the Soviet Union. He went on to encourage Communist parties in Western Europe to political and strike action, producing considerable unrest, particularly in France and Italy.

Between 1948 and 1952, the US provided $13 billion in aid (some $132 billion in October 2017 values) to Western European countries, the largest recipients being the UK with 26 per cent of the total, France with 18 per cent and the western zone of Germany 11 per cent. Of the total, 70 per cent was spent on goods from the US. The British mostly used the money to supplement everyday expenditure rather than to improve means of production, unlike Germany which used it, as intended, to upgrade and rebuild its industrial capacity. The organization behind the Marshall Plan developed into the Organization for Economic Cooperation and Development – the OECD.

In late February 1948 the Soviet Union orchestrated a coup in Czechoslovakia, the last Eastern European country other than Yugoslavia where they had allowed some democratic institutions to survive. A fortnight later, the Czech Foreign Minister Jan Masaryk – one of the leaders of the democratic faction – was found dead in the courtyard of the Foreign Ministry, having apparently fallen or been pushed from a window in what was almost certainly a murder. Also in February that year, the US and UK, which had already merged their zones of occupation in Germany into a single economic unit known as the Bizone or 'Bizonia', proposed creating a new four-power currency to stimulate the German economy and undermine the thriving black market. The Soviet Union rejected their proposal. That June the Soviet Union stopped all land transport into the western zones of Berlin and the US and UK began the Berlin airlift. The airlift kept the supply lines to the western sectors of the city open until the Soviet Union ceased the blockade a year later. In April 1949, the Western Allies created the North Atlantic Treaty Organization as a mutual defence organization – later matched on the Soviet side by the Warsaw Pact.

The US, British and French governments merged their zones of occupation of Germany in May 1949 to create the German Federal Republic (West Germany) with its capital in Bonn. Five months later, the Soviet Union created the German Democratic Republic (East Germany) with its capital in Berlin. In 1952, the German Democratic Republic closed its border with the Federal Republic everywhere except in Berlin. In 1956, the Soviet suppressed the Hungarian uprising. Then in 1961, the Soviet Union and East Germany created the Berlin Wall, closing the last crossing point through which East Europeans might hope to travel freely to the West. The 'Iron Curtain' first referred to ideologically by Churchill in May 1945 in the aftermath of Yalta was now physically complete and would remain in place for three decades. Any pretence on the Soviet part of adherence to the terms of the Declaration on Liberated Europe agreed at Yalta had already long vanished.

EPILOGUE

'The problems of victory are more agreeable than
those of defeat, but they are no less difficult.'

Churchill

'I didn't say the result was good. I said
it was the best I could do.'

Roosevelt on Yalta and Eastern Europe

Whether George Bush was right in 2005 to compare the Yalta
conclusions to the 1938 Munich Agreement as an act of appeasement or 'a sell-out' to dictatorship is a good question. So is
whether Churchill and Roosevelt at Yalta bought Western European stability at the price of Eastern European freedom. The
answers depend on which aspect of the conference agreements
is at issue.

In the immediate aftermath of the conference both Roosevelt
and Churchill admitted privately that on Eastern Europe, and on
Poland in particular, the results were imperfect but were the best
they could achieve. The situation in which they found themselves
had several analogies to that of Crimea itself today, annexed by
Russia, and that of eastern Ukraine where divergent ethnicities
dispute the borders and where in both cases Western leaders have
few viable sanctions against Russia other than moral pressure.
Stalin was confident in his belief that, 'Whoever occupies a territory also imposes on it his own social system. Everyone imposes
his own system as far as his army has power to do so. It cannot

be otherwise.' A major reason for the imperfection in the agreement at Yalta on Eastern Europe, therefore, was that by February 1945 the USSR was in possession of nearly all that territory and therefore held a dominant position, enabling Stalin to stonewall Churchill and Roosevelt on Poland and other issues.

Stalin astutely observed that 'In politics one should be guided by the calculation of forces'. Therefore, as Roosevelt and Churchill sought to balance the demands of their war-weary citizens for peace against the need for justice for the countries of Eastern Europe, they had few levers with which to work on Stalin. Their publics sympathized with the harsh wartime suffering of the Soviet people and would not stand for the use of force against them. In any case, as the British planners who reviewed the prospect for Churchill suggested, military victory over the Soviet Union – even if secured – would take a considerable time and great loss and sacrifice. Aligning themselves with any elements in Germany to oppose the Soviets when Nazi war crimes were becoming ever clearer, ever more horrific, as each day passed was unthinkable. Use of the atomic bomb, unproven at the time of Yalta and unlikely to be available in sufficient numbers, was again out of the question. Although Churchill's 'naughty document' agreement in Moscow, with its endorsement of spheres of influence created without the knowledge or consent of the peoples involved, had removed some of the moral high ground from beneath his feet at least, he and Roosevelt did secure statements such as the Declaration on Liberated Europe and commitments to fair elections against which they could hold Stalin to public account later.

The one lever they might have been able to use to better advantage and to a greater extent than they did was the United States' economic muscle. Stalin recognized the power of the dollar and of American industry when he said, 'the most important things in this war are machines.' The USA was 'a country of machines . . . Without the use of those machines, through Lend Lease, we would lose this war.' If the US had threatened to withdraw Lend-Lease when the problems arose about the Polish government, perhaps at Yalta, perhaps before then, it might have had some effect. However, even at Yalta there was still a war to be won and no one wished to risk fracturing the alliance entirely, particularly when the Soviet Union was doing so much of the fighting and bearing such a disproportionate amount of the casualties. Roosevelt in particular had other issues on his mind such as the establishment of the UN and the entry of the Soviet Union into the war against Japan.

With hindsight it would have proved more advantageous if the conference had been held when originally proposed in the summer of 1944, rather than being postponed first to autumn and then by Roosevelt to Churchill's consternation until after the US presidential inauguration. The USSR would have been in possession of much less of Eastern Europe and more options might have been open to hasten the Western Allies' advance. However, that would have cost lives, and a major element of both American and British strategy was to prevent the loss of their own military's lives, as evidenced by British reluctance to commit to a cross-Channel invasion at an early date and the American wish to avoid an invasion of the Japanese home islands.

Some have suggested that the terminal ill health of Roosevelt and the war-weariness of an ailing Churchill may have contributed to their failure to achieve more at Yalta for Eastern Europe and been a factor in their naivety in trusting Stalin to keep those agreements they made. However, although these elements may have had some impact on their stamina and strength of argument, they had no influence on the outcome: the healthy Truman – albeit inexperienced in international diplomacy – could achieve no more for Eastern Europe at Potsdam. Perhaps surprisingly, given his character, he too would be equally deceived by Stalin's charm into believing, at that time at least, that despite all the evidence accumulating to the contrary, Stalin was someone with whom he could do business.

Ultimately there is much truth in the meaning of the humorous story which circulated among the Soviets, that when Stalin went hunting with the other two leaders and they killed a bear Churchill suggested he would take the skin, leaving the meat for the other two. 'No, I'll take the skin. Let Churchill and Stalin take the meat,' Roosevelt said. When Stalin said nothing, the other two asked what he thought. 'The bear belongs to me – after all I killed it,' he responded.

In other areas, Churchill and Roosevelt did better. Churchill won his pyrrhic short-term victory to preserve the British Empire; a study of the conference proceedings shows how much a single entity all three leaders considered the empire at the time. In one instance – retaining control over Hong Kong – Churchill at least preserved a Western outpost on the coast of China throughout many troubled years. Roosevelt achieved his objective of securing agreement to the establishment of the United Nations. Although the veto arrangements decided at Yalta would cripple it on most occasions when dealing with disputes among the great powers, it would have some success in peacekeeping elsewhere.

Roosevelt succeeded, too, in agreeing terms and a timescale for Soviet entry into the war on Japan, something by which he and his advisers at the time set great store both to reduce US casualties and to shorten the war. However this too was a pyrrhic victory. If Roosevelt and his advisers and indeed Churchill – there were senior British members of the Manhattan Project – had been better briefed so that they better understood the potential and progress of the atomic bomb project, they might not have felt the same imperative to draw the Soviet Union into the Pacific war. After the first successful atom bomb test, the diminished requirement for Soviet assistance was clear to all three powers, not least to Stalin, who hastened his plans to attack Japan and move into Korea. Without a Soviet advance to the thirty-eighth parallel in Korea, and Soviet occupation of the Kurile Islands and Sakhalin, the Korean War would not have happened and Korea would be likely to be united and democratic.

One perhaps less expected area where the Yalta Conference had a lingering influence is the UK's relationship with France and thereby the European Union. Not only de Gaulle but other senior French personnel resented the prominence Britain had gained by fighting on after the fall of France. Towards the end of the war a French general told British General Hastings 'Pug' Ismay, 'There will be Frenchmen who will not forgive you for two generations. You made our shame so great by fighting on.' Such sentiments probably underlay de Gaulle's inability to appreciate Churchill's efforts to enhance France's status. Instead he hubristically resented what he considered slights to himself and France. One clear example is that after the unanimous agreement of the Big Three not to invite him to Yalta, he out of pique refused to meet Roosevelt in Algiers.

De Gaulle's resentment at his exclusion from Yalta persisted for the rest of his life and resulted in his distrust of what he saw as Anglo-American hegemony, for example in the way they kept atomic weapons information to themselves. It led not only to de Gaulle's withdrawal from NATO's active command structure in 1966, seventeen years after the organization's foundation, but also to his absolute veto of Britain's entry into the European Community in 1963 and 1967. In 1963 he asserted 'L'Angleterre ce n'est plus grand chose' – 'England isn't much any more'. Arguably, had Britain been involved in the European Union at an earlier date, it might have had a greater influence on its development and just perhaps meant that a Brexit referendum might never have been called and – even if it had – the result might have been different.

Yalta did not put an end to 'the system of unilateral action, the exclusive alliances, the spheres of influence, the balances of power' as Roosevelt claimed it should in his speech to Congress on 1 March 1945. It was generally, as he said specifically of the Polish agreements in the same speech, 'a compromise'. As such, it is open to criticism, some of it justified at the time and more of it justified with the complacent benefit of the hindsight of history. However, the aspirations drafted by Roosevelt for his Jefferson Day speech, scheduled for the day after he died, 'The work, my friends, is peace . . . an end to the beginnings of all wars . . . to this impractical, unrealistic settlement of the differences between governments by the mass killing of peoples' remain as valid today as they did then.

ACKNOWLEDGEMENTS

My husband Michael shared with me all aspects of the writing of this book. We would like to thank the many people who helped with this project, giving generously of their time, energy and enthusiasm.

In the UK we are very grateful to Allen Packwood, Director of the Churchill Archives Centre, Churchill College, Cambridge and to Heidi Egginton and her colleagues at the Centre for their help and advice during our visit; Elizabeth Piper, Christ Church Archives, Oxford, for advice on relevant documents in the Portal Papers; Dr. Dobroslawa Platt, Director, The Polish Library, Polish Social and Cultural Association for insights into the period; the staffs of the London Library, British Library, Bodleian Library and the UK National Archives for, as ever, helping smooth the task of research.

In the US, we are indebted to David Olson, Archivist for the Columbia Center for Oral History, Columbia University for advice on the collection, and to his colleagues at the Center who made our research visit so rewarding; Dr. David Woolner, Senior Fellow and Hyde Park Resident Historian, the Roosevelt Institute, for his very helpful guidance on source material in the FDR Presidential Library and Kirsten Carter, Supervisory Archivist, and her colleagues at the FDR Library for all their considerable assistance both during and following our visit; the staff of the Library of Congress in Washington DC, both in the manuscript archives and in the main reading room, and the staff of US National Archives and Records Administration in Maryland.

Our thanks go also to our friends St. John Brown, Ginny Covell, Kim Lewison and Neil Munro for their kind and helpful insights on text, Robin Binks for the loan of books and Donald and Ingrid Wallace and Alice Munro for advice on medical questions.

Finally, we are very grateful to our editors, Georgina Morley of Picador in the UK and George Gibson of Grove Atlantic in the US, and to our agents Bill Hamilton in London and Michael Carlisle in New York for their help and encouragement, and of course, to all the other people involved within their organizations.

NOTES AND SOURCES

ABBREVIATIONS USED IN THIS SECTION:

CCC   Churchill Archives Centre, Churchill College, Cambridge, UK.

COHP   Columbia University Oral History Project, New York, USA.

FDRL   Franklin D. Roosevelt Presidential Library, Hyde Park, NY, USA.

FRUS/B   *Foreign Relations of the United States, The Conference at Berlin*, vols 1 and 2. Washington: United States Government Printing Office, 1960.

FRUS/MY   *Foreign Relations of the United States: The Conferences at Malta and Yalta*. Washington: United States Government Printing Office, 1955.

IWM   Imperial War Museum, London, UK.

LOC   Library of Congress, Washington DC, USA.

NARA   US National Archives and Records Adminstration, College Park, MD, USA.

UKNA   UK National Archives, Kew, London, UK:

     CAB –   Cabinet Office Papers.

     FO –   Foreign Office Papers.

     PREM – Prime Minister's correspondence.

Soviet/TYP   *The Teheran, Yalta and Potsdam Conferences*. Moscow: Progress Publishers, 1969 (official Soviet records).

The wartime correspondence between the three leaders, Churchill, Roosevelt and Stalin, is available from a number of sources. The three-volume *Churchill and Roosevelt – The Complete Correspondence* edited by W. F. Kimball published by Princeton University Press in 1984 is exactly what its name implies. S. Butler's *'My Dear Mr. Stalin' – The Complete Correspondence Between Franklin*

D. Roosevelt and Joseph V. Stalin published by Yale University Press in 2005 fulfils a similar function. The Churchill Archives at Churchill College, Cambridge, and the UK National Archives at Kew contain all official communications to and from Churchill, and the US National Archives in Maryland and the FDR Presidential Library at Hyde Park in New York State do the same for correspondence to and from Roosevelt. Therefore, in each case, for correspondence between the three leaders the source is given simply as sender, recipient and date and number according to Kimball for FDR/WSC correspondence and Butler for FDR/Stalin exchanges.

The Churchill/Truman correspondence is similarly available in the archives and in *Defending the West — The Truman–Churchill Correspondence, 1945–1960*, edited by G. W. Sand and is referenced in the same manner.

This book draws on many diaries, letters and memoirs, published and unpublished, of participants on all sides and at all levels to illuminate the dry, sometimes selective, official accounts of the three sides. In doing so, however, I have borne in mind the purpose for which other material was written, sometimes — in the case of published memoirs — self-justification or even self-glorification; in the case of letters to loved ones or friends to reassure, to catch a mood or to amuse; in the case of private diaries to release exasperation. The British Field Marshal Sir Alan Brooke, for example, often criticized Churchill in his diary, even calling him 'a public menace', but reminded readers when it was published, 'my diary was the safety valve and only outlet for all my pent up feelings . . . I thank God that I was given an opportunity of working alongside of such a man, and of having my eyes opened to the fact that occasionally such supermen exist on this earth.'

PROLOGUE

'Statesmen . . . itself': W. Churchill, *The Gathering Storm*, p. 285.
'We . . . war': Quoted Kennedy, *Freedom from Fear*, p. 852.
'as in . . . phaeton': Moran, *Churchill – The Struggle for Survival*, p. 218.
'cut . . . decided': Beria, *Beria, My Father*, p. 104.
'a Sherman . . . going': McIntire, *Twelve Years with Roosevelt*, p. 213.
'divided . . . unstable . . . had . . . expendable': Speech in Latvia, 7 May 2005, widely quoted, e.g. Rees, *Behind Closed Doors*, p. 211.
'I mean . . . right': *New York Times*, 16 February 1996.
'the tragedy of Yalta': Nicholas Sarkozy biography on www.imdb.com
'The revival . . . behind us': www.worldpolitics.review.com
'jaw-to-jaw': For a full discussion of this quote and its precise nature see International Churchill Society, www.winstonchurchill.org
'No more . . . alter!': C-871, Churchill to Roosevelt, 1 January 1945.

CHAPTER ONE 'The Big Three'

'Mr President . . . walk': Quoted Ferrell, *The Dying President*, p. 99.

'You . . . part': George Elsey quoted Meacham, *Franklin and Winston*, p. 163.

'a black . . . back': Widely quoted, for example, ibid., p.35.

'This . . . centimetres': Quoted Stelzer, *Dinner with Churchill*, p. 174.

'really . . . mouthwash': quoted ibid., p. 183.

'I have . . . me': This famous quip is widely quoted, for example by International Churchill Society, www.winstonchurchill.org

'a drunken sot': Quoted Fenby, *Alliance*, p.12.

'he supposed . . . time': Quoted Rees, op. cit., p. 104.

'with . . . chemist': Quoted Bishop, *FDR's Last Year*, p. 15.

'Alright . . . stomach': Quoted Fenby, *Alliance*, p. 238.

'Stalin . . . weakness': Beria, op. cit., p. 134.

'He . . . unhappy': Harriman, *Special Envoy*, p. 191.

'special supports . . . he was': Berezhkov, *At Stalin's Side*, p. 238.

'of . . . mischief': Djilas, *Conversations with Stalin*, pp. 59–60. After being part of Tito's post-war government in Yugoslavia, Djilas became a dissident and was imprisoned.

'a frightening . . . waters': S. Churchill, *A Thread in the Tapestry*, p. 65.

'a rotund . . . bulldozer': Adamic, *Dinner at the White House*, p. 24.

'a strange . . . infectious': Margaret (Daisy) Suckley, ed. Ward, *Closest Companion*, p. 229.

'ruddy . . . broad-shouldered . . . close-set . . . deep': Adamic, op. cit., p. 15.

'thought . . . humour . . . exceptionally corny . . . loved . . . humour': Bohlen's research papers for his book, Box 24, LOC.

'a good . . . actor': Reilly, op. cit., pp. 124–5.

'the Garbo in me': Quoted Meacham, op. cit., p. 27.

'Everything . . . imperturbability': Dean Acheson, quoted Stelzer, op. cit., p. 195.

'play-acting . . . with . . . saying': Quoted Djilas, op. cit., p. 19.

'a sense . . . depth': Ibid., p. 60.

'as much . . . jest': Ibid., p. 103.

'to recover . . . being': Ibid., p. 140.

'never . . . off': Quoted Meacham, op. cit., p. 32.

'a dreadful . . . crawlers': Quoted Rees, op. cit., p. 158.

'He . . . weakness': Beria, op. cit., p. 134.

'never . . . conferences': Gromyko, *Memories*, p. 100.

'a chameleon on plaid': Quoted Edmonds, *The Big Three*, p. 141.

'The President . . . form it': W. Churchill, *The Grand Alliance*, p. 442.

'defence . . . politics . . . domestic . . . reasons': Colville, *The Fringes of Power*, p. 127.

'a sharp . . . argument . . . benign . . . affectionate': Sir Aubrey Montague Brown, quoted Meacham, op. cit., p. 228.

'lovable . . . human': Eleanor Roosevelt, quoted Lehrman, *Churchill, Roosevelt and Company*, p. 274.

'was . . . naturally': Mary Soames, quoted Meacham, op. cit., p. xvii.

'Patience . . . unfamiliar': Colville, op. cit., p. 126.

'Energy . . . qualification . . . it . . . trick': Quoted Attlee, *Attlee's Great Contemporaries*, p. 162.

However . . . wholesome': All quotes about Attlee's letter to Churchill come from Colville, op. cit., p. 554–5.

'when . . . listening': Quoted Kimball, *Forged in War*, p. 142.

'a great . . . situation': Eleanor Roosevelt, oral history, session 9, reel 1, pp. 10–11, Graff Papers, FDRL.

'almost . . . wisdom': Quoted Beschloss, *The Conquerors*, p. 219.

'strictly opportunistic': Henry Wallace, COHP.

'by . . . indirection . . . very . . . time' Quoted Lelyveld, *His Final Battle*, p. 15.

'great . . . moves': Soames, *Clementine Churchill*, p. 448.

'the coldest . . . see . . . liked . . . other': Quoted Beschloss, op. cit., pp. 219–20.

'he would . . . them': Elsey, quoted Rees, op. cit., p. 129.

'You . . . war': Quoted Kimball, *The Juggler*, p. 7.

'I think . . . too': Arthur Krock, COHP, p. 45.

'a master . . . oratorial . . . He . . . proposition': Eisenhower in 'Churchill as an Ally in War', in ed. Eade, *Churchill by his Contemporaries*, p. 159.

'to stir . . . dough': Quoted R. Holmes, *In the Footsteps of Churchill*, p. 97.

'A man . . . words': E. Roosevelt, *This I Remember*, p. 349.

'a fortunate relationship': Ibid., p. 255.

'to keep . . . on': widely quoted, e.g. www.winstonchurchill.org

'Human . . . years': Quoted Dobbs, *Six Months in 1945*, p. 26.

'Stalin . . . raise': Beria, op. cit., p. 147.

'set . . . art': Ibid., p. 46.

'I was . . . uncomfortable': Gromyko, op. cit., p. 99.

'could . . . army . . . a bloodright . . . cause': W. Churchill, *The Grand Alliance*, p. 537.

'I am . . . me': Quoted Massie, *Dreadnought*, p. 754.

'has little . . . believe': Quoted R. Churchill, *Youth*, p. 190.

'If . . . existence': Quoted Massie, op. cit., p. 755.

'Restless . . . originality': Ibid., p. 766.

'The Dardanelles . . . grief': Quoted Gilbert, *Challenge of War*, p. 429.

'a stinker . . . over us': ed. A. Smith, *Hostage to Fortune: The Letters of Joseph P. Kennedy*, p. 411.

'foul baboonery': Widely quoted, for example on International Churchill Society, www.winstonchurchill.org

'a pestilence . . . Typhus': Quoted Edmonds, op. cit., p. 40.

'half-naked fakir': Churchill to his constituents, 23 February 1931, quoted R. Holmes, op. cit., p. 14.

'similar . . . ago . . . I am . . . Indian': Quoted French, *Liberty or Death*, p. 90.

'Parliament . . . freedom': Hansard, 5 October 1938.

'A second-class . . . temperament': Quoted Kimball, *Forged in War*, p. 4.

'I was . . . politics': Quoted Edmonds, op. cit., p. 45.

'The United . . . trust': Quoted Morgan, *FDR*, p. 213.

'Japanese . . . results': Ibid., p. 276.

'If . . . list': Ibid., p. 321.

'the only . . . itself': Quoted Dobbs, op. cit., p. 105.

'a reconciler . . . feminine . . . people . . . at . . . present': Wallace, COHP.

'They . . . Georgia': The hut in which Stalin was born is preserved in Gori, incorporated into a Stalin Museum where one can even buy snow globes containing the hut, a figure of Stalin or both.

'Stalin . . . childhood': Quoted Montefiore, *Stalin – 1878–1939*, p. 27.

'Don't be . . . mother . . . I'll . . . watchman': Ibid., p. 26.

'a ruthless . . . hand': Ibid., p. 33.

'has concentrated . . . caution . . . Stalin . . . Secretary': Quoted Edmonds, op. cit., pp. 50–1.

'Socialism in one Country': Ibid., p. 56.

'God . . . have': Quoted Montefiore, *Stalin – 1878–1939*, p. 92.

'the indiscriminate . . . victims': Quoted Butler, *Roosevelt and Stalin*, p. 7.

CHAPTER TWO 'We Ended Friends'

'the most . . . nation': Quoted Kimball, *Forged in War*, p. 74.

'No lover . . . Roosevelt': Colville, op. cit., p. 624.

'if . . . me . . . Historic . . . enormously': Harriman, op. cit., p. 75.

'not a law . . . star': Quoted Kimball, *Forged in War*, p. 317.

'If Hitler . . . Commons': Colville, op. cit., p. 404.

'bluntness . . . insult': FRUS/1942, p. 618.

'No risks . . . Germans': Berezhkov, op. cit., p. 299.

'I was . . . otherwise . . . Have. . . . God': W. Churchill, *The Hinge of Fate*, p. 399.

'very . . . necessary': Ibid., p. 403.

'this . . . of a man': Churchill, quoted Moran, op. cit., p. 63.

'I was . . . friends': Ibid., p. 64.

'be more . . . explore . . . ambitions': R-297, Roosevelt to Churchill, 28 June 1943.

'a poor . . . donkey . . . the great . . . buffalo . . . way home': Winston Churchill to Violet Bonham Carter, eight months after the Teheran Conference and widely quoted.

'always . . . dog': George Elsey, quoted Rees, op. cit., p. 13.

'I did . . . exchanges': Bohlen, *Witness to History*, p. 146.

'As . . . brothers': In her book *The Roosevelt I Knew*, pp. 70–1, Frances Perkins recounts how Roosevelt told her of his wooing of Stalin.

'My father . . . think': Quoted Meacham, op. cit., p. 266.

The substance . . . returned: All quotes in these two paragraphs come from W. Churchill, *Closing the Ring*, p. 298.

'the day . . . consciences': Quoted Fenby, *Alliance*, p. 260.

'It is . . . develop': Harold Macmillan's diary, 5 June 1944, quoted Kimball, op. cit., p. 259.

'You . . . nation': Churchill, quoted Moran, op. cit., p. 177.

'unnatural . . . unnecessary': Quoted Beschloss, op. cit., p. 125.

'The German . . . civilization': Roosevelt Memorandum to Secretary of War, 26 August 1944.

'so much to ask': W. Churchill, *Triumph and Tragedy*, p. 138.

'The plan . . . field': Quoted Rees, *Behind Closed Doors*, p. 307.

'Roosevelt . . . Plan': Quoted Fenby, *Alliance*, p. 319.

'nonsense . . . not . . . approved it': Quoted Beschloss, op. cit., p. 141.

'naughty': Quoted widely, for example Gilbert, *The Road to Victory*, p. 992 and Fenby, *Alliance*, p. 323.

'the US . . . itself': Ibid.

'Might . . . paper': W. Churchill, *Triumph and Tragedy*, p. 198.

'We . . . together': Quoted Fenby, *Alliance*, p. 326.

'you could . . . coast': Stalin to Roosevelt, 19 October 1944.

'come . . . desire': C-801, Churchill to Roosevelt, 22 October 1944.

'Do you . . . Cyprus': R-632, Roosevelt to Churchill, 22 October 1944.

'there would . . . coming in': C-804, Churchill to Roosevelt, 23 October 1944.

'From what . . . our ships . . . where . . . for all . . . Will you . . . message?': Ibid.

'I would . . . ship': Telegram 252, Roosevelt to Stalin, 23 October 1944.

'If the . . . to that': Telegram 253, Stalin to Roosevelt, 29 October 1944.

On 2 November . . . near future': All quotes in this paragraph are from R-641, Roosevelt to Churchill, 2 November 1944.

'from dysentery . . . plague': Harriman, op. cit., p. 368.

'Here . . . security . . . with . . . precaution . . . and throw . . . refusing': C-814, Churchill to Roosevelt, 5 November 1944.

'about . . . January . . . My naval . . . Black Sea': Telegram 256, Roosevelt to Stalin, 18 November 1944.

'Your message . . . moulder': C-825, Churchill to Roosevelt, 19 November 1945.

'by Russian . . . Fahrenheit': Quoted Plokhy, *Yalta*, p, 27.

'I liked this': W. Churchill, *Triumph and Tragedy*, p. 268.

'I shall . . . alter!': C-871, Churchill to Roosevelt, 1 January 1945.

'You have . . . everything': C-874, Churchill to Roosevelt, 5 January 1945.

'I do not . . . seven': C-884, Churchill to Roosevelt, 10 January 1945.

'pertinacity': Ibid.

American-educated Meiling Soong: Meiling led discussions with the Americans of China's equipment requirements and secured considerable aid. When

Congress dispatched Wendell Wilkie, Roosevelt's defeated Republican opponent in the 1940 presidential election, to China on a bipartisan fact-finding mission, Meiling arranged lavish receptions for him, thinking he might run for president again in 1944 and at the least that he was capable of exerting great influence in Washington on China's behalf. Their relationship prospered to such an unprecedented extent that an American accompanying Wilkie told how after an evening reception an angry Chiang Kai-shek appeared, demanding to know where his wife was. At four in the morning, the married Wilkie turned up 'very buoyant . . . cocky as a young college student after a successful night with a girl, . . . giving me a play by play account of what had happened between him and Madam.' Their affair soon became the subject of much gossip. Despite this, an infatuated Wilkie invited Meiling to visit the US. Her visit was a great success and Chiang received much further aid.

With her husband, Meiling attended the pre-Teheran Allied summit between Churchill and Roosevelt in Cairo in November 1943. The acerbic British Field Marshal Sir Alan Brooke described Chiang as 'a cross between a pine marten and a ferret . . . a shrewd but small man . . . very successful in leading the Americans down the garden path'. Of Meiling, then in her forties, he noted that when she showed 'the most shapely of legs' through the slit in the skirt of her black satin dress it caused 'a rustle amongst those attending the conference and I even thought I heard a suppressed neigh come from a group of some of the younger members!' The discussion ended with the promise of more aid for Chiang, the return of Formosa (Taiwan), seized by Japan in 1895 and a decision on a joint Allied advance into north-west China through Burma.

'quick . . . wrong': Quoted Fenby, *Chiang Kai-shek*, p. 387.

'China . . . side': Quoted Clemens, *Yalta*, p. 49.

'I cannot . . . Empire': Churchill to Eden on America's Four Power Plan, 21 October 1943, quoted Clemens, op. cit., p. 48.

'four . . . pigtails': Quoted Fenby, *Alliance*, p. 7.

'Great . . . Illusion': Quoted Woolner, *The Last 100 Days*, p. 55.

'all . . . back': Quoted Rees, op. cit., p. 219.

'What . . . Dover?': Quoted Beschloss, op. cit., p. 92.

'an improbable . . . gaze': Moran, op. cit., p. 80.

'Oh, don't' . . . burn him': Quoted Meacham, op. cit., p. 211.

'[He] . . . to please': Quoted Plokhy, op. cit., p. 104.

'treachery in battle . . . to Algiers . . . necessary': Quoted Fenby, *Alliance*, p. 297.

'De Gaulle . . . the invasion began': On another occasion when de Gaulle was arguing for Churchill to take a stronger line with Roosevelt on behalf of himself and France, Churchill told him, 'Each time I must choose between you and Roosevelt, I shall always choose Roosevelt'.

'a well . . . figure': Quoted Meacham, op. cit., p. 201.

'a narrow . . . good': Quoted Lehrman, op. cit., p. 200.

'and would . . . opportunity': R-288, Roosevelt to Churchill, 17 June 1943.

'Roosevelt . . . arbitrator': Quoted Meacham, op. cit., p. 208.

'forever intriguing . . . the work': Quoted Gilbert, *Road to Victory*, p. 1155.

CHAPTER THREE Argonaut

His inaugural . . . in war': The full text of Roosevelt's Fourth Inaugural Address – both the prepared text and, as quoted here, as delivered , is on File No. 1570, FDRL Franklin database.

'and especially . . . arm': Wallace, COHP, vol. 21, p. 3632.

'I feel . . . decline . . . She . . . lips': Frances Perkins, COHP, p. 286.

'I need it': Ibid., p. 280.

'Reilly had . . . taken aboard': Among the crew of the *Catoctin* were twelve Russian-speaking US naval personnel, one surnamed Romanov – the family name of the Russian Tsars – specially selected to help with interpreting.

'We ain't . . . parachutes . . . as . . . crazily': Reilly, op. cit., p. 202.

'Who . . . map': Ibid., p. 204.

'gallons . . . vodka . . . if any . . . contest . . . early . . . heavy . . . It must . . . patriotism': Ibid., p. 205.

'did nothing . . . pain': Ibid., p. 206.

'a lead-lined . . . bathtub': Meiklejohn, World War II diary, part II, p. 616, LOC.

'entrusted . . . entourage': S. Beria, op. cit. p. 104.

'contained . . . metal . . . undetectable': S. Beria/IWM/interview 19548.

'it was . . . well': E. Roosevelt, *This I Remember*, p. 265.

'The President . . . say': Daisy Suckley's diary, 30 September 1933, quoted Persico, *Franklin and Lucy*, p.285.

'an ordeal to be borne': Eleanor made this remark to her daughter. It is widely quoted, for example in Rowley, *Franklin and Eleanor*, p.52.

'If you . . . fuss . . . be simpler': E. Roosevelt, *This I Remember*, p. 265.

'Daddy's girl . . . Daddy': *Life Magazine*, 5 March 1945.

'probably . . . Pitt': Jenkins, *Churchill*, p. 448.

'mobilising . . . battle': Quoted Edmonds, op. cit., p. 36.

'in the case of his father . . . with Pamela': After the war and her divorce, Pamela Churchill had long relationships with several other prominent men including Gianni Agnelli of the Fiat motor family, Prince Ali Khan and Baron Ellie de Rothschild. Subsequently she married a Broadway producer and, after his death, in 1971 went back to and married Averell Harriman and became a major fundraiser for the Democratic Party. After Harriman's death in 1978, by then a US citizen she became US ambassador to Paris where she died in 1997.

'She . . . crippled me': Quoted Montefiore, *Stalin – 1878–1939*, p. 20.

'My mother's . . . back': Quoted Edmonds, op. cit., p. 57.

'and not . . . types': Beria, op. cit., p. 139.

'bloated . . . power . . . force . . . countries . . . aggressiveness . . . action':
Harriman, op. cit., p. 341.

'three . . . stations . . . and every . . . sweep': Ibid., p. 392.

'It . . . DDT': Letter 4–10 February, 1945, Harriman Papers, LOC.

Throughout . . . meal: All quotes from Meiklejohn, World War II diary, part II,
p. 610, LOC.

'hanging . . . everywhere': Ibid., p. 165.

'I never . . . best . . . being . . . things . . . full . . . state': Harriman, op. cit.,
p. 393.

Kathleen . . . to one': All quotes in these three paragraphs are from Bright, *The
Inner Circle*, pp. 178, 182, 184–5 and 188. Telegrams about the British
arrangements at Yalta are in PREM 4/77/1B, part II, UKNA.

'if we . . . world': C-894/1, Churchill to Roosevelt via Hopkins, 24 January
1945.

'most . . . experience': C-896, Churchill to Roosevelt, 26 January 1945.

'Papa sat . . . much': Letter to Clementine Churchill, 31 January 1945, CCC.

'It was . . . hours . . . The hospital . . . laid on . . . the bed . . . way . . .
sat . . . lump': Ibid.

'we flew . . . good': Eden, *Memoirs*, p. 509.

'A poisonous . . . sunshine': Brooke, op. cit., p. 651.

'I don't . . . Staff': Ibid., p. 649.

'as a fine . . . life': W. Churchill, *Triumph and Tragedy*, p. 223.

'We are . . . me': Quoted Bishop, op. cit., p. 237.

'You're deafened . . . to . . . Seeing . . . experience . . . There . . . lungs': BBC
News Website, 7 September 2004.

'like autumn leaves': Colville, op. cit., p. 549.

'as a . . . arriving': BBC News Website, 8 September 2014.

'These latest . . . straw . . . It is . . . going': WW2 People's War, BBC online
archive of Second World War memories, www.bbc.co.uk/ww2peopleswar

'Only the belief . . . kept us going':Innovations recently deployed by the
American forces included the world's first series produced helicopter, the
Sikorsky R4, first used for convoy protection in the Atlantic in January 1945.

'the largest naval engagement . . . in history': 282 ships took part in the Battle of
Leyte Gulf, compared with some 250 at World War One's largest naval battle
– Jutland in 1916. The Japanese lost four aircraft carriers, three battleships,
ten cruisers and eleven destroyers.

    Kamikazes were named after 'the divine wind' with which the Japanese
deities were reputed to have forestalled two thirteenth century invasions of
Japan by the Mongols under Kublai Khan. They were explosive-packed planes
– usually Zero fighters – and boats which their single occupants crashed into
US vessels in suicide attacks.

'the stormiest . . . war': Quoted Woolner, op. cit., p. 32.

'brutally . . . Eisenhower': Ismay, op. cit., p. 385.

'pencil-like thrust': www.armchairgeneral.com, quoting Eisenhower deriding
    Montgomery's plan.
'the . . . conclusion': Brooke, op. cit., p. 653.
'heavy . . . Chemnitz . . . most . . . fronts': Quoted Gilbert, *Road to Victory*,
    p. 1165.
'a proposal to launch . . . high explosive': During a lull in the discussions,
    Chevalier Hannibal Scicluna, the Librarian of Malta, showed Kuter and Portal
    some of the island's treasures including some Gobbelin tapestries. When he
    commented that the British had been expected to relinquish sovereignty of
    Malta around 1880 but 'in recognition of the great desire of the
    overwhelming majority of the Maltese' had decided not to, an amused Portal
    whispered to Kuter, 'If you will study English history, you will find that sort
    of thing happened all over the world. We have had a terrific time with natives
    who insisted that their countries be turned over to British sovereignty'.
'in recognition . . . Maltese . . . If you . . . sovereignty': Kuter, *Airman at Yalta*,
    pp. 72–3.
'cheerful . . . reach . . . Surely . . . chance?': Moran, op. cit., p. 217.
'my heart . . . ending . . . Tender . . . husband': 1 February 1945, ed. Soames,
    Speaking for Themselves, p. 513.
'marching . . . grip': Quoted Gilbert, *Second World War*, 631.
'God . . . Jewesses!': Ibid., pp. 633–4.
'We lay . . . defeat': Ibid., p. 634.
'some . . . ordeal . . . At first . . . freed': *Washington Post*, 27 January 2015.
'very light . . . overturned . . . snow': Quoted Gilbert, *The Second World War*, p. 634.
'Ten-year-old . . . kindness': All quotes in this paragraph are from *Daily Mail*
    online, 2 February 2010. Eva Mozes Kor, who publicly forgave her Nazi
    persecutors, died in July 2019 during her annual visit to Auschwitz.
'I expect . . . fanaticism!': Adolf Hitler's last radio speech, 30 January 1945,
    author's own translation but many translations available including full text on
    https://archive.org
'I cannot . . . more': Quoted Dobson, *The Cruellest Night*, p. 120.
'She left Danzig . . . 1,000 U-boat crewmembers': Some have claimed without
    obvious evidence that the *Wilhelm Gustloff* was carrying the looted panels of
    the Amber Room from the Catherine Palace just outside St. Petersburg, last
    heard of in Konigsberg at around this time. The Polish government have
    banned all diving on the wreck as a war grave.
'They were . . . differently': Quoted Rees, op. cit., p. 325.
'The worst . . . Hungary': Ibid., p. 324.
'Can't [one] . . . trifle?': Djilas, op. cit., p. 88.
'the highest . . . Cross . . . if I am not . . . wing . . . Looking . . . eyes . . . the
    sheet . . . smile': Quoted Aldrich, *Witness to War*, p. 596.
'a madhouse . . . typical': von Kardorff, *Berliner Aufzeichnungen*, p. 243. Author's translation.
'recognised . . . state': Quoted Gilbert, *Second World War*, p. 629.

CHAPTER FOUR 'One Tiny Bright Flame in the Darkness'

'too . . . ornate': Gold Coast Railroad Museum website.

'a little . . . comfortable': Ibid.

'The Pullman Company's . . . comfortable': The *Ferdinand Magellan* is the only passenger railcar to be designated a national Historic landmark by the US government and is in the Gold Coast Railroad Museum, Miami, Florida.

'got . . . soot': Letter to John Boettiger, 23 January 1945, John Boettiger Papers, Box 6, FDRL.

'God-awful': Post-war interview with Ferrell, quoted Ross, *How Roosevelt Failed America in World War II*, p. 141.

'Many . . . favorite': Raymond Clapper, quoted Sherwood, *Roosevelt and Hopkins*, p. 2.

'almost . . . moods': Ibid.

'cookie . . . boot': Bohlen, op. cit., p. 135.

'like . . . blanket': Quoted Butler, *Roosevelt and Stalin*, p. 14.

'a catalytic . . . donnas': Quoted Morgan, op. cit., p. 579.

'the perfect . . . "protocol"': Quoted Kimball, *Forged in War*, p. 77.

'Lord . . . Matter': Ibid.

'worth . . . battleship': Harriman, op. cit., p. 128.

'an animated . . . Wheat': *New Yorker*, 7 August 1943.

'deplorably untidy . . . his clothes . . . on it': Ismay, op. cit., pp. 213–14.

'small . . . respect': Quoted Meacham, op. cit., p. 92.

'I want . . . wear it': Quoted Woolner, op. cit., p. 27.

'little . . . Conference': Byrnes, *Speaking Frankly*, p. 23. Many briefing notes are in FRUS/MY.

'field meet': Rigdon, *White House Sailor*, p. 134.

'a lot . . . gadgets': Anna Boettiger's letter to John Boettiger, 30 January 1945, John Boettiger Papers, Box 6, FRDL.

'all the money': Ibid.

'the game . . . else': Draft book, p. 185, Flynn Papers, FDRL.

'more modest': Letter to Clementine Churchill, 4 February 1945, CCC.

'standing . . . attention': Yalta Notes, Anna Halstead Papers, Box 84, Folder 11, FDRL.

'hands . . . history': Eden, op. cit., pp. 511–12.

'in best . . . spirits': Quoted Gilbert, *Road to Victory*, p. 1167.

'as if . . . at all': Marian Holmes, diary, 2 February 1945, CCC.

'a decent . . . innocence . . . unware . . . nuances . . . no intriguer . . . politician . . . as his . . . affairs . . . would not . . . to do . . . Boy Scout enthusiasm': Bohlen research papers for his book, Box 24, LOC, and his published book *Witness to History*, p. 166.

'good clerk': Quoted Beschloss, op. cit., p. 167.

'a douche . . . Administration': Ibid.

'about . . . Spain': Ibid.

'stark . . . bath': Attributed to Hopkins, see richardlangworth.com for wider
    context.

'The Prime Minister . . . United States': Ibid. (Churchill later denied to Robert
    Sherwood – Roosevelt's speechwriter and biographer of Harry Hopkins –
    having made such a statement.)

'The United Nations . . . Good!': Ibid.

'with . . . decency . . . to take . . . needed': Eden, op. cit., pp. 510–11.

'Pleasant . . . done': Ibid., p. 512.

'a lot . . . Malta"': Anna Boettiger, COHP, pp. 42–3.

'man to man': Quoted Kimball, *Forged in War*, p. 238.

'My father . . . [with Roosevelt]': S. Churchill, *Thread in the Tapestry*, p. 76.

'He must . . . cigar': Moran, op. cit., p. 218.

'thought . . . trip': Letter to Clementine Churchill, 4 February 1945, CCC.

'The immense . . . war': Yalta Notes, 2 February 1945, Anna Halstead Papers,
    Box 84, Folder 11, FDRL.

More junior . . . breakfast': All quotes in this paragraph are from J. Rogers,
    IWM/00000881.

'was no . . . luncheon . . . were going . . . mind': Eden, op. cit., p. 512.

'loves Winston . . . war': Quoted Lehrman, op. cit., p. 135.

'a child . . . stronger': Quoted Meacham, op. cit., p. 34.

'We will . . . sea': Churchill to Charles Taussig, one of Roosevelt's foreign policy
    advisers, quoted Dallek, *FDR and American Foreign Policy*, p. 430.

'I hate . . . religion': Quoted French, op. cit., p. 170.

'Hitler-like . . . India . . . shouting . . . breeding . . . rabbits . . . on . . . war':
    op. cit., pp. 188–9.

'scandalous': Ibid., p. 182.

'to hold . . . population': C-665, Churchill to Roosevelt, 29 April 1944.

'yield . . . flag': Quoted Kimball, *Forged in War*, p. 139.

'He's awfully . . . strike . . . There are . . . Empire': Quoted Meacham, op. cit.,
    p. 213.

'I have . . . wheel': Quoted Gilbert, *Road to Victory*, p. 1166.

'I never . . . unnecessary': Quoted Dobbs, op. cit., p.3.

'a cold starlight night': John Mitchell's diary, 3 February 1945, part 18, the Yalta
    Conference, 24 Sqn RAF Association blog book.

'the planes . . . Africa': Stettinius, *Roosevelt and the Russians*, pp. 28–9.

'all . . . day': Nel (née Layton), *Churchill's Secretary*, p. 166.

'slept . . . vibration': Notes on Illness and Death of FDR, Folder 113, Bruenn
    Papers, FDRL.

'being . . . use . . . this . . . ahead': Quoted Rees, op. cit., p. 333.

'The President . . . stage': Moran, op. cit., p. 226.

'care . . . bodyguards . . . It was . . . infirmity': Beria, op. cit., p. 104.

'under . . . snow': Bohlen, op. cit., p. 173.

'was . . . body . . . being . . . exhaust . . . might . . . body . . . The . . .
    attempt': Brown Papers, FDRL.
'so . . . conversation': Yalta Notes, Anna Halstead Papers, Box 84, Folder 11, p.
    14, FDRL.
'to . . . Germans': Letter Anna Boettiger to her husband, 4 February 1945, John
    Boettiger Papers, Box 6, FDRL.
'a few . . . peasants . . . as . . . despair! . . . Christ . . . this': Letter to
    Clementine Churchill, 4 February 1945, CCC.
'Finally . . . snow': Quoted Aldrich, op. cit., p. 605.
'the call . . . now! . . . cars . . . behind !!! . . . obviously . . . died': Letter to
    Clementine Churchill, 4 February 1945, CCC.
'pave[d] . . . Father': Yalta Notes, Anna Halstead Papers, Folder 11, Box 84, p. 16,
    FDRL.
'that . . . bird': Yalta Notes, 3 February 1945, Anna Halstead Papers, Box 84,
    Folder 11, FDRL.
'went . . . fire': Martin, *Downing Street*, p. 179.
'passengers . . . escape': Brown Papers, pp. 185–6, FDRL.
'practically all': Letter to Clementine Churchill, 4 February 1945, CCC.
Twelve . . . arrangements': All quotes in this paragraph are from Bright, op. cit.
    pp. 190 and 192.
'What . . . to!': M. Holmes, interview transcript, WCHL, 15 February 1955,
    CCC.

CHAPTER FIVE 'All the Comforts of Home'
'the great . . . noblemen . . . the bright . . . palaces . . . tall . . . pines': Twain,
    The Innocents Abroad, chapter XXXVII.
'charming situation . . . Naples . . . scale . . . The number . . . Brighton':
    Murray's Handbooks, p. 373.
'the gayest . . . Crimea': Wood, *The Tourist's Russia*, p. 213.
'two peculiarities . . . generals': Chekhov, 'The Lady with the Dog'.
'when a . . . head . . . striking': R. Hopkins, *American Heritage*, vol. 56, no. 3.
'like animals . . . Sea': Quoted Plokhy, op. cit., pp. 43–4.
'though . . . untouched . . . there . . . deported': Birse, *Memoirs of an Interpreter*,
    p. 179.
'We . . . Russian . . . our . . . town': Korniyasenko, *Emel*, no. 205, p. 31.
The deportations . . . shoes': Arire Idrisli's account of the Tatar deportations in
    these paragraphs is from *Emel*, no. 210, p. 36.
'When . . . drive': Yalta Notes, Anna Halstead Papers, Box 84, Folder 11, p. 17,
    FDRL.
'understand . . . home': Quoted Plokhy, op. cit., p. 47.
'cubicle-like room . . . a funny . . . lock . . . methinks . . . it . . . tried . . . me':
    Yalta Notes, Anna Halstead Papers, Box 84, Folder 11, p. 18, FDRL.
'a most . . . pest': Quoted Beschloss, op. cit., p.179.

'Harry . . . cereal': Quoted Meacham, op. cit., p. 316.

'packed . . . ward': Quoted Plokhy, op. cit., p. 46.

'the most . . . rage': Brooke, op. cit., p. xlviii.

'Ernie . . . shock!': Richards, *Portal of Hungerford*, p. 287.

'a time . . . system': Quoted Mosley, op. cit., p. 316.

'closely . . . plants . . . lurking . . . They . . . guest': Rigdon, op. cit., p. 147.

General Kuter . . . subject': According to Robert Meiklejohn, when some of the American team asked an NKVD general 'how come' there were so few facilities, he replied that 'in Leningrad there was one palace of the Czars that had no toilet facilities at all. When the Czar wished to satisfy his natural requirements, a servant brought in an elegant mother of pearl "throne" which was completely self-contained and which was removed when he had finished . . . I guess servants were cheaper than plumbing'.

'excepting . . . subject': Kuter, op. cit., p. 122.

'practically nil': Letter, 1 February 1945, Harriman Papers, LOC.

'There was . . . too': ed. Resis, *Molotov Remembers*, p. 48.

'with . . . waist': Yalta Notes, 3 February 1945, Anna Halstead Papers, Box 84, Folder 11, FDRL.

'The President . . . displeased': Kuter, op. cit., p. 121.

'3 or 4 . . . effects': Yalta Notes, Anna Halstead Papers, Box 84, Folder 11, p. 17, FDRL.

'the maitre . . . wounded': Ibid.

'The Soviet . . . raise': Quoted Butler, op. cit., p. 348.

'for a . . . talk': Note of conversation, 4 February 1945, Harriman Papers, LOC.

'The setting . . . year': W. Churchill, *Triumph and Tragedy*, p. 303.

'ugliest place . . . ever seen': Hanging on the walls of the Vorontsov were portraits of the aristocratic English Herbert family which Churchill recognised as copies of the originals he had seen at the Herberts' ancestral home, Wilton House. The reason was that Prince Mikhail Vorontsov's sister had married into the Herbert family. Vorontsov's architect Edward Blore was first introduced into fashionable circles by Princess Diana's ancestor Earl Spencer. His other commissions included modifications to Buckingham Palace and Windsor Castle.

'fantastic! . . . outside!': Letter to Clementine Churchill, 6 February 1945, CCC.

'quite . . . seen': Stuart-Clark, letter to sister written after return from Yalta, February 1945, stuart-clark/ww2today.com

'so as . . . chair': Quoted Plokhy, op. cit., p. 71.

'Bowls . . . vodka!': Cadogan, *The Diaries of Sir Alexander Cadogan*, p. 706.

'there is . . . at 6 a.m!': Ibid.

'If you . . . bucket!': Letter to Clementine Churchill, 4 February 1945, CCC.

'in case . . . down': W. Churchill, *Triumph and Tragedy*, p. 311.

'Everything . . . rubble': Drake, IWM/8250.

'When a . . . orders': General Information Bulletin, Anna Halstead Papers, FDRL.

'very . . . braid': Stuart-Clark, letter to sister, February 1945, stuart-clark/ ww2today.com

'a tin . . . it': Evans, 'A Bird's Eye View of the Yalta Conference by a Wren', BBC People's War.

'we have . . . happened': Yalta Notes, Anna Halstead Papers, Box 84, Folder 11, p. 17, FDRL.

'When his corpse . . . the river': Autopsy photographs show three bullet wounds to Rasputin's body, one of which, some have alleged, was caused by a bullet from a British Webley revolver indicating British complicity. Two British secret agents were indeed in St. Petersburg at the time – Lieutenant Oswald Rayner, who had known Prince Yusupov at Oxford and visited his palace several times that day, and Captain Stephen Alley whose father had been one of Prince Yusupov's tutors. The British authorities certainly had a motive for wanting Rasputin out of the way because he was urging the withdrawal of Russian troops from the world war.

'One . . . them': Yusupov, Lost Splendour, p. 264.

'much . . . Lenin': Eden to Cabinet colleagues, 1 January 1942, quoted Kimball, Forged in War, p. 204.

'Perhaps . . . kopeck': Djilas, op. cit., p. 70.

'he . . . negotiation': E. Roosevelt, This I Remember, p. 266.

'a careful . . . negotiator . . . a man . . . mystery . . . Although . . . talks': Bohlen, op. cit., p. 130.

'a confidence . . . regarded': Eden, op. cit., p. 515.

'You say . . . shelter?': Quoted Rees, op. cit., p. 81.

'A man . . . diplomatist': Quoted Dobbs, op. cit., p. 175.

'a rather. . . . man . . . in Stalin's . . . himself . . . somewhat . . . pince-nez': Djilas, op. cit., p. 100.

'He undressed . . . now"': Quoted Rees, op. cit., p. 329.

'Roosevelt . . . English . . . a friend . . . U.S.': S. Beria/IWM.

'every . . . boards': Quoted Rees, op. cit., p. 202.

'My . . . me': Andrew, The Mitrokhin Archive, p. 145.

'this was . . . planes': L. Streitfield, Hell from Heaven, chapter 20, www.398th.org. Streitfield was a bombardier from 600th Squadron.

'Why . . . salvation': von Kardorff, op. cit., p. 241. Author's translation.

'the fate . . . hands . . . has been . . . democracies . . . you will . . . Poland': Letter from Tomasz Arciszewski, 3 February 1945, Plohky, op. cit., p. 152.

CHAPTER SIX 'Uncle Joe and Stone Arse'

'wonderfully mild': Brooke, op. cit., p. 655.

'repeated negatives': Eden, op. cit., p. 514.

In fact . . . Harry is': All quotes in these paragraphs are from Yalta Notes, Anna Halstead Papers, Box 84, Folder 11, pp. 18–19, FDRL.

'too . . . Oxford': Quoted Reynolds, *From World War to Cold War*, p. 160.

'Worth . . . store': Quoted Harbutt, *Yalta 1945*, p. 38.

'half . . . woman': Sir Charles Petrie, *Lords of the Inland Sea*, p. 272 wrote, 'Anthony's father was a mad baronet and his mother a very beautiful woman. That's Anthony – half mad baronet, half beautiful woman.'

'Nothing . . . them': Eden, op. cit., p. 509.

'delight . . . frightfully . . . sails': Cadogan, op. cit., p. 699.

'his . . . smile . . . Anthony . . . pretext': Gromyko, op. cit., p. 155.

'diplomatic skills . . . very suave . . . the British . . . frivolity . . . touch . . . petulance . . . not . . . harmonious': Bohlen research papers for his book, Box 24, LOC.

'it was . . . States': Eden, op. cit., p. 513.

'rather . . . partner': Quoted Kimball, *Forged in War*, p. 130.

'which . . . need for it': Quoted Edmonds, *The Big Three*, p. 411.

'represents . . . right': Ibid.

'both . . . friends . . . the helpless . . . Prussia': Birse, op. cit., p. 182.

'the perfection . . . conciseness . . . as if . . . job!'": Ibid., pp. 182–3.

'Churchill's . . . enterprises': General Albert Wedemeyer, quoted Woolner, op. cit., p. 51.

'the Red . . . operation': W. Churchill, *Triumph and Tragedy*, p. 276.

'his powerful . . . strength': Stettinius, op. cit., p. 99.

'The two . . . again': Bohlen, op. cit., p. 180.

'I scrambled . . . them . . . he . . . lemon . . . 200 . . . fruit': R. Hopkins, *American Heritage*, vol. 56, no. 3.

'he had . . . Manila': Bohlen, op. cit., p. 180.

'bloodthirsty . . . ago': FRUS/MY, p. 571.

'everyone . . . savages': Ibid.

'would again . . . 50,000': Ibid. For the full account of the exchanges between Stalin and Roosevelt see FRUS/MY, pp. 570–3.

'a very . . . person . . . unrealistic . . . had . . . all': Ibid., p. 572.

'only . . . kindness': Ibid., p. 573.

'something . . . army . . . The British . . . people . . . have . . . too . . . seemed . . . France . . . a . . . trouble . . . British': Ibid., pp. 572–3.

Towards . . . doorway': All quotes in these three paragraphs are from R. Hopkins, *American Heritage*, vol. 56, no. 3.

'like butterflies': Spiridovich, *Les Dernières Années de la Cour de Tzarskoïë Sélo*.

'the splendour . . . occupants': Birse, op. cit., p. 180.

'the most . . . assembled': Leahy diary, Box 6, p. 33, LOC.

'that . . . listening': Bohlen, op. cit., p. 137.

'We are . . . hands': Birse, op. cit., p. 144.

'Will . . . home . . . sphinx-like': Birse, op. cit., pp. 113 and 184.

'to vent . . . spleen': Yalta Notes, Anna Halstead Papers, Box 84, Folder 11, p. 21, FDRL.

'Whenever . . . world': Harriman's recollections around the time of his ninetieth
     birthday, Terkel, *The Good War*, p. 329.
'they . . . world': FRUS/MY, p. 574.
'that . . . peoples': Bohlen, op. cit., p. 180.
'they . . . on': Quoted F. Taylor, op. cit., p. 218.
'much . . . know': Brooke, op. cit., p. 655.
'I didn't . . . Washington': Quoted Plokhy, op. cit., p. 88.
'destroyed . . . transport . . . robot . . . rockets': FRUS/MY, p. 585.
'were . . . warfare': Stettinius, op. cit., p. 108.
'He spoke . . . gestures': Ibid., p. 107.
'that . . . doing now': FRUS/MY, p. 587.
'the future . . . any': Soviet/TYP, p. 65.
'somehow . . . reappeared': Stettinius, op. cit., p. 111.
'It was . . . finality': Kuter, op. cit., p. 136.
'A tantrum . . . eyes . . . At . . . enough': Yalta Notes, 4 February 1945, Anna
     Halstead Papers, Box 84, Folder 11, FDRL.
'storming . . . home': Harriman, op. cit., p. 395.
'Okay . . . dinner!' Yalta Notes, 4 February 1945, Anna Halstead Papers, Box 84,
     Folder 11, FDRL.
'If you . . . badly': Harriman, op. cit., p. 395.
'would . . . fits!': Yalta Notes, 4 February 1945, Anna Halstead Papers, Box 84,
     Folder 11, FDRL.
'an extreme . . . important': Harriman, op. cit., p. 395.
'The . . . Gaulle's . . . reflecting . . . deliberations': R. Hopkins, *American Heritage*
     56, no. 3.
'listening to everyone': Quoted Clemens, op. cit., p. 128.
'that . . . prefer': Stettinius, op. cit., p. 111.
'What . . . here? . . . You . . . it!': Quoted Hastings, *Finest Years*, p. 549.
'After . . . bad?': Quoted Fenby, op. cit., p. 359.
'just . . . leg': Quoted Clemens, op. cit., p. 129.
'We have . . . Poland . . . But . . . vote': Stettinius, op. cit., p. 113.
'The eagle . . . sang': FRUS/MY, p. 590. Churchill was rephrasing the lines where
     Tamora tells her husband the Roman Emperor Saturninus: 'The eagle suffers
     little birds to sing/And is not careful what they mean thereby,/Knowing that
     with the shadow of his wings/He can at pleasure stint their melody.'
'to . . . world': Harriman, op. cit., p. 396.
'beaten up': Ibid.
'Far . . . fit': Ibid.
'the American . . . do . . . would . . . people': Bohlen, op. cit., p. 181.
'Whenever . . . defendants': Ibid., p. 130.
'I know . . . State?': Birse, op. cit., p. 185.
'I don't . . . him . . . like . . . hound': Quoted, Montefiore, *Court of the Red Tsar*,
     p. 492.

'Dinner . . . sinister': Eden, op. cit., p. 512.

'he . . . matters . . . was . . . vote': Bohlen, op. cit., p. 181.

'success . . . prestige . . . The crucial . . . Europe': Quoted Reynolds, *From World War to Cold War*, p.99.

CHAPTER SEVEN 'To Each According to his Deserts'

'our . . . gone': Cadogan, op. cit., p. 704.

'very carefully . . . unnecessary': Anna Boettiger's letter to her husband of 7 February 1945, John Boettiger Papers, Box 6, FDRL.

'She had . . . conversations': Perkins, *The Roosevelt I Knew*, pp. 316—17.

'an enormous . . . mother . . . the usual . . . can': Meiklejohn, World War II, diary, part II, p. 627, LOC.

'manage . . . She . . . out"': Perkins, COHP, p. 287.

Anna . . . likes': All quotes in these three paragraphs are from Anna Boettiger's letter to her husband of 7 February 1945, John Boettiger Papers, Box 6, FDRL.

'send . . . Papa': Telegram Fleece 36, PREM 4/78/1 Pt 1, UKNA.

'presents . . . o'clock!': Letter to Clementine Churchill, 8 February 1945, CCC.

'Britain . . . Greece . . . Great . . . Greece': Quoted Plokhy, op. cit., p. 146.

'this . . . Raj': Quoted Lowe, *Savage Continent*, p. 299.

'hesitate . . . necessary': Quoted Bishop, op. cit., p. 216.

'giving . . . liberation . . . boil[ed] . . . Charter': Quoted Harbutt, op. cit., p. 213.

'All . . . things . . . Sawyers . . . glasses . . . You . . . sir': Moran, op. cit., p. 224.

'a Russian . . . scent': Pawle, *The War and Colonel Warden*, p.352.

'a sliding . . . shut . . . I . . . lizard': M. Holmes, diary, 5 February 1945, SPCR 23/3, CCC.

Other . . . thirst . . . In our . . . time': All quotes in these four paragraphs are from Stuart-Clark, letter to sister February 1945, stuart-clark/ww2today.com

'bigwigs . . . bath': Adams, IWM/18163.

'an adequate . . . parts': Quoted Fenby, *Alliance*, p. 348.

'the most . . . bedding': Moran, op. cit., p.221.

'a horde . . . battalions': R. Hopkins, American Heritage, vol. 56, no.3.

'a couple . . . D. D. T. . . . I haven't . . . doing so': Moran, op. cit., p.221.

'I . . . Russians . . . necessary . . . operations': Quoted Butler, op. cit., pp. 389—90.

'After . . . Japan': Gromyko, op. cit., p. 83.

'after . . . sentries . . . had . . . themselves . . . into . . . hug . . . to . . . friends': Brooke, op. cit., p. 656.

'great . . . uniform . . . thoroughly informed . . . The . . . sailors': Leahy, *I Was There*, p. 353.

'as . . . permitted': FRUS/MY, p. 597.

'the . . . air . . . everything . . . success': Ibid., pp. 598–9.

'we . . . bombed': Quoted F. Taylor, op. cit., p. 218.

'no . . . forces': FRUS/MY, p. 604.

'to . . . air': Ibid., p. 605.

'cormorants . . . ducks . . . My . . . all!': Brooke, op. cit., p. 657.

'a . . . countries': FRUS/MY, p. 608.

'the . . . news': Stettinius, op. cit., p. 118.

'Any . . . desired': Ibid., p. 119.

'The . . . States . . . less . . . problem . . . the . . . anytime': Bohlen, op. cit., p. 186.

'It's . . . scattered': Cadogan, op. cit., p. 705.

'first . . . Sarah': www.worldhistory.biz

'Hasn't . . . decision?': FRUS/MY, p. 625.

'scattering . . . tribes': Quoted Buhite, *Decisions at Yalta*, p. 21.

'impotent . . . war': Quoted Kimball, *Forged in War.*, p. 249.

'reunite . . . nation . . . the . . . years': Quoted Beschloss, op. cit., p. 28

'the . . . Germany . . . which . . . war': Soviet/TYP, pp. 48–9.

As . . . distance: All quotes in these paragraphs are from Bohlen, op. cit., p. 183.

'make . . . harder': FRUS/MY, p. 627.

'Await . . . future': Ibid., p. 626.

'what . . . them': Ibid., p. 615.

'Mr. President . . . Harry': Ibid., p. 633.

'he . . . years': Ibid., p. 617.

'momentous statement . . . to occupy . . . strength': W. Churchill, *Triumph and Tragedy*, p. 279.

'opened . . . enemy': Stettinius, op. cit., p. 127.

'All . . . Roosevelt . . . not . . . true': Ibid., p. 129,

'his . . . meeting': Gromyko, op. cit., p. 85.

'reparations . . . manpower': FRUS/MY, p. 630.

'the . . . manpower': Soviet/TYP, p. 72.

'using . . . matter': Leahy, op. cit., p. 354.

'a big day!': Quoted Plokhy, op. cit., p. 102.

'quite astronomical': Soviet/TYP, p. 73.

'First. . . . On . . . aviation . . . enterprises': Byrnes, op. cit., p. 26.

'He . . . nation': Violet Bonham Carter quoted Meacham, op. cit., p. 30.

'If . . . hay': W. Churchill, *Triumph and Tragedy*, p. 279.

'That's . . . you': FRUS/MY, p. 621.

'If . . . go': Byrnes, op. cit., p. 27.

'The Germans . . . machines': Soviet/TYP, p. 75.

'America . . . machinery . . . estimated . . . dollars': Leahy, op. cit., p. 355.

'he . . . Union': FRUS/MY, p. 622.

'first . . . reparations': Ibid., p. 623.

'the . . . France': Ibid.

'each . . . needs . . . he . . . deserts': Soviet/TYP, p, 80.

'getting . . . of': Quoted Meacham, op. cit., p. 318.

'missed nothing . . . no . . . notes': Gromyko, op. cit., pp. 85 and 100.

'Marshal . . . obdurate . . . liked . . . on': Eden, op. cit., pp. 514–15.

'Uncle . . . restrained . . . without . . . temper': Cadogan, op. cit., p. 706.

'the . . . possessed': Beria, op. cit., p. 105.

'Do . . . history . . . He . . . civilization . . . when . . . wind': Moran, op. cit., p. 224.

'only . . . world . . . a . . . bones': Ibid., p. 226.

'it . . . Council . . . it . . . friend': Bohlen, op. cit., pp. 184–5.

'I . . . World': Letter to Clementine Churchill, 6 February 1945, CCC.

'German . . . them': Lucy Ash reporting on Vladimir Gelfand's war diary, BBC News Daily Digital Magazine, 1 May 2015.

'both so weak . . . by stretcher': The George Cross awarded posthumously to Violette Szabo is in London's Imperial War Museum.

CHAPTER EIGHT 'The Monstrous Bastard of the Peace of Versailles'

'much . . . more': Telegram Jason 151, 6 February 1945, PREM 4/78/1 Pt II, UKNA.

'Papa . . . strength . . . You . . . Wow': Letter 6 February 1945, CCC.

'eating . . . toast . . . lovely . . . chocolates . . . You . . . line': Letter to parents, 5 February 1945, CCC.

'an . . . closer . . . feeding . . . library!!': Letter to Clementine Churchill, 6 February 1945, CCC.

'At . . . time': Richards, op. cit., p. 284.

'to do . . . string': Ibid, p. 283.

'I am . . . right!': Ibid., pp. 286–7.

Later . . . unbroken': All quotes in this paragraph are from letter to Clementine Churchill, 6 February 1945, CCC.

Foreign . . . end: the text of the press release is in FRUS/MY, p. 659.

'no . . . given': CAB/120/70, UKNA.

'to . . . 2.45 . . . not . . . end': Anna Boettiger's letter to her husband of 7 February 1945, John Boettiger Papers, Box 6, FDRL.

'Quite . . . aged . . . It's . . . madhouse': Cadogan, op. cit., pp. 704–5.

'the . . . Conference . . . the . . . Alliance': W. Churchill, Triumph and Tragedy, p. 290.

'the . . . Versailles': Speech by Molotov to the Supreme Soviet, 31 October 1939.

'in . . . power': Hansard, 31 March 1939. The formal agreement was not signed until 25 August 1939. It is widely available e. g. www.avalon.law.yale.edu

As the Poles . . . concerned: The quotes in these two paragraphs come from Rees, op. cit., pp. 10 and 16.

After . . . them: Davies, God's Playground, p. 321 gives the text of the secret protocol.

'I . . . population': Quoted Rees, op. cit., p. 17.

With Russian . . . at Yalta: The quotes in this paragraph are from ibid., p. 32.

'the hunger . . . animal': Ibid., p. 49.

'for . . . NKVD': Ibid., p. 58.

'[An] orchestra . . . then': Quoted Davies, *God's Playground*, p. 333.

'the black . . . stench . . . We . . . camps': Quoted Rees, op. cit., p. 182.

'the methodical . . . skull': Telegram 25 January 1944 from US Embassy in Moscow to FDR and State Department, Harriman Papers, LOC.

'The . . . Lithuania': Quoted Rees, op. cit., p. 185.

'Corpses . . . bodies': Quoted Gilbert, *Second World War*, p. 526.

'the . . . criminals': Quoted Rees, op. cit., p. 287.

'I . . . Allies': Quoted ibid., p. 289.

'from . . . us': Quoted Davies, *Rising '44*, p. 249.

'The SS . . . stairs': Quoted Rees, op. cit., p. 290.

'This . . . live': Mikolajczyk, *The Pattern of Soviet Domination*, pp. 95–6.

'a deeply moved . . . I know . . . never': Quoted Davies, *God's Playground*, p. 347.

'Poland . . . helped': Quoted Edmonds, op. cit., p. 352. Soviet/TYP p. 47 also describes Churchill's suggestion.

'suffering . . . fighting . . . expected . . . intact': Eden, op. cit., p. 434.

'Your . . . done': Mikolajczyk, op. cit., p. 61.

'friendly . . . did . . . moment . . . agreed . . . Line . . . the . . . same': Quoted Rees, op. cit., p. 315.

'I . . . quietly': Mikolajczyk, op. cit., pp. 107–8.

'We . . . care': Ibid., p. 109.

'You . . . you': Ibid., p. 110. Official Polish accounts of both the discussion with Stalin and of the subsequent private meeting with Churchill are given in Sikorski Institute, *Documents on Soviet-Polish Relations, Vol. 2*, pp. 405–22.

'shocked surprise': Quoted Rees, op. cit., p. 318.

'Poland . . . Germany': Cadogan, op. cit., p. 683.

'almost . . . agreement . . . domination . . . Poland . . . consisting . . . fled': Bohlen, op. cit., p. 169.

'absurdly . . . government': Ibid., p. 187.

'alone . . . Germans': W. Churchill, *Triumph and Tragedy*, p. 280.

'That . . . organisation': Moran, op. cit., p. 225.

'A . . . change . . . we . . . them': Stettinius, op. cit., p. 140.

'not . . . clear': W. Churchill, *Triumph and Tragedy*, p. 280.

'in . . . Governments . . . as . . . war': FRUS/MY, p. 664.

'conflict . . . ourselves . . . secure . . . years': W. Churchill, *Triumph and Tragedy*, p. 280.

'the . . . aggression': FRUS/MY, p. 666.

'talked . . . Russia . . . show . . . it': W. Churchill, *Triumph and Tragedy*, p. 282.

'a distant . . . question': Ibid., p. 290.

'like . . . face"': Soviet/TYP, p. 90.

'the . . . Poland': Ibid.

'all Poles': Ibid.

'the . . . Poland': FRUS/MY, p. 677.

'representative government': Stettinius, op. cit., p. 151.

'After . . . right . . . a . . . Power . . . had . . . life . . . mistress . . . soul': W. Churchill, *Triumph and Tragedy*, pp. 312—22.

'blunt, stubborn': Leahy, op. cit., p. 358.

'a matter . . . death . . . would . . . shameful': W. Churchill, *Triumph and Tragedy*, pp. 292—3.

'the Soviet . . . Curzon . . . very . . . pleased?': Soviet/TYP, p. 94.

'It . . . mind': W. Churchill, *Triumph and Tragedy*, p. 293.

'a slip . . . tongue': Soviet/TYP, p. 95.

'I . . . consulted . . . bandits . . . criminals': FRUS/MY, pp. 669—70.

'traitors . . . turncoats': Soviet/TYP, p. 95.

'equal . . . Gaulle': FRUS/MY, p. 670.

'should . . . behind': Soviet/TYP, p. 96.

'keep . . . Army': W. Churchill, *Triumph and Tragedy*, p. 293.

'bitterness . . . deportations': Ibid., p. 294.

'Poland . . . years . . . All . . . troubles': Ibid.

'very dusty': Eden, op. cit., p. 516.

'I . . . bayonets': Quoted Plokhy, op. cit., p. 176.

'the Red . . . will': Bohlen, op. cit., p. 188, summarizing the pessimistic British and American mood on Poland that evening of 6 February 1945.

'We . . . off': Moran, op. cit., p. 219.

'the . . . speeches': Quoted Bishop, op. cit., p. 348.

'shrewdly . . . unity': Harriman, op. cit., p. 408.

'greatly disturbed . . . in Poland . . . other . . . people . . . If . . . future?': Stettinius, op. cit., pp. 157—8.

'on the . . . enough': Eden, op. cit., p. 518.

'We . . . difficult': Telegram 'Jason' 178, Churchill Papers, 20/223, CCC.

'On . . . inch': Beria, op. cit., p. 106.

'Stalin . . . swallow': Moran, op. cit., p. 225.

'radiant' : Plokhy, op. cit., p, 129, quoting Martin Bormann, head of the Nazi Party.

'these . . . hour': Quoted Bishop, op. cit., p. 235.

'and . . . Jap': 'February 6, Close Shave with a Stay-Behind Japanese Suicide Bomber', WW2today.com/macdonaldfraser

CHAPTER NINE 'The Riviera of Hades'

'Russian . . . food': R. Hopkins, *Witness to History*, p. 151.

'We . . . system': George Kennan, diplomat US Embassy in Moscow in 1944, in Kennan, *Memoirs*, pp. 195—6, quoted Plokhy, op. cit., p. 325.

'There . . . coffee . . . vainly . . . preferred . . . they . . . eggs . . . caviar . . .
 wine': R. Hopkins, *American Heritage*, vol. 56, no. 3.
'when . . . warm': Rigdon, op. cit., p. 147.
'hurriedly . . . could': Evans, 'A Bird's Eye View of the Yalta Conference by a
 Wren', BBC People's War.
'admired . . . fish': W. Churchill, *Triumph and Tragedy*, p. 275.
'as the . . . me . . . There . . . night . . . young . . . spies . . . not . . . time':
 Evans, 'A Bird's Eye View of the Yalta Conference by a Wren', BBC People's
 War.
'intelligence men . . . to assume . . . talked': Rigdon, op. cit., p. 153.
The daily . . . each': All quotes in this paragraph are from Gromyko, op. cit., p.
 86.
'one . . . another': Cadogan, op. cit., p. 705.
'This . . . daylight': US General Information Bulletin, Harriman Papers, LOC.
'where . . . brewed': The slightly surreal guide to local attractions is in PREM
 4/77/1B, UKNA.
The site . . . guise': All quotes in this paragraph are from Brooke, op. cit., p. 658.
'he . . . time': FRUS/MY, p. 699.
'tried . . . Hades"!': Letter to Clementine Churchill, 8 February 1945, CCC.
'a closer . . . white': Ibid.
'Uncle . . . Oaks': Stettinius, op. cit., p. 172.
'the . . . Government': FRUS/MY, p. 709.
'We . . . air': Soviet/TYP, p. 97.
'European ... hostilities': The decision to set up the European Advisory
 Commission was taken at a meeting of the Foreign Ministers of the US, UK
 and the Soviet Union in Moscow in 1943. The original suggestion came from
 the British who advocated establishing a body to act as a clearinghouse for
 any European problems of common interest associated with the war apart
 from military issues. Under US pressure – Roosevelt was reluctant to agree
 to anything that might restrict US freedom of action in post-war Europe –
 the EAC's finally agreed remit was narrowed to deal only with problems
 associated with surrender terms and zones of occupation.
'the . . . correspondence?': FRUS/MY, p. 711.
'only . . . before': W. Churchill, *Triumph and Tragedy*, p. 294.
'he . . . Crimea . . . which . . . ideas': Harriman, op. cit., p. 408.
'the . . . peace . . . entirely acceptable': FRUS/MY, pp. 711–12.
'smiles . . . lips': Quoted Plokhy, op. cit., p. 184.
'England . . . country': Quoted Dobbs, op. cit., p. 87.
'in . . . impulse': Beria, op. cit., p. 106.
'would . . . two . . . had . . . enemy': FRUS/MY, p. 712.
'he . . . States': Sherwood, op. cit., p. 857.
'This . . . good': Stettinius, op. cit., p, 174.
'if . . . member': FRUS/MY, p. 713.

'Mr. . . . Harry': Ibid., p. 729.

'could . . . them . . . profound sympathy . . . might . . . Assembly': W. Churchill,
    Triumph and Tragedy, p. 313.

'to . . . Nations': Bohlen, op. cit., p. 194.

'The . . . war . . . would. . . . Holland . . . undertake . . . world': FRUS/MY,
    pp. 714–15.

'not unnaturally . . . since . . . meeting. . . . another . . . tasks': Eden, op. cit.,
    p. 517.

'The . . . thing': Cadogan, op. cit., p. 706.

'There . . . mind . . . *All* . . . *rot* . . . *rot* . . . *politics* . . . I . . . Britain': FRUS/
    MY, p. 729.

'of . . . decision': FRUS/MY, p. 715.

'to . . . aggression': Quoted Plokhy, op. cit., p. 274.

'unselfish . . . policy': Ibid., p. 275.

'support[ed] . . . concessions': Quoted Kimball, *Forged in War*, p. 261.

'By late . . . politcally': Among the senior American 'advisers' to serve in Iran at
    this time was the ex-Superintendent of the New Jersey State Police, Colonel
    H. Norman Schwarzkopf, who trained and led Iranian police. His son H.
    Norman Schwarzkopf Junior led the coalition forces in the first Iraq War.

'all . . . basis': Quoted Kimball, *Forged in War*, p. 261.

'had . . . time': FRUS/MY, p. 715.

'Stalin . . . notebook': Quoted Plokhy, p. 277.

'some . . . circles . . . as . . . possible': FRUS/MY, p. 716.

'went . . . wishes': Ibid.

'the basis . . . Poland': Bohlen, op. cit., p. 190.

'Poles . . . Poland': FRUS/MY, p. 716.

'brutal . . . attack . . . Poles . . . abroad': Ibid., p. 717.

'It . . . indigestion . . . frankly shocked': W. Churchill, *Triumph and Tragedy*, p. 295.

'most . . . Red Army': FRUS/MY, p. 717.

'Moreover . . . war': Soviet/TYP, p. 104.

'the . . . them . . . to . . . problem': FRUS/MY, pp. 717–18.

'cheerful': Eden, op. cit., p. 517.

Churchill . . . Moscow': The telegram to War Cabinet of 8 February 1945 quoted
    in these two paragraphs is given in W. Churchill, *Triumph and Tragedy*, pp.
    284–5.

He . . . Government': Churchill's telegram to Attlee is ibid., p. 296.

'Uncle . . . accommodating': Cadogan, op. cit., p. 706.

'Russians . . . be': Eden, op. cit., p. 517.

The President . . . vote': All quotes in this paragraph are from Stettinius, op. cit.,
    pp. 187–8.

'I . . . Roosevelt': Quoted Plokhy, op. cit, p. 222.

In front . . . hill': Account of Edgar Valderrama, C Company 11th Infantry
    Regiment, 5th Division, www.joedemadio.com

'a God-awful . . . back ': Reminiscences of Peter Zwack, 'World War II: Siege of Budapest', www.historynet.com

CHAPTER TEN 'The Broad Sunlit Plains of Peace and Happiness'

As the . . . soda!': All quotes in this paragraph are from letter to Clementine Churchill, 8 February 1945, CCC.

'a grand . . . Americans': Letter 4–10 February 1945, Harriman Papers, LOC.

'and a life-size . . . hand . . . grim': Moran, op. cit., p. 226.

'looked ghastly . . . began . . . verve . . . The President . . . Stalin': Ibid., pp. 226–7.

'was all right . . . a definite conclusion': Stettinius, op. cit., p. 193.

'sympathetic consideration ': Ibid., p. 191.

'an amendment . . . agreed. . . . Republics': Ibid., p. 193.

'favorably impressed . . . the United . . . day': Ibid.

'reserved . . . position . . . somehow . . . proposal': Ibid., pp. 195–6.

'Yes': Ibid., p. 196.

'a good omen': FRUS/MY, p. 733.

'excellent': Leahy, op. cit., p. 361.

'by intensive . . . lives': FRUS/MY, p. 766.

'difficult': Ibid.

'the British . . . ideas': Ibid., p. 768.

'a remarkable . . . delayed': Ibid.

'there . . . whatsoever': Ibid.

'If . . . easily': Bohlen, op. cit., p. 196.

'he knew . . . objections': FRUS/MY, p. 769.

'the pre-eminent . . . country': Bohlen, op. cit., p. 197.

'Roosevelt . . . me in': Berezhkov, op. cit., p. 240.

'it would . . . powers': FRUS/MY, p. 769.

'Let him wait': Dobbs, op. cit., p. 70.

'delicate . . . they . . . resent this': FRUS/MY, p. 770.

'Prime . . . us': Ibid.

'of small. . . . warlike': Ibid.

'complete success': Ibid., p. 771.

'You . . . place': Stettinius, op. cit., pp. 196–7.

'a . . . talk': FRUS/MY, p. 992.

'to attempt . . . security': Ibid., pp. 772–3.

'but had . . . about it': Ibid., p. 773.

'had wavered . . . side . . . who . . . suffered': Ibid.

'having . . . Germany': Ibid., p. 774.

'had . . . in': Ibid., p. 775.

'not . . . logical' . . . small . . . moment': Soviet/TYP, p. 108.

'the martyrdom . . . sufferings': FRUS/MY, p. 775.

'embarrass': Ibid.

'giving . . . one': Ibid.

'wrestled . . . Poland': Harriman, op. cit., p. 410.

'very close': FRUS/MY, p. 776.

'represent . . . Republic . . . Polish . . . Unity . . . representative . . . abroad':
    Ibid., pp. 792–3.

'a sharp confrontation': Gromyko, op. cit., p. 91.

'the existence . . . Poland': Stettinius, op. cit., p. 212.

'great authority': FRUS/MY, p. 786.

'would . . . Government': Stettinius, op. cit., p. 212.

'the . . . doubt': FRUS/MY, p. 787.

'Now . . . of it': Quoted Lelyveld, op. cit., p. 281.

'the crucial . . . Conference . . . the whole . . . failure . . . If . . . outcry . . .
    had been . . . stage': W. Churchill, *Triumph and Tragedy*, pp. 298–9.

'a new . . . London': FRUS/MY, p. 779.

'Molotov is right': Ibid., p. 781.

'tragic': Soviet/TYP, p. 113.

'geniuses': FRUS/MY, p. 780.

'truly tremendous': Soviet/TYP, p. 111.

'a great . . . history': Ibid., p. 112.

'who . . . popular?': FRUS/MY, p. 789.

'Why . . . France?': Soviet/TYP, p. 113.

'In about . . . defeat us . . . I do not . . . happen': FRUS/MY, p. 790.

'The other . . . me': Ibid.

'very . . . affairs': FRUS/MY, p. 782.

'We shall . . . more': Beria, op. cit., p. 106.

'February 8th . . . Poland': Eden, op. cit., p. 517.

'arduous . . . emotionally disturbing . . . worried . . . upset': Clinical Notes on
    Illness and Death of FDR, Bruenn Papers, Folder 113, FDRL.

'one . . . vodka': Brooke, op. cit., p. 659.

'All . . . alert . . . that . . . ankles': Leahy, op. cit., p. 365.

'the good . . . good': Gromyko, op. cit., p. 89.

'excellent . . . spirits . . . for . . . smile': Stettinius, op. cit., pp. 219 and 221.

'regular . . . jacket . . . occasionally . . . drink . . . unless . . . uniform':
    Cunningham, *A Sailor's Odyssey*, p. 628.

'I had . . . alert': Stettinius, op. cit., p. 221.

'saturnine . . . he . . . water': Cunningham, op. cit., p. 628.

'Ah . . . Himmler': Quoted Fenby, *Alliance*, p. 369.

'irritation . . . bitterness': Bohlen, op. cit., p. 182.

'even . . . mood': W. Churchill, *Triumph and Tragedy*, p. 287.

'caviare . . . bit': Cadogan, op. cit., p. 706.

'the bravest . . . world . . . when . . . Hitler . . . to . . . world . . . his . . .
    man': FRUS/MY, pp. 797–8.

'the British . . . fight': W. Churchill, *Triumph and Tragedy*, p. 288.

'Stalin . . . determination': Moran, op. cit., p. 227.

'the mighty . . . soil': FRUS/MY, p. 798.

Stalin next . . . wellbeing': All quotes in this paragraph are ibid.

'I am . . . views': W. Churchill, *Triumph and Tragedy*, p. 286.

'not . . . difficult . . . as . . . wartime': Stettinius, op. cit., p. 221.

'buckets . . . man': Cadogan, op. cit., p. 707.

'were all . . . us . . . to lead . . . carelessness': Stettinius, op. cit., pp. 221–2.

'extraordinarily . . . oratory . . . a great . . . translation . . . While . . . produce':
    Bohlen research papers for his book, Box 24, LOC.

However . . . laughing': All quotes in these paragraphs ibid., from numbered
    pages of drafts of his book, pp. 184–5.

'The "Bear" . . . form': Letter from Sarah Oliver to Clementine Churchill, 9
    February 1945, CCC.

'that the . . . Russian': Letter 4–10 February 1945, Harriman Papers, LOC.

'to make . . . comfortable': Letter from Sarah Oliver to Clementine Churchill, 9
    February 1945, CCC.

'Jesus . . . scared': Letter 4–10 February 1945, Harriman Papers, LOC.

'very friendly . . . Can . . . please . . . I . . . in you': Ibid.

'man . . . bodies . . . Archie . . . toast': Quoted Dobbs, op. cit., p. 75.

'None . . . careful': Letter 4–10 February, Kathleen Harriman, Harriman Papers,
    LOC.

'In these . . . cards': Letter 6 April 1943 to Lord Pembroke, Foreign Office,
    www.lettersofnote.com

'sentimental and emotional': Moran, op. cit., p. 227.

'while . . . settle . . . a very . . . wit': Richards, op. cit., p. 288.

'Stalin . . . himself . . . the standard . . . dragged': Brooke, op. cit., p. 660.

'with . . . Pacific': Stettinius, op. cit., p. 204.

'awe-inspiring . . . troops . . . they . . . forward': Horrocks's graphic account of
    Operation Veritable is on www2today.com

'All . . . troops . . . Strike . . . West': Quoted Gilbert, *Road to Victory*, p. 1190.

In a slave . . . died': The extraordinary story of Devyataev and his companions is
    told in full in Hastings, *Armageddon*, pp. 453–6.

'Do you . . . end': Quoted Gilbert, *Second World War*, p. 639.

CHAPTER ELEVEN 'Quite a Decent Arrangement
About Poland'

'It sounds . . . unnecessarily?': Stettinius, op. cit., p. 205.

'The President . . . people?': Gromyko, op. cit., p. 98.

'Such a . . . ill': Quoted Bishop, op. cit., pp. 318–19.

'sit . . . rummy': Boettiger letter to her husband, FDRL.

'a world . . . security': Stettinius, op. cit., p. 223.

'Papa's . . . back': Letter 9 February 1945, CCC.

'at . . . Japan': FRUS/MY, p. 827.

'to . . . unconditionally . . . the overwhelming . . . powers . . . mitigation . . . surrender . . . the saving . . . out . . . would . . . attack': Ibid., p. 826.

'meandered . . . delay': Brooke, op. cit., p. 660.

'formula': FRUS/MY, p. 804.

Reading . . . elections': All quotes in this paragraph ibid.

'hardly . . . Britain': Ibid.

'I fairly . . . wanted': Eden, op. cit., p. 518.

'of course . . . they . . . representatives': FRUS/MY, p. 806.

'for the moment': Ibid., p. 808.

'might . . . less': Ibid.

'Thank . . . remarks . . . a great . . . tuppence': Cadogan, op. cit., p. 708.

'very useful . . . in . . . tone . . . vigorously pursued': FRUS/MY, pp. 835–6.

Shortly . . . shrugged': All quotes in these four paragraphs are from R. Hopkins, *American Heritage*, vol. 56, no. 3.

'During . . . thread': Quoted Plokhy, op. cit., p. 242.

Despite . . . Poles: All quotes in this paragraph are from FRUS/MY, p. 842.

'the urgent . . . Poland: Ibid., p. 843.

'there . . . meetings': Soviet/TYP, p. 115.

'to . . . off': W. Churchill, *Triumph and Tragedy*, p. 302.

'the whole. . . . failure': Soviet/TYP, p. 115.

'great agitation': Ibid., p. 116.

'would . . . heritage': FRUS/MY, p. 844.

'got . . . applause': Eden, op. cit., p. 514.

'the Japanese . . . Pacific . . . never . . . never': Stettinius, op. cit., p. 238.

'dramatically . . . Stalin': Ibid.

'if . . . resort': Soviet/TYP, p. 117.

'would . . . conferences': Ibid.

'now . . . drafting': FRUS/MY, p. 846.

For example . . . details': All quotes in this part of the paragraph are in FRUS/MY, p. 846.

'to try . . . forces . . . usual . . . kindness': Ibid., p. 847.

'six . . . States': Ibid., p. 848.

'not . . . Poles': Ibid., p. 853.

'We . . . quarrelsome': W. Churchill, *Triumph and Tragedy*, p. 303.

'did not . . . anything': Quoted Plokhy, op. cit., p. 265.

'all . . . hearing': W. Churchill, *Triumph and Tragedy*, p. 303.

'liberated . . . choice . . . the right . . . live . . . By this . . . mankind': The text of the final Joint Declaration is in FRUS/MY, pp. 977–8.

'This . . . far! . . . Don't . . . forces': ed. Resis, op. cit., p. 51.

'one small change . . . to . . . invaders': FRUS/MY, p. 848.

'need . . . Greece . . . complete . . . Greece': Stettinius, op. cit., p. 244.

'to any . . . needed': Ibid., p. 244.

'like . . . wife . . . above . . . suspicion': Soviet/TYP, p. 122.

'Caesar's . . . lily-white': Ibid., p. 123.

'already applied': FRUS/MY, p. 848.

'that . . . Wilkie': Ibid., p. 849.

'has. . . . France . . . now . . . time': Moran, op. cit., p. 224.

'Three . . . four': FRUS/MY, p. 849.

'an egg . . . myself': Ibid.

'sent . . . done': Quoted Beschloss, op. cit., p. 21.

'grand criminals': Quoted Gilbert, *Road to Victory*, p. 1201.

'nothing . . . war': Soviet/TYP, p. 124.

The . . . desired': All quotes in this paragraph are from McIntire, op. cit., pp. 221–2.

'Marshall's . . . direction': Brooke, op. cit., p. 660.

'informing . . . point . . . be . . . out': Quoted Harbutt, op. cit., p. 303.

Meanwhile . . . State': All quotes in this paragraph are from Moran, op. cit., p. 208.

'British Revised Formula': Stettinius, op. cit., p. 246.

'reorganised . . . abroad . . . the question . . . day': Ibid., p. 248.

'quite . . . Poland . . . get . . . hurdle . . . none . . . sense': Cadogan, op. cit., pp. 707–8.

'support . . . invaders': Stettinius, op. cit., p. 249.

'We leave . . . 18th': Cadogan, op. cit., p.707.

'one . . . stand it': Ibid., p. 708.

CHAPTER TWELVE 'Judge Roosevelt Approves'

'P. M. . . . Higher''': M. Holmes, diary, 10 February 1945, SPCR 23/3, CCC.

'Have . . . days': Quoted Gilbert, *Road to Victory*, p. 1203.

'Spirits . . . cough': Clinical Notes on Illness and Death of FDR, Bruenn Papers, Folder 113, FDRL.

'do . . . Conference . . . the three kings. . . . interminably . . . the Russians . . . case': Stettinius, op. cit., pp. 252, 257 and 258.

'Americans . . . warning . . . Certainly . . . agree': FO 954/20C/424, UKNA.

'the Polish . . . Union': Stettinius, op. cit., p. 252.

'a new . . . Government': FRUS/MY, p. 872.

'who . . . occupation': Ibid., p. 863.

'appropriate machinery . . . mutual consultation': Ibid., p. 873.

'would . . . work . . . to take . . . possible': Ibid., p. 874.

'could . . . agree': Ibid., p. 875.

After . . . authorities: All quotes on Iran in this paragraph are from ibid., pp. 819–20.

'Mr. Eden . . . suggestion': The exchange between Eden and Molotov is ibid., pp. 877–8.

'possession': Ibid., p. 896.

'the concurrence . . . Kai-shek': Ibid., p. 897.

'you . . . Government': W. Churchill, *Triumph and Tragedy*, p. 304.

'would . . . Poland . . . the best . . . get': Ibid.

'as . . . possible . . . could . . . with': Quoted Tolstoy, *Victims of Yalta*, p. 119.

'there . . . repatriation': Quoted Gilbert, *Road to Victory*, p. 1204.

'begged . . . sons': Ibid.

'very few': Ibid.

'would . . . impossible': Ibid., p. 1205.

'welcome . . . good': W. Churchill, *Triumph and Tragedy*, p. 308.

'intolerable': Quoted Gilbert, *Road to Victory*, p. 1205.

'I believe . . . situation': Stettinius, op. cit., p. 258.

'will . . . Poland': FRUS/MY, p. 898.

'Mr. President . . . breaking it . . . I know . . . time': Leahy, op. cit., p. 370.

'otherwise . . . decided': FRUS/MY, p. 898.

'up . . . desired': Ibid., p. 898.

'a good . . . West': Ibid., p. 899.

'raised . . . surrender!'": Bohlen, op. cit., p. 185.

'a very severe telegram': Quoted Gilbert, *Road to Victory*, p. 1207.

'far . . . exports . . . bombed . . . dismembered': Ibid. for full text of the
    telegram.

'The beautiful . . . stream': Stettinius, op. cit., p. 264.

'about . . . money': Soviet/TYP, p. 127.

'that . . . knuckles . . . spat . . . most': Moran, op. cit., p. 229.

'Was . . . at all?': Soviet/TYP, p. 127.

'Not . . . contrary': Ibid.

'even . . . reparations': Ibid.

'Mr President . . . to': FRUS/MY, p. 920.

'the whole . . . Moscow': Ibid., p. 902.

'Judge . . . accepted': Stettinius, op. cit., p. 266.

'ironically . . . You . . . tomorrow?': Soviet/TYP, p. 128.

'had . . . throat': FRUS/MY, p. 903.

'I tried . . . question . . . I had . . . government': Quoted Plokhy, op. cit., p. 281.

'he did . . . boundaries': Stettinius, op. cit., p. 268.

'the Heads . . . Governments . . . the Three Governments': Soviet/TYP, p. 128.

'ancient . . . Oder . . . how . . . Polish . . . very long ago . . . this . . . Britain':
    FRUS/MY, p. 905.

'considered . . . with . . . digressions . . . substantial . . . West . . . felt': FRUS/
    MY, p. 905.

'thoroughly tired': Leahy, op. cit., p. 374.

'great . . . pomp': Stettinius, op. cit., p. 272.

'what . . . business': M. Holmes, diary, 10 February 1945, SPCR 23/3, CCC.

'wild . . . steppes': Anna Halstead Papers, Yalta Conference Miscellaneous Folder,
    FDRL.

'hordes . . . table . . . Red . . . Palace': M. Holmes, diary, 10 February 1945, SPCR 23/3, CCC.

'They . . . walls': W. Churchill, *Triumph and Tragedy*, p. 309.

'all . . . hall': Sturdee, letter 11 February 1945, ONSL/1, CCC.

'in his tropical . . . wheeled in': M. Holmes, diary, 10 February 1945, SPCR 23/3, CCC.

'surrounded . . . men . . . dark . . . suspicion': Nel, op. cit., p. 168.

'The P. M. . . . up"': M. Holmes, diary, 10 February 1945, SPCR 23/3, CCC.

'dreadfully ill': Bright, op. cit., p. 198.

'hard . . . President': M. Holmes, diary, 10 February 1945, SPCR 23/3, CCC.

'happened . . . sight': Sturdee, letter 11 February 1945, ONSL/1, CCC.

'he . . . Teheran': Bright, op. cit., p. 198.

'remained . . . background . . . may . . . you': M. Holmes, diary, 10 February 1945, SPCR 23/3, CCC.

While . . . away: All quotes in this paragraph are from Stettinius, op. cit., p. 206.

'in a . . . liking . . . always . . . people': W. Churchill, *Triumph and Tragedy*, p. 309.

'tell . . . to it . . . for the . . . caused': FRUS/MY, pp. 921–2.

'There . . . about us': W. Churchill, *Triumph and Tragedy*, p. 310.

'a Russia . . . peace': FRUS/MY, p. 922.

'they were . . . people': Ibid., pp. 922–3.

'the zenith . . . career': Quoted Gilbert, *Road to Victory*, p. 1208.

'which . . . Rhine . . . the British . . . Russians . . . The Prime . . . Road" . . . Tell . . . weapon': Captain Pim's account quoted ibid., p. 1209.

'of even . . . think': FRUS/MY, p. 923.

'he did . . . do . . . since . . . with': Ibid.

'experience . . . state': Ibid.

'any . . . needs . . . the United. . . . shelter . . . since . . . States': Ibid., p. 923.

'British . . . state . . . in war . . . state': Ibid., p. 924.

'he had . . . East': Ibid.

'recognised . . . difficulty': Ibid.

'middlemen . . . parasites': Bohlen, op. cit., p. 203.

'But . . . prize . . . in . . . tone': Stettinius, op. cit., p. 278.

Jo Sturdee . . . go': All quotes are from Sturdee, letter 11 February 1945, ONSL/1, CCC.

'we . . . scream"': Nel, op. cit., p. 169.

'the Soviet . . . campaign': Quoted Gilbert, *Road to Victory*, p. 1208.

'Just . . . Mother?': Quoted Aldrich, op. cit., p. 607.

CHAPTER THIRTEEN 'A Landmark in Human History'

'Joe . . . first': Cadogan, op. cit., pp. 708–9.

'INTO . . . Nutterden . . . bunker . . . Germany': February 1945, war diary, 131st (City of Glasgow) Field Regiment Royal Artillery, www.131stfieldregimentroyalartillery.co.uk

'a sour look . . . The President . . . to do': Moran, op. cit., p. 230.

'impatient . . . indifference . . . he . . . man': Ibid., p. 785.

'conscious . . . impotence': Ibid., p. 233.

'flabbergasted': Hopkins Papers (Sherwood Collection), Box 337, FDRL.

'Ibn . . . Churchill': Telegram Fleece 163, 5 February 1945, CAB 120/170, UKNA.

'My . . . him': Telegram Jason 504, 9 February 1945, PREM 4/78/1 Pt II, UKNA.

'in . . . world . . . thought . . . areas': Hopkins Papers (Sherwood Collection), Box 337, FDRL.

A genuine . . . discussions': All quotes in this paragraph are from Eden, op. cit., pp. 513–14.

'an American . . . secondary': W. Churchill, *Triumph and Tragedy*, p. 309.

'The British . . . resentment': Beria, op. cit., pp. 105–6.

'in the closest secrecy': Bohlen, op. cit., p. 198.

'the Heads . . . defeated': The full text of the secret agreement is given in FRUS/MY, p. 984.

'I need . . . you': Ibid., p. 967.

'Roosevelt weather': Ibid., p. 558.

'this . . . thing': Moran, op. cit., p. 231.

'the Sunday . . . mutton': Ibid.

'our . . . Nazism . . . our . . . purpose': FRUS/MY, p. 930.

'OK . . . *Khorosho*': Quoted Dobbs, op. cit., p. 91.

'clearly . . . off': Quoted Gilbert, *Road to Victory*, p. 1210.

'raise . . . outcry': Quoted Dobbs, op. cit., p. 92.

'on . . . view . . . to . . . ability': FRUS/MY, p. 928.

'he . . . lunch': Quoted Plokhy, op. cit., p. 320.

'Together . . . significance?': *Life*, 12 March 1945.

'general . . . personal' : FRUS/MY, p. 930.

'any . . . peace"': Ibid.

'Not . . . toasts': Cadogan, op. cit., p. 709.

'such . . . host': Harriman, op. cit., p. 417.

'sharp-tongued press . . . had . . . lead': Soviet/TYP, p. 131.

'everyone . . . spirits': Letter to Clementine Churchill, 12 February 1945, CCC.

'We . . . Berlin': Quoted Beschloss, op. cit., p. 188.

'Like . . . cigar': Quoted Palin, *New Europe*, p. 188.

'looked . . . had': Leahy, op. cit., p. 377.

'the only . . . hate': Quoted Fenby, op. cit., p. 379.

'having . . . off!" . . . sprang . . . arrived . . . tears . . . me!" . . . genial . . . come on!"': Letter to Clementine Churchill, 12 February 1945, CCC.

'The P. M. . . . spirits . . . grand . . . meals': Moran, op. cit., p. 231.

'in a . . . leave . . . we . . . time': Letter to parents, 11 February 1945, CCC.

As Churchill . . . nothing': All quotes in this paragraph are from Bright, op. cit., p. 198.

'Believe . . . Sebastopol': Letter to Clementine Churchill, 12 February 1945, CCC.

'in a . . . luggage . . . winding . . . road': M. Holmes diary, 11 February 1945, SPCR 23/3, CCC.

'like . . . genie . . . three . . . party': Letter to Clementine Churchill, 12 February 1945, CCC.

'great . . . squabbling': Bohlen, op. cit., p. 200.

'It . . . two . . . having . . . President': FRUS/MY, p. 932.

'could . . . axe': Quoted Plokhy, op. cit., p. 322.

'a last . . . Conference': Stettinius, op. cit., p. 284.

'With . . . hand': Bright, op. cit., p. 199.

'Please . . . hosts': US General Information Bulletin, Harriman Papers, LOC.

'every . . . station': Reilly, op. cit., p. 213.

'of . . . importance': Quoted Harbutt, op. cit., p. 321.

'All . . . Yalta': Quoted Gardner, *Spheres of Influence*, p. 241.

'The whole . . . results': Quoted Harbutt, op. cit., p. 335.

'romantic . . . exhibitionism . . . influential': Ibid.

'An . . . end': Quoted Plokhy, op. cit., p. 253.

'the alliance . . . tomorrow . . . the greatest . . . day': Quoted Toland, *The Last 100 Days*, p. 130.

'let . . . understand': Quoted Harbutt, op. cit., p. 335.

'Dresden . . . can do . . . refugees . . . winter': Quoted F. Taylor, *Dresden*, p. 3 and Hastings, *Armageddon*, p. 387.

'how many . . . number?': Quoted Gilbert, *Second World War*, p. 641.

'other . . . spectacle': Quoted F. Taylor, op. cit., p. 322.

'our . . . water tub . . . we . . . to and fro': Survivor Lothar Metzger interviewed May 1999, www.timewitnesses.org

'only . . . thick': Victor Gregg, interviewed in the *Independent*, 12 February 2015.

'the semi-liquid . . . dust': Quoted in Lindqvist, *A History of Bombing*, items 214 and 215.

'It seems . . . impressive': Quoted F. Taylor, op. cit., p. 430.

CHAPTER FOURTEEN Elephants in the Room

'We have . . . think': Quoted Plokhy, op. cit., p. 322.

'something . . . behave': Quoted Dallek, *FDR and American Foreign Policy*, p. 521.

'We really . . . Kremlin': Sherwood, op. cit., p. 870.

'a sense . . . satisfaction': Bohlen, op. cit., p. 200.

'When . . . Japan . . . We've . . . Americans': Quoted Meacham, op. cit., p. 317, author's interview with Kathleen Harriman.

'We have . . . gained': Soames, op. cit., p. 515.

'I think . . . impressed!': Cadogan, op. cit., p. 709.

'make . . . war': Leahy's diary, 11 February 1945, quoted Rees, op. cit., p. 341.

'were . . . words . . . was . . . himself . . . a difference . . . intention': Eden, op. cit., p. 518.

'Everything . . . well . . . Let's hope . . . him': Beria, op. cit., p. 106.

'traitors . . . will receive . . . mercenaries': Mikolajczyk, op. cit., pp. 122–3.

'you . . . factory': Quoted Teller, *Memoirs*, p. 142.

'tended . . . tons . . . about a pound . . . thousands . . . explosive . . . an . . . isotopes': Peierls, *Bird of Passage*, pp. 152–4.

'about 1 kg . . . bomb . . . the centre . . . city . . . fatal . . . explosion . . . may . . . country . . . even . . . attack': From the Frisch–Peierls Memorandum quoted in full as an appendix to Szasz, *British Scientists and the Manhattan Project*.

'although . . . improvement': Churchill to Ismay, 30 April 1941, PREM 3/139/8a, UKNA.

'What . . . physics?': Quoted Jungk, *Brighter Than a Thousand Suns*, p. 174.

'ought . . . mortal crimes': Churchill to Lord Cherwell, 20 September 1944, PREM 3/139/8a, UKNA.

'It was . . . schoolboys': Jones, *Biographical Memoirs of Fellows of the Royal Society*.

'Roosevelt . . . allies': Quoted Butler, op. cit., p. 495.

'found . . . survivors': Quoted Gilbert, *Auschwitz and the Allies*, p. 337.

'photographic . . . cordwood . . . print . . . Belsen': Mikolajczyk, op. cit., p. 137.

'fantastic nature' Quoted J. Smith, *FDR*, p. 608.

'a wild . . . fears . . . might . . . citizens': Quoted Morgan, op. cit., p. 713.

'Get . . . necessary': Churchill to Eden, 7 July 1944, Quoted Beschloss, op. cit., p. 63.

'There is . . . Europe': Churchill to Eden, 11 July 1944, quoted ibid.

'bombing . . . business': Quoted Beschloss, op. cit., p. 66. The notes to Beschloss describe in detail the origins of this quote.

'The most . . . earth': *Encyclopaedia Britannia* online entry for 'Majdanek Concentration Camp'.

'I had . . . sufferings': *Washington Post*, 27 January 2015.

'We . . . undo it': FRUS/MY, p. 94.

CHAPTER FIFTEEN 'A Fraudulent Prospectus'

'The *Catoctin* . . . fare': FRUS/MY, p. 560.

'I appreciate . . . questions': George Stroganoff-Scherbatoff, COHP.

'the royal . . . scullions': Bohlen, op. cit., p. 202.

'next . . . hoist': Ibid.

'whole . . . scream': Letter from Roosevelt to Daisy Suckley from Algiers, 18 February 1945, ed. Ward, op. cit., p. 396.

'He denied . . . culture': Bohlen, op. cit., p. 203.

'gravely . . . bystander': Ibid., and unpaginated Bohlen papers, LOC.

'Give . . . them': Quoted Lelyveld, op. cit., p. 291.

'he would . . . people': Bohlen, op. cit., p. 204.

'with a . . . Arabia': Ibid., p. 203.

'the meal . . . gift': Rigdon, op. cit., p. 168.

'"The King . . . Roosevelt smiled': Contained in several drafts of Bohlen's book, *Witness to History*, e.g. carbon paper draft pp. 299–300, Box 13, LOC.

'a terrific . . . port!': Cadogan, op. cit., p. 710.

'Our host . . . pleasantly': W. Churchill, *Triumph and Tragedy*, p. 312.

'how . . . incredible! . . . It's . . . churches': Letter to Clementine Churchill, 12 February 1945, CCC.

'No wonder . . . reparations': Letter 13 February 1945, CCC.

'Let right . . . all!': Quoted Pawle, *The War and Colonel Warden*, p. 359.

'the ovation . . . attention': Holmes diary, 19 February 1945, SPCR 23/3, CCC.

'one . . . surface . . . enormously . . . Poor . . . butted in': Cadogan, op. cit., p. 712.

'The President . . . farewells': W. Churchill, *Triumph and Tragedy*, p. 314.

'My admiration . . . Prophet . . . As . . . tasted': Ibid., pp. 348–9.

'to concentrate . . . before': CAB 65/51, folio 79, UKNA.

'we can . . . pot . . . insulting': Bohlen, op. cit., p. 205.

'not . . . discussions': Sherwood, op. cit., p. 585.

'grouchy': Quoted Lelyveld, op. cit., p. 294.

To help . . . trust: All quotes in these paragraphs are from Rosenman, *Working with Roosevelt*, pp. 478–9.

'I hope . . . trip . . . I come . . . peace . . . spells . . . failed': Roosevelt's speech to Congress on 1 May 1945 – both the prepared text and as delivered as quoted here – is in File 1572, FDRL, Franklin database.

'the cold . . . eyes': Quoted Beschloss, op. cit., p. 190.

'quite sure . . . meant . . . Poland . . . any . . . country': CAB/65/51, folio 77, UKNA.

'as a fifth . . . allies': Cadogan, op. cit., p. 718.

'in French . . . kind': Anders, *An Army in Exile*, p. 255.

'Both . . . at first': Cadogan, op. cit., p. 749.

'a great calamity . . . We . . . them': Anders, op. cit., p. 256.

'calmed down . . . the meeting . . . good': Cadogan, op. cit., p. 749.

'Poor . . . Stalin': Quoted Cadogan, op. cit., p. 716.

'So . . . themselves': ed. Wing, *Mass-Observation*, p. 260.

On 27 February . . . rule': The quotes from Churchill's report to the Commons are from Hansard, 27 February 1945.

'to ensure . . . power': Ibid., 28 February 1945.

'How . . . mendacity': Cadogan, op. cit., p. 721.

'in his heart . . . position': Colville, op. cit., p. 565.

'Great . . . eating': Telegram 24 February 1945, PREM 3/356/4, UKNA.

News . . . Russia"': All quotes in these paragraphs are from Colville, op. cit., pp. 565–6.

In an exchange . . . secured: All quotes in this paragraph are from R-714, Roosevelt to Churchill, 11 March 1945.

'this . . . graphically': Brooke, op. cit., p. 667.

'Most satisfactory': Quoted R. Holmes, op. cit., p, 271.

'heatedly . . . I . . . acknowledge': E. Roosevelt, *This I Remember*, p. 268.

'pressed . . . of him': Interview with Anna Halstead, Lash Papers, Box 44, Folder 22, FDRL.

'the test case . . . elections . . . a farce . . . prospectus': C-905, Churchill to Roosevelt, 8 March 1945.

'Poland . . . freedom?': C-910, Churchill to Roosevelt, 13 March 1945.

'plain . . . pike staff . . . to drag . . . democracy?': C-925, Churchill to Roosevelt, 27 March 1945.

'We must . . . know it': Harriman to Roosevelt, 21 March 1945, quoted Berthon and Potts, *Warlords*, p. 296.

'The Soviet . . . friendly': 303, Stalin to Roosevelt, 7 April 1945.

'behind . . . Union . . . not . . . worse': Quoted Bishop, op. cit., p. 505.

'no political . . . surrender': 295, Roosevelt to Stalin, 24 March 1945.

'fully informed': 300, Stalin to Roosevelt, 3 April 1945.

'it . . . involved . . . Frankly . . . subordinates': 301, Roosevelt to Stalin, 4 April 1945. Text also contained in R-734, Roosevelt to Churchill, 5 April 1945.

'A beaten . . . Victory': Quoted Gilbert, *Second World War*, p. 652.

'It was . . . nothing': Brooke, op. cit., p. 678.

'absolutely . . . weight': Reilly, op. cit., p. 227.

'bright blue hair': Ibid., p. 102.

'She was . . . Franklin"': Anna Halstead Papers, Folder 1, Box 84, FDRL.

'Lucy . . . immature . . . *so* . . . difficulties': ed. Ward, op. cit., pp. 415–16.

'I would . . . correct': R-630, Roosevelt to Churchill, 11 April 1945.

'so that . . . names': ed. Blum, *Morgenthau Diaries*, vol. 3, p. 416.

'recalling . . . Churchill': Shoumatoff, *FDR's Unfinished Portrait*, p. 111.

'like . . . longer': Ibid., p. 114.

'We . . . work': ed. Ward, op. cit., p. 418.

'constantly . . . the Boss . . . that . . . nothing . . . whims . . . we . . . work': Diary, 12 April 1945, Hassett Papers, FDRL.

'Have . . . cigarette? . . . looked . . . head!"': ed. Ward, op. cit., p. 418.

CHAPTER SIXTEEN 'I Liked the Little Son of a Bitch'

'the President . . . dead . . . very . . . shocked': Truman, *Mr. President*, p. 94.

'perhaps . . . with him': Halifax to Churchill, 13 April 1945, Churchill Papers 20/214, CCC.

'PM . . . airport': Cadogan, op. cit., p. 727.

'You . . . hit me': Quoted Meacham, op. cit., p. 344.

'I . . . war': W. Churchill, *Triumph and Tragedy*, p. 372.

'I feel . . . Franklin': Ibid.

'in Franklin . . . old': Churchill's eulogy to the House of Commons for the President is contained in Hansard, 17 April 1945.

'I regret . . . affairs': W. Churchill, *Triumph and Tragedy*, p. 376.

'his . . . seconds . . . appeared . . . distressed': Harriman, op. cit., p. 441.

'My Fuhrer . . . point': Quoted Moran, op. cit., p. 766.

'Fate . . . time': Quoted Fenby, *Alliance*, p. 398.

'My . . . strength': Churchill to Eden, 20 April 1945, Churchill Papers 20/215, CCC.

'An . . . word': Quoted Fenby, *Alliance*, p. 399.

'enjoyed . . . probably . . . official': Bohlen, op. cit., p. 213.

'I gave it . . . jaw': Joseph Davis journal, 30 April 1945, LOC.

'there were . . . but little': Ed Murrow's CBS broadcast, 16 April 1945.

'and doling . . . children . . . and begged . . . few yards': Quoted Gilbert, *Second World War*, p. 664.

'This British . . . Yalta': Churchill to Stalin, 29 April 1945, PREM 3/356/6, folio 443, UKNA.

'An iron . . . others': Telegram 44, Churchill to Truman, 12 May 1945.

'This evening . . . Europe': Brooke, op. cit., p. 693.

'that psychological . . . released': Minutes of Interim Committee, 31 May 1945, File 100, Harrison Bundy Files M1108, NARA.

'to soften . . . Russians': Sherwood, *Roosevelt and Hopkins*, p.851.

'fundamental mistake': FRUS/B, vol. 1, p. 33.

'Despite . . . made': Sherwood, op. cit., p.851.

'not . . . terms:' Telegram 60, Churchill to Truman, 31 May 1945.

'In . . . manner': Quoted Rees, op. cit., p. 369.

'None . . . Potsdam': Quoted Beschloss, op. cit., p. 246.

'charming . . . clever . . . soft-soap': Truman, *Off the Record*, p. 51.

'liked . . . language': Soames, *Clementine Churchill*, p. 422.

'like most . . . inadequate': FRUS/B, vol. 2, President's Log.

'unfortunately . . . view': Cadogan, op. cit., p. 763.

More . . . road': All quotes in these paragraphs and the footnote are from Meiklejohn, who also noted another major activity of the Soviet troops – buying watches. The Soviets authorities had postponed paying their men till this point and were now loading them with 'fabulous sums in occupation marks' which they wanted to spend before being sent home. Even 'a broken down and tired watch with a cracked crystal, as long as it ticks real loud, will bring the equivalent of $400 in occupation marks'. US soldiers bought watches from the German population to meet Russian demand, then exchanged the occupation marks they received for dollars at the US Adjutant General's offices at the official exchange rate which had been set artificially high. World War II diary, part II, p. 701 and 704, LOC.

'a little . . . made': Quoted Szasz, *The Day the Sun Rose Twice*, p. 89.

'I am . . . worlds': Quoted Pharr Davis, *Lawrence and Oppenheimer*, p. 240.

'The brilliant . . . job': BBC radio broadcast by Rudolf Peierls on 'Atomic Energy and its Present Possibilities', 1948.

'Operated . . . expectations': M.1109/NARA.

'I hope . . . of it': Truman, *Off the Record*, pp. 52–3.

'babies . . . born . . . Now . . . same way': Stimson's diary, 22 July 1945, microfilm, Cambridge University Library (original at Yale University).

'completely . . . Germany': Brooke, op. cit., p. 309.

'It is . . . Japan': Ehrman, *Grand Strategy*, vol. 6, p. 292.

'couldn't . . . compared . . . neither . . . clever': Quoted Montefiore, *Stalin – 1939–1953*, p. 204.

'could . . . hell . . . looked . . . you . . . either . . . Argentina': Quoted Dobbs, op. cit., p. 296.

'had . . . garden': Bohlen, op. cit., p. 227.

'nothing . . . solid': Quoted Montefiore, *Stalin – 1939–1953*, p. 204.

'he . . . him . . . business-like . . . ear': Eden, op. cit., p. 545.

'The P. M. . . . point': Cadogan, op. cit., p. 765.

'Churchill . . . means': Quoted Fenby, *Alliance*, p. 410.

'want . . . decide . . . You . . . day': Quoted Kennedy, op. cit., p. 842.

In response . . . Greece: All quotes in this paragraph come from the two United States accounts of this meeting of the Potsdam Conference, FRUS/B, vol. 2, pp. 362 and 371.

'I have . . . thumbing . . . sick . . . business': Truman, *Dear Bess*, p. 520.

'they . . . away . . . hang them': Quoted Dobbs, op. cit., p. 304.

'casually . . . Japanese'": Truman, *Memoirs, Vol. 1: The Year of Decisions*, p. 416.

'Stalin . . . war? . . . we . . . anything'": Quoted Holloway, *Stalin and the Bomb*, p. 125.

an opportunity . . . war . . . unconditional surrender . . . the alternative . . . destruction': The text of the Potsdam Declaration of 26 July 1945 is widely available, for example in FRUS/B, vol. 2 and on Columbia University's online resource http://afe.easia.columbia.edu

'laughable': Quoted Kurzman, *Day of the Bomb*, p. 403.

'much overrated': Letter from Truman to wife, 29 July 1845, Truman, *Dear Bess*, p. 520.

'like Stalin': Truman, *Dear Bess*, p. 522.

'I liked . . . bitch': Truman, *Strictly Personal*, p. 33.

'strengthened . . . governments . . . renewed . . . peace': The text of the Potsdam Communiqué is contained in FRUS/B, vol. 2 and widely reproduced.

'beautifully horrible': *Veterans of Foreign Wars Magazine*, November 1959.

'like . . . molasses': Quoted Thomas and Witts, *Ruin from the Air*, p. 326.

In Hiroshima . . . them': All quotes in this paragraph are from Futaba Kitayama's account in 'Bombing Eyewitness Accounts' on the Hiroshima Peace Memorial Museum website.

'They're . . . they?': Elsey, *An Unplanned Life*, p. 92.

'the longhairs . . . smokeless powder': Bohlen, op. cit., pp. 236–7.

'the bomb . . . over': Elsey, op. cit., p. 92.

'military convenience': Byrnes, op. cit., p. 222.

CHAPTER SEVENTEEN The Iron Curtain Descends

'Whenever . . . children': Quoted Lowe, op. cit., p. 212.

'people . . . again': Quoted ibid., p. 235.

'out of . . . place': Ibid., p. 239.

'The prisoner . . . feet up': Quoted Plokhy, op. cit., p. 305.

'could . . . business': Quoted Tolstoy, op. cit., p. 259.

'inhuman': Ibid., p. 262.

'of small . . . warlike': FRUS/MY, p. 770.

'Unless . . . Soviets': Truman to Byrnes, 5 January 1946, Truman, *Off the Record*, p. 80.

In February 1946 . . . world': The quotes from Byrnes's speech come from Harbutt, op. cit., p. 386.

On 5 March . . . world: Churchill's Fulton, Missouri, speech is widely available e.g. on International Churchill Society www.winstonchurchill.org

This speech . . . collapse: Stalin's *Pravda* interview is available on www.marxists. org

With tensions . . . elsewhere: Truman's speech presenting the 'Truman Doctrine' is given in full on www.avalon.law.yale.edu

EPILOGUE

'The problems . . . difficult': Hansard, 11 November 1942.

'I didn't . . . do': Roosevelt to Adolf Berle, 5 March 1945, ed. Berle, *Negotiating the Rapids*, p. 476.

'Whoever . . . otherwise': Stalin, April 1945, quoted Djilas, op. cit., p. 105.

'In politics . . . forces': Quoted Cadogan, op. cit., p. 778.

'the most . . . machines . . . a country . . . war': Harriman, op. cit., p. 277.

'No . . . meat . . . The bear . . . killed it': Quoted Fenby, *Alliance*, p. 384 and widely.

'There . . . fighting on': Ismay, op. cit., p. 381.

'L'Angleterre . . . chose': Quoted *Independent*, 2 June 2017.

'the system . . . power . . . a compromise': Roosevelt's speech to Congress on 1 March 1945, File 1572, FDRL, Franklin database.

'The . . . peoples': The draft of Roosevelt's undelivered Jefferson's Day Speech is in File 1577, FDRL, Franklin database.

BIBLIOGRAPHY

ARCHIVES CONSULTED

Cambridge University Library

Henry Stimson's diary, 22 July 1945, microfilm

Churchill Archives Centre, Churchill College, Cambridge (CCC)

Winston Churchill, papers
Flight-Sergeant Geoffrey Green, conference diaries
Marian Holmes, diary, interview transcript and taped interview
Hugh Lunghi, papers including transcript of tribute speech to Churchill
John Martin, papers
Sarah Oliver, née Churchill, letters to Clementine Churchill
Nina Edith Onslow, Countess of Onslow, née Sturdee, 'Jo', letters to family
Admiral James Somerville, papers including pocket diary

Columbia University Oral History Project (COHP)

Anna Roosevelt Halstead
W. Averell Harriman
Arthur Krock
Frances Perkins
George Stroganoff-Scherbatoff
Henry Wallace

Franklin D. Roosevelt Presidential Library (FDRL), Hyde Park, New York

Valentin Berezhkov, oral history (Verne Newton Papers)
John Boettiger Papers
Wilson Brown Papers
Howard Bruenn Papers

Edward Flynn Papers
Pamela Churchill Harriman, oral history (Verne Newton Papers)
William Hassett Papers
Harry Hopkins Papers
Ian Jacob, oral history (Verne Newton Papers).
Joseph Lash Papers
John Martin, oral history (Verne Newton Papers)
William Rigdon Papers
Anna Roosevelt Halstead (Boettiger) Papers
Eleanor Roosevelt Papers and oral history (Robert D. Graff Papers)
Franklin D. Roosevelt Papers
Mary Soames, oral history (Verne Newton Papers)

Imperial War Museum (IWM)

Private Papers
T. J. Cowen (15712)
J. Rogers (17645)
Oral Histories
G. I. Adams (18163)
M. C. Beevor (9599)
S. Beria (19548)
C. Bohlen (3020)
A. Eden (2811)
W. A. Harriman (2884)
A. Hiss (2885)
H. Lunghi (15436 and 30929)
G. M. Wilson (16584)

Library of Congress (LOC)

Charles Bohlen Papers
Joseph E. Davies Papers
W. Averell Harriman Papers (including Kathleen Harriman letters)
William Leahy, diary
Robert E. Meiklejohn, diary (contained in Harriman Papers, box 211)

UK National Archives (UKNA), Kew, London

CAB 65/51 (War Cabinet papers)
CAB 99/31 (Cabinet report on political proceedings) available digitally
CAB 120/170 (Argonaut)
CAB 120/171 (Administrative arrangements for Yalta)
FO 954/20C/424
PREM 3/51/2 (Attendance of supreme commanders at Malta/Yalta)

PREM 3/139/8a. (Churchill's correspondence on 'Tube Alloys' (atom bomb
    project)
PREM 3/356/3 (Future of Poland)
PREM 3/356/4 (Dominion views on Yalta results)
PREM 3/356/6 (Telegrams on Poland March/May 1945)
PREM 3/398/6 (Operational correspondence and papers on Yalta)
PREM 4/77/1B (Correspondence and papers relating to Argonaut)
PREM 4/78/1 (Telegrams to and from Argonaut)

US National Archives (NARA)

File 100, Harrison Bundy files M.1108
M.1109

ONLINE RESOURCES

24 Squadron RAF Association Blog Book, https://the24sec.wordpress.com
131st Field Regiment Royal Artillery – www.131stfieldregimentroyalartillery.
    co.uk
Asia for Educators – http://afe.easia.columbia.edu
Avalon Project – www.avalon.law.yale.edu (Yale Law Library documents in law,
    history and diplomacy)
BBC News Daily Digital Magazine
Franklin Database, Roosevelt Presidential Library (FDRL)
Hiroshima Peace Memorial Museum – hpmmuseum.jp
IMDb – www.Imdb.com
International Churchill Society – www.winstonchurchill.org
Letters of Note – www.lettersofnote.com (blog)
Time Witness – www.timewitnesses.org (memories of the last century)
US Holocaust Memorial Museum – www.ushmm.org
World War II Today – ww2today.com (day-by-day eyewitness accounts)
WW2 People's War – www.bbc.co.uk/ww2peopleswar (archive of Second World
    War memories gathered by BBC)
www.marxists.org
www.worldhistory.biz

BOOKS

Primary Sources

Adamic, L. Dinner at the White House. New York: Harper and Bros, 1946.
Aldrich, R. J. Witness to War. London: Transworld, 2004.
Anders, Lt General W. An Army in Exile. London: Macmillan, 1949.
Astley, J. B. The Inner Circle – A View of War at the Top. London: Hutchinson, 1971
    (Joan Bright's account)

Berezhkov, V. M. *At Stalin's Side – His Interpreter's Memoirs*. New York: Carol Publishing Group, 1994.

Beria, S. *Beria, My Father*. London: Duckworth, 2001.

Berle, B. B. and Jacobs, T. B. (eds) *Negotiating the Rapids – 1918–1971, from the Papers of Adolf A. Berle*. New York: Harcourt Brace Jovanovich, 1973.

Birse, A. H. *Memoirs of an Interpreter*. London: Michael Joseph, 1967.

Blum, J. M. (ed.) *The Morgenthau Diaries – Years of War, 1941–1945*. Boston, MA: Houghton Mifflin, 1967.

Bohlen, C. E. *Witness to History, 1929–1969*. New York: Norton, 1973.

Bonham Carter, V. *Winston as I Knew Him*. London: Eyre and Spottiswoode, 1965.

Brooke, A., Field Marshal, Viscount Alanbrooke *War Diaries – 1939–1945*. London: Weidenfeld and Nicolson, 2001.

Butler, S. (ed.) *'My Dear Mr. Stalin' – The Complete Correspondence Between Franklin D. Roosevelt and Joseph V. Stalin*. New Haven, CT: Yale University Press, 2005.

Byrnes, J. F. *Speaking Frankly*. London: Heinemann, 1947.

Cadogan, A. (ed. D. Dilks) *The Diaries of Sir Alexander Cadogan*. London: Cassell, 1971.

Chekhov, A. 'The Lady with the Dog', available online on Project Gutenberg.

Churchill, S. *A Thread in the Tapestry*. London: Deutsch, 1967.

Churchill, S. *Keep on Dancing*. London: Weidenfeld and Nicolson, 1981.

Churchill, W. S. *My Early Life – A Roving Commission*. London: Thornton Butterworth, 1930.

Churchill, W. S. *The Second World War, Vol. I: The Gathering Storm*. London: Folio Society, 2000.

Churchill, W. S. *The Second World War, Vol. II: Their Finest Hour*. London: Folio Society, 2000.

Churchill, W. S. *The Second World War, Vol. III: The Grand Alliance*. London: Folio Society, 2000.

Churchill, W. S. *The Second World War, Vol. IV: The Hinge of Fate*. London: Folio Society, 2000.

Churchill, W. S. *The Second World War, Vol. V: Closing the Ring*. London: Folio Society, 2000.

Churchill, W. S. *The Second World War, Vol. VI, Triumph and Tragedy*. London: Penguin Books, 1988.

Colville, J. *The Fringes of Power: Downing Street Diaries, 1939–1955*. London: Hodder and Stoughton, 1985.

Cunningham, Admiral of the Fleet Viscount *A Sailor's Odyssey – Autobiography*. London: Hutchinson, 1951.

Djilas, M. *Conversations with Stalin*. London: Rupert Hart-Davis, 1962.

Eade, C. (ed.) *Churchill by his Contemporaries*. London: Hutchinson, 1953 [New York, 1954].

Eden, A. *Memoirs – The Reckoning*. London: Cassell, 1965.

Elsey, G. *An Unplanned Life – A Memoir*. Columbia, MO: University of Missouri Press, 2005.

Foreign Relations of the United States, The Conference at Berlin [FRUS/B], vols 1 and 2, Washington: United States Government Printing Office, 1960.

Foreign Relations of the United States, The Conferences at Malta and Yalta [FRUS/MY], Washington: United States Government Printing Office, 1955.

Gromyko, A. (trans. H. Shukman) *Memories*. London: Hutchinson, 1989.

Hansard (UK daily parliamentary record) 1938–45.

Harriman W. A. and Abel, E. *Special Envoy to Stalin and Churchill 1941–1946*. New York: Random House, 1975.

Hassett, W. D. *Off the Record with FDR, 1942–1945*. London: George Allen and Unwin, 1960.

Hickman, T. *Churchill's Bodyguard*. London: Headline, 2006.

Hopkins, R. *Witness to History*. Seattle, WA: Castle Pacific Publishing, 2002.

Ismay, H. L. *Memoirs of General the Lord Ismay*. London: Heinemann, 1960 [New York: Viking, 1960].

Kardorff, U. von *Berliner Aufzeichnungen*. Munich: Biederstein Verlag, 1962.

The Katyn Forest Massacre: Hearings Before the Select Committee to Conduct an Investigation of the Facts, Evidence and Circumstances of the Katyn Forest Massacre, Eighty-Second Congress, 1952.

Kennan, G. F. *Memoirs – 1925–1950*. London: Hutchinson, 1968.

Kimball, W. F. (ed.) *Churchill and Roosevelt – The Complete Correspondence, Vols II and III*. Princeton, NJ: Princeton University Press, 1984.

Kuter, L. S., General, *Airman at Yalta*. New York: Duell, Sloan and Pearce, 1955.

Leahy W. D., Fleet Admiral *I Was There*. London: Victor Gollancz, 1950.

Maisky, I. *Journey into the Past*. London: Hutchinson, 1962.

Martin, J. *Downing Street: The War Years*. London: Bloomsbury, 1991.

McIntire, R. T., Vice-Admiral *Twelve Years with Roosevelt*. London: Putnam and Co., 1948.

Mikolajczyk, S. *The Pattern of Soviet Domination*. London: Sampson Low, Marston and Co., 1948.

Moran, Lord *Winston Churchill – The Struggle for Survival, 1940–1965*. London: Constable, 1966 [diaries of Lord Moran].

Nel, E. (née Layton) *Mr. Churchill's Secretary*. London: Hodder and Stoughton, 1958.

Panter-Downes, M. *London War Notes*. London: Longman, 1971.

Pawle, G. *The War and Colonel Warden*. London: George Harrap, 1963.

Peierls, R. *Bird of Passage*. Princeton, NJ: Princeton University Press, 1985.

Perkins, F. *The Roosevelt I Knew*. London: Hammond, Hammond and Co., 1947.

Reilly, M. and Slocum, W. J. *Reilly of the White House*. New York: Simon and Schuster, 1947.

Resis, A. (ed.) *Molotov Remembers*. Chicago: Ivan R. Dee, 1993.

Richards, D. *Portal of Hungerford*. London: Heinemann, 1977.

Rigdon, W. *White House Sailor*. New York: Doubleday, 1962.

Roosevelt, E. (Eleanor) *This I Remember*. London: Hutchinson and Co., 1950.

Roosevelt, E. (Elliott) *As He Saw It*. New York: Duell, Sloan and Pearce, 1946.

Roosevelt, J. *My Parents – A Differing View*. London: W. H. Allen, 1977.

Rosenman, S. *Working with Roosevelt*. London: Rupert Hart-Davis, 1952.

Sand, G. W. (ed.) *Defending the West: The Truman–Churchill Correspondence, 1945–1960*. Westport, CT: Praeger, 2004.

Sherwood, R. E. *Roosevelt and Hopkins*. New York: Harper and Row, 1950.

Shoumatoff, E. *FDR's Unfinished Portrait – A Memoir*. Pittsburgh, PA: University of Pittsburgh Press, 1990.

Sikorski Institute (ed.) *Documents on Polish-Soviet Relations 1939–45, Vol. 2*. Sikorsky Institute. London: Heinemann, 1967.

Smith, A. (ed.) *Hostage to Fortune: The Letters of Joseph P. Kennedy*. New York: Viking Press, 2001.

Soames, M. (ed.) *Speaking for Themselves – The Personal Letters of Winston and Clementine Churchill*. London: Transworld, 1998.

Spiridovich, A., *Les Dernières Années de la Cour de Tzarskoïë Sélo*. Paris: Payot, 1928.

Stettinius, E. R. Jnr. *Roosevelt and the Russians*. New York: Doubleday, 1949.

Sudoplatov, P. and Sudoplatov, A. *Special Tasks*. London: Little, Brown and Co., 1994.

The Tehran, Yalta and Potsdam Conferences. Moscow: Progress Publishers, 1969 [official Soviet records, Soviet/TYP].

Teller, E. *Memoirs*. Cambridge, MA: Perseus, 2001.

Tibbets, P. W. *Mission Hiroshima*. New York: Stein and Day, 1985.

Trevor-Roper, H. (ed.) *The Goebbels Diaries*. London: Secker and Warburg, 1978.

Truman, H. S. *Memoirs, Vol. 1: Year of Decisions*. New York: Doubleday, 1955.

Truman, H. S. *Mr. President – Personal Diaries, Private Letters, Papers*. London: Hutchinson, 1952.

Truman, H. S. (ed. R. H. Ferrell) *Off the Record: The Private Papers of Harry S. Truman*. New York: Harper and Row, 1980.

Truman, H. S. *Strictly Personal and Confidential – The Letters Harry Truman Never Mailed*. Boston, MA: Little, Brown and Co., 1982.

Truman, H. S. *Dear Bess*. Columbia, MO: University of Missouri Press, 1998.

Tully, G. *F.D.R. – My Boss*. Chicago: People's Book Club, 1949.

Ward, G. C. (ed.) *Closest Companion – The Unknown Story of the Intimate Friendship between Franklin Roosevelt and Margaret Suckley*. Boston, MA: Houghton Mifflin, 1995.

Wing, S. K. (ed.), *Mass-Observation*. London: Folio Society, 2007.

Yusupov, F. *Lost Splendour*. London; Jonathan Cape, 1953.

Secondary Sources

Andrew, C. *The Mitrokhin Archive*. London: Allen Lane, 1999.

Attlee, C. R. (ed. F. R. Field) *Attlee's Great Contemporaries: The Politics of Character*. London: Bloomsbury, 2009.

Barnett, C. *Engage the Enemy More Closely*. London: Hodder and Stoughton, 1991.

Berthon, S. and Potts, J. *Warlords*. Cambridge, MA: Da Capo Press, 2006.

Beschloss, M. *The Conquerors*. New York: Simon and Schuster, 2002.

Bishop, J. *FDR's Last Year*. New York: William Morrow and Co., 1974.

Breur, W. B. *The Great Raid on Cabanuatan*. New York: John Wiley and Sons, 1994.

Brown, A. *The Myth of the Strong Leader: Political Leadership in the Modern Age*. London: Bodley Head, 2014.

Buhite, R. D. *Decisions at Yalta*. Wilmington, DE: Scholarly Resources Inc., 1986.

Burns, J. M. *Roosevelt: The Soldier of Freedom*. New York: Harcourt Brace, Jovanovich, 1970.

Butler, S. *Roosevelt and Stalin*. New York: Alfred A. Knopf, 2015.

Churchill, R. S. *Winston S. Churchill, Vol. I: Youth 1874 –1900*. London: Heinemann, 1966.

Churchill, R. S. *Winston S. Churchill, Vol. II: Young Statesman, 1901–1914*. London: Heinemann, 1967 [this eight-volume biography was completed by Martin Gilbert, see below].

Clemens, D. S. *Yalta*. New York: Oxford University Press, 1970.

Dallek, R. *Franklin D. Roosevelt and American Foreign Policy, 1932–1945*. Oxford: Oxford University Press, 1995.

Dallek, R. *Franklin D. Roosevelt: A Life*. London: Allen Lane, 2018.

Davies, N. *God's Playground – A History of Poland, Vol 2: 1795 to the Present*. Oxford: Oxford University Press, 2003.

Davies, N. *Rising '44*. London: Macmillan, 2003.

Dobbs, M. *Six Months in 1945*. London: Hutchinson, 2012.

Dobson, C., Miller, J. and Payne, R. *The Cruellest Night*. London: Hodder and Stoughton, 1979.

Edmonds, R. *The Big Three*. London: Penguin Books, 1992.

Ehrman, J. *Grand Strategy, Vol. 6: October 1944–August 1945*. London: HMSO, 1956.

Fenby, J. *Generalissimo: Chiang Kai-shek and the China He Lost*. London: Free Press, 2005.

Fenby, J. *Alliance*. London: Pocket Books, 2008.

Ferrell, R. H. *The Dying President*. Columbia, MO: University of Missouri Press, 1998.

French, P. *Liberty or Death*. London: Harper Collins, 1997.

Gardner, L. C. *Spheres of Influence*. London: John Murray, 1993.

Gilbert, M. *Winston S. Churchill, Vol. III: Challenge of War, 1914–1916*. London: Heinemann, 1971.

Gilbert, M. *Winston S. Churchill, Vol. IV: Stricken World, 1917–1922*. London: Heinemann, 1975.

Gilbert, M. *Winston S. Churchill, Vol. V: Prophet of Truth, 1922–1939*. London: Heinemann, 1976.

Gilbert, M. *Winston S. Churchill, Vol. VI: Finest Hour, 1939–1941*. London: Heinemann, 1983.

Gilbert, M. *Winston S. Churchill, Vol. VII: Road to Victory, 1941–1945*. London: Heinemann, 1986.

Gilbert, M. *Winston S. Churchill, Vol. VIII: Never Despair, 1945–1965*. London: Heinemann: 1988.

Gilbert, M. *Auschwitz and the Allies*. London: Michael Joseph, 1981.

Gilbert, M. *Second World War*. London: Phoenix, 2000.

Gillies, D. *Radical Diplomat: The Life of Archibald Scott Kerr, Lord Inverchapel*. London: Tauris, 1999.

Grayling, A. C. *Among the Dead Cities*. New York: Walker and Co., 2006.

Harbutt, F. J. *Yalta 1945*. New York: Cambridge University Press, 2014.

Hastings, M. *Armageddon*. London: Pan Books, 2005.

Hastings, M. *Finest Years*. London: Harper Press, 2009.

Holloway, D. *Stalin and the Bomb*. London: Yale University Press, 1994.

Holmes, R. *In the Footsteps of Churchill*. London: BBC Books, 2005.

Hough, R. *Winston and Clementine: The Triumph of the Churchills*. London: Bantam Press, 1990.

Jackson, A. *Churchill*. London: Quercus, 2012.

Jenkins, R. *Churchill*. London: Macmillan, 2001.

Johnson, D. *V for Vengeance*. London: William Kimber, 1981.

Jungk, R. *Brighter Than a Thousand Suns*. New York: Harcourt, 1958.

Kennedy, D. M. *Freedom from Fear* (Oxford History of the United States, Vol. 9, Part 2). New York: Oxford University Press, 2004.

Kimball, W. F. *The Juggler*. Princeton, N J: Princeton University Press, 1991.

Kimball, W. F. *Forged in War*. Chicago: Ivan R. Dee, 2003.

Kurzman, D. *Day of the Bomb*. New York: McGraw-Hill, 1986.

Lash, J. P. *Eleanor and Franklin*. New York: Norton, 1971.

Lee, C. and Lee, J. *The Churchills*. New York: Palgrave Macmillan, 2010.

Lehrman, L. *Churchill, Roosevelt and Company*. Guilford, CT: Stackpole Books, 2017.

Lelyveld, J. *His Final Battle: The Last Months of Franklin Roosevelt*. New York: Alfred A. Knopf, 2016.

Lewin, R. *The War on Land*. London: Hutchinson, 1969.

Lindqvist, S. *A History of Bombing*. London: Granta Books, 2001.

Lowe, K. *Savage Continent*. London: Viking, 2012.

MacMillan, M. *History's People*. London: Profile Books, 2016.

Manchester, W. and Reid, P. *The Last Lion*. New York: Little, Brown, 2012.

Massie, R. *Dreadnought*. London: Jonathan Cape, 1992.

Meacham, J. *Franklin and Winston*. London: Granta Books, 2004.

Michel, H. *The Second World War*. London: Andre Deutsch, 1975.

Montefiore, S. S. *Stalin – 1939–1953*. London: Phoenix, 2003.

Montefiore, S. S. *Stalin – 1878–1939*. London: Phoenix, 2004.

Montefiore, S. S. *The Court of the Red Tsar*. London: Phoenix, 2005.

Morgan, T. *FDR*. London: Grafton Books, 1987.

Mosley, L. *Marshall – Hero for our Times*. New York: Hearst, 1982.

Murray's Handbooks – Russia, Poland and Finland. London: John Murray, 1875.

Palin, M. *New Europe*. London: Weidenfeld and Nicolson, 2007.

Pelling, H. *Winston Churchill*. London: Macmillan, 1974.

Persico, J. E. *Franklin and Lucy*. New York: Random House, 2008.

Petrie, C., *Lords of the Inland Sea*. London: Lovat Dickson, 1937.

Pfarr Davis, N. *Lawrence and Oppenheimer*. New York: Simon and Schuster, 1968.

Piirimäe, K. *Roosevelt, Churchill and the Baltic Question*. New York: Palgrave Macmillan, 2014.

Plokhy, S. M. *Yalta*. New York: Viking, 2010.

Rees, L. *Behind Closed Doors*. London: BBC Books, 2008.

Reynolds, D. *From World War to Cold War: Churchill, Roosevelt and the International History of the 1940s*. Oxford: Oxford University Press, 2006.

Reynolds, D. *Summits*. London: Penguin, 2007.

Rhodes, R. *The Making of the Atomic Bomb*. New York: Touchstone, 1988.

Rose, N. *Churchill – An Unruly Life*. London: Simon and Schuster, 1994.

Ross, S. H. *How Roosevelt Failed America in World War II*. Jefferson, NC: McFarland and Co., 2006.

Rowley, H. *Franklin and Eleanor: An Extraordinary Marriage*. New York: Farrar, Straus and Giroux, 2010.

Smith, J. E. *FDR*. New York: Random House, 2007.

Soames, M., *Clementine Churchill – The Biography of a Marriage*. London: Doubleday, 2002.

Stafford, D. *Roosevelt and Churchill: Men of Secrets*. London: Little, Brown, 1999.

Stelzer, C. *Dinner with Churchill*. London: Short Books, 2011.

Szasz, F. M. *The Day the Sun Rose Twice*. Albuquerque, NM: University of New Mexico Press, 1984.

Szasz, F. M. *British Scientists and the Manhattan Project*. London: Macmillan, 1992.

Taylor, A. J. P. *The Second World War*. London: Penguin, 1976.

Taylor, F. *Dresden – Tuesday 13 February 1945*. London: Bloomsbury, 2005.

Terkel, S. *The Good War*. New York: Pantheon Books, 1984.

Thomas, G. and Witts, M. *Ruin from the Air*. London: Book Club Associates, 1977.

Toland, J. *The Last 100 Days*. New York: Random House, 1966.

Tolstoy, N. *Victims of Yalta*. London: Corgi, 1990.

Twain, M. *The Innocents Abroad*. San Francisco: H. E. Bancroft and Co., 1869, available online through the Gutenberg Project.

West, N. *Venona*. London: Harper Collins, 1999.

Williams, R. C. *Klaus Fuchs, Atom Spy*. Cambridge, MA: Harvard University Press, 1987.

Wood, R. K. *The Tourist's Russia*. London: Andrew Melrose, 1912.

Woolner, David B. *The Last 100 Days*. New York: Basic Books, 2017.

Zubok, V. M. *A Failed Empire: The Soviet Union in the Cold War from Stalin to Gorbachev*. Chapel Hill, NC: University of North Carolina Press, 2009.

ARTICLES

Hopkins, R. 'How Would you Like to be Attached to the Red Army', *American Heritage*, vol. 56, no. 3 (June–July 2005).

Idrisli, A., *Emel*, no 210 (September/October 1995) [translated by Metin Camcigil for the International Committee for Crimea, Syrgun Stories Series].

Jones, R. V. 'Winston Leonard Spencer Churchill, 1874–1966', *Biographical Memoirs of Fellows of the Royal Society*, vol. 12 (1966), pp. 35–105.

Korniyasenko, O. *Emel*, no. 205 (November/December 1995) [translated by Ayla Onart for the International Committee for Crimea, Syrgun Stories Series].

Schlesinger, S. 'FDR's Five Policemen: Creating the United Nations', *World Policy Journal*, vol. 11, no. 3 (Fall 1994). pp. 88–93.

Veterans of Foreign Wars Magazine (November 1959).

OTHER JOURNALS, NEWSPAPERS AND MAGAZINES

Baltimore Sun
Daily Mail
Economist
Life
Manchester Guardian
Middleton Times Herald
New York Herald Tribune
New York Times
Syracuse Herald Journal
Time
The Times (London)
Washington Post

INDEX

Adams, Gladys 133
Alexander, Harold, Field Marshal 115, 221
Alexander II, Tsar 93
Alexandra, Tsarina 94, 97
Alexandrovna, Nina 55, 251
Alexei Nikolaevich, Tsarevich 94
Allied Control Commission 140–1, 176–7, 232
Alliluyeva, Nadya (Stalin's second wife) 52
Alliluyeva, Svetlana Iosifovna (Stalin's daughter) 16, 52–3
Amery, Leo 82–3
Anders, Władysław, General 157, 159, 161, 279–80
Anderson, Frank, General 52
Antonov, Alexei Innokentievich, General 120–1, 135–6, 185, 191, 204, 213
Arciszewski, Tomasz 163
Ardennes offensive 58–9, 62
Argentina 187, 224n, 303
Artikov (NKVD officer) 47–8, 85
Atlantic Charter 27, 78, 131, 218–19, 278
atomic bomb (Manhattan Project): aircraft modified to carry 62; establishment of 263; Hiroshima bombing 307–8; Nagasaki bombing 308; news of Trinity test sent to Churchill and Truman 302, 305; not discussed at Yalta 261; possibility of use against Soviet Union 324; practising bombing runs 62; production of uranium and plutonium 62; Soviet knowledge of 264–5, 319; target selection 296–7;

Trinity test 298, 301–2, 326; Truman informed of 295; US military expectations of 62
atomic research: Bohr's advocacy of openness 264–5; calculation of critical mass 262; history of discoveries 261; Maud Committee report 263; memorandum to British government 262–3; Quebec Agreement (1943) 265; Quebec Agreement (1944) 32; secrecy issues 265; Soviet intelligence 263–4; splitting the uranium atom 261–2; US/UK collaboration 32, 263, 265, 296, 327
Attlee, Clement: Churchill's messages to 170, 184, 221, 222; government 316; Greece policy 320; Potsdam Conference 300, 306; prime minister 306; relationship with Churchill 14
Augusta, USS 26, 298
Auschwitz (Oświęcim) concentration camp 66, 242, 266–9

Barbarossa, Operation (1941) 27
Belorussia: deportations 314; history 151, 153; territory 153, 158; UN membership question 178, 196, 247, 297n
Belsen concentration camp 267, 268, 294–5
Bengal famine 82–3
Beria, Lavrentii Pavlovich: appearance, background and character 107–9, 201; 'Cambridge Five' spies 109; conversations at banquet 204; deportations 95, 107, 156; NKVD

Beria, Lavrentii Pavlovich (*cont.*)
    command 2, 107, 207, 246; NKVD
    security checks around Yalta 87, 104;
    on Stalin's Poland policy 170,
    199–200; on Stalin's view of public
    opinion 144; on Yalta Conference
    success 260; relationship with Stalin
    107, 156, 182, 201; transcripts of
    American and British conversations
    108; Yalta redecorations and renova-
    tions 98, 100
Beria, Sergo Lavrentievich (son of above):
    bugging American and British conversa-
    tions 108, 173; bugging Churchill 2,
    133, 245; bugging Roosevelt 2, 49; on
    Roosevelt's bodyguards 86; on Stalin
    bugging colleagues' conversations 17;
    on Stalin sleeping 12; on Stalin's atti-
    tude to drinking 10; on Stalin's
    gestures of goodwill 178; on Stalin's
    intelligence and memory 16; on Stalin's
    relationships with opera singers 53; on
    Stalin's sense of humour 12
Berlin: airlift 322; Allied bombing of 64,
    69, 110–11, 135; British strategy
    towards capture of 63; capital of
    German Democratic Republic 322;
    fall to Red Army 295; Hitler's bunker
    in 70, 171, 295; Potsdam Conference
    near 298; ruined centre 300, 301;
    Soviet advance on 60, 115, 116, 121,
    125, 242, 293; Stalin's policy on 115;
    US bombing raids 110–11; Wall 322
Bevin, Ernest 306
Birse, Arthur, Major: chair at dinner
    hosted by Roosevelt 124; conversation
    with Vyshinsky 126; farewell gift to
    Pavlov 248; interpreting for Churchill
    119, 204, 236; journey to Yalta 88,
    95; on Churchill and Stalin's relation-
    ship 115; on Livadia Palace 119
Bloch, Denise 146
Blore, Edward 100
Blunt, Anthony 109
Boettiger, Anna (Roosevelt): character
    128; chocolate gift refused 172;
    concern for father's health 128–9,
    150, 200, 209, 283; father's birthday
    celebrations 76; journey to Yalta 3,
    71–2, 77, 80, 87, 89; Livadia Palace
    experiences 96–7, 99, 102, 133, 174;

lunching with father 143, 213; on
    Byrnes 120, 123–4; on father's rela-
    tionship with Lucy Mercer Rutherfurd
    288–9; on Harry Hopkins 112–13; on
    Stalin 204; press reports 56; relation-
    ship with parents 50–1, 283–4;
    Sebastopol visit 149; Suez visit 272;
    Yalta arrival 96–7; Yalta departure
    248; Yalta role 50–1, 128
Boettiger, John 72, 129
Bohlen, Charles: Churchill's formal dinner
    236; coaching Kathleen Harriman
    204; on Churchill–Eden relationship
    114, 126; on Churchill's oratory 203;
    on Churchill's UN position 179–80;
    on Harry Hopkins 277; on Ibn Saud
    meeting 272–4; on interpreting 119,
    203, 299; on Molotov's attitude to US
    finance 137; on Polish debate 183; on
    Potsdam Conference 303; on
    Roosevelt–Churchill relationship 30;
    on Roosevelt–Stalin relationship 30,
    116; on Stalin's tactics 193, 233; on
    Stalin's view of Iran 247; on Stalin's
    view of Jewish people 240; on
    Truman 294; on Yalta mood 201,
    250, 259–60; reporting Mikołajczyk's
    position 163–4; Roosevelt's draft
    letter to Stalin on Poland 170; secret
    agreement on Japan war 245; view of
    Eden 114; view of Molotov 106;
    view of Roosevelt 139, 192; view of
    Stettinius 77; Vyshinsky encounter
    125–6
Bohr, Niels 261, 262, 264–5
Bór-Komorowski, Tadeusz 159
Braun, Eva 171
Braun, Werner von 206, 207n
Bright, Joan 55, 89, 237, 250, 251–2
Britain (UK): agreement to repatriate
    Soviet citizens 229, 251, 315–16; air
    operations 135–6; alliance with Soviet
    Union 27; atomic research and collab-
    oration with US *see* atomic bomb
    (Manhattan Project) *and* atomic
    research; Baltic states policy 269–70;
    Chiefs of Staff 133, 134–6, 175, 229;
    general election (1945) 180,
    299–300, 306; German reparations
    227, 230; German surrender approach
    285–6; guaranteeing Polish borders,

1939 154–5; Iran invasion 181; Marshall Plan aid 321; Polish forces 156–161, 198, 280; Polish government in exile 157–160, 198; Polish government recognition 197, 229, 297; post-war relationship with France 326–7; responses to Conference Communiqué 253; 'special relationship' with US 320; 'spheres of influence' discussion between Churchill and Stalin 33, 130, 138, 282, 324; ULTRA code-breaking 129, 223; US post-war aid to Western Europe (Marshall Plan) 321; V2 attacks 61, 111, 285; VE Day 295; War Cabinet 32, 179, 184, 221, 232, 233, 279; war losses 308; zone of occupation in Germany 138, 140, 322

British Empire: Churchill's position on 40, 81–4, 216, 221, 244, 278, 316–17, 326; UN membership issues 179, 184, 190

Brooke, Alan, Field Marshal: Balaclava battlefield visit 175; coordination and communication issues for Soviet/Anglo-American offensives 135–6; first tripartite meeting at Yalta 134–5; journey to Malta 57; on Churchill's response to atomic bomb test 302; on possibility of war with Russia 296; on Roosevelt–Churchill debate about Japan ultimatum 210; Potsdam Conference 300; relationship with Antonov 134–5; Siegfried Line visit 283; Stalin's grand dinner 200, 205; strategic discussions in Malta 58, 63; view of Alexander 221; view of Churchill 57–8, 221, 288; view of Marshall 221

Brown, Wilson, Vice-Admiral 86, 98, 150

Bruenn, Howard, Lt-Cdr: diagnosis of Roosevelt's condition 72, 128–9, 200, 225, 283; diagnosis of Watson's condition 151; encounter with Byrnes 123; journey with Roosevelt to Yalta 84, 85; restricting Roosevelt's visitors 200, 208; Roosevelt's death 289–90

Bruni, Carla 3–4

Buchenwald concentration camp 294

Budapest 60, 68–9, 186

Bulgaria 33, 69, 282, 304

Burgess, Guy 109, 110

Burma 63, 171, 194, 303

Bush, George W., President 3, 323

Butler, Rab 113

Byrnes, James: background and career 72–3, 77–8; Conference Communiqué role 231, 252; firm approach to Soviet Union 319; on Roosevelt's Yalta preparations 76; on Soviet Korean position 309; Potsdam Conference 299, 306; relationship with Harriman 299; relationship with Roosevelt 73, 169–70, 283; relationship with Stettinius 73, 175, 208; successor 321; temper tantrums at Yalta 120, 123–4; UN issues 175, 189, 213

Cadogan, Alexander: on Churchill 180, 203, 275, 292, 303; on Churchill–Anders meeting 280; on Eden 113, 275; on Japan war secret agreement 245; on leaders' discussions at Yalta 150; on MPs 281; on news from the front 224; on Roosevelt 243; on Stalin 144, 243, 247; on toasting Vyshinsky 212; on Vorontsov Palace 100–1; on Yalta arrangements 137, 201; on Yalta departure 222; on Yalta progress 185, 222, 260; on Yalta routine 174; Potsdam Conference 300; visiting Chekhov's house 188

Cairncross, John 109, 263

Caron, Bob 307

Casablanca Conference (1943) 29, 83

Catoctin, USS 46, 49, 75, 101, 248, 251, 271, 274

Chadwick, James 261, 263

Chamberlain, Neville 20, 82, 113, 280

Chekhov, Anton 94, 188–9

Chequers 98

Cherwell, Lord 265

Chiang Kai-shek: Cairo meeting 29, 38; defeat by Mao and flight to Taiwan 317; not invited to Yalta 38, 39; performance of armed forces 39; Potsdam Declaration 306; UN Declaration 78–9; UN presence 318; US view of 38–9; Yalta discussions concerning 192–3, 221, 228, 231, 245

Chiang Kai-shek, Madame (Meiling Soong) 39, 317

China: absence from Yalta 38; Council of
Foreign Ministers membership of 305;
Dairen proposal at Yalta 192, 194,
228; Hong Kong issue 165, 326;
Japanese war 38, 39, 63; Nationalist
regime 38; People's Republic
proclaimed by Mao Zedong 317;
Soviet advance 308; Soviet policy
towards 192, 194, 221, 228; UN
Declaration 79; UN role 39, 78, 164,
212, 318; war losses 38, 308; Yalta
secret agreement on Japan 228, 245
Churchill, Clementine (wife of Winston)
14, 19, 51–2, 64, 129, 291
Churchill, Jennie (née Jerome, mother of
Winston) 17–18
Churchill, Mary (daughter of Winston)
13, 30, 292, 300
Churchill, Pamela (Digby) (daughter-
in-law of Winston) 52, 75, 97, 205
Churchill, Randolph (son of Winston) 13,
51–2
Churchill, Lord Randolph (father of
Winston) 17–18
Churchill, Sarah see Oliver
Churchill, Winston: accommodation at
Yalta 99–101; age and appearance 7,
10, 11–12, 78, 137, 213–14, 237;
arrival at Yalta 1–3, 89–90; Athens
visits 131, 275; atomic bomb policy
265, 326; atomic bomb test news 302,
326; background 17–18, 247; Baltic
states policy 269; bitten by bedbugs at
Yalta 133; Cairo meeting with Chiang
Kai-shek and Roosevelt 29, 38; career
18–20, 21, 26; character 4, 12–14,
16, 18, 129, 144, 221, 292, 300, 303;
children 51–2; communications from
Britain at Yalta 129, 174; Conference
Communiqué 246–8; Declaration on
Liberated Europe 218–19, 282, 324;
domestic politics 13, 239–40, 306;
drinking 9, 203; elections (1945)
239, 306; eulogy for Roosevelt
292–3; Far East policy 39–40; France,
policy towards 30, 40, 140–1, 143,
177, 219, 233; German occupation
policy 32–3, 138–41; German reparations issue 141–3, 230, 233–4;
German war criminals issue 219–20;
Greece policy 33, 129–31, 199; Haile

Selassie meeting 276; health 8–9, 57,
64, 188, 209, 225, 325; Hitler's view
of 127; Hong Kong policy 40, 165,
192, 326; hosting final formal dinner
236–40; India policies 82–4, 185; Iran
policy 180–1; 'iron curtain' message
to Truman 296; 'Iron Curtain' speech
(1946) 319–20, 322; Japan war policy
209–10; journey from Yalta to
Franconia 274; journey to Yalta 56–7,
70, 84–9; King Farouk meeting 276;
King Ibn Saud meeting 275–6;
imperialist views 81–4, 179–80, 216,
221, 316–17, 326; last meeting with
Roosevelt 275; learns of Roosevelt's
secret agreement with Stalin 244–5;
lunching with Roosevelt 150; Malta
discussions 79–80, 81; Map Room
100, 115, 132, 239; marriage 51,
129; meeting with Anders 279–80;
meeting with Stalin before Conference
115; melancholia 84, 145; Middle
East visits 244; military strategy 115;
Molotov's visit (1942) 98; Montreux
Convention question 231, 234–5;
Moscow meetings with Stalin 27–8,
32, 33, 130, 138, 282, 324; oil policy
181–2; oratory 15–16, 119, 203;
Placentia Bay meeting with Roosevelt
26–7; plans for second Big Three
meeting 34–7; Polish border policy
162–3, 166–8, 183, 232; Polish
concerns after Yalta agreement 282,
284–5, 295, 296, 304, 305; Polish
elections question 167, 170, 185,
197–9, 217–18, 221, 226; Polish
government policy 164, 168–70,
183–5, 197–9, 215–18, 232; Potsdam
Conference 298, 299–306; prisoners
of war issues 229–30; Quebec meetings with Roosevelt (1943 and 1944)
29, 32, 77, 265; racist views 21, 82;
relationship with de Gaulle 40–2;
relationship with Eden 113–14, 275;
relationship with Harry Hopkins 74;
relationship with London Poles
163–4, 198, 217, 247, 279–80; relationship with Roosevelt 16, 19, 21,
26–7, 30–2, 80, 81, 114, 243–4,
292; relationship with Stalin 17, 28,
30–1, 201–2, 238, 280, 284–5, 303;

relationship with Truman 294, 298, 300, 319; report to Commons on Yalta 280–1; report to War Cabinet on Yalta 279; response to Allied invasion of Germany 64–5; response to Dresden destruction 255–6; response to Roosevelt's death 291–3; response to Siegfried Line breach 283; smoking 10, 141; 'spheres of influence' discussion with Stalin 33, 130, 138, 282, 324; support for White Russians 19, 28; Teheran Conference (1943) 29–31, 117; trusteeships issue for liberated colonies 79, 194, 216, 221; UN policy 78–9, 164–6, 177–80, 184, 189, 213, 245–6; view of France 145, 164; view of Molotov 107; view of Yalta Conference 260, 323; views on rights of smaller nations 125, 126; Warsaw rising (1944) 160, 161; Washington meetings with Roosevelt 27–8, 32, 78–9; Western Front visits 283, 287–8; Yalta departure 249–50
Clark Kerr, Archibald: German peace terms issue 286; on Stalin's view of Churchill 202; Polish government issues 182, 197, 210; sense of humour 204–5; Soviet reports from Auschwitz 266–7; Yalta role 123
Coates, Ed, Major 47
Cold War 3, 4, 318
Colville, John (Jock) 13–14, 61, 281, 282
concentration camps: American liberation of 268, 294; British liberation of 268, 294–5; gas chambers 66; genocide 66, 267–9; inmates forced onto death marches 65–6; liberation of 66, 67, 266, 268; Mikołajczyk's wife in 158; photographic and film records 267, 268, 295; Soviet liberation of 66, 67, 266, 268; survivors 66, 242, 266, 313; used to house German deportees 315; Western knowledge of 267
Conrad, Joseph 152
Control Commission 140–1, 176–7, 232
Cossacks 316
Council of Foreign Ministers 305
Cox, James 21
Crimean War 175, 274
Cunningham, Andrew, Admiral 135, 201
Curie, Marie 152, 261

Curzon, Lord 153
Curzon Line: accepted by Lublin Poles 159, 168; Churchill's policy 166–7, 232, 235; first suggested 153, 162; rejected by London Poles 162–3; Roosevelt's policy 163, 197, 232, 235; Stalin's policy 162, 167–8, 182–3, 235
Czechoslovakia 20, 154, 314–15, 321–2

D-Day (Operation Overlord 1944) 29, 31, 32, 40, 75, 76, 121
Dachau concentration camp 267
de Gaulle, Charles, General: asked for Yalta invitation 38; broadcast on Yalta decisions 277; character 40; D-Day broadcast row 40–1; discussed at Yalta 31; exclusion from Yalta 3, 40, 42, 56, 124; French position in occupied Germany 233; Hopkins meeting 56, 73; relationship with Churchill 40, 327; relationship with Eisenhower 40–1; relationship with Roosevelt 277, 327; resentment at British fighting on after fall of France 326–7; resentment at exclusion from Yalta 327; Stalin's view of 41, 117, 168, 199; Strasbourg defence 59; veto of British European Community entry 327; view of Churchill 16; view of Roosevelt 41; withdrawal from NATO 327
Declaration on Liberated Europe: Eden's proposed amendment 226; France association issue 219, 226, 232; full text in Conference Communiqué 246; Molotov's amendment 226; praised by Byrnes 252; provisions ignored by Stalin 282, 318, 320, 324; Soviet policy 322, 324; Stalin's proposed amendment 218, 222, 226; Yalta discussion and agreement 218–19, 226, 232, 318, 324
Delano, Laura Polly 50, 288
Devyataev, Mikhail Petrovich 206–7
displaced persons 31, 65, 273, 313–14
Djilas, Milovan 10, 12, 108
Djugashvili, Yakov 52, 301
Dönitz, Karl, Grand Admiral 67
Dresden, Allied bombing 64, 121, 136, 254–6

Dumbarton Oaks meeting on United
    Nations (1944) 79

Eastern Front 88, 94–5, 120, 122,
    135–6
Eden, Anthony: appearance, character and
    career 113, 114, 214; Athens visit
    222, 275; Auschwitz bombing question
    267; Declaration on Liberated Europe
    222, 226, 232; discussions with
    Molotov 112; end of Yalta Conference
    247, 251; Foreign Office telegram on
    Ibn Saud 244; France policy 140, 176,
    226, 232; German reparations issues
    212, 226–7, 230; Iran policy 227–8;
    journey to Malta 56, 57, 77; Malta
    discussions with Stettinius 77, 78, 79;
    'Moscow Declaration' on war crimes
    220; Moscow visit (1941) 162; opposi-
    tion to German 'pasturalization' policy
    32; Poland issues 78, 79, 112, 162,
    169–70, 185, 200, 210–11, 217, 221–2,
    226, 229, 232; Potsdam Conference
    300, 302–3; relationship with Churchill
    113–14, 126, 275; relationship with
    Molotov 112, 137; repatriation of pris-
    oners of war 230; response to secret
    agreement on Japan war 245; return
    from Potsdam 306; Roosevelt's funeral
    292; son's death 303; 'spheres of influ-
    ence' discussions 33; Suez Crisis 317;
    Truman's view of 306; UN issues 180,
    189–90, 194–5, 212, 238, 251; view of
    Churchill 144, 180; view of Roosevelt
    77, 114, 126, 139, 303; view of Stalin
    104, 126, 143–4, 216; view of Stalin–
    Molotov relationship 106–7; view of
    Truman 303; view of US 114; views
    on future relations with Soviet Union
    260; views on Yalta preparations 79,
    81, 112; views on Yalta progress 126;
    Warsaw rising (1944) 160; Yalta
    working arrangements 119
Edward VII, King 18
Egypt: Churchill's visit 275–6; King
    Farouk 225, 271, 276; Roosevelt's
    visit 244, 266, 271–4; Suez Canal
    165, 317; UN issues 179, 195–6
Eisenhower, Dwight D., General: D-Day
    landings (Overlord) 29, 40–1, 121;
    relationship with de Gaulle 40–1, 59;

relationship with Montgomery 58, 63;
    Strasbourg strategy 59; strategy for
    advance into Germany 63, 117, 206;
    view of Churchill 15; view of
    Roosevelt 14
'Enola Gay' (bomber) 307
Estonia 155, 261
European Advisory Commission 176
European Union 326–7
Evans, Joan 102, 173–4

Farouk, King of Egypt 225, 271, 276, 317
Ferdinand Magellan (railcar) 71, 75, 88,
    319
Ferebee, Tom 307
First World War: Churchill's career 19;
    Eden's career 113; German repara-
    tions 142; Polish situation 152;
    propaganda about German atrocities
    267; Stalin's career 8; Stalin's distrust
    of British 104; Truman's career 291;
    Versailles Peace Conference 22, 152,
    153, 269
Fleming, Ian 55
France: Allied invasion of (1944) 58;
    capitulation (1940) 26, 326; Control
    Commission role 141, 145, 176–7,
    232–3; Council of Foreign Ministers
    305; de Gaulle's role 3, 31, 40–1,
    277, 326–7; German occupation zone
    117, 140–1, 145, 176–7, 233, 246;
    German reparations issue 143;
    Indochina issue 194; Joint Declaration
    question 219, 226, 232; Marshall Plan
    aid 321; Poland relations 155, 156;
    role 30, 31, 147, 219; UN role 78,
    164, 212; US aid 321; war losses 308
Franco, Francisco, General 304, 305
Franconia (liner/troopship) 101, 174, 236,
    274
Fraser, George MacDonald 171
Frederick the Great 224
Freisler, Roland 110
Frisch, Otto 262–3
Fuchs, Klaus 264

Gandhi, Mohandas 20, 83
Gelfand, Vladimir 146
George VI, King 80, 83, 205, 238
Germany: Allied advance into 64–6;
    Allied invasion strategy 63–4; Berlin

airlift 322; captured naval ships 304; death marches 65, 242; dismemberment 138–40, 150, 176, 233, 246; division into three zones 138; forced labour for Soviet Union 171; future of 32–3 ; German Democratic Republic (East Germany) 322; German Federal Republic (West Germany) 322; gold reserves 242; jet fighters and bombers 62; Marshall Plan aid 321; 'pasturalization' policy 32; reparations amount and nature 141–2, 212, 226–7, 233–4, 238; reparations commission 143, 176–7, 226, 233–4; reparations demanded by Soviet Union 141–2, 211–12, 230; reparations discussed at Potsdam 304–5, 306–7; reparations discussed at Yalta 137, 138, 141–3, 211–12, 226–7, 230, 233–4, 238; separate peace plan issue 105–6, 127, 285–6, 288; surrender 295; surrender terms 127, 138, 139–40, 150, 164, 176, 285–6; U-boats 60–61, 75, 122, 223, 304; US and UK zones of occupation 322; war criminals 219–20; war losses 308

Goebbels, Joseph 32–3, 69, 139, 224, 293–4, 296n

Gorky, Maxim 93

Greece: British 'sphere of influence' 33, 130; British troops in 59, 130; Churchill's policy 33, 129–31, 199; Churchill's visits 131, 244, 275; civil war 320–1; foreign observers 217; Stalin's policy 33, 130, 199, 218, 282, 304; US support 320–1; war losses 308

Greek National Liberation Front (EAM) 130

Greek People's Liberation Army (ELAS) 130, 131

Greenglass, David 264

Gregg, Victor 255

Gromyko, Andrei Andreyevich: arrangements for Yalta Conference 34, 123; Japan war policy 134; on Churchill 141; on Polish discussions 197; on Roosevelt 208–9; on Stalin 12, 17, 143, 174; Roosevelt's death 293; view of Eden 114

Gurary, Samary 214–15

Gusev, Fedor Tarasovich 123, 200–1

Hahn, Otto 261–2

Haile Selassie, Emperor 225, 271, 276

Halifax, Lord 20, 291

Hall, Theodore (Ted) 264

Hannibal, Operation 67, 241

Harding, Warren, President 21

Harlan, Veit 70

Harriman, Averell: affair with Pamela Churchill 52; appearance, background and career 53, 299; card playing with Churchill 64; dealing with Byrnes 124, 299; France policies 233; journey to Malta 54; journey to Yalta 53–4, 87; lunching with Roosevelt 150, 213; Moscow meeting 28; news of US Manila entry 137; on Roosevelt 10; on 'spheres of influence' letter 33; on Stalin 28, 120; Placentia Bay meeting 26–7; Polish issues 162–3, 170, 182, 197, 210, 285; Potsdam Conference 299; report on Yalta site for Conference 36–7; Roosevelt's death 293; Soviet terms for joining Japan war 192, 228, 245; UN issues 189, 293; Yalta Conference arrangements 99, 112, 123; Yalta departure 248

Harriman, Kathleen: accompanying father to Yalta 50; affair with Roosevelt's son 52; chocolate gift refused 172; Japan war news 260; journey to Yalta 53–4, 87; Katyn visit 158; Livadia facilities 98, 133; lunching with Roosevelt 213; meeting Chekhov's sister 188; on Livadia dining arrangements 99; on Roosevelt 143; preparing Livadia Palace for Roosevelt's arrival 54–5, 89, 96, 97; Sebastopol visit 149, 170; speech at Stalin's grand dinner 204; Yalta departure 248

Hassett, William 290

Heisenberg, Werner 261, 264

Hess, Rudolf 55, 109–10, 220

Hessen, Edith van 242

Himmler, Heinrich 70, 147, 156, 160, 201

Hindenburg, Paul von, Field Marshal 60, 152

Hiroshima 70, 297, 307–8
Hiss, Alger 109, 189, 195
Hitler, Adolf: anti-Jewish policies 261,
    267, 273; appeasement 20, 113, 319;
    assassination attempt 60, 111; bunker
    70, 171, 224, 300; death 295, 300;
    Eva Braun's birthday 171; giving
    Livadia Palace to von Runstedt 94;
    invasion of Russia 27; planning recon-
    struction of birthplace 207; Poland
    invasion plans 154; response to
    Roosevelt's death 294; Soviet attack
    on Berlin 115; Soviet pact
    (Ribbentrop/Molotov) 155; Stalin
    insists still alive 303; view of
    Churchill 127; war with US 27;
    'Wolf's Lair' headquarters 60
Ho Chi Minh 317
Holmes, Marian: Churchill's Athens visit
    275; Churchill's grand dinner 236–7;
    office room 132, 205; on Churchill
    132, 205, 225, 236; on Roosevelt 77;
    Yalta arrival 90; Yalta departure 250
Holmes, Oliver Wendell 20
Hong Kong 27, 40, 165, 192, 326
Hoover, Herbert, President 22
Hopkins, Harry: absent from first plenary
    session 119–20; appearance, character
    and career 73–5, 145; Black Sea coast
    choice for Conference 34; break-
    fasting at Livadia 173; death 299;
    finding a bed for Churchill's siesta
    150–1, 176; France policy 145, 219,
    232, 277; German reparations issue
    232–3; health 75, 81, 113, 119, 145,
    277; Japan war issues 297; meeting
    with de Gaulle 56, 73; Moscow
    meeting with Stalin (1945) 297–8,
    303; on Roosevelt–Churchill relations
    81, 112–13; on Roosevelt's views 39,
    81, 189; on Stalin 165; on Stalin's
    offer to son Robert 214; Placentia Bay
    meeting 26; Polish question 297–8;
    Potsdam arrangements 297; relation-
    ship with Churchill 56, 74, 145, 244,
    292; relationship with Roosevelt
    73–4, 77–8, 139–40, 145, 179–80,
    219, 277; relationship with Stettinius
    77–8, 175; reporting Mikołajczyk's
    wishes to Roosevelt 163–4; resigna-
    tion 299; role at plenary sessions

119, 138, 139–40, 179–80, 232–3;
    talks with Pope 56, 73; UN issues
    175, 179, 189, 297; view of Stalin
    259, 260; views on colonies 221; Yalta
    departure 271; Yalta optimism 259
Hopkins, Robert (son of above): at Yalta
    118, 133, 172–3; photographing
    attendees 116, 124, 137, 213–14,
    247; Stalin's offer to 214
Horrocks, Brian, Lieutenant-General 206
Hull, Cordell 77, 181, 220
Hungary 33, 69, 267, 304, 322

Ibn Saud, King of Saudi Arabia 225, 244,
    251, 272–3, 275
Ichigo, Operation (1944) 39
Ickes, Harold 78
Idrisli, Arire 95–6
India 82–4, 316
Indianapolis, USS 307
Indonesia 317
Iran (Persia) 78, 180–2, 227–8, 247,
    319–20
'Iron Curtain' 319–20, 322
Ismay, Hastings 'Pug', General 55, 74,
    326
Istomina, Valentina 'Valechka' Vasilevna 53
Italy: African colonies 305; Allied
    campaign in 29, 59, 115; Communists
    59, 321; elections issue of 304; possi-
    bility of German forces' surrender
    285–6; surrender of 29, 59; transfer
    of Allied troops to Western Front from
    135; transfer of British troops to
    Greece from 59; war losses 308
Iwo Jima, US campaign 283, 287

Japan: atomic bomb targets in 296–7;
    British forces fighting 63, 64;
    Churchill's policy towards 40,
    209–10, 230, 245, 302; Hiroshima
    and Nagasaki bombing 307–8;
    Hiroshima wartime activities in 70;
    invasion of China 38–9; kamikazes
    70; Korea occupation 194, 309;
    Manila campaign 145–6, 171, 191;
    Okinawa campaign 287; Pearl Harbor
    attack 27; rejection of Potsdam offer
    306; responses to Soviet involvement
    in Pacific war 260; Roosevelt's poli-
    cies towards 190–1, 194, 209, 210;

Roosevelt's views on Japanese immigration to US 21–2; Soviet non-aggression pact with 193, 288; Soviet planning for Pacific war against 213; Stalin's policy towards 27–8, 104, 134, 185, 191–4, 200, 306; surrender 308, 309; terms for Soviet entry to war with 3, 192–4, 200, 228, 294; Tokyo bombing 287; US policies towards 62–3, 78, 134, 190–1, 302; war against 62–3, 187, 287; war crimes 146; war losses 308; Yalta agreement 245, 260, 283, 294; Yalta discussions 78, 133–4, 190–4, 209, 221

Jewish people: Churchill's attitude to bombing Auschwitz 267–8; concentration camps 66–7, 242, 267–8; death marches 65, 242; deportations 267; emigration of German scientists 261; genocide 66, 261, 266–7; German responses to Morgenthau Plan 33; homeland for 240, 266; Molotov's wife 106, 107n; Palestine immigration question 273, 276; Polish population 153; Roosevelt's attitude to 240; Roosevelt's response to extermination reports 267; saved by Wallenberg 60; Stalin's attitude to 106, 240; Truman's attitude to 299

Jodl, Alfred, General 295

Jones, Ron 242

Kardorff, Ursula von 69, 110–11

Karlik, Agnes 68

Katyn massacre 156–8

Kennedy, Joseph 19

Kerensky, Alexander 94

See Clark, Kerr, Archibald

Khrushchev, Nikita 261, 306

Khudykh, Dimitry 158

Kientopf, Anna 314

Kim Il-Sung 318

King, Ernest, Admiral 97, 135, 185, 208, 260

Kitayama, Futaba 307–8

Kohl, Helmut, Chancellor 4

Kolberg (film) 70

Kor, Eva and Miriam Mozes 67

Korea 3, 194, 309, 318, 326

Korean War 309, 318, 326

Korniyasenko, Olga 95

Krock, Arthur 15

Kurile Islands 192, 309, 326

Kuter, Laurence, Major-General 64, 98–9, 110, 123

Kuznetsov, Nikolai Gerasimovich 135, 185

Latvia 155, 156, 261

Layton, Elizabeth 85, 132, 237, 241

League of Nations 21, 78, 147, 166, 179

Leahy, William, Admiral: Chiefs of Staff meetings 135; journey to Yalta 86; on atomic bomb 308; on first plenary session 119; on Ibn Saud 274; on Polish agreement 232, 281; on Roosevelt 249; on seventh plenary session 236; on Soviet slave camps 141; on Stalin 260; on Stalin's grand dinner 200; on support needed for war with Japan 191; relationship with Roosevelt 283; Soviet entry into Japan war 245, 306; view of Kuznetsov 135

LeHand, Marguerite 'Missy' 50

Lend-Lease programme: British renewal hopes 32; Byrnes's role 73; ended 321; extended to Soviet Union 28; institution of 26; possible use as bargaining tool at Yalta 297, 324; Roosevelt's idea 26, 191, 202; Stalin's view of 191, 202, 297; supply routes 181

Lenin, Vladimir Ilyich (Ulyanov) 12, 23–4, 94, 104, 106, 167

Levi, Primo 66–7

Leyte Gulf, battle (1944) 63

Lincoln, Abraham 71

Linz 207

Lithuania 151, 152, 158, 178, 261, 314

Litvinov, Maxim 106

Livadia Palace: ballroom (the 'White Hall') 118–19, 210, 231; bathrooms and lavatories 97–8, 101; bedbugs and lice 49, 133; bomb shelter 98, 103–4; central heating 98, 101; cleaners 98; communications with White House 128; courtyard photo call 213–14; dining arrangements 99; fifth plenary session 193, 194–9; first plenary session 118–22; food and drink 172–3; Foreign Ministers' meeting

Livadia Palace (*cont.*)
210; formal dinner after first plenary session 99, 123–6; fourth plenary session 176–83; gardens 48, 98, 102, 246; history 48, 93, 94–5; lemon tree 116, 251; listening devices 48–9, 174; overcrowding 55, 97; packing up 252; preparations for US delegation 48–9, 54–5, 96, 98; resort for NKVD staff 246; Roosevelt's arrival 89, 96; Roosevelt's departure 248–9; Roosevelt's rooms 96; second plenary session 137–45; seventh plenary session 231–6; Stalin's departure 248; Stalin's visits 115, 116–18, 190–4; US delegation departure 251

London, meeting of Foreign Ministers (1945) 318

London Poles (Polish government in exile): borders policy 159; Churchill's plans 184; Churchill's view of 163, 198, 217, 247, 279; denounced as traitors 261; formation of government in exile 157; hopes for Yalta Conference 111; Katyn massacre issue 158; leadership 162–3; Moscow meeting 162–3; relations with US and UK 163, 216; relationship with Lublin Poles 168, 261; response to Yalta terms 279; Stalin's view of 168; Warsaw rising 160; Yalta debate 167–8, 182–3, 197–9, 222; Yalta visit question 170, 177

Lublin Poles (Sovet-backed provisional government): Churchill's view of 169, 217; established by Soviet authorities 159, 198; expulsion of Germans 314; Moscow meeting 162; non-Lublin Poles inclusion in government 294, 297; recognized by Soviet Union 159; relationship with London Poles 168, 261; Roosevelt's view of 169, 216–17; Soviet policy 285; Ukraine deportations from 313; US public opinion against 166; Yalta debate 167–8, 182–3, 197–9, 210–11, 222; Yalta visit question 170, 177, 183

Ludendorff, General Erich 301

Lunghi, Hugh, Captain 86, 108, 121, 126, 136, 160

MacArthur, Douglas, General 62–3, 134, 137, 145

McCloy, John 268

McIntire, Ross, Vice-Admiral 3, 35, 46, 72, 129, 220

MacLean, Donald 109, 110

MacLeish, Archibald 279

Macmillan, Harold 32

Maisky, Ivan Mikhailovich: appearance and character 141, 204; conversation with Churchill about Poland 169; on Iran issues 182; on UN issues 177; reparations issues 141–2, 212, 226–7

Majdanek concentration camp 268

Malenkov, Georgi 12

Malta: Brooke's journey to 57–8; Churchill's journey to 56–7; Churchill's melancholia 84, 145; Eden's discussions with Stettinius 77–8; Eden's journey to 57; Harriman's journey to 54; Luqa aerodrome 46; Roosevelt–Churchill meetings at 80, 81, 112; Roosevelt's departure from 85–6; Roosevelt's journey to 75–7; Roosevelt's sightseeing drive 80; stopover on way to Yalta 37–8; strategy discussions at 63–4, 110; wartime experiences 80–1

Manchuria 134, 192, 228, 309

Manhattan Atomic Bomb Project *see* atomic bomb (Manhattan Project)

Manila, US campaign 63, 116, 137, 145–6, 171, 191, 242

Mao Zedong 38, 39, 317–18

Marinesko, Alexander, Captain 67, 241

Marshall, George, General: Brooke's view of 221; career 121, 321; Chiefs of Staff meetings 135, 191, 213; food problems at Yalta 173; Plan 321; report on Allied position in the west 121–2; strategy talks with British 63; UN issues 208; Yalta accommodation 97

Martin, John 275

Martynushkin, Ivan, Lieutenant 66, 69

Marx, Karl 143

Masaryk, Jan 322

Mass Observation Project *see* Rutherford, Edie

Meiklejohn, Robert 54, 128, 300–1

Meitner, Lise 262

Mengele, Josef 67
Mercer, Lucy *see* Rutherfurd
Michael, King of Romania 282
Mikołajczyk, Stanisław: denounced as
    traitor by Lublin Poles 261; evidence
    of German Jewish genocide policy
    267, 268; forced into exile 297;
    Moscow meeting with Churchill and
    Stalin 162, 168; Polish border issues
    162, 163, 168; Polish deputy prime
    minister 297; Polish government and
    election issues 163–4, 184, 197, 211,
    217; Polish Prime Minister 158; possi-
    bility of invitation to Yalta 170;
    resignation 163; wife 158
Mitchell, John 84
Mitterrand, François, President 4
Molotov, Vyacheslav Mikhailovich
    (Scriabin): appearance 106, 107, 214;
    background and career 23, 106; Baltic
    states policy 155–6; character 2,
    106, 107, 112, 144, 199, 201, 227;
    Churchill's view of 107; Declaration
    on Liberated Europe 218, 226; discus-
    sions with Eden 112; German
    surrender question 286; gift to Eden
    251; gifts to Stettinius 248, 251;
    Harriman's view of 53; Iran policy
    227–8; lunch for Foreign Ministers
    136–7; Marshall Plan rejection 321;
    Moscow Declaration on war crimes
    220; name 106; on Chequers bath-
    rooms 98; on German
    dismemberment 176; on German
    reparations 176–7, 212, 226, 230,
    306; on Stalin 9–10; on Stalin's view
    of Roosevelt 193; Polish borders
    policy 162–3, 182, 197, 232, 235,
    306–7; Polish elections policy
    210–11, 215, 222, 284; Polish govern-
    ment policy towards its creation 168,
    182–3, 197–9, 216–17, 226, 229,
    284–5, 294; relationship with Eden
    114; relationship with Stalin 106–7,
    125; secret agreement on Japan war
    193, 228; 'spheres of influence' discus-
    sions 33; Teheran Conference 31;
    Truman meetings 293, 294; UN poli-
    cies 175, 177–8, 189–90, 195–6,
    212, 247, 251; UN San Francisco
    conference 237–8, 293; US shipping

sales question 191; view of Poland
    153; von Ribbentrop pact 48, 154;
    wife 106, 107n; Yalta agenda question
    99; Yalta arrivals 2; Yalta working
    arrangements 89, 119; Yugoslavia
    policy 215
Montgomery, Bernard, Field Marshal
    58–9, 63, 206, 220, 283
Montreux Convention 230–1, 234
Moran, Lord (Charles Wilson): journey to
    Malta 56–7; on bedbugs 133; on
    Churchill's health 8, 57, 64, 209; on
    Churchill's love of France 145; on
    Churchill's moods 131, 205, 221,
    243–4, 249; on Churchill's Polish
    policy 169; on Conference location
    35–6; on de Gaulle 40; on Harry
    Hopkins 189, 219, 221; on Roosevelt
    2, 86, 145, 171, 221, 243; on Stalin's
    views 170–1; visit to Chekhov's house
    188–9
Morgenthau, Henry 32–4, 78, 109, 142,
    289, 299
Morgenthau Plan 32–4, 109, 142
Moscow commission on reparations 212,
    233, 234
Moscow Declaration on war crimes 220
Mountbatten, Lord Louis 316
Munich Agreement (1938) 3, 20, 154,
    323
Murphy, USS 272
Murrow, Edward R. 52, 294

Nagasaki 308
Napoleon 152
Nasser, Gamal Abdel 317
Nehru, Jawaharlal 82
Netherlands, war losses 308
Nicholas II, Tsar 89, 94, 96
NKVD: Beria's role 107; Katyn massacre
    156–7; treatment of Soviet escapees
    207; warnings to local citizens 172,
    252; Yalta preparations 47–9, 87; Yalta
    security 54, 85, 102, 104, 116, 123,
    303
North Atlantic Treaty Organization
    (NATO) 322, 327
Norway, 'Black Friday' 223

oil 23, 78, 122, 136, 142, 166, 181–2,
    227, 247, 256, 276, 319

Okinawa, US landing on 287

Okunevskaya, Tatiana 108

Olga, Grand Duchess 119

Oliver, Sarah (Churchill): at Yalta 100–1, 129, 137, 148–9, 176, 188, 204, 213, 248, 274–5; journey to Malta 56–7, 77; journey to Yalta 87–9; 'Little Three' 204; marriage 51; on Churchill 129, 148, 188, 209; on Stalin 10; relationship with Winant 51; sightseeing in Malta 80; Yalta attendance 50; Yalta departure 249–50

Oliver, Vic 51

Oppenheimer, Robert 264, 296, 301

Orion, HMS 57, 77

Orwell, George 318

Overlord, Operation (1944) see D-Day

Paraguay 179, 187

Paris-Match 124

Patton, George, General 58, 186

Pavlov, Vladimir Nikolaevich 116, 236, 239, 248

Pearl Harbor attack (1941) 27, 114, 263

Peenemünde 206–7

Peierls, Rudolf 262–3, 301

Perkins, Frances 46, 128

Philby, Kim 109

Philippines 27, 63, 83, 116, 137, 145–6, 171, 191, 242, 288

Pim, Richard, Captain 100, 239, 242

Pius XII, Pope 56, 73

Placentia Bay 26–7, 298

Planck, Erwin 60

Poland: Bolshevik invasion (1920) 153; borders 31, 153, 162, 167–8, 176, 183, 232, 235, 284, 304, 305, 306–7, 313; British guarantee of borders (1939) 4, 154; Curzon Line 153, 159, 162–3, 166–8, 182, 197, 232, 235; deportations 156, 157, 313–14; Eden's concerns 78, 79, 112, 169–70; elections issue 197, 210–11, 215, 217–19, 221–2, 225–6, 284, 304; 'émigrés' 166, 183, 200; geography 151; German invasion (1939) 154–5; Government of National Unity 197; government recognized by US and UK 232, 297; history 151–2; home army 159–60, 217, 285; independence under

Versailles Treaty 152–3; Katyn massacres (1940) 156–8; London government 198; London Poles see London Poles; Lublin Poles see Lublin Poles; massacre of Ukrainians 314; Polish forces fighting for Allied cause 4, 59, 157, 160, 161, 198; Polish voters in US 125, 152; population (1939) 153; Presidential Council proposal 166, 197; Provisional Government (Lublin) 197–9, 215, 217; Provisional Government of National Unity 226, 232, 235; provisional government proposals 164, 170, 176, 182–3, 197–9, 215; resistance fighters 159–61, 313; responses to Yalta agreements 259, 261; Riga Treaty (1921) 153; Soviet advance (1944) 36, 53, 144; Soviet invasion (1939) 155; Soviet–Nazi non-aggression pact (1939) 155; Teheran Conference 162, 163; war losses 308; Warsaw rising (1944) 159–61, 285; Western leaders' goal at Yalta 164; Western Neisse border issue 168, 182, 197, 232, 305, 307; Yalta agenda 143, 147, 151, 176, 182–3, 210; Yalta agreements 247, 260, 279–81, 284, 294, 295, 323–4, 327; Yalta debate 166–9, 210–11, 216–7, 221–2, 225–6, 229, 232

Polish government in exile see London Poles

Portal, Charles (Peter), Marshal of the RAF: Chiefs of Staff meetings 135; feeding goldfish 149, 173; Malta talks 64, 110; on dinner conversation of 'Big Three' 205; on Livadia arrangements 97; picking lock of bathroom 149; relationship with Pamela Churchill 52

Potsdam Conference: accommodation 299, 300, 301, 303; achievements 325; agenda 304; arrivals 298, 299, 300–1; Attlee's return 306; British delegation 299–300, 306; chairman 303; Churchill's departure 306; Communiqué 307, 318; conclusion 307; Declaration on Japan 306; first plenary session 303–5; news of atomic bomb test 302, 306; postponement 298; Truman at 303–5, 325; US delegation 298–9

Prince of Wales, HMS 26
prisoners of war: camps 65, 315; death marches 65, 242; Dresden clear-up 255; German 287; liberation 260, 285, 313; Peenemünde escapees 206–7; repatriation 229–30, 251, 315–16; Romanian 48, 102, 149; Russian Liberation Army 223; Soviet 158; Stalin's son 52; Tatars 95

Quebec conferences (1943 and 1944) 29, 32, 77, 265
Quincy, USS 75–7, 79, 116, 134, 271–2, 275, 277–8, 283

Radescu, Nicolae 282
Rasputin, Grigori 97, 103
Ravensbrück concentration camp 146
Reilly, Mike 2, 11, 46–9, 71, 85, 252, 288
Rhine River: Allied advance on 117, 122, 206, 239, 242, 283; Allied crossing of 63, 115, 287; Churchill's visits 283, 287–8
Ribbentrop, Joachim von: Kremlin visits 154–6; on British and American readiness to fight 201–2; on Churchill 254; Poland partition line 155, 162; Soviet–Nazi non-aggression pact 48, 107, 154–5; 'spheres of influence' agreements 155–6
Rigdon, William, Lieutenant 173, 273
Rogers, Joyce 81
Rolfe, Lilian 146
Romania: defection from German alliance 69, 281–2; Potsdam agenda 304; prisoners of war 48, 102, 149; Soviet coup 161, 282; Soviet influence 33
Roosevelt, Eleanor: character 49, 128; husband's death 290, 291–3; on Churchill 13, 16; political activities 50, 51; relationship with husband 14, 49–50, 105, 129, 283–4, 288; Yalta attendance question 49, 50
Roosevelt, Elliott 31, 50
Roosevelt, James 45, 46, 76
Roosevelt, Franklin Delano, President: accommodation at Yalta 96–7; affairs 49–50; age 7; appearance 11, 77, 86, 200, 213–14, 237, 290; appointment of Stettinius 77–8; arrival at Yalta 2–3, 96–7; atomic bomb policy 265, 326; background 20, 247; birthday 76; Cairo meeting with Chiang Kai-shek and Churchill 29, 38; career 13, 20–2, 26; character 4, 10, 13, 14–15, 16, 143–4; children 50, 51; China policies 39–40; cocktails 98, 116; Conference chairman 120; Conference Communiqué 246–8; death 290, 291–3; Declaration on Liberated Europe 218–19, 282, 324; dog 12; domestic politics 13; drinking 9; Far East policy 193–4, 200, 209–10, 228, 231, 245; farewell tour of Livadia grounds 246; first plenary session 118–22; France policy 30, 117, 140–1, 143, 177, 219, 232–3; German occupation policy 32, 138–41; German reparations issue 141–3, 233–4; health 2, 7–8, 21, 35, 46, 77, 86, 128–9, 138, 200, 208–9, 225, 243–4, 278–9, 283–4, 288–90, 325; Ibn Saud meeting 272–4; Iran policy 181; Japan war policy 134, 192–3, 200, 209–10, 228, 231, 245, 325, 326; journey from Yalta to Egypt 271; journey to US 277–8; journey to Yalta 70, 71–2, 75–7, 84–9, 319; last meeting with Churchill 275; Lend-Lease programme 26, 73, 191, 202; marriage 49–50, 129, 283–4; meeting with Stalin before Conference 99, 115, 116–18; Middle East visits ('three kings') 225, 240, 244; Montreux Convention question 234–5; oil policy 181–2; opening Conference 120; oratory 15, 45–6; Placentia Bay meeting with Churchill 26–7; plans for future of Germany 32–3; plans for second Big Three meeting 34–7; Polish agreement at Yalta 232, 281, 284–5, 324–5, 327; Polish issues, policy towards 162–4, 166–70, 176, 197–9, 216–17, 225, 232, 235; preparations for Yalta 76, 79–80, 81, 112–13; presidential inauguration (1945) 45–6, 325; proposed meeting with Stalin 29; Quebec meetings with Churchill (1943 and 1944) 29, 32, 77, 265; railcar (*Ferdinand Magellan*) 71–2;

Roosevelt, Franklin Delano, President (*cont.*)
relationship with Churchill 16, 19, 21, 26–7, 30–2, 80, 81, 117–18, 243–4, 278; relationship with de Gaulle 41–2, 117, 277; relationship with Harry Hopkins 73–4; relationship with Lucy Mercer Rutherfurd 49–50, 288–9; relationship with Stalin 17, 30–1, 116–18, 120, 125, 202, 278, 284–6; response to Iwo Jima casualties 283; Romania policy 283; second plenary session 137–43; secret agreement with Stalin on entry into Japan war 193, 228, 230, 245; segregation policy towards 73; smoking 10, 87; speech to Congress (1 March 1945) 278–9, 327; Teheran Conference 29–31, 117, 125; UN inaugural conference 179, 180, 189, 196, 208; UN membership policy 178–9, 185, 189–90, 195–6, 213; UN vision 21, 76, 78–9, 182, 325, 326; UN voting policy 164–6, 213, 236, 245–6, 326; view of Churchill's imperialism 83, 278; view of Stalin 25, 259, 278; view of Vietnamese 317; view of Yalta Conference 259, 279, 323, 327; Washington meetings with Churchill 27–8, 32; White House communications 128, 174, 220; working hours 12; Yalta departure 236, 240, 248–9; Zionism question 240
Roosevelt, Franklin Delano Junior 52
Roosevelt, Theodore, President 16, 20, 85
Rosenman, Sam 277–8
Rudel, Hans-Ulrich 69, 224
Ruhr 63, 115, 117, 138–9, 187, 287
Runstedt, Karl von, Field Marshal 94–5
Russian Liberation Army 223
Rutherford, Edie 280
Rutherford, Ernest 261
Rutherfurd, Lucy Mercer 49–50, 76, 288–9, 290
Rutherfurd, Winthrop 49

'*Sacred Cow*' (aircraft) 2, 84–6, 271, 298
Sakhalin 192, 309, 326

Saki airfield 1, 47, 85–6, 116, 128, 129, 231, 271
Sarkozy, Nicolas, President 4
Saturnus, Wiesława 156
Saudi Arabia 240, 244, 251, 272–4
Sawyers, Frank 131, 149, 188, 231, 240–1, 249–50
Scobie, Ronald, General 275
Sebastopol: capture and recapture 102, 175; Churchill's return journey 250, 274; communication links with Yalta 101–2; Roosevelt's return journey 248, 271, 274; trips to 149, 174; war damage 102, 149
Seele, Gertrude 69–70
Setaro, Harry 7
Shaw, George Bernard 141
Shoumatoff, Elizabeth 289–90
Siegfried Line (West Wall) 126–7, 186, 243, 283
Silvermaster, Gregory 109
Simpson, William, Lieutenant-General 283
Somerville, James, Admiral 88
Soviet Union (USSR): atomic intelligence 263–4; Baltic states 156, 269–70; Berlin blockade 322; Berlin Wall 322; Chiefs of Staff 134–5; Cold War 318; Czechoslovakia coup (1948) 321–2; Declaration on Liberated Europe 318, 322; deportations 31, 95–6, 107; Eastern bloc 321; Eastern Europe policies 304, 318, 321; exclusive trade treaties 321; expulsion from League of Nations 166; fall 264; famine (1932/3) 24; forces advance into China 308; German forced labourers 171; German invasion 27, 157; German reparations 137, 141–3, 212, 230, 238, 307; Hitler's view of 154; Iran invasion 181; Japan war needs 213, 228, 230–1, 245; Japan war policy 38, 62, 134, 191–2, 221; Jewish national home 240; Katyn massacre 157–8; Korea position 3, 309, 326; Lend-Lease 2–3, 28, 53, 87, 191, 202, 297, 321; liberation of Allied prisoners of war 285; non-aggression pact with Nazi Germany 141, 154–5; Polish government recognition 226; relationship with China 309; repatriation of liberated citizens and

prisoners of war 229, 251, 315–16; 'republics' 105, 178; responses to Conference Communiqué 253–4; spies 109–10, 306, 319; Truman's approach towards 294, 319; UN membership 178, 179, 190, 195, 236, 297n; UN role 78–9, 164, 213; war losses 106, 308, 325; westward advance (1945) 59–60; zone of occupation in Germany 138, 322

Spain 304, 305

Spychalski, Marian, Colonel 261

Stalin (Joseph Vissarionovich Djugashvili): aims at Yalta 104; anxieties about separate German peace deal 105–6, 127, 285–6, 288; appearance and age 7, 10, 17, 87, 116, 123, 213–14, 233, 237; atomic bomb 265, 306, 326; background and career 22–5, 247, 259; bear hunting story 325–6; character 4, 9–10, 12, 16–17, 87, 143–4, 243; children 52–3, 301; China policy 192–4; collectivization policy 24, 28; Cominform 321; Conference Communiqué 246–7; Declaration on Liberated Europe 218–19, 222, 318, 320, 324; deportation of Tatars 95–6; doodles 122; drinking 9–10, 124; famine (1932/3) 24; Far East policy 193–4, 200, 213, 221, 228, 230, 245; France policy 117, 140–1, 143, 177, 219, 233; German captured naval ships question 304; German occupation policy 138–41; German reparations issue 141–3, 230, 233–4, 238; German war criminals issue 220; Greece policy 130, 131, 320; health 8, 12–13, 35; hosting grand dinner at Yusupov Palace 200–5, 207; Iran policy 182, 247, 319, 320; Japan war policy 134, 185, 191–3, 200, 213, 221, 228, 245, 297, 306, 326; journey to Yalta 87–8; Katyn massacre 156–8; Korea position 309; late-night parties for Soviet delegation 174; Lend-Lease dependence 324; marriages 52; meeting with Churchill before Conference 115; meeting with Harry Hopkins in Moscow (1945) 297; meeting with Roosevelt before Conference 99, 115, 116–18;

memory 143; military strategy 115, 136, 144–5, 220; mistress 53; Montreux Convention question 230–1, 234–5, 305; Moscow meetings with Churchill 27–8, 32, 33; name 23; naval strategy 185; negotiating abilities 143–4; oil policy 181–2; pact with Nazis (1939) 105; plans for second Big Three meeting 34–7; Poland policy 162, 166–71, 177, 182–3, 198–200, 217–18, 229, 231–2, 297–8, 304, 305; Polish campaign (1920) 153; Polish partition agreement (1939) 154–5; political beliefs 323–4; Potsdam Conference 298, 301–7; prisoners of war issues 230; proposed division of influence in Eastern Europe 33–4; purges 24–5; rejection of Marshall Plan aid 321; relationship with Churchill 28, 30–1, 201–2, 216, 238, 303; relationship with de Gaulle 41–2, 117; relationship with Molotov 106–7; relationship with Roosevelt 30–1, 116–18, 120, 125, 202, 208–9, 286; relationship with Truman 302–3; relationship with Vyshinsky 126; reputation in US and UK 144, 278; response to Churchill's 'Iron Curtain' speech 320; response to Red Army rapes 69; response to Roosevelt's death 293; Ribbentrop discussions (1939) 154–5; second plenary session 137–43; secret agreement with Roosevelt on Japan 193, 228, 230, 245; seen as victor of Yalta 260; sense of humour 12, 94, 144, 200–1, 204; smoking 10, 87, 122, 124, 143; speaking English 124; speech on Capitalism and Communism (1946) 319; 'spheres of influence' discussion with Churchill 33, 130, 131, 138, 324; spies 109; support for Communist parties in Western Europe 321; Teheran Conference 29–31, 117, 125; translating for 119; 'Uncle Joe' nickname 30, 125; UN policy 79, 164–6, 177–80, 189–90, 194–6, 221, 245–6, 297; view of Churchill 83, 104–5; view of Roosevelt 105, 209, 261; view of Yalta 260–1; views on rights of smaller nations 125, 126;

Stalin (*cont.*)
  Warsaw rising (1944) 159–61; westward campaign (1945) 59–60; Yalta accommodation 103–4; Yalta arrival 3, 88; Yalta departure 248; Zionism question 240; zones of occupation policy 305
Stalin, Vasily 53
Stauffenberg, Claus von 60
Stettinius, Edward: appearance 77, 214; appointment 73, 78; background and career 77–8, 299; Declaration on Liberated Europe 222, 226; France policy 176; Iran policy 227–8; journey to Yalta 84; Malta talks 38, 78, 79; on Beria 201; on British attitude to America 114; on Churchill's grand dinner 236; on Churchill's oratory 233; on German reparations 211–12; on German surrender terms 164; on NKVD guards 123; on repatriation of Soviet citizens 229; on Roosevelt–Churchill relationship 193–4; on shipping sale 191; on Stalin 116, 122, 124, 141; on trusteeships 216; on UN inaugural conference 189, 205–6, 208, 212, 237–8, 251; on UN membership 190, 194–5, 196; on UN voting 164–6, 175, 176, 177, 178, 185, 189–90; Polish government policy 183, 198, 209–11, 215–16, 222, 225–6; secret agreement on Japan war 245; souvenirs of Yalta 248, 251; Yalta departure 251, 271; Yalta working arrangements 119
Stilwell, Joseph 'Vinegar Joe', General 39
Stimson, Henry 297, 299, 302, 306
Stone, Harlan 45
Strasbourg, defence (1945) 59
Strassmann, Fritz 261–2
Stroganoff-Scherbatoff, Count 271
Stuart-Clark, Maureen 88, 100, 102, 132
Sturdee, Jo 132, 148, 231, 237, 240, 249
Stutthof concentration camp 65
Suckley, Margaret 'Daisy' 11, 50, 76, 272, 288–9, 290
Sudoplatov, Pavel 264
Suez Canal 130, 165, 271, 275, 317
Szabo, Violette 146

Taiwan 317
Tatars, deportation from Crimea 95–6, 107
Tedder, Arthur, Air Chief Marshal 59
Teheran Conference (1943): Beria's role 49; Churchill–Roosevelt–Stalin relationships 29–31, 80, 83, 105, 117; communiqué 31; first 'Big Three' conference 23, 29; France discussions 58; German zones of occupation 138; interpreters 88, 106; Iran policy 181–2; Japan war policy 134; Jewish homeland issue 266; Nazi speculation on 147; opening conference 120; Polish border issue 162–3, 166; Stalin's journey to 87–8; Stalin's request for ports 192
Theresienstadt concentration camp 242, 315
Tibbets, Paul 62, 307
Tokyo, US bombing raid 287
Tolstoy, Leo 93, 188
Trotsky, Leon 23, 24, 28, 264
Truman, Harry, Vice-President, *then* President: background and career 291; Council of Foreign Ministers 305; desegregation of US military 73; 'Doctrine' 320; European waterways scheme 305; Iran policy 319; letter to Stalin 294; Manhattan Project 295; Molotov meeting 293, 294; news of atomic bomb test 302, 305, 306; Poland policy 294, 297, 305; Potsdam chairman 303–4; Potsdam Conference 298–300, 302–8, 325; presidency 291; relationship with Churchill 292–3, 298, 300, 303–4, 319; relationship with Soviet Union 294, 319; relationship with Stalin 302–3; replacement of Stettinius 78; response to Soviet advance into China 308; Roosevelt's death 291–2; Taiwan policy 317; telling Stalin about atomic bomb 306; Vice-President 46, 291; view of Eden 306; view of Roosevelt 14; view of Stalin 17, 307, 325
trusteeships 78, 79, 194, 212, 216, 221, 318
Tukhachevsky, Mikhail 153
Turkey 19, 196, 231, 234–5, 321
Twain, Mark 93

Ukraine: border disputes 323; deportations 313–14; famine (1932/3) 24; history 151, 153; Nazi collaborators 313; territory 153, 158; UN membership question 178, 185, 196, 247, 297n; war losses 308

United Kingdom (UK) see Britain

United Nations (UN): Charter 297, 319; Declaration 78, 194, 196; General Assembly 79, 178, 185, 189, 196, 213, 236, 246; inaugural conference 178–80, 189–90, 194, 196, 212, 216; membership issues 178–80, 184, 189–90, 194–6; origins 39, 78–9; Potsdam Conference 307; Roosevelt's advocacy of 21, 76, 78, 182, 325, 326; San Francisco Conference 205, 208, 237–8, 246–7, 251, 252, 288, 293–5, 297; Security Council 39, 79, 185, 212, 216, 246; Security Council voting procedures 164–6, 175, 176, 177, 297, 318; Soviet boycott 318; Soviet participation 221, 282–3; trusteeships 78–9, 194, 212, 216, 318; veto arrangements 79, 164–5, 297, 326; voting 189–90, 195, 236, 245–6, 297

United States (US): aid to Turkey 321; Berlin airlift 322; British policy towards 114; Chiefs of Staff 133–4; China relations 38–9, 317; desegregation of military 73; discussions on future of Germany 32; German surrender approach 285–6; Hitler declares war on 27; Iran policy 181; Korea position 309; Korean War 309, 318, 326; Lend-Lease programme 3, 26, 28, 32, 53, 73, 87, 181, 191, 202, 297, 321, 324; Manhattan Project see atomic bomb (Manhattan Project); Marshall Plan 321; Polish government recognition 297; Polish voters in 125, 152, 163, 166, 217; press conference after Yalta 252–3; public opinion 13, 33, 140, 144, 164, 166, 279, 295, 297; responses to Conference Communiqué 252–3; Saudi Arabia base 273; secret agreement on Soviet entry to Japan war 193, 228, 230, 245; secret agreement with UK on atomic research 32; support for

Greece 320–1; 'Truman Doctrine' 320; Truman's presidency 291; UN role 78, 164, 236; Vietnam War 317; war losses 308; zone of occupation in Germany 138, 322

V2 missiles 61–2, 122, 206, 285

VE Day 295

Venturer, HMS 223

Veritable, Operation 206, 220, 243

Versailles Peace Conference (1919) 19, 21, 22, 152–4, 269

Vietnam War 317

Vonnegut, Kurt 255

Vorontsov, Mikhail, Prince 100

Vorontsov Palace: bathrooms and lavatories 101, 149, 250; bedbugs 133, 250; British Administrative Office 174; British delegation 48; British delegation's arrival 89–90; British delegation's departure 251–2; Churchill's departure 249–50; Churchill's grand dinner 236–41; Churchill's view of 90, 99–100; communications with London 129; Foreign Ministers' meetings 189, 225–6; goldfish 149, 173; history 48, 100; NKVD guards 102; overcrowding 55, 101; packing up 252; porch 231; preparations for British delegation 48, 55, 100; Stalin's visit 115; surveillance 173; white marble lions 248

Vyshinsky, Andrei Yanuarievich 125–6, 212, 247, 282

Wallace, Henry 14, 22, 25, 46

Wallenberg, Raoul 60

Warsaw, Soviet capture (1945) 60

Warsaw Pact 322

Watson, Edwin 'Pa', Major-General: death 277; health 150–1, 175–6, 277; relationship with Anna Boettiger 128; relationship with Byrnes 120; relationship with Roosevelt 72

Wavell, Archibald, Lord 83

Weary Willie, Operation 64

Webb, Beatrice 18

Welles, Orson 11

Welles, Sumner 9

Wells, H. G. 141

Wells, Stan 65
Western Front 122, 135–6, 287–8
White, Dexter 109
Wilhelm Gustloff (liner) 67–8, 241
Wilson, Henry, Field Marshal 88
Wilson, Woodrow, President 21, 46, 78
Winant, John 51
Wolff, Karl, General 127, 285–6, 288
'Wool' secret plan 127

Yalta: accommodation 3, 48–9, 54–5,
96–104; agenda for Conference 99,
112; arrivals 3, 88, 89–90; baths,
showers and lavatories 132–3; bedbugs
and lice 49, 133, 250, 300; bugging
equipment 48–9, 108, 173–4; Chiefs
of Staff meetings 133–6, 175, 191,
209–10, 213; choice of location for
Big Three meeting 34–7; code-name
3, 37, 129; communications 101–2,
104; Conference Communiqué 231,
236, 238, 243, 246–7, 252–3;
Declaration on Liberated Europe *see*
Declaration on Liberated Europe;
departures 248–52; eighth and final
plenary session 240, 246–7; female
roles 49–51; fifth plenary session
194–9; first plenary session 118–22;
food and drink 132, 148, 172–3, 201,
236–7; Foreign Ministers' meetings
122–3, 150, 164, 174–7, 189–90,
194–6, 210–12, 215–22, 225–8;
Foreign Ministers' role 136–7, 140–1,
143, 179, 180, 187, 214, 236, 238,
248, 250–1; formal dinners 123–6,
200–5, 236–40; fourth plenary session
176–83; history 93–6; interpreters
119, 132, 165, 203–4, 214, 248,
250–1; issues ignored by Conference
261–70; leaders' photo call 213–14;
Livadia Palace *see* Livadia Palace; military discussions 120–1, 122–3;
minutes 119; opening of Conference
120; photographers 118; postponement of Conference 36, 325; press
speculation on location of Conference
146–7; seating arrangements 119;
second plenary session 137–45;
seventh plenary session 231–6; sixth
plenary session 215–20; third plenary
session 151, 164–9; travel arrangements 37–8, 46–7, 53–4, 56, 84–9;
views on agreements 3–4, 259–61,
281; Vorontsov Palace *see* Vorontsov
Palace; war damage 48; weather 48,
148, 246; Yusupov Palace *see* Yusupov
Palace
Yugoslavia 33, 199, 215, 217, 315, 321
Yusupov, Felix, Prince 103
Yusupov Palace: Beria's accommodation
107; bomb shelter 103; Chiefs of Staff
meetings 134–6, 191; Churchill's visit
229, 231; Eden's discussions with
Molotov 112; Foreign Ministers'
meetings 175, 221; history 103;
Molotov's accommodation 106; secret
agreement on Japan war 228; Soviet
delegation 99; Stalin's grand dinner
200–5, 207; Stalin's lodgings 103;
Stalin's routine 174; US draft on
Poland 170

Zhemchuzhina, Polina Semyonovna 106,
107n
Zhukov, Georgii Konstantinovich, Marshal
60, 120–1, 145